Ten Thousand Saints
A Study in Irish & European Origins

'This adventurous book could stimulate a revival of interest in Irish hagiology.'   —*Times Literary Supplement*

'A work of great wit and erudition and no reference library should be without a copy.'   —*The Irish Press*

'Enchanting. Mr. Butler approaches his subject with the fundamental reverence it deserves and is not anti-saint but anti-humbug.'   —*The Daily Telegraph*

'This book is ambitious, unusual, provocative.'   —*Hibernia*

'A work in which sound learning is combined with distinctive literary grace.'   —*The Church of Ireland Gazette*

'I am completely convinced by the argument that our 10,000 saints were "not real people but ingenious and necessary fabrications of the mind".'   —*The Irish Times*

'Has the allure of a detective story.'   —*The Irish Independent*

'The book has the courage and simplicity one expects from a private scholar. Mr Butler has just one outstanding theory. He sets it out and if he's wrong the book will be thrown away. How many professors have such courage?'   —*Westmeath Examiner*

'A writer of rare elegance and grace, and with an even more rare moral and intellectual courage. He was a literary artist of vivid and often exquisite prose.'   —*The Washington Post*

Ten Thousand Saints
A Study in Irish & European Origins

HUBERT BUTLER

THE LILLIPUT PRESS
DUBLIN

Copyright © 2011 Literary Estate of Hubert Butler

First published in 1972 by
The Wellbrook Press, Kilkenny, Ireland

This edition published 2011 by
THE LILLIPUT PRESS
62–63 Sitric Road, Arbour Hill,
Dublin 7, Ireland
www.lilliputpress.ie

All rights reserved. No part of this publication may
be reproduced in any form or by any means
without the prior permission of the publisher.

A CIP record for this title is available from
The British Library.

ISBN 978 1 84351 148 9

3 5 7 9 10 8 6 4 2

Set in 12 on 14.5 pt Fournier by Marsha Swan

To

JACQUES BOUCHER DE PERTHES
(1788–1868)
The customs officer of Abbeville
who grew prize pears,
wrote plays that were never produced,
joined the Kilkenny Archaeological Society,
shunned scientists
and founded
the science of prehistory

and

RICHARD BUTLER
(1794–1862)

I am far from claiming to be a savant or even a very clever man, but I am not blind ... What seemed to me ten times worse than any criticism was this obstinate refusal to investigate the facts and the cry, 'Nonsense! It can't be so!' without bothering to go and see.

Hatred and persecution at least can be fought; but indifference is a wall between you and the light, it buries you alive; I'd sooner have an enemy who flung Truth back into her well and crashed the bucket down on her head.

Nothing is more difficult to eradicate than old errors. What is most strange is that Science, when it has adopted and above all professed them, holds to them ten times more tenaciously than does Ignorance. That is because Ignorance has nothing to unlearn; it is a field that has not yet been taken over by the thistle and the nettle. There is no need for it to be harrowed.

Jacques Boucher de Perthes

But it is not likely that legends so widely propagated and so fondly cherished had no foundation in fact; that they were altogether either poetical fictions, or moral and political parables and myths. It is more reasonable to conjecture that they were the forms of historical narrative used by one people, which, falling into the hands of another people of different language, of other habits of thoughts and turns of expression, were understood by them in a sense which they were not intended to bear, and in which they were not used by their authors. We would look upon these strange and portentous narratives as the hieroglyphic records of forgotten but substantial history.

Harriet J. E. Butler
A Memoir of the Very Reverand Richard Butler,
Dean of Clonmacnoise and Vicar of Trim,
from Butler, R. Introduction to Annals of Clyn
Irish Archaeological Society, 1849
(privately printed, 1863, pp. 242–3)

Note on the Second Edition

The first edition of *Ten Thousand Saints* was scanned by staff at the Scholars' Laboratory in the Alderman Library, University of Virginia. This was then correlated line by line, with errors corrected both in the original text and the digital version by Richard S. Crampton.

The integrated text was edited by Crampton, following Hubert M. Butler's expressed wishes for the second edition. Butler had kept seven much-marked copies of the first edition at Maidenhall, Kilkenny. They contained his corrections, new text, new titles for chapters, new footnotes, additional references for the bibliography and new entries for the indexes. These changes have now been inserted to form a definitive edition. An added sixth index was developed by Crampton, cross-referencing additional items of Butler's research. Maps and tables have been numbered and referrals indicated where appropriate.

The dedication has been expanded at Butler's request to include comments by his great uncle, Richard Butler (1794–1862), Dean of Clonmacnoise and Vicar of Trim.

An Afterword by Richard Crampton reconciles Butler's pioneering research with modern DNA findings in bio-archaeology and linguistics.

Contents

Introduction, Alan Harrison, 2005 — xv
In Memoriam: Alan Harrison (1943–2005), Ross Hinds, 2011 — xxiv
Preface to the Original Edition, Hubert Butler, 1972 — xxv
Bibliography and Abbreviations — xxix

Part I

1. Saints and Scholars — 3
    Saints — 3
    Scholars — 6

2. Why did St Locheni Menn Stammer? — 13

3. Puncraft, an Ancient Art and an Explanation of the Glossary — 19
    My Glossary — 22

4. How Ancestors and Saints Were Made — 25
    In South Leinster — 28
    Some Ancestor Saints — 30
    How Saints Were Made — 32

5. Who was Lug? — 35

6. The First Invaders of Ireland — 39
    Macalister and the Idols — 41
    O'Rahilly and the Gods — 42

7. *Les Hommes Elégants de la Forêt*:
    Tribal Implications of Gaulish Proper Names — 46
    Country Methods — 49

CONTENTS

8. Where Did the Irish Come From? ... 52
   The Bebryces ... 53
   Iberians and Ligurians ... 54
   The Veneti ... 55
   The Thracians ... 56
   The Getae ... 56
   The Briges ... 57
   The Thyni ... 58
   The Mygdones ... 58
   Other Peoples ... 59

9. Tribal Maps ... 61
   Amalgamated Tribes ... 62
   Irish Analogies ... 66
   Mug Ruith and his Iberian Relations ... 69

PART 2

10. Tribal Charts and Tables of Name Variants ... 73
    The Goban Saints and the Cruithne ... 73
    Kenneth Jackson and St MoChuda ... 75
    St Cronan and St MoChua ... 75
    Terminations ... 76

11. St Brigit and the Breac Folk ... 77
    The Brig Folk in Scotland ... 79
    The Breac Folk in Decies ... 81

12. St Patrick: His Family and Household ... 84
    St Patrick's Missionary Journeys ... 88
    St Lupita, St Patrick's Sister ... 91
    St Erc, St Patrick's Embroideress ... 93
    The Erc Folk and the Thracians ... 96
    Restitutus, St Patrick's Brother-in-Law ... 98
    St Martin, St Patrick's Uncle ... 100

CONTENTS

13. Saints of the Vascones	108
St Mescan, St Patrick's Brewer, and St Bescna, his Chaplain	108
St Escon and the Fish	110
Continental Relations: Ulysses and Aesculapius	111
14. Some Saints of the Cunesioi	114
St Finncu and the Dogs	114
St Canice and the Head Folk	116
St Conchind and the Dog Heads	119
15. Saints of the Veneti	122
St Fintan Munnu and Others	124
Their Relations with Other Saints	126
The Board-Faced Saints and the Birds	130
St Aenboin and the Units	131
Aine the Sun Goddess	132
St Enda	133
The Gwynn Saints	135
16. The Carpic Saints	137
St Corba and the Chariots	137
(A) THE CHARIOT FOLK	137
(B) ST CORBA AND ST COBRAN	139
(C) CONTINENTAL SAINTS	140
St Fuinche Garb and the Rough Folk	140
St Gabhran and the Goats	149
St Seighin Gabal and the Forks	150
St Crebriu and the Branches	151
St Gregory and the Greeks	152
St MacCreiche and the Plunder	155
St Corcaria and the Purple Folk	157
St Cruithnechan and the Wheat	159
St Mac da Cerda and the Craftsmen	161
St Cairbre Crom and the Crooked Folk	162
St Gnavan and the Bones	163
St Cearc and the Hens	165
St Goban and the Smiths	166
A Greek Epilogue	171

CONTENTS

17. The Sons of Mil 175
    St Maelcu and the Bald Folk 175
    The Bald Folk 175
    Leitrim and Longford 176
    Sligo and Mayo 178
    Wicklow 180
    Wexford 180
    Westmeath 181

18. The Tigurini 182
    St Kentigern and the Princes 183
    St Luchtigern and the Mice 186
    St Foirtchern 187
    The Saintly Sons of Vortigern 189
    Some Miscellaneous Tigern Saints 191
    St Tigernach of Clones 192

19. Saints of the Daii 195
    Da Saints 199
    Who was St Da Goban? 200

20. St Brendan 202

21. St Ailbe and the Apples 204
    Apples 207

22. St Sciath and the Shields 208

23. St Tartinna and the Heifers 215
    The Tartessii 215
    In County Louth 216
    In Meath and Wicklow 216
    The Dartraige 217
    Other Traces 217

24. St Fursa and the Frisians 218
    St Fursa's Irish Family 218
    Irish Stories of Fursa 220

CONTENTS

Fursa's Companions	222
Fursa and his Companions in Ireland and Gaul	224
St Meldan	225
St Faelan	226
St Goban	226
St Algisus	227
Fursa in East Anglia	227
St Fursa in Gaul	228
Could the Frisians Have Reached Ireland?	229

25. The Cicones — 231

26. The Colours of the Winds — 233

27. The Saints Leave Ireland
    A Poem — 240

Afterword: *Irish Saints, Heroes and Tribes: Bio-Archaeology and Hubert Butler*, Richard S. Crampton — 246

Glossary — 288

INDEX 1: *Saints* — 303

INDEX 2: *Ancestors and Heroes* — 309

INDEX 3: *Irish Tribes (and their Ancestors)* — 319

INDEX 4: *Continental Tribes (and their Ancestors)* — 325

INDEX 5: *Historians and Historic Figures* — 330

INDEX 6: *Miscellany* — 333

Tables, Maps, Illustrations

TABLE 1:	*Irish Tribal Names*	18
TABLE 2:	*Ancestor Saints*	31
TABLE 3:	*Tribes of Gaul*	65
TABLE 4:	*Continental Tribes with Irish Kinsmen*	67
TABLE 5:	*The Thracians and their Variants*	97
TABLE 6:	*The Brig-Bard Tribes and their Variants*	98
TABLE 7:	*Fer Names*	104
TABLE 8:	*Chart of the Carpetani*	142
TABLE 9:	*The Carp Folk and their Variants*	174
TABLE 10:	*Saints of the Daii*	196
MAP 1:	*Spain*	63
MAP 2:	*Central Europe*	64
MAP 3:	*Gaul*	65
MAP 4:	*Britain*	68
MAP 5:	*Decies in Waterford*	80
ILLUSTRATION 1:	*Scythian Bronze Horse-Trapping from near Amiens, Ashmolean Museum*	210
ILLUSTRATION 2:	*From a Cross at Moone, Co. Kildare*	210
ILLUSTRATION 3:	*From a Purse in a Ship Burial, Sutton Hoo, Suffolk*	211
ILLUSTRATION 4:	*From South Cross Castledermot, Co. Kildare*	211
ILLUSTRATION 5:	*From a Cross at Kells, Co. Meath*	211

Introduction

ALAN HARRISON, 2005

There is an expression in the Irish language which goes *'Bheadh sé molta dá mbeinn I mo thost'* and this can be translated as 'If I were silent he would still be praised.' Hubert Butler (1900–91) needs no words of mine to establish or defend his reputation. His own writings are the most eloquent proof of his standing as a thinker and scholar. Since the publication in 1985 of the first collection of essays, *Escape from the Anthill*, Lilliput Press has published three more volumes of his writings and a fifth one, *The Appleman and the Poet*, is in preparation at present. The range of subjects, the style that speaks of such a sharp mind, and the sheer humanity of these works produced over a long period display a consistently high standard that is equalled by few other Irish writers. Most of these would fall into the category of essays, which is a medium that lies sometimes uneasily between literature and scholarship. In fact, somewhat like his Irish predecessor Jonathan Swift (with whom he is often compared), the writing itself is so good, the argument so logically produced, that the evidence or scholarship behind them seems to have a secondary place. Nothing could be further from the truth. Hubert Butler based his writings on both experience and evidence and had a natural scholar's approach towards collecting, collating and assessing his sources. Even a cursory look at his papers confirms this.

About a year ago I came across a collection of essays commemorating Hubert Butler. These were the papers given at a centenary celebration of Hubert Butler's birth held in Kilkenny in October 2000. Among these essays was one by Dick Crampton, Hubert's son-in-law and a medical professor at the University of Virginia, in which he discussed the only full-length book published by Hubert, *Ten Thousand Saints: A Study in Irish and European Origins*. The collection of papers as a whole confirmed my enjoyment and admiration of Hubert's writings but I returned in my mind often to the statement by Dr Crampton that Hubert Butler considered his work on the saints and Irish origins as his most important contribution to scholarship and that it was a great disappointment that it had been greeted by the scholarly community only with disapproval and with little or no engagement with the ideas he was propounding. I had read the book cursorily when it came out in 1972 and like most of my comrades in Celtic Studies I had subscribed to the orthodoxy that nobody but a person who had spent a lifetime absorbing the intricacies of the Old Irish language could speak with any authority on the meaning of the traces of ancient Ireland contained in the Irish lives of the saints, Irish mythology, Irish genealogy, Irish place names and, of course, according to the dogma of Irish cultural nationalism the folklore and mind of the Irish people required a knowledge of the modern Irish language and all that it entailed. From that viewpoint Butler was an easy target, and he knew it and sought to deflect, it as I will discuss below.

Hubert's disappointment with the book's critical reception was even more poignant when we consider the circumstances behind his research and the production of the book. In the aftermath of the event known as the 'Papal Nuncio Affair', which resulted in his retirement from the Kilkenny Archaeological Society in 1952, the project he devoted much of his intellectual life to was this study of Irish and European origins. During this period of twenty years Hubert familiarized himself with much more primary material for his study, begun in 1941, and starting classically from the questions of what meaning the material had for Ireland, and the generations of scholars through whose hands and minds it had passed, he began to formulate his theories of Irish origins. He understood better than anyone his own shortcomings – no formal training in Old Irish or in the arcana of Early Irish history – but he also knew his strengths – a formidable intellect, a training in the Classics and a knowledge of other cultures.

He called his approach 'country scholarship' and I believe it will be worthwhile to look at what he meant by that and to compare it to the methods of official academic learning. The country scholar, according to Hubert Butler, has no axe to grind and (if the reader can bear the mixing of metaphors) everything is grist to his mill. The so-called 'trained' scholar is bound by the conventions of his discipline and must conform to the process that has been laid down for him. In many cases the process itself seems to be more important than the resulting evidence or truth. I have seen some instructions to young scholars, especially in the sociological field, which grant a greater proportion of the marks to the precise adherence to a prescribed process than to the originality of the approach or the value of the outcomes. Butler saw the country scholar approach in the work of several of his predecessors like Edward

INTRODUCTION

Ledwich, George Petrie and even Eoin Mac Neill. Though he doesn't make much mention of them he would also have recognized many of the traditional scholars of the seventeenth and eighteenth centuries as belonging to the same mould. I suspect he was intentionally provocative and perhaps defensive in his coining and usage of the expression. He understood the challenge his ideas would be to those who followed a purely philological or culturally national historical approach and he wished to engage them in debate. He must have been sadly disappointed when his carefully constructed ideas were dismissed as the ravings of one of the charlatan band that inevitably become attached to matters 'Celtic' and 'Irish'.

The shelves of bookshops are now full of so-called Celtic spirituality, mysticism, new-age medicine and the like. There is an industry producing these which has little if anything to do with scholarship let alone Celtic scholarship. The Scottish scholar Donald Meek, from the Department of Celtic at Aberdeen University, has recently written a description and critique of this movement that seeks to piggyback on the genuine article. His was a welcome intervention, authoritative and fair. In connection with this I remember encouraging my colleague in the Archaeology Department at UCD, George Eogan, to write a book for the general public on his research at the mound at Knowth, Co. Meath. I said to him that if he didn't do it the vacuum would be filled by others without his expertise. And this is the nature of charlatan scholarship.

Whatever else may be said about Hubert Butler he was not a charlatan and the dismissal (by people like me) mentioned above of his life's work on the Irish saints was unjustified. That is not to say that he is right in every detail and that we were wrong. He would not have expected that himself. Indeed there is plenty of evidence in the book that he anticipated and would have welcomed vigorous debate. For my part, my interest in what he has to say and my confidence in the value of producing it again is strengthened greatly by the discovery that he consulted his 'friend James Carney' whom he was certain would disagree with some of his findings. For the non-Celtic/Old Irish scholar I should explain that Professor James Carney of the School of Celtic Studies at the Institute of Advanced Studies could be described as a great speculator and a shining light of interpretation of the culture and history contained in the old texts. Hubert also used texts such as M.A. O'Brien's *Corpus Genealogarium* and Ellis Evans's work on Gaulish personal names. He quotes from Kenneth Jackson's work but not from that scholar's *Language and History in Early Britain*, a book I believe that might have given him support for some of his ideas and that would have delighted him. I can only guess how much he would have welcomed the publication of several books by Pádraig Ó Riain and the speculations of scholars like Joseph Nagy. Butler's ideas did deserve consideration and if we believed they were wrong we should have supplied other explanations for the evidence he produced.

Hubert Butler's work involved speculations, guesses if you like, but they were based on a painstaking study of an enormous corpus of evidence. He also had an unusual understanding of the nature of this material that had passed through the minds and imaginations of generations of Irish scholars. As we will see below, this reference to minds and imaginations is of crucial importance for our understanding of his theories and for our acceptance of their validity. During the twenty years from the early 1950s to the publication of *Ten Thousand Saints* Butler amassed, by hand, every possible reference to every possible saint in the Irish corpus in Irish and Latin. In *Ten Thousand Saints* he only showed one example of his methodology from about 250 pages of the type of basic research he had done. Had I realized the extent of this I don't believe I would have written off his speculations as readily as I must have done in the early 1970s.

Let me give a brief description of this material. It is a single page, larger than foolscap, more like the size of the page of a large folio book divided horizontally into seven columns; the first column deals with a tribal name; the next with the key word associated with that name; then we have the names of saints who also have this key word as part of their makeup; then there is a list of places associated with the saints; followed by heroes that are associated with them; and other places with the same or similar elements; the sixth column mentions possible continental tribes (Celtic or otherwise) that could be related; and the final column gives a commentary on the foregoing material taken from other authors and from his own thoughts on the subject. Each page has between ten and fifteen entries in each column. This was all done by hand and represents itself a valuable corpus for future scholars. Incidentally there is a copy of this material among other papers of Hubert's in the library of Trinity College, Dublin.

Having pleaded guilty to ignoring at best and at worst belittling Hubert Butler's work when it came out in 1972, perhaps I can say a little about my own engagement with Irish language scholarship and Early Irish history. I do this in the expectation that the debate and dialogue that Hubert wished for might belatedly be initiated now. In order to do this most effectively I must be more personal than is usual in academic discourse. But then discourse between academia and country scholarship probably leaves room for one's own individual experiences. First of all, although I am an academic who has spent all his professional life working with material mainly in the Irish language, I am not an Old Irish scholar, nor am I an expert in Early Irish history. Having said that, ever since the early days of my apprenticeship I have read nearly all there is available in and about both domains out of sheer interest. I don't think of these subjects and my own areas of interest (the late Middle Ages and the seventeenth and eighteenth centuries) as a continuum or a seamless garment, but I am very aware of the connections between them. My training was, first and foremost, linguistic, textual and philological. My instincts as a scholar and my academic output have been primarily literary, interpretative, contextual and cultural. That statement alone should explain why the former approach based on what certainly used to be the common training in Celtic Studies is not sympathetic to Butler's speculations and why the present me is more open to them.

The philological scholar can find faults in Hubert's reasoning and the textual scholar can reject the authenticity of the texts he uses. For example one's immediate reaction on seeing some of Hubert's 'interpretations' of Irish names is to ridicule them. To give an example of one of the most famous of Irish names, that of the hero Cú Chulainn, Butler tells us this means 'dog-holly'(from *cú*, hound and *cuilleann*, holly). This is nonsense to the philologist, especially if he hasn't followed the argument that has been made about punning (see below for a fuller discussion of this). Hubert will be told that the 'l' in the name of the blacksmith Culann is 'broad' while the one in *cuileann* is 'slender' and therefore they are not the same word. According to this explanation the name means 'the hound of Culann' though there seems to be no explanation of what Culann's name may have meant. My answer to the philologist is try it with a native speaker of Irish and see if he/she can make the semantic leap proposed by Butler's theory of word-play. I have heard jokes in the Gaeltacht that demand much greater shifting of sounds to supply the meaning of a funny story. Then to turn to the case of textual scholarship I have plenty of evidence that the best editors (i.e., those who best reproduce the authentic texts as they were originally written) are not always those who understand the importance and significance of their material. Their role is extremely important but the explanation of the cultural meaning of the texts are often provided by others. Indeed Hubert praises very highly M.A. O'Brien's editions of the genealogical corpus but remarks on the lack of commentary other than the critical apparatus. Too rigorous adherence to the philological or textual orthodoxy can lead one to misinterpret the subtlety of Butler's arguments and his defence of them. I believe each area of expertise could be used, rather, to refine what Hubert has proposed as a possible model for, not early Irish history but for proto-Irish history.

The canvas on which Hubert Butler has chosen to draw his story is larger than Old Irish language, larger than Early Irish history, larger than folklore and archaeology; it is in short part of the story of Europe. There is no scholarship nowadays that embraces all the disciplines necessary to deal with such a canvas – that is the *raison d'être* for the 'country scholar'. In recent years I studied a number of characters from the seventeenth and eighteenth centuries who were intimately associated with the rise of Enlightenment learning; men like James Ussher, James Ware, Narcissus Marsh, William King, Jonathan Swift, Edward Lhwyd, Humfrey Wanley, John Toland and others from the Dublin Philosophical Society and from the Royal Society. All of these touched on the subject areas mentioned above but none of them was an expert in all of them – they were the equivalent of the country scholars of their day. In fact all scholarship then was country scholarship, seeing that the line of distinction between the several disciplines was not drawn as strictly as it is now. When I read Hubert Butler I think of these multi-disciplined, dilettante (not in the pejorative sense of being superficial) scholars. His competencies are wide, embracing Irish (despite his apology for his lack of knowledge of that language), Latin, Greek, Russian, French, German, Serbo-Croatian and several other European histories, languages and cultures. His understanding of Ireland as part of the bigger picture of prehistoric Europe is refreshing and his ability to trace the traditions of the historical Irish back to that picture is exciting. He may sometimes be incomplete in his evidence, even inaccurate in his use of it, but the overall result is ingenious.

At a ceremony to celebrate the life of the great scholar of the early Irish landscape Frank Mitchell, Professor Fergus Kelly compared him to the Irish god/hero Lugh arriving at the royal court at Tara. He knocks at the door and the doorkeeper tells him that everyone who enters must be the possessor of a special skill. Lugh mentions his several skills one by one and after each recitation the doorkeeper informs him that there is already someone inside who excels in that skill. When the list is finished Lugh asks the doorkeeper if there is anyone inside who is master of all the skills already mentioned, and he is thus admitted as a supreme hero because of his versatility. It is not incongruent to mention Hubert Butler in connection with this story also. I don't believe Frank Mitchell would have been unhappy to be compared with Hubert and I am sure the latter would have admired greatly the country scholar in Mitchell.

The preceding paragraphs are intended to make the case for the decision to re-edit *Ten Thousand Saints*. I hope I have indicated my own enthusiasm for the project. 'Re-editing' is not really the right word for what is necessary. In fact the book was published at Butler's own expense and apart from others who may have read it in proof, it was never edited. In my experience as an editor it is practically impossible to edit one's own work. Either the content, the presentation or the copy-editing will suffer. I have no doubt that Hubert Butler's reputation, which is based on the collections of his essays, owes much to the work of his editors. I say this not to take away from him but rather to affirm my belief that good writing deserves good editing and that there is a synergy between the two that is greater than the two together. There is a difficulty editing work of someone who is no longer alive to avail of an editor's advice. As an editor I am torn between my desire to interfere as little as possible with the author's original text and the necessity to impose consistency and clarity on his arguments. I will explain the editorial approach later but I would first of all like to try and summarize and synthesize Hubert Butler's work on Irish prehistory.

In presenting Butler's thesis I will often use his own words. He starts with the great number of Irish saints, and especially the fact that saints with the same and similar names tend to cluster in great numbers in contiguous territories. He says of them:

> Indeed it is through them [the saints] that I feel myself to be on the trail of a beauty and a truth more ancient, abundant and durable than theirs. If I am wrong I will surely be corrected. Or will I? I do not believe any Celtic scholar will accept my conclusions, which derive from the conviction that the saints had no human reality and must be otherwise explained. The way to refute me totally is to defend their historicity. Will anyone try? I doubt it.

The saints therefore were not real people but rather a 'Christian by-product of the dying art of ancestor-making'. Ancestor-making or cooking the genealogical books was not an unknown art throughout the Irish Middle Ages. Even as respected historians as the Four Masters or Geoffrey Keating were not above reconstructing history to suit their own biases. The key to understanding Butler's theory of ancestor-making is to consider seriously the possibility that he is right about what he calls 'puncraft'. Frankly I don't like this coinage but the concept and his application of it is quite ingenious. He is referring to the fact that names can change as they travel over territory and over time and that these changes reflect the needs of the different people who use them. And the verbal changes may not obey all the rules of etymology, morphology or phonetics. Language that passes through the 'mind and imagination' mentioned previously has no imperative to conform to post-hoc linguistic analysis. When he applies this to the names of saints and the names of people who share elements that are similar, it enables him to speculate that these elements reflect an ancestral memory that can take us back to the tribes that roamed through Europe in pre-historic times. The word 'tribe' itself can be confusing, but it generally can be taken to represent a group that derive their origin from a common ancestor. Thus the chain is: ancestor > name > phonetic rationalization > variety of puns/word play > stories that explain the name. This is just a complex form of what has happened in the case of some well-known place names formed within relatively recent times. For example in Dublin 14 there is a road now known as 'Birches lane' but it was originally 'Butchers' lane', being close to where the goats were kept in Goatstown. Similarly 'Leperstown' has changed into the more genteel 'Leopardstown'. And if you want to witness the folkloric creativity at work look at the surname 'Buckley'. This is Ó Buachalla, or 'grandson of the cowman' in Irish and as such is commonly anglicized as 'Buckley'. In his history of the Protestants of Ireland in the eighteenth century Toby Barnard tells of a Cornelius Buckley from Co. Cork who is called 'Buckley' because of the silver buckles he wore on his shoes. This is a typical example of a folk rationalization story that arises when the original meaning of the name no longer has any currency. It leaves a vacuum readily filled by those skilled in 'ancestor-making'.

This concept is not dependent on close correspondence of the original stem of the words or their phonetic realizations. It is a form of etymology that is based on approximations – unloved by those of us trained to have a philological frame of mind, but quite realistic to those who allow the imagination to have sway. Fortunately such approaches are not without parallel in the Irish tradition. Hubert Butler mentions one of the best known of these, namely Cormac's *Glossary*. In fact it is a trump card that he underplays. Cormac's *Glossary*, attributed to Cormac Mac Cuilleanáin (d. 908), king/bishop of Cashel, includes a large list of old and rare Irish words and names and explains them in Irish often citing stories to illustrate the meanings and origins of them. Many of these fall exactly into the category of Butler's 'puncraft' and to the modern philologist are plainly incorrect. The same could be said of many of the stories in the *Dinnshenchas* (the lore of famous places). Hubert does not overtly allude to this feature though his list of sources shows us that he consulted the five volumes of the metrical *Dinnshenchas* edited by Edward Gwynn.

Hubert Butler uses this wordplay device to point to similarities between saints, families, place names in Ireland and on the continent, and connects them to movements of peoples across Europe in prehistoric times. For him the coincidences are too great to ignore and it must be admitted that even when one eliminates some of the more doubtful correspondences the evidence is considerable. Even if he is only half correct, there is a case to answer as he says himself: 'I do not claim that I am right but that I am looking in the right direction.' This is a modest enough claim for the result of thirty-one years' research, especially in an age when the career of a professional academic presses him/her into claiming that his/her findings are the final word on the subject. It would indeed be a fitting ending to his work if this re-edition were not the last word!

As I have already said, my objective in the editing will be to present the author's own text and make as few changes as possible to it. We have Hubert's own corrections that should be incorporated. He refers to other writings on the subject that he has not included here due to the exigencies of space imposed by publishing the book himself. These will be consulted with a view to seeing if their inclusion would result in any improvement of the original. Footnotes and other references are not consistent throughout and a uniform style will be applied to these. The book was published without the index – a real loss and its inclusion could, I believe, have lessened the criticism that we can infer from the silence its publication invoked. The printing and publication separately of an index went unnoticed. It looks like an amateur publication – the right hand margin is not justified, the maps are attractive but some of the names on them unreadable. It has a naïve attractiveness and with time will become a book-collector's item. These are technical matters and easily rectified by a modern publisher. Sometimes the text reads as a collection of discrete pieces and I feel also the text requires some contextualization and linkages. These I will supply as I feel the need through footnotes explaining references or through supplying summaries of the most important points at the end or beginnings of chapters.

In Memoriam: Alan Harrison (1943–2005)

Alan Harrison, Professor of Irish at Trinity College Dublin, died on 22 April 2005. He had written the Introduction to this new edition of *Ten Thousand Saints*, but had not supplied the footnotes to explain references in the text nor provided the summaries of chapters that he intended to write. Alan and I had known each other since we were twelve years old, and we considered our personal bookshelves as holding mutual property, with no need for duplicate volumes. One of the few exceptions was the essays of Hubert Butler – we both wanted to own a copy of each of them! The Butler commemorative volume, *Unfinished Ireland*, was another exception, and it was Richard Crampton's paper there that persuaded Alan to revise, in 2003, his initial dismissal in 1972 of *Ten Thousand Saints*.

Hubert Butler's absence of relevant academic qualifications would not have meant much to Alan in his mature years; the supervisor for his PhD at Trinity, Professor David Green, had simply a primary degree, and one of his lecturers in Modern Irish, Martín Ó Cadhain, did not have even a primary degree. Alan was especially keen on interdisciplinary studies; he founded, with Andrew Carpenter and Ian Campbell Ross, the Eighteenth Century Ireland Society in 1986, to provide a space where scholars of history, of literature in both English and Irish, and of the arts, could learn from each other. He had therefore a respect for Butler's achievement and was an ideal person to relaunch Hubert Butler's magnum opus. It is sad that he was not able to complete the task, but his Introduction can serve as an invitation to his colleagues in the field to re-examine Butler's work and begin the long postponed debate (now including the discipline of DNA analysis – see Afterword) on whether Butler was indeed 'looking in the right direction'.

Ross Hinds
Brussels, January 2011

Preface to the Original Edition

Hubert Butler, 1972

When I first began to speculate about the Irish saints, I was secretary of the revived Kilkenny Archaeological Society and hoped to model it on the pattern of its famous predecessor, which still survives as a Dublin-based national society. The motives and methods of the old county societies were already forgotten but they seemed to me more enlightened than the current ones. Without any conscious striving after 'social therapy', the local scholars had stressed the continuity of our regional history and reminded us that we and our neighbours were the heirs of the people and problems we investigated. The focus of their enquiries was mostly man himself and not his artefacts and his material debris, his food vessels, ashpits, collar bones. Within a restricted area their minds worked with agility and few inhibitions. The past was not so dead that it could not strike sparks out of the present.

I have used these antiquated methods in my study of the ten thousand saints and the fifteen thousand ancestors, on whom, I believe, they depended. These methods are nowadays so peculiar that I must explain them.

Perhaps a jigsaw puzzle addict would understand me best. Spilling on the table a mass of queerly shaped pieces, he assumes they form a picture. It is an enormous puzzle and the reproduction on the lid and many of the pieces are missing. It should have a dozen people working on it, but these co-operative and neighbourly diversions are now unfashionable. Sometimes he groups the pieces by colour, sometimes by shape; he never stops guessing, because every recorded failure, by elimination, brings success a little nearer. Often he fits together a dozen pieces but the interlocked fragment may be upside down; it may be a segment of the setting sun, it may be the red of a woman's cloak. He has only one rule. Go on guessing!

This analogy is imperfect. I have one conviction so strong that I treat it as an axiom. I believe that the ten thousand saints, though key figures in the unravelling of our past, were, except for a well-known handful, not real people but, like the ancestors, ingenious and necessary fabrications of the mind. And I suspect that, if today the professional scholar, by and large, accepts the 'historicity' of the Irish saints, whose lives were mostly written some six centuries after they are said to have died, there is no fresh fervour of belief behind this acquiescence. It is because the saints bore him deeply and because among the pots and bones science has opened up for him a more prestigious field, in which he can reach a sort of certainty with his foot-rule and annoy nobody.

Few men will have even heard of 99 per cent of the ten thousand who come under discussion, though they may revere the 1 per cent that some accident of social history has brought to their attention and those whose human existence no one could dispute. Like the pieces of the jigsaw puzzle, like the fifteen thousand ancestors of the genealogical tables, they all belong to the same picture and not one can be excluded.

In a preliminary way I have grouped the ancestors and saints with different continental tribes, which I believe must have come to Ireland. My groupings must often be wrong but about some I have a dogged certainty. We know that the Brigantes and Menapii reached Ireland, so I hold that their neighbours the Veneti must also have come. They were famous seafarers and left their names wherever they settled in Europe. Among the Iberian tribes. I am confident about the Cunesioi and the Draganum Proles. What about the Carpetani? Is it possible that so large a tribe from central Spain, so closely mingled with the Celts, failed to precede them or accompany them? I am almost confident about the Tigurini, the Scythians, the Vascones, open-minded about the others.

My chapter on the Daii is a grouping of enigmas with an obvious family resemblance. Should the whole group be turned upside down and identified differently? Maybe.

About the Cicones I reckon there is only one chance in five that I am right, but less than one chance in fifty that this group of ancestors, saints and tribes had peculiar breasts, yet that is the alleged meaning of their names. To the Greeks, Amazons were 'breastless' and so male-female. My most extravagant guesses are seldom sillier than the accepted explanations.

I am a classical scholar with only ad hoc Irish. I have studied the lives of the saints in the original Latin or in translations from the Irish and I will have made many mistakes, which a Celtic scholar, sympathetic to my arguments, could have helped me correct. Yet I do not believe that the names of the saints and ancestors were originally 'Celtic', so though my mistakes may spoil the presentation of my theory, they will not invalidate it.

PREFACE TO THE ORIGINAL EDITION

The way of a country archaeologist in Ireland in 1972 is a very hard one and I hope that I and my tribe will be forgiven for faults that belong to our circumstances. We are forced to depend on secondary sources, to be niggardly and erratic in our references and inconsistent in our spelling of names. What can be expected, when the most obvious books like *The Tripartite Life of St Patrick*, *The Martyrology of Òengus* or *Silva Gadelica* can no longer be bought but must be borrowed from Dublin? Some generations ago an arrogant and suicidal policy of centralization robbed us of our libraries, our museums, our dignity and our independence of mind and made the whole idea of unsubsidized, or, as the subsidized prefer to call it, 'amateur', scholarship ridiculous.

The jigsaw addict sits alone at his vast table, shifting the pieces round and round, hoping that an arm will sometime reach across the table and an indignant voice say: 'Look! you're wrong! That large block of blue you've got there is the sea, not the sky!' No arm comes, yet some perverse sense of duty keeps him glued to the table, addressing to himself all the reproofs, all the congratulations that are so much sweeter shared.

I have frequently published articles about the saints and tribes, often saying provocative things that would have thrown our ancestors into hysterics of disagreement or approval. But even when I make absurd mistakes, no voice is raised to correct me. Is it that archaeology, as our grandfathers knew it, is dead? Did it succumb to some lethal pox, after first science and then Himmler embraced it?

Or is it that the old reverence for the Irish saints is totally gone? I think this is only half true. We all of us still have an affection for the mysterious beings after whom our churches, Catholic and Protestant, are named. Even the most fabulous of them have always seemed emblems of unworldliness, protectors of innocence and poetry, and nothing I say can make them negligible. Indeed it is through them that I feel myself to be on the trail of a beauty and a truth more ancient, abundant and durable than theirs. If I am wrong I will surely be corrected. Or will I? I do not believe any Celtic scholar will accept my conclusions, which derive from the conviction that the saints had no human reality and must be otherwise explained. The way to refute me totally is to defend their 'historicity'. Will anyone try? I doubt it.

For practical reasons I cannot here offer an index, but I have already written a sequel, in which I have dealt with some twenty continental tribes, which seem to me as relevant as the Veneti and the others to early Irish history and hagiography. The Thracians and Ligurians would each need a book, still unwritten, to themselves.

PREFACE TO THE ORIGINAL EDITION

Writing as a country scholar, I am proud that my book is printed and its cover designed by friends and neighbours in my own county. If there are misprints, they are surely due to my careless proofreading. No writer could hope for a more careful and conscientious printer of a difficult text than Desmond McCheane of the Wellbrook Press.

I must mention here my old friend, Eric Dorman O'Gowan, a solitary scholar of Cavan, who tried in the old way to relate the history of his county and of Ireland to prehistoric Europe. I owe much to his encouragement and to the many friends who gave me good practical advice. To none do I owe more than to Eleanor Burgess, who both understood what I was trying to say and helped me to say it.

The maps and the drawings, except the untidy one of Britain, are by my wife, Susan Butler, who went on believing in me, when everyone else said I was chasing a will o' the wisp.

Bibliography and Abbreviations

I have deliberately given a meager bibliography and see no point in referring the reader to the huge corpus of Irish material with which Celtic scholars are familiar. My thesis is a very simple one and even those who can only read what is translated into English or written in Latin and who know no Greek or German, will find enough evidence in the list below to condemn my arguments or to confirm them.

Short as my list is, it is perhaps for the country reader deceptively long. Many of the books such as *The Martyrology of Òengus*, *The Tripartite Life of St Patrick*, and *Silva Gadelica* are unpurchasable and must be borrowed from Dublin libraries. I have not mentioned Baring-Gould's important *Lives of the British Saints*, 1907–13 or Rhys's *Early Britain*, because even libraries do not usually have them.

A. Arribas, *The Iberians*, 1960	A
H. Butler (ed) *Journal of the Butler Society*, 1973–4.	B
S. Baring-Gould, *Lives of the Saints*, 1914. Sixteen volumes.	BG
P. Bosch-Gimpera, *Les Indo-Européens*, 1961.	G
J.B. Bury, *Life of St Patrick*, 1905.	Bury
J. Rhys, *Celtic Britain*, 1882.	CB
Canon Carrigan, *History of the Diocese of Ossroy*, 1905. Four volumes.	Carr
M.A. O'Brien, *Corpus Genealogiarum Hiberniae*, 1962.	CGH
O'Donovan & Stokes (eds.), *Cormac's Glossary*, 1868.	Cormac
W. Ridgeway, *Early Age of Greece*, 1901&1931. Two volumes.	EA of G
Chadwick & Jackson (eds) *Early British Church*, 1958.	EBC
T.F. O'Rahilly, *Early Irish History and Mythology*, 1946.	EIHM
W.H. Hennessy (ed), *Book of Fenagh*, 1875.	FEN
H. Hubert, *Greatness and Decline of the Celts*, 1934.	GDC
D.E. Evans, *Gaulish Personal Names*, 1967.	GPN
R. Graves, *The Greek Myths*, 1955.	Graves
T. O'Rahilly, *Genealogical Tracts*, 1932.	GT
E. Hogan, *Onomasticon Goedilicum*, 1910.	H
H. Cary, *Herodotus*, 1882	HDT
A. Holder, *Alt-Keltischer Sprachschatz*, 1896&1961. Three volumes.	HOL
P.W. Joyce, *Irish Names of Places*, 1920	INP
J.H Todd (ed), *Irish Nennius*, 1848.	Ir Nenn

BIBLIOGRAPHY AND ABBREVIATIONS

John O'Donovan, Complete works.	J.O'D
Journal of Royal Society of Antiquaries, formerly Kilkenny Archaeological Society, 1848 to present day.	JRSAI & KAJ
R.A.S Macalister (ed), *Lebor Gabala (Book of Invasions)*, 1938–1956.	LG
C.H. Plummer, *Lives of Irish Saints*, 1922. Two volumes.	LIS
E. MacLysaght, *The Surnames of Ireland*, 1969.	MacL
E. MacNeill, *Phases of Irish History*, 1919.	MacN
R.E. Matheson, *Surnames and Christian Names in Ireland*, 1901.	Math
E. Gwynn, *Metrical Dindshenchas*, 1903–1935.	MD
O'Donovan, Todd & Reeves (eds), *The Martyrology of Donegal*, 1864.	M of D
The Martyrology of Òengus.	M of Oe
C.H. Plummer, *Miscellanea Hagiographica Hibernica*, 1925.	Misc
E. O'Curry, *Manners and Customs of the Ancient Irish*, 1873. Three volumes.	OC
J. O'Hanlon, *Lives of the Irish Saints*, 1875–1897. Nine volumes.	OH
H. d'Arbois de Jubainville, *Premiers Habitants de l'Europe*, 1889.	Prem.
Canon Power, *Place Names of Decies*, 1952.	Power
R. Butler (ed) Clynn's *The Annals of Ireland*, 1849.	RB
W. Reeves (ed), Adamnan's *Life of Columba*, 1857.	Reeves
G. Murray, *The Rise of Greek Epic*, 1911.	RGE
G. Petrie, *Round Towers of Ireland*, 1845.	RT
H.L. Jones (tr.) *The Geography of Strabo*, 1949. Eight volumes.	S
S.H. O'Grady, *Silva Gadelica*, 1892. Two volumes.	SG
Rev. J.F. Shearman, *Loca Patriciana*, 1879.	SH
W.F. Skene, *Celtic Scotland*, 1876. Three volumes.	SK
C. O'Rahilly (ed), *Tain Bo Cuailgne*, 1967.	TBC
R. Thurneysen, *Die Irische Helden- und Konigsage*, 1921.	THU
J.H. Todd, *St Patrick, Apostle of Ireland*, 1864.	Todd.
W. Stokes, *Tripartite Life of St Patrick*, 1887.	TRIP
C.H. Plummer, *Vitae Sanctorum Hibernae*, 1910.	VSH
W.R. Wilde, *Lough Corrib*, 1867.	Wilde
W.J. Watson, *Place names of Scotland*, 1926.	WJW

Part I

CHAPTER 1

Saints and Scholars

Saints

I call this book *Ten Thousand Saints*, because I am an Irish country scholar and the saints have always seemed to me the central mystery of our past, as they once seemed to the Irish antiquarians of 150 years ago. For them they were the focus of a lively sceptical controversy out of which Irish archaeology, which was then based on country societies, developed. Yet the reader will see I could have called it several other names equally well. For beyond the saints, but attached to them, lie other mysteries, challenges, which only those in whom curiosity is dead could fail to take up. I could call it 'Fifteen Thousand Ancestors' or 'Fifty Tribes' for instance, or 'The First Invaders of Ireland', for it is about all these things. But the saints are the first challenge. Though I have never, since I was a boy, believed they were real people, they are nearest to me and hence dearest.

Looking out of my window as I write I have been able, since the leaves fell, to see the sixteenth-century castle of Kilbline, though the last vestige of St Blaan's church, from which it took its name, disappeared some years ago. To the south of it I can see the woods, where St Paan's now unroofed church stands in the demesne of the great house of Kilfane, and under the distant hills I can vaguely locate the cult centres of other saints, St Scothin under Slieve Mairge, St Moling under Brandon, half a dozen at least around Mount Leinster, and, if the mist thins, I will see the round tower of Tullaherin, which belongs to St Ciaran, who before Patrick preached Christianity in Ossory, and within a short walk along the river bank is the well of St Fiachra, who is deeply revered in France. When night comes, the sky to the north is red with the lights of Kilkenny, the city of St Canice, who succeeded St Ciaran in the diocese. And within ten miles of my home I could count at least fifty others. And what I could do every Irishman could do, for every parish in Ireland has one saint or more.

It is still a domestic and settled scene. Though it is the age of the aeroplane, the clergy, Protestant and Catholic, seldom leave their parishes. It is the age of census forms and card-indexes, yet, when they die, they are not remembered for very long and few local sages could tell you their mother's maiden name. In contrast, the saints I have mentioned all travelled far and wide, in Scotland, Wales, Cornwall, Gaul, Italy, and always came home to Ireland, leaving their names behind them for centuries in the places they visited. And we know the pedigrees of their father and their mother often for twenty generations and the names of all their sisters, brothers, nephews, nieces, both religious and secular. St Paan was the uncle of St David of Wales, and was one of the forty-eight children of Braccan, a buccaneering Irishman, who gave his name to Breconshire, and, though he was a very worldly man, gave it also to Kilbricken church on Hook Head, thirty miles south of here. All forty-eight children were saints, twenty-four of either sex, and many of them have cult centres both in Ireland and Wales.

As for St Blaan or Bledenus, his principal church was at Dunblane in Perthshire, but he was born in Bute and culted in Inverary and Aberdeen. Irish saints, it must be noted, are supposed to have founded or ruled the monasteries and churches that bear their names. The idea of an honorary dedication is a late one.

St Ciaran was also in Bute and Kintyre. In Brittany he is called Sezin and in Cornwall Piran. He died in at least two countries.

Though St Moling's chief church is here at St Mullins, he is also culted in Kerry and in the Scottish island of Arran.

St Scothin was educated in Wales and twice walked across the sea to visit old friends there. Giraldus Cambrensis identified him with St Swithin of Winchester, and though St Swithin lived some centuries later, he too is a fabulous saint, whose only biography was written close on two centuries after his *floruit*. So, as Irish saints often lived to be immensely old, Giraldus may well be right.

St Fiachra had several namesakes scarcely distinguishable from himself and cult centres in Carlow and Donegal before he set sail for Gaul, where he established himself as a wonder-working anchorite in a cell at Meaux near Paris.

St Canice is as widely travelled as any other Irish saint. He covered five Irish counties and as many Scottish and Welsh ones with his monasteries and miracles. With St Columba he converted the Picts and their king. For him the Grampians split in half to let light upon Laggankenny and the little toe of his right foot was preserved in a monastery he founded in Italy. The monks had been inconsolable when they learnt that St Canice was to die and leave his relics to Aghabo, until a fiery dragon had come down from heaven and scissored off this modest memento. He may also be that St Kenneth, who stood on one leg and was fed by seagulls in the Gower Peninsula.

Every October St Canice is commemorated in Kilkenny as a busy Irish prelate with widespread diocesan responsibilities. Is this a true picture of him and his saintly colleagues? I do not think so. Can I show that they were not, as we are asked to believe, a dim foreshadowing of a bench of bishops, but the dying echoes of an immemorially old world, which the bishops have superseded? It was pre-Roman, pre-Greek, almost certainly pre-Celtic and it is in the most fabulous passages, which the modern hagiologist rejects, that the features of that world can be most plainly distinguished.

If I were to succeed in this, I do not believe I would be damaging the *pietas* with which these venerable figures have been regarded for centuries. There are sanctities that depend not on belief but on a long tradition of reverence. By suggesting that these cult centres were holy places centuries before Christianity, am I mocking at the love and respect with which they are still regarded? Am I injuring belief? I do not think so. Last August the bishop of Meaux and a group of French scholars attended the Pattern of St Fiachra at Kilfera. St Fiachra also had a cult centre at Meaux. I cannot think that one of them believed more than a line or two of St Fiachra's recorded history. Some must have been complete sceptics. Yet they had a good reason for coming. For something important once happened which we can neither remember accurately nor wholly forget, which linked our small neighbourhood forever with theirs. If we could get closer to the truth, we would not be weakening these pleasant ties. We would be strengthening them enormously.

The main impediment to discovery is the refusal to see that the early saints and the vast company of Irish ancestors, with whom they are allied, belong to a single pattern. They were one and all moored to history and to each other by long chains, and, if one chain snaps, they all snap. What happens then to the ten thousand saints and the fifteen thousand ancestors? A whole system collapses (or rather our dull-witted comprehension of it) and we are confronted with the problem of twenty-five thousand imaginary beings, who neither lived nor were gratuitously invented. There is far too much inner consistency among them for them to be the product of druidic or monastic doodling.

Who were they then? The question is never asked and, since without curiosity there is no scholarship, the study of the saints has languished and is almost dead. If it is to be revived, one must spend some pages seeking the reason for the crippling burden of apathy that has extinguished it.

Scholars

A couple of centuries ago, when Irish archaeology started, it was not at all democratic. The first antiquarians were mainly country gentlemen and their clients, doctors, solicitors and the clergy were with few exceptions of the Protestant Church. Being intellectuals, they were real rationalists or real believers and propagated their faith with passion. Historical facts were either true or false and the idea that an untruth could be seen as a beautiful and elevating allegory or a phase in man's development or something of the kind appealed to nobody. 'It is corrupting to the mind,' said one of them, 'to believe that which is not true.' Vallancey, one of the great pioneers, a retired civil servant, belonged to the Age of Reason; Ledwich, his chief opponent, was a Protestant clergyman. Neither they nor their disciples thought of the saints as real people. The rationalists thought that the saints were deities, which the Irish had brought with them from the Mediterranean, and Ledwich, who was only sceptical in a sectarian way, believed they were 'monkish fictions', from which it was the mission of the Protestant Church, under 'the fostering care of Britain', to purge religion (*Antiquities of Ireland*, Edward Ledwich, 1803). Of Irish descent himself, Ledwich was rector of St Canice's chief cult centre at Aghaboe and canon of St Canice's Cathedral Kilkenny, yet he called St Canice 'an imaginary personage' and the tales of the other saints, even St Patrick himself, he held to be '*nugae nugacissimae*', which it was 'consummate hypocrisy and wickedness to inculcate upon the ignorant'.

This controversy raised provincial archaeology from its torpor. Ledwich's outburst provoked a violent reaction, in which Anglo-Irish chivalry played as big a part as scholarship or Gaelic sentiment, for many scholars had been influenced by the Young Ireland movement, which was largely Protestant in origin. Out of the commotion some of the great figures of Victorian archaeology, Petrie, O'Donovan, O'Curry, emerged, some of them ascendancy Irish, some native, all of them champions of the Irish saints. In my parish the rector, James Graves, and John Prim, the editor of our local newspaper, started the famous Kilkenny Archaeological Society. For nearly a hundred years this society exercised a dominating influence over the study of the Irish past. Before long it had swollen into a national society; museum, library, journal and administration were gradually transferred to Dublin. Like Frankenstein constructing his monster, these rural enthusiasts had built up the metropolitan organizations, which were later to professionalize archaeology and drive out the provincial 'amateur'. In the meantime the new archaeology was more cautious and neighbourly than the old, and the society soon repudiated Ledwich, who never appears in the pages of the journal except as 'a foul-mouthed charlatan', or an 'ignorant calumniator'. As the century wore on less and less was said against the Irish saints. The Marquess of Ormonde, the President of the Kilkenny Archaeological Society, who edited and presented to each of its members a life of St Canice, is very tactful about the first founder of our noble cathedral of St Canice. As the Anglo-Irish and their Church began to feel the draught of doom, a reticence, which had originated in chivalry, continued from discretion.

For all the middle years of the *Journal of the Royal Society of Antiquaries of Ireland*, as this organ now called itself, the Irish saints became the unchallenged property of Father Shearman, a delightful writer, to whom the saints and their complicated family ramifications were as real as his own parishioners. His work is of lasting value, for even if the people and events, which he co-ordinates so ingeniously, do not belong to this world, the texture of his argument is sound, his learning and industry beyond praise.

The Prince Consort was invited to be Patron of the Society and he sent twenty-five pounds. By many delicate adjustments harmony was maintained among its members. I am sure no one was so crude as to say: 'You be nice about our Royal family and we'll be nice about your saints', but the scandal of Ledwich was never repeated, and, in one of Father Shearman's genealogical trees, he demonstrated that both St Mochop of Kilchop and St Aedan the Leper were distant cousins of Queen Victoria.

Ledwich and Vallancey continued to have their disciples, sceptics and romantics, like Henry O'Brien, Sir William Betham, Dr Beaufort, Marcus Keane, but the archaeological societies mostly cold-shouldered them. O'Brien and the others had a proud and personal interest in the Irish saints whose cult centres often lay upon their estates. In their remote country houses they peopled the past, which reason had emptied of its saints and heroes, with Phoenicians, Etruscans, Cuthites. Unlike the orthodox, they were conscious of a vacuum, which had somehow to be filled. Marcus Keane, a land agent from Co. Clare, was among the last of these rural polymaths. Most of his theories are now absurd, but he had a sturdy scepticism that merits respect. He complained that the total ages of ten representative saints amounted to 3090 years, that eleven had leprosy, that they were all of them aristocrats and related to each other. The same names recurred over and over again. There were twenty-seven St Fintans, twenty-five St Senans, thirty St Cronans, twelve St Bridgets, ten St Gobans, fifty-eight St Mochuas, forty-three St Mo-Laises and Colmans uncountable. All their recorded activities were supernatural and often, by Victorian standards, very wicked. Keane argued that this state of affairs could only be explained by assuming that a limited quantity of imported deities had acquired different attributes and personalities in different regions, so that, when the time had come to christianize them, a handful of gods and goddesses dissolved into many thousands of saints. In its negative aspect his argument seems to me unassailable and I even find it hard to condemn the exuberant dogmatism, whereby he identifies St Ciaran with Chiron, the Centaur, St Cronan with Cronos, St Bolcan with Vulcan, St Nessan with Nessus and so on. However wrong he may have been, he was more adult or else more honest than many of his contemporaries. His most fantastic conjectures had the merit of a clumsy boot shoved in a doorway and kept open questions that more prudent scholars have been eager to close.

In Keane's time the country house library was already decaying and the travelled and learned amateur was giving place to the salaried metropolitan specialist. George Petrie, a prudent Scotsman, who measured, counted, parsed and dated, reacted strongly against the loose and lordly ruminations of the country sages. Was his acrimony purely intellectual? He claimed to believe in the Irish saints. Did he really? There are passages in his great book on the round towers of Ireland, which can only derive from insincerity or from babyish credulity. He deduces from the fabulous life of St Mo-Chua of Balla that the saint was the architect not only of his own round tower but also of St Fechin's mill. But turn to St Fechin's life and you will read that St Fechin built the mill himself and supplied it with a mill stream by flinging his crozier through a mountain. St Mo-Chua and his fifty-seven namesakes were fully as fantastic in all their doings.

Petrie, of course, wished to dissociate himself from Irish ascendancy arrogance, but, until Ledwich wrote his famous book, this had not been a characteristic of the early antiquarians. They had mostly seen the saints not as objects of superstition but as numinous beings, who linked their neighbourhood and their neighbours with a Mediterranean world more ancient than Greece or Rome, to which their classical learning gave them special access. Catholic scholars like Bishop Lanigan understood them and imitated them.

Richard Butler, fascinated by the pre-Norman Irish traditions that were slighted in all the Anglo-Norman chronicles, refused to believe as Clyn did that 'the strange and portentous legends' of the early Irish had no factual foundation. He thought they were sober historical narratives of one people, interpreted by their successors, whose language and habits were different [RB]. An idea like this, obvious as it may seem, germinates best in the free air outside the academic forcing-house. Yet to formulate it in 1849 without access to metropolitan libraries was difficult. He carried it no further [B].

Canon O'Hanlon was the last and most ambitious of the traditional hagiologists who followed upon Petrie. On every day of the year the feast of five or six or seven of the Irish saints can be celebrated and whole lifetimes have been spent collating their biographies, miracles, floreats and obits. '*The Book of Life*, alone,' wrote Cardinal Newman, 'is large enough to contain them.' Canon O'Hanlon tackled them all. He was non-committal and sometimes caustic, when they struck sinners dead with an eyelash or when their vomit turned to gold, but deeply respectful of their vast missionary journeys, their complicated kinships, and their innumerable church foundations. Only when he reached September, did his health begin to flag and public interest to wane. His eight published volumes are a magnificent achievement, full of country learning and regional knowledge, which no later scholar has been able to ignore.

Since his death no one has treated the saints except individually or considered that, real or fabricated, they constitute a unitary problem.

The late Professor Macalister is fairly typical of recent scholarship. His mind was essentially a sceptical and original one and he approached hagiography like a game of spillikins. How many saints can one by delicate manipulation extract from Celtic Christianity without bringing the whole edifice toppling? This technique involved a different method for the disposal of different saints. One can count at least three. He argued, for example, that St Bridget was the priestess and alleged incarnation of a pagan goddess, Brigit. She became a Christian and managed to christianize the pagan shrine. This curious notion has had the approval of J.F. Kenney, a foremost writer on the Irish saints, and of many contemporary scholars. 'And though,' wrote Macalister, 'it is probable that she herself changed the official name, Bridget, which hitherto she had borne (for no Christian lady would willingly continue to bear a name so heathenish while Christianity was still a force), it was too deeply rooted in the folk memory and continued to be used locally to designate her.'

In a different vein he suggests that St Ibar was a very good and real man, who got confused with a sacred yew tree (for *ibar* means yew), whose shrine in Co. Wexford he had appropriated.

> Let it be clearly understood that the historicity of these saints is not in question. That is amply attested by the ruins of the religious houses associated with them. But their names have suffered the usual fate of names handed down by tradition and have become confused with other names, which by reason of a much longer history, stretching far back into unknown abysses of pagan ages, had made a deeper impression on popular memory.

With equal delicacy he argues that the famous St Ruadan of Lorrha, who cursed Tara, was really a christianization of the red god (for *ruad* means red). That is to say the three saints have to be coaxed out of history by three different doors.

Surely the devices by which Macalister tried to bring his heresies into line with orthodoxy are abject? Do the ruins of religious houses 'amply attest' the existence of the saints to whom they are dedicated? Had Macalister never heard of the twelfth-century saint factory at Cologne, at which a succession of abbots 'recovered' the bones and built the tombs of many of the eleven thousand virgins, who accompanied St Ursula on her voyage? Baring-Gould, who believes St Ursula to have been a Norse deity, records 213 of these miraculous discoveries. Attacking the saints piecemeal and greatly preoccupied with manners, Macalister never comes to grips with his problem. Ledwich, at least, was aware that truth always creates new sanctities to replace the old, and, if, in the pursuit of truth, we demolish a few altars, we had better not stop to patch them up again, for we shall do it very badly. I doubt whether Macalister himself can really have believed in the holy duplicity of this priestess of Brigit, who managed to keep her job, while neglecting all its obligations. There is, of course, no particle of evidence for her tragic dilemma. St Bridget is said to have travelled all over Ireland and there are many legends of her ministry in Scotland and Wales. If in a long life, spent in far places, she nowhere succeeded in disentangling herself from her former employer, the fire goddess of Kildare, her message must have been a very confused one.

Such absurd theories have value as evidence of the climate of opinion. The Irish scholar is today so conditioned by education and environment that he could scarcely argue differently. Our most eminent hagiologist, Father John Ryan, has written: 'Our race ... has shown itself capable of producing in unique abundance the very highest type of which humanity is capable, the saint. Therein lies our chief claim to recognition and to glory as a nation.' That is to say to be sceptical about our saints would be to be sceptical about the reputation of our country. Naturally our scholars have to tread carefully.

I. SAINTS AND SCHOLARS

In his influential book, *Irish Monasticism*, Father John Ryan shows how the Irish saints can be tidied up for history. Omitting from the lives everything that is grotesque or improbable, he has tried to make a plausible picture out of such statements as do not outrage common sense. Arguing as he does, one might say that, while the cow certainly did not jump over the moon, we have no grounds for denying that Miss Muffett sat on a tuffett and Jack Horner in a corner. For example, in illustration of the rigours of Irish monasticism, he quotes the '*gravissima regula*', which St Sinell of Lough Erne imposed on his monks. They had to eat straw bread made of unthreshed corn. But the evidence for this comes from the life of St Munnu, a completely fabulous work of great charm. Its writer would have been as likely to intrude a real fact into the narrative, written many centuries after the supposed lives of St Munnu and St Sinell, as an upholsterer to patch a chintz cover with a piece of linoleum. Dr Ryan would have shown the quality of the story, had he related how St Munnu, after eating St Sinell's peculiar bread for eighteen years, had gone to a synod to decide whether the Irish or the Roman date for Easter should prevail and how he advised the assembled saints that two monks, Irish and Roman, should be simultaneously burnt, and that the monk who survived would know the true date for Easter. Why should we suppose that St Sinell's methods of baking bread are more 'historical' than St Munnu's of baking monks, seeing that the same historian is the authority for both?

In the books that are now written about the Celtic saints the question 'Did they ever live, and, if not, what do they represent?' is, if posed at all, a subordinate and almost shamefaced one. It is no longer, of course, a daring or original question but incurious and conciliatory people have rigged up around our saints a protective wall of good manners, which is more impenetrable than the old idolatries. One is not now expected to believe in the Irish saints but our respect for the possible beliefs of others acts on our faculties like a gentle drug. In fact it is some generations now since an unsurpliced scholar has tiptoed very far into the vast Valhalla of the Irish saints and, when, like the late Professor Macalister, they occasionally intrude, it is with immense circumspection. It is obvious that the movement for the rehabilitation of the Irish saints, which began in chivalry, has ended in sterility. It is not only that Ledwich wrote much better than his more tactful successors, but his ideas acted like leaven on those who disagreed with him, while the insipid or pedantic hagiological writings of today could only have been published in a society in which the last bubble of intellectual ferment had long ago died down.

Maybe I have been unfair to some learned and important books. Lately

Professor Kenneth Jackson wrote eighty-four pages about the biographies of St Kentigern of Glasgow, about sources, scribal errors, orthography, Cumbric roots and epenthetic vowels. There was one sentence about his reality. It ran 'One may reasonably accept that he was a real person.' But no reasons were offered.

Jackson's offence is not that he is wrong – he is, of course – but that he thinks the question secondary. To us mortals life is a primary concern, and, if Kentigern lived, then so did his ten thousand colleagues, who are not a scrap more incredible than he is. And it would then be evident that once upon a time men had discovered the secret of irresistible goodness but lost it after five generations. Here would be a real subject to discuss, not for eighty-four pages but for eighty-four thousand, and one could spare a line or two for the Cumbric roots and the epenthetic vowels.

Yet I cannot believe in this lost secret of goodness. The good men we know are not like that. They do not go about in droves; they are seldom irresistible or long remembered.

Plainly these saints were superimposed with great care over something more ancient, beautiful and interesting than themselves. It would need still greater care to scrape away even the upper layer of an endless palimpsest. But roughly I would argue that the saints were a Christian by-product of the dying art of ancestor-making.

As an art, ancestor-making surpassed any succeeding mode of chronicling what would otherwise have been forgotten. If we were to read the ancient notation correctly, we should one day learn of the wanderings and minglings of all the great tribes of Europe and how every parish in Ireland and many in Britain and in Europe were settled. We would acknowledge without regret that, while Ireland had only the average number of good men, it had superb practitioners of an ancient art who survived the ruin of their class elsewhere in Europe.

CHAPTER 2

Why did St Locheni Menn Stammer?

Twenty-five years ago I started to puzzle about the Irish saints, not only because of their huge numbers but because of their deliberate, gratuitous oddity. Why, for example, were St Ultan Tua, St Locheni Menn and Colman Got, the monk who rose from the dead at Rahan, all of them dumb or stammerers, for that is what their afternames mean (the attributes which Irish saints wear after their names are not exactly nicknames, so I have chosen to call them 'afternames')? And why did so many of their secular kinsmen (they were all closely interrelated) suffer in the same way and all have such peculiar explanations for their afflictions? St Ultan's trouble came from keeping a stone in his mouth during Lent. Cuscraid Menn and Menn mac Salcolga stammered because Cet, the great hero-ancestor, had slit their windpipes. If one counted all these dumb people, there were over forty of them, all of them distinguished men and not seriously handicapped by their disability. That is to say they managed to convert many heathens and defeat formidable foes.

At that time, T. F. O'Rahilly, the great philologist, had just expounded his theory that the P-Celts had inhabited Ireland before the Q-Celts had arrived. Overwhelmed by his learning and the severe scornful treatment which he meted out uncontradicted to rival scholars in his voluminous footnotes, I assumed he might be right. If he was, one could argue that Q-Celts found P-Celts unintelligible and vice-versa, so that one set of Irishmen considered the other set dumb or stammering. That for instance was why the Greeks called foreigners barbarians (those who said 'Bar bar bar' instead of speaking). It was thought to be why the Russians called the Germans *njemtsi* or the dumbfolk. I wrote an article about this in *Antiquity*, March 1949, for its editor and founder, my friend O.G.S. Crawford. I am a classical scholar and I adduced all the instances I could find from Greek and Roman sources and I followed it up with an article in the *Journal of the Royal Society of Antiquaries of Ireland*, 1950. But nobody seemed bothered by my problem or interested in my solution and soon I decided that not only was O'Rahilly altogether wrong but I was wrong myself. For all the afternames of all the saints and all the heroes were equally odd.

Not only were there saints with oddly pleasant epithets like *bind*, sweet, *ban* and *finn*, white, *caem*, beautiful, *beo*, lively, *cass*, curly, but there were fourteen called *cael*, thin, six were *garb*, rough, ten were *breac*, speckled. Others were called *baeth*, stupid, *cam* and *crom*, crooked, *caech* and *dall*, blind, *mael*, bald, *goll*, one-eyed and very many were called *liath*, grey and *dub*, black, *derg*, red, *odar*, dun-coloured. They were also called *dorn salach*, dirty fist, *glunsalach*, dirty kneed, *cosfada*, long legged, *brocainech*, badger faced, and Marcus Keane had not exaggerated the number of leper (*lobhar*) saints. There were many more than eleven.

The Irish explanations for these names were so ingeniously contrived that one knew they were invented. St Ethcen Dornsalach, Dirty-fist (11 Feb.), had just come in from ploughing to greet St Columba. St Ninnidh Lamhglan, Pure Hand (2 Apr.), kept his hand in an iron glove so that it would be pure for consecrating St Brigit. St Glunsalach, Dirty-knee (3 Jun.), a reformed robber, was assiduous in prayer.

Not only did the saints have all these afternames but the heroes and ancestors had twice as many of an identical pattern. And soon I observed that the first names were composed of the same elements as the afternames. There was St Caelfinn, Thin-white, St Maelodar, Bald-dun. There was a limited number of these attributes and saints, heroes and ancestors used them all singly or in double and treble combinations.

Moreover these names were not very stable. St Fiachra Goll, the One-Eyed, was also St Fiachra Cael, the Thin. Erc Culbuidhe, the Yellow-haired, was Erc Caelbuidhe, the Thin-yellow, Maine Mal, the Prince, was the same as Maine Mall, the Slow, and, if you followed some of these equations to the end, you might find that each particular aftername had ten or a dozen variants, so that it was a matter of luck whether a saint or a hero had a flattering epithet or an ugly one.

The explanation came when I discovered that Maine, who had alternative afternames, Mal, prince, and Mall, slow, was ancestor both of an Ui Maine tribe in the west and the Ui Mael tribe in Wicklow, which left its name in the Glen

2. WHY DID ST LOCHENI MENN STAMMER?

of Imaal. These Mael folk provoked a number of anecdotes about bald, *mael*, people. That is to say when you said that any particular saint or hero was *mal*, prince, *mall*, slow or *mael*, bald, you associated him with the Mael folk. And I soon discovered that *mael* could mean tonsured as well as bald, so there were a great many holy men among the Ui Mael.

At the same time I noticed that St Caeman Breac, the speckled, was associated with a midland tribe, the Breacraige, and St Aed Glas, the green, with the midland Glasraige. St Cairbre Caem, the handsome, lived close to the Ui Caem (now the O'Keeffes) near Fermoy. I no longer had any doubts.

The same process repeated itself among what appeared to be compound tribes, whose names are reversible (e.g. the Clann Flann Dub is also the Clann Dub(f)lann). In Leitrim there was the Maelciarain, whose name would normally be interpreted, 'the tonsured or dedicated to St Ciaran', but in the same area was an aggressive saint called Ciaran Mael or the Bald, who by a miracle chased away another saint's plough team across the Shannon. He was clearly a former ancestor of the Maelciarain and, saint as he was, was anxious to protect their arable rights [LIS II. 38].

It was very difficult to coordinate these speculations until Michael O'Brien's *Corpus Genealogiarum Hibernicae*, Volume I, appeared in 1965. I had, of course, seen and used many Irish genealogies before, but this is the most complete, even though he died after only one volume was published. It is written for Celtic scholars, as all such books now are, and, since, as a country scholar myself, I am writing primarily for country scholars, I have to warn them that no concessions are made to us. There are long passages in difficult Irish and an intimidating system of indexing, which I have had to replace by a page index of my own. But it is an essential book, with which one soon finds oneself at ease. The genealogies can be understood without any vocabulary, except of the words that are used, I maintain, to give tribal names an Irish meaning. These words are easily memorized and I have listed them, to the best of my ability, according to tribes in my Glossary.

Tribal names are formed by the following prefixes:

Aes	Dal	Sil
Cenel	Fir	Tuath
Clann	Muinter	Tellach
Corcu	Moccu	Ui (the modern O')

And the suffix -raige or -rige.

It should be known too that *mo* meaning my, and *do* and *to* meaning thy, are used as prefixes to saints' names and held to be terms of respect.

As with the saints 150 years ago, the first question a country scholar will ask is 'Were all these men and women real? And if not, how did they evolve?' Michael O'Brien in his short introduction, naturally does not raise this issue, nor does any other editor. Though to the country scholar it is a primary question, we should be grateful that to the trained Celtic scholar it is usually secondary, for the huge task of recording accurately, with all their variants, the names of these fourteen thousand men and women would be impossible, if the editor were to interrupt his labours with fundamental questions like these.

The country scholar, able to enjoy the fruits of these labours, would deserve the contempt with which he is now regarded everywhere, if he did not ask continuously all those primary questions from which the academics abstain. Were these ancestors real? After reading a few pages, one can have no doubt. One should not have to resurrect Ledwich and Vallancey from the dead, so that an emphatic 'no' can be said, and one can pass on to the next country question: 'How then did they come into being?'

Before the answer came to this, I had to become familiar with O'Brien's and other genealogies and ask myself fresh questions. There were large families of brothers, Aeds, Maines, Lugaids, two, five or ten of each, where each brother has the same name but a different epithet. Often such brothers come in pairs. Linge Finn, the fair, was brother of Linge Dub, the black, Cairthenn Finn was brother of Cairthenn Dub and there are eight of these Finn-Dub pairs.

Dark brothers and fair brothers might recur constantly in any family but why not distinguish them by their first name rather than by their colouring? Other pairs had odder epithets still, and even the oddest epithets recur again and again.

Here are four significant pairs of brothers:

From south-west Munster
    Cairpre Blai and Cairpre Dub   CGH 263   sons of Oengus Bolg
From the Dessi in Waterford
    Muindech Blai and Muindech Dub   CGH 396   sons of Fintat
From the midlands
    Guaire Blaith and Guaire Garb   CGH 165   sons of Laoghaire
From the north-west
    Amalgaid Blaithe and Amalgaid Menn LG 319

2. WHY DID ST LOCHENI MENN STAMMER?

Dub means black, *garb* means rough and *menn* means stammering, but what do *blai, blaith, blaithe* mean? *Blath* means flower and St Blath, who was Bridget's cook, was called Flora but surely all these people were not flower-like?

It does not take long to be sure that all these afternames like Mal, Mall and Mael were tribal. There were Cairpre tribes, Blai tribes, Dub tribes, Muindech and Menn tribes, Guaire tribes, Garb tribes, Amalgaid tribes all over Ireland, and the Muindech and Cairpre tribes are located just where they should be in the Dessi country of Waterford, within easy reach of the Ui Blait of Clare, who are also called the Cenel Blai.

These people are all composite ancestors of composite tribes. *Garb* did not really mean rough nor *dub* black nor *menn* stammering. And, if we read further, we see that the genealogists have told us this as explicitly as they could.

There were, for example, six brothers called Lugaid. Their father, Daire, called them all by the same name, because it had been prophesied that one of his sons called Lugaid would reign over all Ireland. Daire's sorcerer said that the son who captured a golden fawn would succeed him, and another condition of success appears to have been that he should sleep with a certain hideous old hag. The six Lugaids took their name from the tribe whose ancestor they were. Thus from Lugaid Cal descended the Calraige, from Lugaid Corp the Corpraige, and so on.

But though Lugaid Cal was obviously called after the Calraige, a Sligo tribe, when he was fabricated as their ancestor, it had to appear that the tribe was called after him. There had to be a personal explanation not only for Cal, but also for Corp. Thus Lugaid Cal slept, when he ought to have been hunting, because *colladh* means sleep and Lugaid Corp ate the fawn's offal, because *corp* suggests corruption. Lugaid Cosc, *ex quo* the Coscraige, 'broke up' the fawn, because *coscar* means breaking up.

Lugaid, the son of Ith, the son of Breogan, was the grandfather of them all (see p. 40). One may disagree about the methods by which these pedigrees were composed (probably the genealogist used both tradition and caprice), but manifestly they were concerned with tribes and not people, and neither sons nor grandsons nor fathers had more than symbolic existence.

In this case it seems that Lugaid represented some ancient tribe or amalgam of tribes and his grandchildren indicated by their afternames the new tribes with which the old stock had interbred.

Lugaid himself possibly came into being when the tribe of Lug met the tribe of Ith (which is also Fid, Id and Aed) and Lug both became Ith's son and added Ith's name to his own. Something similar happened with Fidcorb, the son of Corb, where Corb, which was also Corp, was ancestor, I believe, in the first place, of the Carpi, an Iberian tribe. Lugaid Corp would result from a triple combination.

To return to St Caeman Breac, St Ultan Tua, and St Locheni Menn, they were neither speckled nor silent nor did they stammer. All these attributes were tribal, not personal. I have tabled below some of the more frequent afternames and suggested also the Irish tribe that corresponds most nearly to them. In each case I have chosen one variant out of many.

TABLE I: IRISH TRIBAL NAMES

AFTERNAME	SUPPOSED MEANING	IRISH TRIBE
Bind	Sweet	Cenel Bindigh
Breac	Speckled	Breacraige
Gael	Thin	Caelraige
Crom	Crooked	Ui Crommain
Dub	Black	Dubraige
Finn	White	Ui Finn
Garb	Rough	Garbraige
Mael	Bald	Ui Mael
Menn	Stammering	Mennraige
Odar	Dun-coloured	Odraige
Ruad	Red	Rudraige
Dubh finn	Black-white	Corcu Duibne, ex Dubh finn [SG, 535]
Maelgarb	Bald-rough	Ui Maelgarb
Maelodhar	Bald-dun	Sil Maelodhar
Maelruad	Bald-red	Ui Maelruad
Mennbric	Stammering-speckled	Sil Mennbric

The next step is to guess from which continental tribe these Irish tribes originally derive.

CHAPTER 3
Puncraft, an Ancient Art and an Explanation of the Glossary

So the two brothers, Cairpre Blai and Cairpre Dub, were neither flowerlike nor black, but resulted from an ancient genealogical practice. They were 'amalgamated ancestors'. A natural human process had been pushing the meaningless tribal names towards meaning, and entire life stories were built out of tribal puns. I use the word 'pun' instead of the more scholarly 'word play'. Pun is shorter and perfectly adequate. In my Glossary I have tried to relate the puns to the tribes that inspired them.

These pun-biographies were habitual with Greeks and Hebrews. It has long been thought that Perseus and Medea [HDT VII 61–2], adopted by the Greeks from the Persians and Medes, were under the influence of their names when they slew dragons and intrigued, for *perthein* means to destroy and *medea* means counsels.

And in the Old Testament this process is universal and often explicit. The ancestors of the twelve tribes of Israel all had adventures which their mother deduced from their names. Thus Issachar means both 'hire' and 'shoulder', so various hirings (a concubine and some mandrakes) were done and he had to bear burdens on his shoulder. Jacob, his father, who supplanted Esau, because his name means 'supplant', put Hagar, ancestress of the Hagarites of Arabia, to flight because Hagar means 'flight'.

With our twenty-five thousand ancestors and saints the usual pun was Irish, Latin or on rare occasions English. The same puns were used again and again. Can we work back from the pun-biography to the ancient tribe whose name inspired it? My Glossary is intended to help towards this.

Let me set out the problem more clearly. As I am writing in English, let us take first the Cornish St Sidwell (1 Aug.), who, because of her name, it is thought, was decapitated with a scythe and thrown into a well. She had a sister St Jutwell (13 Jul.) whose head was also thrown into a well and a third sister was St Vulvella. Can we work back from the scythe and the wells to the tribes whose names inspired this simple pun? Sometimes it's easy. On this occasion it is not. Guessing as boldly as the hagiographer did, I would suggest that St Sidwell's scythe corresponds to the word *sioth* or peace, which we meet in the name of Cu Sidhe, dog of peace, ancestor of the Clann Consithe of Fife. I would then suggest that the ancestress of the Sigovellauni of Valence might have made a new life for herself at St Sidwell in Cornwall. She would be a cousin to the ancestor of the Catuvellauni of East Anglia and Chalons, and to St Syth of Islay, who found lost jewels, *sead*, if prayed to [WJW 333]. I will write later of the saints of the Siginni and Vellauni, to whose amalgamation I trace Sigovellauni (see Glossary).

Now take a Latin pun. There were several saints of Tipperary called Lactan, with heroes and tribes to match. They had many adventures with cows, which miraculously gave or withheld their milk, *lac*. I have related them to the Lacetani, a small tribe in Iberia west of Barcelona, but I believe it to be a Ligurian offshoot.

Finally an Irish pun. St Moelgubi, whose name is translated Calvus Tristitiae, the bald or tonsured one of sorrow, was crucified in Wicklow [VSH I 247] and it was certainly because of his name that this sad fate befell him. Yet Moelgubi was no casual invention. His father, Dimma mac Fergna, had nine sons of whom Moelgubi was the youngest, and he had a minutely recorded genealogy reaching before and after him for many generations [CGH 46, 356]. A vast number of the tribes of Wicklow were descended from Dimma or his brothers or uncles. Among them were the Ui Mail or Nepotes Moel, who, as I have said, provoked innumerable puns about baldness, for *moel* means bald. Dimma was also ancestor of the Ui Gobain or Gubain, whose name recalled *guba*, mourning. So it was natural enough that, when the two tribes associated, a joint ancestor, Moelgubi, came into being and his sad fate was already sealed.

The next stage of interpretation is to discover the most likely continental affinities of these two Wicklow tribes. For this I refer the reader to 'The Sons of Mil' (see p. 176) and 'St Goban and the Smiths' (see p. 167).

If we accept that biographies were written from tribal puns, many problems

3. PUNCRAFT, AN ANCIENT ART AND AN EXPLANATION OF THE GLOSSARY

that have puzzled scholars for generations become clear. There is a famous story of a terrible curse that was laid upon King Conchobar and all the Ulster leaders except Cuchullain. Whenever battle threatened, they suffered Noinden Ulad or the Nine Days (Debility) of the Ulstermen, akin to the debility of a woman in childbirth. If we observe that there were Conchobuir tribes [CGH passim] and Noinden tribes [CGH 47] and that a Conchobar was son of a Noindenach [CGH 168], we see how it all came about. Noindenach also suggests Nine Days or Terms and its variant Noidenaig suggests *naoidhe*, infant. Probably most of the Ulster tribes had common ancestors, so the dread disease of Noinden would have affected them all. Yet scholars are still trying to explain the Debility of the Ulstermen by the practice of '*couvade*' among the Polynesians, by vegetation rituals and the hibernation of the Phrygian god.

There are echoes of tribal puns on every page of Irish legend so that it is plain that the making of genealogies and pun biographies was the main task of druids, poets, hagiographers.

Why did Cuchullain meet a wizard, *sirite*, in the Irish midlands [THU 466]? Well, clearly it was because of the Muinter Siriten (later the Sheridans) of the midlands whose genealogy we know from *The Book of Fenagh*, page 383.

Why did he do strange things with holly twigs in the *Tain Bo Cuailgne*? It was because *cuillend* means holly and his name suggested 'Dog-holly'.

Again why are we told in *The Book of Rights* (p. 201) that the famous Cathair, ancestor of the Clann Cathair, left a set of chessmen (*fithcellacht*) to Crimthann, one of his thirty-three sons? Well, it was because an Ui Fithcellach tribe, of which there were many, was, as often, connected with an Ui Crimthann tribe [CGH 48].

It is here that the real problem begins. Why should any tribe be called Ui Fithcellach after chessmen? My Glossary can help here; I try to collate and coordinate the multitude of puns by which the names of composite ancestors and tribes are explained. In this way we can break them up into their component parts and reassemble them again according to their true affinities, Fid with Fith and Id, Cell with Gel and Cael, and so on. A simpler, earlier pattern of European tribes then pushes its way through the superimposed complexities with which the genealogists and storytellers were familiar.

The art of the genealogist-punster (or is it a science?) is intensely introverted. He buries the truth, where it is safe but almost indiscoverable. Is it absurd to see in this the first symptoms of the Irish obsession with words? When Joyce in *Finnegans Wake*, with sick and sterile nostalgia, buried the names of Dublin streets, shops, suburbs in polyglot puns, did he anticipate that one day foreign students, in pursuit of Ph.Ds, would work out that Lucalizod certainly meant Lucan plus Chapelizod and that Cabinhogan probably meant Cabinteely plus Sallynoggin?

The ancient punsters certainly one day expected to be interpreted. But who is now to do the interpreting? The burial of the tribal truth was a country craft and its effective unburial should be a country craft too, as it was a hundred years ago. Possibly it may have to wait until curiosity is once more allied with intimacy and affectionate commitment to people and places.

My Glossary

Cormac Mac Cullinan, a ninth-century king-bishop of Cashel, made a famous glossary; he was learned and ingenious and he chose those explanations that were edifying and entertaining. He cannot possibly have believed any of them. He was dealing with fancies, his own and those of others. When he came to proper names, it was clear that he was giving an Irish shape to swiftly changing, totally inscrutable pre-Celtic words. One of his aims may have been to offer ideas, both fresh and traditional, to the learned men who composed the genealogies and bardic stories.

For example, he said that the Benntraige got their name from *binit*, rennet or whey, because they brought whey as a tribute to the king of Cashel. Alternately it was because their founder, Fer Bend or Fer da Beann, was either a 'man of two peaks (or mountains)' or because he wore 'two horns' on his head.

My Glossary is Cormac's in reverse. I want to work back from the puns to the reality behind them. By taking the Benntraige or Benndraige tribe, the first on my list, as an example, you will see that the puns can illuminate as well as obscure. I have not associated it with any of the great and known tribes, because I do not know where it belongs, but it is so widespread and important that I think its name must be a multiple distortion of one that is known to history; Veneto-Thracian perhaps? Let others do the guessing. The evidence comes from Derry and Donegal, Wexford, Cork and Roscommon. The Benntraige gave their name to the two rivers Bann, one in Derry, the other in Wexford and to Bantry Bay in Cork.

There is a hill over Coleraine in Derry called Dun da Beann or Fort of two Peaks, now named Mount Sandel. Its tribal associations are confirmed by a recorded visit from Fer Bend [LG 106].

Neighbours to the Benntraige in Derry were the Fir Li, so we meet with

3. PUNCRAFT, AN ANCIENT ART AND AN EXPLANATION OF THE GLOSSARY

a compound tribe, the Li Benndrigi, where the two tribes merged along the Bann. Their compound ancestress may have been the fairy LiBan (Beauty of Women). The corresponding saint St Liban (White-beauty) was an Ulster mermaid with three alternative names (27 Jan.). All three suggest the names of Ulster tribes or compound tribes. You will see later that the Munster Benntraige also produced compound ancestors.

A straightforward ancestor-saint of the Benntraige was St Bind (Sweet), another name for St Mac Carthenn of Clochar, Co. Tyrone (15 Aug.). A branch of the Cenel Binnig lived in Tyrone and had an ancestor, Bind or Eochu Binnech, for whom St Mac Carthenn clearly deputized in Christian times. As I explain elsewhere he did the same for three other local tribes, whose ancestors' names he wore in addition to his own.

I have thus suggested in my Glossary that *bind*, sweet, and *ban*, white, in proper names and nicknames were tribal elements related to the Benndraige. For example Ethne, mother of St Columba, was also called Derbind Belfada or 'Sweet-tear-long-mouth'. Could any revered lady really have such a name? You will see in my Glossary that all four syllables, which constantly recur in proper names, could be 'tribal elements'. Bind is an appropriate syllable for the highly mythological Eithne to wear, for she is said to have been born in Donegal, where the Cenel Bindigh had a settlement. Her nickname is not odder than that of St MoLaisse of Loch Erne, which is Broc-ainech-bind-corach, meaning Badger-faced-sweet-tuneful. That in its turn is no odder than the name of a Munster ancestor, Broc-salach-crion-gluinech or Dirty-badger-dry-kneed. These after-names are composed of recurring elements, whose tribal connotations I have guessed at in my Glossary.

The tribal use of *ban*, white, can be illustrated by St Emine Ban (23 Dec.) who lived among the Benntraige in Wexford (barony Bantry).

There were Benntraige at Bantry in west Cork too and the Munster tribal pattern is wonderfully clear in the pedigree of their neighbours. For Ded, *ex quo* the Ui Deda, had two sons, Glas *ex quo* the Ui Glassin and Binn, *ex quo* the Benntraige and a grandson Glassben.

He had another son, Tet or Teith, *ex quo* the Aes Teith, a variant I believe of Ded himself. So I suggest that Tedbendach, the aftername of the patriarch of East Munster, Tigernach Tedbendach, is a tribal amalgam, in which both the Aes Teith and the Benntraige were involved. Those who disagree with this are invited to suggest what Tedbendach really meant.

More reading and more knowledge could clarify the question enormously but in fact I have felt that until my general principles and, in particular, the fact of amalgamated ancestors are accepted, I am more likely to suffocate the reader with detail than convince him. So I have eliminated much that seems to make assent unavoidable.

The reader will be puzzled by the enormous quantity of pun elements in my Glossary. Every conceivable colour for example has a corresponding tribe, every member of the body, every beast and plant and physical attribute. This does not mean that there was an enormous number of tribes and tongues. It only means that in pre-literate days, when strangers pronounced a tribal name in a new way, there were no dictionaries to correct them. Such consistency as existed came from the fixed belief that all proper names had a meaning, so the variants all varied in the direction of a familiar word.

In my Glossary I have invented no interpretations. They are all traditional puns and most have been used many times. I have tried to sort out according to tribes the pun elements out of which the relevant proper names are composed. Some are obvious or explicit, some only probable, many may be wrongly attributed. But one thing is sure, none of them have the meaning which scholars, ancient and modern, ascribe to them.

CHAPTER 4

How Ancestors and Saints Were Made

There are thousands of books written on the Irish saints, but the Bibliography I have provided is small. A very few books will suffice for the reader to make up his mind as to whether what I say is probable or improbable. Turn a few pages of any martyrology, any volume of genealogies, and you will find enough evidence to condemn me or acquit me.

All I have tried to do is to make out of obvious facts a sort of base camp from which more adventurous explorers can take off into the unknown. One day, as I have said, they will learn who the first peoples were who came to our islands and where they settled and when, how poetry began and religion and how different races first learnt to live in harmony.

What is most obvious must come first. Early races all had imaginary ancestors, whose names derived from their tribal names ('eponymously', if you like that word), and he or she was the brother, sister, father, uncle or nephew of the ancestor of the neighbouring tribe. We meet this in the Bible, where Heth, ancestor of the Hittites, was father of Canaan, ancestor of the Canaanites, where Moab, ancestor of the Moabites, was brother of Ammon, ancestor of the Ammonites, and Eber and Kret were ancestors of Hebrews and Cretans. We meet it in Greece and Asia Minor, where Aeolus and Ion, Lycius, Mysus, Lydus, Mygdon, Bithynus, each had his own large tribe and they were all suitably related to each other. We meet the same family pattern among the Germans, where Cheru ancestor of the Cherusci, Ingaevo ancestor of the Ingaevones, Suebus of the Suebi, affiliated huge and ancient tribes to each other. To the east of them we find Scythes, ancestor of the Scythians, and his brothers, Gelon of the Geloni and Celtos of the Celts.

It is not so easy to discover the ancestors in those lands that were overrun by the Romans before their history had been recorded. But in Gaul we can discern Tricoria of the Tricorii, Nemetona of the Nemetes, Esus of the Essuvii, and Turonus of the Turones. In Spain there was of course Eber of the Iberians, and his daughter Bera, who perhaps was ancestress of their neighbours the Berones. He is distinct from Eber, son of Salah, ancestor of the Hebrews. But the Romans, who had no interest in preserving tribal loyalties among their subjects, liked to treat these Gaulish ancestors as gods, to whom their own gods could be affiliated.

In Ireland the ancestral pattern is a broken one, disorganized not by Roman invaders but by the arrival of Christianity. Nonetheless, among the early recorded invaders were Nemed, father of the Children of Nemed, Eber, ancestor of the Children of Eber, Mil of the Milesians and a group of imaginary beings like Scota, Lug, Baeth, Traig, Finn, who were half god, half man, and whose tribal affinities seem to me obvious but are seldom asserted. And, when we come to the genealogies of the settled tribes of Ireland (O'Brien's *Corpus* is the best record of them), it is clear that almost every tribe, however small, had its imaginary ancestor, related in the traditional continental way to a thousand tribal colleagues. Thus in Munster, Mella, Belocc and Cindiu, ancestresses of the Sil Mella, Ui Belchae and Ui Caindeann, were sisters, and that pattern is everywhere repeated [CGH 345].

If we are to interpret these genealogies correctly, we must first study the mechanics of ancestor-making. What happened to ancestors when their tribes merged with other tribes or spread in small groups to distant lands? There were many problems.

When the Persians allied themselves with the Medes, Perseus did not just marry Medea, for the Medes then preferred a male ancestor, Medea's son, Medus. And, when a small group of Hittites settled among the Canaanites, Heth, son of Canaan, had to distinguish himself from the great Heth, ancestor of the Hittites, who lived very far away. He surely became a distinct person, but a cousin. That is to say there was an infinite duplication of ancestors of the same name and their pedigrees became increasingly complicated.

And that was only the beginning of complications. As time passed and tribes wandered, their names subtly changed. If you look at my Maps 1 to 4, you will see scattered over them a host of names that only differ slightly: Suardones and Sordi, Nemetes and Nemetavi, Lusi and Lusitani. In Ireland too we get tribes whose names run the same gamut of variations; Lig-Lug-Ling-Long

4. HOW ANCESTORS AND SAINTS WERE MADE

is the beginning of an almost infinite series with ancestors to match.

But, as if to arrest the immense proliferation of ancestors, new methods of naming them were used. Two ancestors sometimes amalgamated into one. Thus when some Celts and some Iberians in Spain became 'Celtiberians', an ancestor appeared, Celtiberus, son of Arar, son of Brigulus. I think that such amalgamated ancestors were frequent on the continent and especially in ancient Greece, but they have no status with scholars and, though I should like to talk of Aesculapius and Ulysses and Hercules, my concern is with Ireland; it is there that I wish to prove their frequency and their significance. And it is in Ireland that the evidence is richest and most easily checked.

That is where both Lug, the foster son of Mind, and Lug-Mind were at home; and where Guaire Garb, the rough, had a brother, Guaire Blaith (the Flower-like?). That is to say one ancestor became the aftername of the other. Alternatively, when two tribes came together, they might decide on one common ancestor with two names. Thus Cuchullain (a composite ancestor himself) is also Lug and Setanta.

I can illustrate best the different ways in which Irish ancestors were made and related to each other by the pedigree of Ded, ancestor of the Ui Dedad of Kerry, a tribe with wide British and Scottish extensions, which is thought to have left its traces in England, Scotland and Wales, not only in the names of rivers and towns but also in the ogam stones of Munster and Wales and parts of Scotland, where Daig, son of Corc from Munster, settled with his sons. Surely so great a tribe must have been known in Europe. If we guess what it was, we must guess boldly.

The following pedigree is much simplified, for in fact, Ded had forty sons and daughters and each had variants to their names.

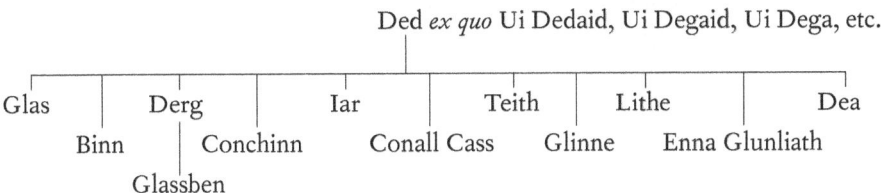

We observe here:

1— Simple ancestors
    Glass *ex quo* Ui Glaissin.
    Binn *ex quo* Benntraige.

Conchinn *ex quo* Ui Conchinn.
Iar, Derg, etc.

2— Amalgamated ancestors
Glassben, nephew of Glass and Binn.
There is in Kerry a tribe called Ui Mac Iair Conchinn, which must derive from both Iar and Conchinn.

3— Ancestors as adjectives
Conall Cass (the curly), *ex quo* Casraige.

4— Ancestors as multiple adjectives
Enna Glunliath. Glunliath (grey knee) derives from the Glunraige and the Ui Liathain. Other brothers were Glinne and Lithe.

5— Ancestors deriving from tribal name variants
Teith, *ex quo* Aes Teith, and Dea, *ex quo* Ui Dega, are male and female variants of Ded.

It was in such ways that ancestors developed out of tribes and acquired from them their afternames and life stories.

There are many stories about all these ancestors, in which considerable liberties have been taken with this pedigree. For instance, there is a story about Ded carrying away as his mistress Conchinn, daughter of Binn. But in the pedigree Binn and Conchinn were both sons of Ded. That is to say the ancestors like the saints would fly away on the wings of fancy, if they were not securely anchored to the ancient tribes.

All the ancestors of the Ded pedigree had saintly counterparts. There were Deg saints and Glass saints: simple or compound they were all there, Binn, Derg, Conchinn, Iar, Cass, Teith, Enna, Glun and Liath.

In South Leinster

How far would the saints outside my window conform to this Kerry pattern? Let us examine one of them, St Moling or Mo Ling of St Mullins. What would one look for and does one find it? I would look for:

(a) A local tribe.
(b) Its ancestor.
(c) The mythological hero who succeeded the ancestor.

4. HOW ANCESTORS AND SAINTS WERE MADE

(d) The saint who succeeded the hero.
(e) Afternames, simple or multiple, indicating the neighbouring tribes, to which the tribe of the hero and the saint are affiliated.
(f) Alternative names for the saint, signifying the ancestors of the tribes, with which his tribe has merged.
(g) A life story based on tribal puns.
(h) A continental tribe from which the Irish tribe would seem to derive.
(i) And then one expects the modern scholar's 'sensible' explanation of it all, to contrast with the ancient scholar's fantastic one.

We have them all at St Mullins:

(a) The Ui Linga tribe lived nearby at the junction of the Barrow and the Nore.
(b) Their ancestor was Ling, son of Mal, ancestor of the Ui Mail [CGH 130], who had many brothers, who were ancestors of tribes. One of them, Fothad, was ancestor of the Ui Fothaid, who left their name in the barony of Forth. Another brother, Cronn or Cronan, was ancestor of the Ui Cranna (barony Crannagh in Kilkenny).
(c) At St Mullins lived the hero Molling or Malling, a pre-Christian warrior friend of Finn. He looks like an amalgamated ancestor to match Ling son of Mal.
(d) Next comes St Moling himself (17 Jun.).
(e) They both had afternames. First came Molling Luath. Then there was St Moling Luachra. Luath is swift, Luachra suggests rushes, and I believe both afternames have the same tribal derivation as Slieve Luachra, a mountain in Kerry, where St Moling is also culted.
(f) St Moling has two other names, Dairchell and Cronan; there were tribes with both these names in Leinster.
(g) He is said to have jumped over some rushes to escape from spectres. He did this because *ling* means jump, *luachair* means rush, and the Fotharta tribe got its name, we are told, from *fuath*, a spectre.
(h) Next there is the question of tribal associations outside Ireland and here you will find that Holder's *Wortschatz* derives the name of the much travelled Lingones from *ling*, a jump. I am sure that Holder is wrong because the Lingones, as they moved across Gaul, north Italy and Spain, had many variants to their name

and who is to say that Lingones is the original one or that it was only when they acquired it that they began to 'jump'? But Holder's testimony is important for it links the modern nonsense explanations for Gaul with the ancient nonsense explanations for Co. Carlow. It is obvious to me that the Ui Linga were an Irish settlement of the Lingones. And you will see in my Glossary that I have gone further; I have placed them with considerable confidence among the Ligurians, for both on the continent and in Ireland Lig and Ling were interchangeable; for example a word for amber was *lingurium* because it came from Liguria.

Finally we have the scholarly approach. My friend Professor Carney calls St Moling 'an undoubtedly historic Irish saint'. He ignores Ling, son of Mal, and the Ui Linga and the Lingones, but he is bothered by the pagan Moiling, Finn's half brother, and says of him: 'He is of course identical with the saint of the same name but by a genealogical fiction is made to belong to an earlier period.' This theory seems to rival Macalister's in improbability. Is it conceivable that our Christian predecessors would turn a real saint into a pagan warrior, who lived many generations earlier?

I have not seen any other suggestion that the Lingones reached Ireland, so it is interesting that W.J. Watson guesses at them in Scotland on the west coast [WJW 45], where St Moling was culted in the island of Arran and in Lewes. He suggests that they gave their name to the river Longus recorded by the second-century geographer Ptolemy and the river Ling in Ross and to Loch Long. Some Welshman should investigate why St Moling was also culted on his feast day, 11 June, at Llannfyllin in Montgomeryshire.

Then there was the usual range of amalgamated ancestors with prefixes and suffixes, which recur again and again. There were Bec Loinges, Conleng, Loingsech, Dunlang, Eolang, Ercleng, Longbardan. In my Glossary I have given the meanings attributed to those added syllables and suggested the tribes from which they derive.

Some Ancestor Saints

Naturally the evidence that the saints derived from ancestors is deeply concealed but sometimes the tribal connection penetrates every disguise. Here is a list of some twenty saints, who were more obviously than others tribal ancestors christianized. They are all of them fabulous and there is nothing to

4. HOW ANCESTORS AND SAINTS WERE MADE

suggest that a tribe in later times chose a genuine saint as patron and named itself after him. Usually the tribe is noted in the same spot in which the saint is culted or in its immediate neighbourhood. Some links are closer than others, but I have not mentioned associations that are merely probable. These are innumerable and I could extend the list indefinitely.

TABLE 2: ANCESTOR-SAINTS

SAINT	TRIBE	LOCALITY
St Mo-Aedoc	Ui Aeda	Clonmore, Co. Carlow
St Berchan		
(a) of Clonamery	Ui Berchain	Rosbercon, Co. Kilkenny
(b) of Clonsast	Ui Berchain	Co. Offaly
St Blad	Bladraige	Isle of Man
St Conchinn	Nepotes Conchinn	Kerry
	Magunihy (MagConchinn)	
St Cuach	Ui Cuaich	Ui Bairrche, Co. Carlow
St Damhin	Clann Daimhin	Loch Erne
St Eochaid	Ui Eochaid	Cluain Ratha
St Erc	Ui Erc	Adech, Co. Donegal
St Lachtan	Ui Lachtnan Ele	Templemore, Co. Tipperary
St Lappan	Ui Lapen	Baltinglass, Co. Wicklow
St Mo-Ling	Ui Linga	St Mullins, Co. Carlow
St Mac Cairthenn		
(a) Ui Maic Cairthinn Clogher		Co. Tyrone
(b) Ui Maic Cairthinn Tir Cairthinn		Loch Foyle
Bishop Maine	Ui Maine	Co. Roscommon
St Muiredach	Ui Muiredach	Tirawley, Co. Mayo
St Neman		
(a) of Dairinis	UiMaic Neamain	Both on river Nem
(b) of Lismore		(Blackwater, Co. Waterford)
St Sillan	Ui Sillain	Ui Dega and Ui Garrchon,
St Sinell	Ui Sinell	Co. Wexford and Wicklow
St Suibhsech	Clann Suibne	South Donegal

I have ignored whatever differences there may be in the size or standing of these social groups and for simplicity referred to them all as 'tribes'.

Investigations like mine belonged once to the province of the country scholar, a man who combined a wide general education with a narrow but intimate local knowledge. I have written my later chapters as though this figure from the past still existed or might be resurrected. I have persuaded myself that the saints and ancestors, whom I have sorted into rough, preliminary groups, would one day be studied group by group by people with a close interest in a particular neighbourhood, tribe, family, community. I have assumed a regional dedication which only this now imaginary person will have.

How Saints Were Made

Let me recapitulate in slightly different terms how, in my view, it came about that ancestors developed into saints. The genealogists had evolved a highly complex technique of neighbourliness, which kept as close as it could to the sources of instinctive love and mutual tolerance. The social virtues start surely between parents and children and have to be stretched a little in order to embrace the extended family and the tribe. The next step, mutual forbearance between alien tribes, must have been the hardest. Reaching beyond the ordinary limits of feeling and habit, an image of a wider solidarity had to be created by the invention of marriages that had never happened and all kinds of imaginary affinities and shared experiences. It must have been a golden age for the poet and social planner. The genealogies had to be kept perpetually up to date, for their message was that all men are brothers or at least that their ancestors had been brothers, sisters, cousins to those of their neighbours.

But sooner or later the ancestor system will have become unworkable under the weight of its own complexities. Society will have become more sophisticated and individualized and real men and women will have competed with symbolic ones for places in the interminable pedigrees. As the old technique of neighbourliness broke down there will have been a readiness to adapt it to a gospel, whose message is that we should love our neighbours as ourselves. As the tribes merged and disintegrated and sharp distinctions became blurred, a celibate saint could have been a useful full stop to a progression that had become meaningless.

Yet neighbourliness remained the form in which Christianity presented itself. In the lives of the saints there is almost nothing, except what is a late intrusion, about universal love or the fatherhood of God or the salvation of the world. Abstract ideas like these seem to belong to the faceless urban conglomerations of imperial Rome, in which, as today, neighbours were of diminishing importance. Until the Normans with their universalist pretensions arrived, the Irish were not well-disposed to any centralized ecclesiastical uniformity. Of course, we are told, the saints went to Rome in droves and, shaming the Popes with their superior piety, often became Popes themselves and brought back to their cult centres in Ireland relics of all the apostles and cartloads of holy Roman soil. But most of this ecumenical flurry happened in the imagination, the old tribal code words being applied to the new systems and new scriptural homonyms being invented. The midland tribe, the Fir Cell, became Viri Ecclesiarum; Cape Clear Island was Insula Clericorum; Ardee (Ath Fir Dead) was Atrium Dei; Bangor (Bend Chor) was De Choro Benedicto. St Kessog wrote a catechesis, St Nem became St Nehemiah, St Lua St Luke, and St Grigoir of Aran became Pope Gregory the Great and adopted his feast day. St Martin of Tours, St Hilary of Arles, St Germanus of Auxerre and Pope Sylvester all had Irish counterparts, who shared their names and feast days.

There were no martyrs, no crusades, no heretics to speak of, and, if one contrasts the coming of Christianity to the continent, one can have no regrets about this. The continental methods of spreading the gospel are vividly described in a letter from Alcuin, Charlemagne's Anglo-Saxon adviser, to a certain Irishman, Caelcu or Colgu. There were mythological Caelcus, holy men, who linked the Caelcu tribes of Iona with those of Galway Bay, very interesting people about whom I wish I have time to write in my chapter on the Geloni. This Caelcu, lector in Scotia, is surely a real person and the letter belongs to our real world, well intentioned, violent, hypocritical.

> Your delight will be gratified by knowing that, through the mercy of God, His Holy Church has peace, prosperity and increase in certain parts of Europe. For the old Saxons and Frisians have been converted to the Faith of Christ, through the instrumentality of King Charlemagne, some being led to this course by rewards and some owing to threats. During the last year the same king made an onset against the Sclaves, whom we call Venedi and subjected them to his power.

This paragraph shows how tenaciously the ancient peoples clung to their beliefs and what drastic methods were used to convert them. A couple of generations earlier St Willibrord and St Boniface and St Wulfram had preached to the Saxons and Frisians, had burnt idols, hewn down sacred trees and assailed Forseti, the Frisian 'deity' himself, in his sacred island of Heligoland. With the armed might of Pepin and Charles Martel behind them, they had made hundreds of thousands of converts. And here it was to be done all over again by Charlemagne (see p. 224).

Plainly the attack on Forseti and his island had not, except as a military adventure, been successful. It was clear that subtler tactics had to be used and, in my chapter on St Fursa, I show that there is evidence that both St Willibrord and Charlemagne had considered the Irish method of turning tribal ancestors into saints and that Forseti and the tribal ancestors, who were his colleagues, had been subjected to it with varying degrees of success.

How lucky the Irish were that no foreigners forced Christianity down their throats and that they were allowed to make these adjustments in their own way at their own time! Their sacred trees were never hewn down, nor were their holy wells polluted, nor the immense and detailed genealogies of their tribes treated with contumely. The wise men of the Celts had a time-honoured skill in correlating seemingly contradictory hypotheses. They knew how to make old enemies sit side by side on the same branch of the family tree; pagan and Christian beliefs were dovetailed into each other with expert ingenuity. The towering fabric of genealogical make believe, which led to epic poetry in Greece, led in Ireland to the most elaborate and abundant hagiography that any country possesses.

CHAPTER 5

Who was Lug?

Much has been written of the Celtic gods but they are few, grotesque and altogether unsatisfactory. They are earthy people with odd and earthy adventures and if, like Taranis, they preside over thunderstorms, or Catubodua over war, it is because that is what their name implies. If one or two of them like Esus, ancestor of Esuvii and Atesui, of northern Gaul were known to have had tribal connections, that is never mentioned. Becoming a god or a saint was a routine metamorphosis, which, I believe, every tribal ancestor had to face when he lost his tribe. The best known of the Irish gods was Lug and what I have said about Ling, St MoLing, the Lingones and the Ligurians is a good introduction to him.

Some fifty miles from St MoLing's cult centre on the Barrow is Clonfert Molua under the Slieve Bloom mountains. St Molua or MoLua mac Oiche (4 Aug.) belongs, I believe, to the same group as MoLing and can illuminate its origins. St Molua is of north Tipperary. He is also called Lugid and probably began his career as ancestor of the Clann Lugdach Ui Oichri. He had a multitude of namesakes (St Comgall of Bangor had fifty monks all called Molua) and he himself had the art of being in three places at once. The Scottish Moluas, sometimes called St Luke, reached up the west coast to the Hebrides.

Our St Molua got his name in this way. St Comgall was walking through some rushes (*luachair*, rush, often comes into the story of these Lug-Ling notabilities) and gave a kick, *lua*, to a baby who happened to be lying there. He picked it up and put it under his armpit (*oiche*) and called it Molua Mac Oiche, or 'My kick, son of armpit'. *Lua*, kick, is a well tried pun. Uachtair Lua in

Monaghan got its name because an old man kicked his doctor for giving bad advice [TBC 3768].

This is the sort of story that Ledwich called 'barbarous' and Macalister 'childish rubbish', but it fills me with excitement. An ancient writer is trying to communicate something too complicated for current speech. It has to be pickled against oblivion in pun language, the precursor of poetry. The puns preserve it safely but the dictionary for pun language has not yet been written.

We have to grope behind the phantoms, the saint, the hero, the ancestor, for the reality, the ancient tribe that once lived here.

Some 120 years ago some scholars of the Kilkenny Archaeological Society visited the mouldering graveyard of Kyle Clonfert and they noted that St Molua's feast is celebrated at Kyle not on his own day, 4 August, but on Lugnasa, 1 August, which is the festival of Lug, the greatest of the pan-Celtic gods. At the same time it was observed that St Molua's well at Emlygrennan was earlier associated with Lugaid, a pagan warrior of fable [JRSAI 117; MD, Met. Dind. Cend Febrat]. It was suggested that he might be identical with Lug, but such speculations had become unpopular and were not pursued.

But was Lug a god originally or did he become one, like the tribal ancestor Esus, and if so what tribe was he ancestor of? As I have said, there were a dozen Lug-Lig-Ling tribes reaching from the Oder through Gaul, north Italy and Iberia to the north of Scotland and the whole of Ireland, and they were all very careless of their vowels. There were the Lugii or Lygii in eastern Europe. There were the Ligyes near Cadiz, the Lugones or Lungones in Asturias, Lougi on the Moray Firth, and when we come to Ireland there are Lig-Lug tribes galore and a huge number of alternative spellings is revealed (see p. 62).

In classical times Ligurians lived around the Gulf of Genoa, where they left their name at Lucca, but it was known that they had once extended far to the north and west, and many thought they had reached Spain and Britain. We get an echo of their struggles in the story of three warriors, Ligys, Draganes and Alebion, battling with Hercules on the borders of Spain. They were clearly the ancestors of the Ligurians, of the Draganum Proles (a tribe of Portugal) and of the Albiones, whom my Map 1 (p. 63) shows in Asturias and who also gave their name Albion to Britain. I believe that ancestors seldom fight anything but ancestors and I think that Hercules, well known in Ireland, was one himself.

There are different views as to how far the Ligurian domain extended. To the Greeks Ligurian history like all other early history was told in puns, for since *ligus* means shrill, the king of the Ligurians became a swan. Nowadays,

5. WHO WAS LUG?

perhaps because of the predominance of Celtic studies, the Ligurians are an unpopular people and I have never seen it suggested that the Liger (the Loire) took its name from them. And it is heresy to argue that they had anything to do with Lugdunum, the ancient name of Lyon, Leyden and various cities in Provence and in central Europe or with Luguvallum, Carlisle. It is firmly fixed in the mind of all reputable scholars that Lug was an ancient pan-Celtic god. But, in fact, neither Gauls nor Romans said much about this god. The Romans called Lyon 'Mons Lucidus' and the Gauls connected it with *lougos*, a raven, and the arms of the city was a raven. In Ireland itself Lug is grotesque rather than divine. His widespread cult could merely be evidence of the power that the Ligurians once exercised in Ireland. He behaved precisely like the other ancestors; there were many of him, each with different parentage and he had other reincarnations, as tribal ancestors did, when their tribes were assimilated out of existence. He was reborn as Cuchullain and, as Lug mac Eithlenn, aided him to kill 130 kings and maim for life two-thirds of the people of Ireland [TBC 203]. Cuchullain's own tribal affinities can be deduced from my Glossary. And the genealogies show dozens of compound ancestors, in whose names Lug has a prefix or suffix that is plainly tribal: Aedlug, Baethlug, Caemlug, Caslug, Erclug, Ferloga, Findlug, Iarlug, Trenlug, Lugmael, Lugtigern, Lugid, Lugdech, Lugbrand, Lugmind, Lug Scieth (lynx of the shield) and so on [CGH X 7]. A good instance of an association of ancestors, both single and compound, comes in a midland pedigree [CGH 96] where Lug is the son of Cas, the son of Caslug.

There are of course Lig ancestors too, but the predominance of the Lugs could be explained if a contingent came from the Lugones, Lingones or Lungones of northern Spain. Indeed Lug mac Eithlenn's great-great-grandfather, Miled, came from Spain [CGH 55] and was not a god but a tribal ancestor.

Of course if they were in Ireland they were most probably in England too. This is outside my province but, if two ancient names are explained by scholars (wrongly) in the same way, it is fair to suspect an affinity. The Lougi of Sutherland are like Lugdunum derived from *lougos*, a raven.

Luguvallum is also Caer Ligualid (Carlisle) and Geoffery of Monmouth, reinforced by the Welsh triads, says that the Loegrians came from Gascony and left their name Lloegyr to the English midlands. Their ancestor was Locrine. To the same family party surely belonged Lud of Caer Lud (London) and Lot or Loth, king of Lothian and Norway, who was St Kentigern's cruel grandfather.

Was Lug himself ever a saint? In Ireland there was St Lugh (19 Nov.); in England St Lucius, king of Britain (3 Dec.) might qualify. He was baptized by

Timothy, disciple of St Paul, and converted all the heathen temples in Britain to Christian churches.

The British say he was buried at Gloucester but the Swiss claim to have his relics at Chur in the Grisons. He had laid aside his crown and sceptre and preached there to the heathen, who had thrown him into a hot spring. He had emerged unhurt and withdrawn with his sister, St Emerita, to a neighbouring cave, the Luciuslochlein.

Baring-Gould gives an excellent and detailed account of his story. To me his Swiss missionary travels are of interest, because there were certainly Ligurians in the Grisons. Chur lies south of the Vindelici, who bordered on Lake Constance and whom I have compared to the Sil Findloga with their ancestor, Findlug.

That is to say Lug was ancestor of the much-travelled Lig-Lug folk, whom we know as the Ligurians. I note that the presence of Ligurians in Ireland is more widely accepted than I had thought. Myles Dillon, *Celtica* Volume VII, quotes in a review of Whatmough's *Dialects of Ancient Gaul*: 'The suggestion that Goidelic Celts were Ligurians is not altogether implausible.'

Chapter 6

The First Invaders of Ireland

The Irish had very definite ideas as to who the first invaders of Ireland were and where they came from. First before the flood came Cessair, daughter of Bith, son of Noah, with her fifty maidens. Then came Partholon from Mygdonia and northern Greece, via Sicily and Spain. After him were the Conchind or Dog Heads, who killed all living men in Ireland. Then came Nemed of the Greeks of Scythia. He and his people died of plague at Ard Nemed, which is Little Island in Cork and only three of his following, Simeon Breac, Iobath, son of Beothach, and Briotan Mael, survived. Beothach went to Boeotia or else to the 'north of the world' (Bothnia). Simeon Breac went to Thrace and Briotan Mael went to Britain and became the ancestor of all the Britons.

The next invaders were the Fir Bolg, descendants of Simeon Breac in Thrace. They included two other peoples, the Fir Domnann and the Gaileoin. They covered the whole of Ireland, but were eventually driven to the islands of the west by the next invaders, the Tuatha De Danann.

The Tuatha De Danann who came after the Fir Bolg are the descendants of Beothach from Boeotia and came from Athens and Achaea to FionnLochlann, which is Norway, and thence to Alba, which is Scotland. They were a magical people landing from clouds in the mountains of Connaught.

They were succeeded by the Gaedel or Sons of Mil, who came from Scythia via Spain and remained the dominant aristocracy of Ireland.

This is an extravagantly condensed summary, for it is impossible not to be exasperated by these tales told with endless repetition and variation in several different texts. We owe it to Macalister's dogged persistence that the mechanical work of editing a story that he obviously found silly and distasteful was carried nearly to its conclusion. Death took him as it took Canon O'Hanlon, before he had reached the index volume. In the end five volumes were published. And we now know the names of all the invaders, of their wives, their servitors, their jesters and their oxen. Even the plough share and its coulter had a personal name. There are many monstrous and mysterious anecdotes. None of it of course is true in the ordinary way and Macalister, who detected real people behind the fantastic stories of the saints, found most of the invasion stories 'empty of historical significance'. The labour of editing this vast collection would have been unendurable, if he had not been sustained by the scholar's interest in orthographical oddities, in the correcting of corrupt texts and careless transcripts and in various notions he had about totemism and matriarchy and 'rustic polydaemonism' (that was how he explained the naming of plough shares and coulters) and a theory he had about idols, to which I will return.

In fact most of the grotesque stories could, I believe, be explained in my usual way without recourse to anthropology. There is an elaborate genealogical background to the invasion stories. The family tree, which started before the Flood, had the ancestors of all the ancient tribes of Europe in its branches, some of them early medieval fantasies, some of them far older. There was Eber of the Iberians, Assur of the Assyrians, Longbardus of the Lombards, Persius, Grecus, Saxus and cohorts of the Irish ancestors, whom we shall meet in the lives of the saints or have already met. After their distant travels and frequent minglings, many of the Irish ancestors, being amalgamated, were hard to identify. Such a one was Lugaid, son of Ith, who was uncle of Mil and led the Sons of Mil to Ireland. At the end of Chapter 2, I suggested that he was a composite figure. Rereading the *Book of Invasions*, I find this expressly stated. 'Lugaid means Lug Ith,' writes the chronicler, but, since an amalgamated ancestor, though a genealogical necessity, is a biological absurdity, he adds, 'that is to say Lug, who was *luga*, or less, than his father Ith' [LG 41] (see p. 17).

Most of the anthropological oddities arose, I believe, from dilemmas like this. The idols, the totemism, the vegetation rituals, the 'pastoral polydaemonism', the matriarchal survivals and all the rest, were, if they existed, of only secondary significance. In the foreground was the genealogical tree, which grew on its own roots and had been nourished for centuries according to ancient traditions. The strange fruit it bore were natural to it, and Macalister, who grumbles about 'childish nonsense', is grumbling about life itself. The basic facts were the ancestors and the punful interpretations of them. Not only ploughs and ploughshares but chessboards and shields and bells and reliquaries

6. THE FIRST INVADERS OF IRELAND

all had personal names. The reason for this and for the long catalogues of servitors and wives and oxen, which infuriated him, was not polydaemonism, pastoral or otherwise; it was due to the superabundance of venerable ancestors, whose names had survived long after the tribes which they had fathered had merged or disappeared. If you were a chronicler who revered the past, what could be more fitting than to apply these time-honoured syllables, where relevant, to the heroes, the saints and all their possessions?

There was a vast pool of such names, timeless and ageless as all ancestors were. Macalister thought the long catalogues of peculiar names that fill the pages of the *Book of Invasions* were senselessly invented. But the names recur again and again, dealt out to different people like cards in a pack. Mil was not only father of the Sons of Mil, the last recorded invaders, he was also a female attendant of Cessair, the first invader; Mil's uncle, the mighty Ith, son of Bregon, was not only a leader of the Sons of Mil, he was also a servitor to Partholon. Servitors, wives, oxen, mostly have names that are familiar even when they are odd: Milchu, Dorcha, Carthenn, Liger, Aine, and afternames Breac, Mael, Liath, Lethderg, Echruad, Lamfin, Lamglan, Glunfind. There were the same impossible explanations for them. For example Lamfind or White Hand had luminous hands (so that he steered by night); his son Eber Glunfind, White Knee, had white spots on his knees; Cridenbel, Heart-mouth, had his mouth in his breast; names for which my Glossary will give tribal explanations.

If Eber Glunfind had no white spots on his knees but was as I believe an amalgamated Ibero-Gelono-Venetic ancestor, Macalister's idol theory is unnecessary. But it is easier to prove that he is wrong than that I am right and this proof is a first necessary stage.

Macalister and the Idols

Macalister takes as an illustration of his idol theory a grotesque figure called Fer Caille, who had a wife Cichol, who was, with a different sex in a different fable, one of the invaders of Ireland. There was a Gallic notability, Cicol, whom Macalister and others take to be a god, but I hold to be some sort of ancestor, perhaps connected deviously with the Thracian Cicones.

Fer Caille (Man of the Wood) had buttocks like cheeses and only one arm and one leg and a nose that could be looped across a branch of a tree. Macalister considers [LG II 263] that all this would be 'a dreary piece of silliness', if Fer Caille was not some sort of idol, who was given a shrine in a pagan temple because of 'a chance freak of tree growth, which made him look like a misshapen man'. But Fer Caille was just an ordinary ancestor with two quite ordinary namesakes. One of them was also called Fer Fuilli and descended with many tribal uncles and cousins from Dallan of the Cenel Dallain [CGH 226]. Another Fer Caille was an ordinary mythological warrior in the Cuchullain Saga [THU 483]: That is to say Macalister's Fer Caille was certainly never 'a freak of tree growth'; he owed his tree-like excrescences to a pun on his name – dreary and silly maybe, but not idolatrous. If I am right Fer Caille would have represented both the Fer tribe and the Caille or Cael tribe. He could be associated with Caelfer, ancestor of the Caelrige and with Gelfer (FerGel) [THU 654], and with all those folk who were thin, *cael*, or one-eyed, *goll*, or white, *gel*, or concerned with hazel, *coll*, or holly, *cuillean*, or *cuilen*, puppy, all of them deriving as I suggest in my Glossary, from the Geloni. Nor was Fer Caille's one hand and one leg an arboreal freak; there were other invaders with Cichol, who had one arm and one leg [LG III 13], and Cuchullain once disabled himself in this way [TBC 150]. If you investigate the genealogies closely, you will even find ancestors named Aenlam and Aencos, deriving from One-tribes, One-hand or One-arm tribes and One-leg tribes. Aengus (now Angus) owed his name, we are told in a fable [THU 606] to *aen gus*, one strength, but, as we are clearly dealing in puns on the untranslatable, is not *aencos*, one leg, just as valid?

O'Rahilly and the Gods

What the idol theory was to Professor Macalister, the god theory was to Professor O'Rahilly, who devotes many pages [EIHM 43–84] to proving that the Fir Bolg were Belgae speaking a P-Celtic tongue and claiming descent from a Celtic thunder god, called Bolg (lightening) and having many divine aliases, such as Oengus Bolg. But Oengus Bolg and his brother, Oengus Dublesc, were perfectly normal tribal ancestors; they were plainly composite and belonged to three neighbouring tribes of South Munster, the Ui Oengusa [CGH 260], the Ui Builc [262] and the Ui Duiblesc [263]. In other genealogies Bolg was Bolc, and Bolc was Bloc and a female Bloc was also Beloc and ancestress of the Ui Belchae [CGH 345]. If they were all manifestations of a lightening god, why could they not get his name right?

On the other hand the name of a wandering tribe is likely to be as unstable as a family name is today. (Do not most anglicized Irish surnames have a dozen

6. THE FIRST INVADERS OF IRELAND

variants?) So if we are looking for continental relations for the Fir Bolg, why pick on the Belgae rather than the much-travelled Volcae of Provence, the Balkan peninsula and Asia Minor, or the Volciani and the Olcades of Iberia? Why invent a Bolg god and omit Vulcan, who surely started as a tribal ancestor himself? Whether the Fir Bolg were proto-Volcae or late Belgae or, as I believe, a hybridized offshoot, does not concern me here. They clearly linked up with a great European fraternity, which included all the Bolg-Volc-Olc peoples. The poet Ausonius said that the Volcae were Belcae, the historian Mela said the Belgae were Celto-Scythians from the Baltic. They may have been wrong; what is certain is that the attempt to solve this problem by philology is bound to fail.

On the other hand the saints have, as always, their evidence to contribute. As I show in a later section 'St Bolgan and the Bags', St Bolcan of Drumbulcain in Co. Antrim (20 Feb.) was also called Olcan, because *olc* means evil. He had had the evil experience of being born in the tomb from a dead mother.

St Bolcan of Roscommon (4 Jul.) was similarly called both Volcan and Olcan and both saints came from Bolg territory, where there were secular ancestors called Bolc and Olcu. That St Bolcan (20 Feb.) was an ancestor who did not impersonate a saint very satisfactorily, is clear. St Patrick had made him a bishop but was later obliged to curse him and his church [OH II 647].

Macalister shows that these invasion chroniclers were greatly influenced by the fifth-century ecclesiastical geographer, Orosius, and the seventh-century ecclesiastical etymologist and historian Isidore, and inspired by a pious desire to link the ancestors of the Irish with Adam and Noah and the Tower of Babel. St Isidore was Archbishop of Seville; he won back Spain from Arianism to the Church and was the only important writer on secular subjects in two centuries. Yet he argues as men argued a thousand years before Strabo, and centuries before Herodotus. He writes like an arrested child, who shrinks from the adult world, whereas the Irish are happy primitives using a current idiom. When Isidore writes of the Sciopodes or Shadefeet in Ethiopia, who lay on their backs in the sun shading themselves with their single monstrous foot, one can infer nothing except intellectual decay, but, in the invasion stories of Ireland, behind the Isidorean facade real secrets are hidden.

Most of the tribal names in the invasion stories are historic: the Fir Bolg, the Fir Domnann, the Gaileoin and the Conchind or Dogheads. Mi, Lug, Ith, Bregon and Nemed are just as much ancestors as Assur of the Assyrians and Briotan of the Britons, and there must be equally substantial tribes behind them. Who were they? No one will dispute that Bregon was of the Brigantes and Conchind of the Ui Conchind. No one ought to dispute that Lug was of the Ligurians, and Nemed was of the Nemedes. You will see from Map 2 (p. 64) that the Nemed folk wandered as widely as did the Lig-Lug-Ling folk. They were Nemetes at Memel on the Baltic, Nemedes in Germany, Nemeturii in north-east Spain. They changed their race as rapidly as they changed their name and address and I am sure that in their Celtic phase, they considered themselves to be *nemed*, holy. O'Rahilly, the philologist, thought as they did.

Ith na n'ech [LG 106] or Ith of the horses is a profound mystery and a more important one. For Ith or Ech or Aed had five or six other name variants and clearly represented some great tribe once dominant in Europe. To them, I believe, belonged the 'horse' folk of Britain, that is to say the Iceni of East Anglia and the Epidii of Galloway and many Id-Fid-Aed folk of Gaul. According to the theory of P-Celts and Q-Celts, Ech-ich is the same as Ep. Could they be the Picts, distinct from the Cruithne but related to the Pictones of the Gaulish coast? Could they have lost their 'P', when they crossed to Britain, leaving traces of themselves in Vectis or Icta, the Isle of Wight, and in Inish Pich, which is Spike Island near Cork? That is for the philologist to decide.

These invasion tales are unanimous that by different routes the Irish came from Thrace and Scythia, from Mygdonia, Greece, Gaul, Iberia, Dacia and the Caucasus, and Macalister is confident that they were simply copying down lists of names from Orosius and Isidore. Possibly, but all they are saying is that over centuries and millenia all the tribes of Europe were in motion, dispersing and merging and replacing each other. Orosius and Isidore no doubt affected the general plan of the *Book of Invasions*, but the detailed working out was done in the traditional Irish way. That is to say there was an ancestor to take the place of every tribe and to illustrate its wanderings and its minglings in his complicated life. I believe that the invaders reached Ireland in confused driblets over an immense period of time: many of the eggs had been already scrambled in Europe and, for the purpose of unscrambling, the genealogies of the ancestors and the stories of their successors, the heroes and the saints, are the most effective instruments we have.

Once we are used to the idea that the fifteen thousand ancestors were neither real people nor invented fantasies but eponymously bore the names of real tribes, often much compounded and battered, our method of enquiring what those tribes were instantly changes. Since the ruling tribes of Europe, who are likely to have used the ancestor system in the centuries before Christ, are mostly known to us, it is fair to examine the index of O'Brien's *Corpus* and to guess the tribal origins of the long columns of names that fall into twenty or thirty distinct groups.

6. THE FIRST INVADERS OF IRELAND

Without accepting the full range of variants that enlarged the bounds of every name group, there are seven or eight predominant elements in the names of the ancestors, each of them with some 400 representatives or more. There were:

1– the Cu-Con-Cind group
2– the Lig-Lug-Ling group
3– the Brig-Brec group
4– the Ith-Ech-Aed group
5– the Mil-Mael group
6– the Finn-En group
7– the Carp-Corb group

I believe that the first three were Cunesioi, Ligurians, Briges, and the last two Veneti and Carpi or Carpetani. I believe there was a very large Thracian group but the name of the Thracian ancestor was shattered among the Treg-Derg-Erc-Draig-Rig groups.

The Iber group (Iberians) is very small, since there are only twenty or so Ibar, Eber, Faebar ancestors. I do not know how to explain this scarcity. Nor is there much point in discussing it, until it is agreed that the saints and ancestors were not real people or 'folklore', but scholarly fabrications. To refute this and all my arguments that depend on it, it is only necessary to prove that even one per cent of the twenty-five thousand early saints and ancestors, whom I treat as fabricated, were real people. Can this be done?

CHAPTER 7

Les Hommes Elégants de la Forêt: Tribal Implications of Gaulish Proper Names

I have suggested that the tribal names of Ireland and the tribal ancestors were all integrated from the broken-down names of older tribes. If this is so and if, for example, the Sil Findloga and its ancestor Findlug really derived from an amalgam of Veneti and Ligurians, one would expect the same process to operate elsewhere in Europe. Did it? Almost all the authorities from Holder, whose great three-volume work covers all the proper names of Celtic Europe, to D.E. Evans in his recent *Gaulish Personal Names* think the opposite. They believe that all this profusion of names is translatable, mostly in a Celtic tongue, and they use Irish analogies. Even so Mr Evans has to admit that there is hardly a single name about which there can be any certainty.

Nor are the Irish analogies helpful. When Holder accepts a French scholar's explanation of the Viducasses as 'les hommes élégants de la forêt' (*fid* is wood and *cass* is curly), apart from the mistaken notion that tribes give themselves names and very fanciful ones at that, he has not reckoned with Bishop Fid of Ath Fadat in Carlow, or the three brother saints, sons of Fidbadach, St Fidmuine, St Fidgus and St Fidairle. He has not dealt with the odd coincidence that the Vadicassii are obviously related neighbours in Gaul of the Viducasses and that *fad* means long not wood. In none of the Irish Fid folk does wood offer any but a highly fanciful explanation and Fid is always highly variable: Fid is the same as Aed and Fith and Ith and Id. St Fidgus is to me an Irish version of the ancestor of the Viducasses and his two brothers and his father ancestors of three related Fid tribes.

The belief that Cass could in these proper names mean curly is surely disproved by the large range of Cass tribes that reach from the Chatti or Cassi of Hesse right across Gaul to the Cassi of Hertfordshire and the Dal Cass or Cais of Clare. If Bodiocasses meant yellow curls, what kind of curls did the Durocasses have or the Tricasses, the Diicasses, the Bellocasses and the Baiocasses?

Mr Evans thinks the proper name, Cassitalos, might mean Curly-brow, but the clue to its real meaning lies in Co. Clare, where the Clann Tail had an ancestor Tal and the Dal Cais had an ancestor Cas. Between the two of them they had the shared ancestor, Cas mac Tail, also known as Cassius Tallius.

In Ireland there was now and again a pun about *tal*, an axe, and *tul*, a brow [GPN], but the true meaning was tribal. Cas Mac Tail, (Curly, son of Axe) was not originally, as alleged, a carpenter.

Similarly in Gaul Cassibodua was ancestor of the Bodiocasses and her understudy Catubodua or Bodb Catha was not really the 'Raven of War'. Bodb Catha was, I suggest, amalgamated ancestress of the Bodbraige or Ui Bodbain [CGH 52] and the Clann Cathrae [CGH 312]. She became a war goddess because of her name, not vice versa.

There are, of course, occasions when Mr Evans claims to have certainly found 'a meaning' for one of these Gaulish names, but I believe he finds it because it was 'planted' there by some early philologist, who was as eager as he is for meanings and less exacting. Mr Evans is confident, for example, that the tribal name of the Eburones meant Yew folk; he says that this meaning is 'virtually implied' in Caesar's story [BG 6 31], that the king of the Eburones poisoned himself with berries of the yew, *ibar*. This argument transports us surely to the enchanted twilight in which Cormac composed his glossary and the monks the lives of the saints. Is it not far more probable that a venerable tribal pun was being invoked, either by druids and courtiers, who invented the story of the king's death or less probably by the king himself, who chose this form of death as being the most symbolic? We can find a parallel to this story in the life of St Ibar, whose mother, when pregnant with the saint, had a face as red as a yew tree, *ibar*. This story 'virtually implies' that St Ibar's name derives from a yew tree and dissociates him effectively from Eber, ancestor of the Iberians. In effect all that is proved by the two tales is that the thousand years that elapsed between Julius Caesar and the medieval hagiographers had not altered the technique of interpreting ancient proper names. The more inscrutable they were, the greater freedom one had to invent, but naturally certain meanings became hallowed by long usage and these were the ones that Cormac tabulated in his glossary.

Is it possible for a sober-minded philologist to pick his way through this jungle of ancient proper names, in which fantasy so frequently reshaped the word it claimed to interpret? Can one advance very far by the light of 'dental affricates' and 'case syncretisms'? Can they help us investigate a society where there was an insatiable appetite for meanings, but fantastic ones were preferred? I do not think they can help us much, as is proved by Mr Evans' grim struggle with the name of Caesar's great Gaulish opponent Vercingetorix. The Romans thought it a meaningless name, 'to inspire terror', and about its meaninglessness they were probably right. But Mr Evans divides it traditionally in three parts: Fer, intensively, Chinged, hero or champion, Rix, a king, and he mentions as an analogy an Irish hero Ferchinged.

In fact this Fer Ching or Chinged had a father called Fer Mac, ancestor of a county Clare tribe, the Ui Fermaic, and a brother called Fer Domnach. Is it likely that a man called 'Intensively a Son' would have two sons called 'Intensively a Champion' and 'Intensively Sunday'? As I show later, personal names beginning in Fer had this odd habit of clustering in groups of two or three, which is only explicable if they were divergent forms of the ancestors of a tribe that had allied itself with two or three different neighbouring tribes. Elsewhere I suggest that this tribe was the Verones of central Iberia.

There are many hundreds of such Fer names in Irish and Fer is never translated 'intensively' but always as 'Man'. Thus Fer Det or Vir Fumi (man of smoke) was a fireman. By similar playful stories it was shown that Fer meant neither intensively nor man. Fer Det had a brother called Fer Diad and clearly the two were different forms of the ancestor of the Fer folk amalgamated with Ded, ancestor of the Clann Dedaid of Kerry.

To prove that Cingit was a tribal word without the meaning champion should not be hard. There are two Cingits in Ireland, both of them female and both of them pronouncedly genealogical figures, with very unstable names. One was also called Cindiu and was ancestress of the Ui Chaindean of Waterford [CGH 345]. The other was also called Cennait and was the daughter and mother of famous ancestors of the south-west [CGH 16]. What ancient tribe lay beyond the Ui Chaindean? My guess would be that Cingit, like her brother Cu Roi mac Daire, belonged to the Cu folk, the Cynetes or Cunesioi. And I believe that Vercingetorix too bore with him an echo of their name.

Finally there is the last syllable of Vercingetorix, -rix. Mr Evans says that for *rig* 'the meaning king is certain'. But, in fact, *rig* often occurs in Irish proper names and, as often as not, it means 'wrist'. Thus Cairbre Rigfada, ancestor of the Dal Ri (gf)ada, of Ulster and Scotland, had a long wrist, other tribal ancestors had yellow, brown, white wrists and two shades of red (*ruad* and *derg*). It would have been much easier to say they were kings but the punsters chose rather to give them this strange deformity.

There are, of course, thousands of tribal names in which *rig* occurs and in which the meaning king is not inappropriate. Cormac in his glossary says the Benntraige tribe had a Rennet or Curd Kingdom, Binit-rige. But there are just enough tribal names like Duro-triges and Allo-triges to suggest that the termination was once -troighe or -traige and the Muscraige of Cork were said to have been Musc-troighe and the Calraige were Cal-troighe. Troighe, according to the ancients' explanation, meant Clann [SG 537]. The way is open to my suggestion that *raige* is a variant of the tribal word for Thracian.

Mr Evans, in his most valuable work, analyses some sixty elements of Gaulish names, which have equivalents in Ireland. I believe that with each one of them it would be possible to show that 'the meaning', which the Gauls or the Irish or the modern scholar attributes to them, is pun-provoked and that the reality behind them is all tribal.

Country Methods

I believe that many scholarly misapprehensions came about when archaeology was divorced from the countryside, where it arose, and where men had some instinctive understanding of how their country predecessors behaved. We notice how from decade to decade our neighbours modify their names in defiance of linguistic laws. And we guess that our ancestors were as wilful. In his book *Surnames and Christian Names in Ireland* (1901), R.E. Matheson, once a country registrar, dealing with births, deaths and marriages in Ulster, showed how even in our relatively literate days, names are liable by progressive attrition to turn into something totally different. Everything depends on local idiosyncrasies and associations. For example, the Scottish names Alexander and Archibald vary in Ireland from district to district. Alexander became Kelshenter in Tandragee, Elchinder in Ballymoney, McClatty in Cookstown; Archibald is Esble in Ballymoney, Aspel in other places, and each name has many variants. Every vowel and every consonant is liable to change. Indigenous names are as variable. Quigley, for instance, is Cogley, Kegley and Twigley, and a brother would often choose one form and a sister the other. And money made a difference. Certain names were 'better' than others. The Mac Parlands, aspiring socially, became Parnells, just as in the south the Welshes became Walsh.

Our predecessors were even more unpredictable in their handling of names, for they expected a name to have a meaning, so that, when time distorted it, it was pushed on beyond a new noise to a new significance. One can see from English analogies how this could be done. Supposing, let us say, one had to work out careers for two mythical figures, the first Elchinder and the first Kelshenter, Elchinder could have been Elk-hunter, a great hero, while Kelshenter, as Kill-Sinners, would have been a fanatical saint. And one could easily imagine alternatives.

The scholars of a later day would have to work back from the hero and the saint to the Alexander family. Philology, that subtle science, would be useless. It would be like trying to mend a bicycle tyre with a sewing machine. One would have to go to north-east Ulster and talk to a great many people, or better still live there. That is country archaeology. It is not superior to the academic kind, but its aims and its methods are totally different. Its decay is a great intellectual disaster.

I have throughout used the country methods, correlating ancient tribal names not by philology but by biographical facts. The Quigleys, Cogleys, Twigleys and Kegleys were grouped together, because Matheson had found a Kegley, whose grandfather had been Quigley, or a Cogley who had been a Twigley in his youth. If Quigley ever had a meaning, it had been lost and only poets and punsters would associate these names with cogs, twigs and kegs or their Irish equivalents.

The philologist's approach is bound to be different. In deciphering ancient names, there are no living people to catechize, so he pounces eagerly on meaningful syllables, the cogs, twigs and kegs. Yet a solicitor in Cookstown or a priest in Tandragee has a better idea of what men are like.

Are all these learned interpretations of proper names wrong? Dare one say such a thing of Holder's majestic *Alt-Keltischer Sprachscatz*, which explores for their root meanings all the 'Celtic' proper names of antiquity and which has recently been republished? Yes, one dare. If you feel appalled at your presumption, turn to Volume II page 739 and you will see that Holder thought Enniskillen was in Co. Kilkenny and that his recent editors have been unable to correct him. The mistake is of no consequence to philology but it emphasizes the great gulf that yawns between the archaeology of the countryside and the archaeology of academies and institutes.

To say that these books are based on wrong premises is no more damaging to them than it is to O'Hanlon or Baring-Gould or O'Rahilly, whose conclusions have all been rejected but whose learning is still valuable. Yet, in regard to proper names, the academic obsession with cogs and twigs and kegs is a real obstacle to the imaginative understanding of our ancestors.

CHAPTER 8

Where Did the Irish Come From?

From where, in fact, did the Irish come? The Irish answer was that they came from almost every country known to them, from Iberia and Gaul and Thrace and Scythia and Greece and Scandinavia and Asia Minor. And, in fact, that is not a bad answer. Reflect that invaders must have been coming in driblets for millennia. There must have been an established civilization in Ireland when Newgrange and the other megalithic monuments were built, centuries before the Celts arrived. The Celtic invasion may well have been the last and smallest. They will have merged with the others and the Irish language will have been a blend of many tongues. Even if a Celtic language dominated all the others, as English did in Ireland, the tribal and territorial names of their predecessors will have survived. For men shed their language long before they shed their names. Look at our telephone books and you will see that Irish names are in an overwhelming majority anglicized but not displaced.

The wanderings of early peoples lasted for centuries. Gilbert Murray [RGE 66] once tried to enumerate the tribes that in early Greek times passed through a single portion of Phrygia, the Troad. He counted fourteen and each of them had an ancestor for whom the Greeks found a place in their own heroic hierarchies. There was Tros of the Trojans, Aeneas of the Aeneadae, Dardanus, Teucer, Cilix, Lycus, Lelex, Mygdon, and Pelasgus, each with a widely ranging tribe to match [S V 249]. And how many other invasions there must have been by tribes whose names are unknown to us.

Victorian archaeologists used to smile at the Irish stories of their Scythian and Greek ancestors, for they pictured boatloads of horsemen from the Russian

8. WHERE DID THE IRISH COME FROM?

steppes or Athenian hoplites disembarking from triremes in Dublin Bay. And the picture was ridiculous.

Yet, if you look at my maps, you will see that all the tribes were everywhere, with slightly differing names and speaking, it must be assumed, slightly different tongues. From Scythia to Gibraltar, the Celts mingled with all the people they met. Each tribe that reached Ireland carried portmanteau fragments of other tribes and knew that fragments of itself coexisted in other tribal portmanteaus. There were Thracian and Iberian and German and Scythian portmanteaus with Celts in all of them, and the Celtic portmanteaus will have been as capacious and well-stocked as any. Fighting and merging its way across Europe, each tribe will have lost most of its cultural distinctiveness, as a Finn or a Bulgar does in Massachussets. Only through their ancestral pedigrees will they have hung on to their identities. So, if we study seriously those long lists of obviously invented beings, the tribal ancestors, every genealogy becomes a table of ingredients in a cookery book. We know how each tribal dish was composed and there are no limits to what we can learn about our past.

The Bebryces

As an instance of a small people that travelled over Europe changing its language and its culture but retaining its name, observe the Bebryces. In Roman times they were settled on either side of the Pyrenees, to which Pyrene, daughter of 'King' Bebryx, had given her name (Map 1, p. 63).

They had earlier been settled in Macedonia, in Colchis and the Black Sea, where they were visited by the Argonauts in their search for the Golden Fleece. Castor and Pollux were aboard the *Argo* and Bibrax, the local king-ancestor, challenged Pollux to a boxing match and was killed by him.

Henri Hubert thinks they were Celts, because *bebros* is an Irish word for beaver. He finds kinsmen for them in Britain among the Bibroci, after whom Berkshire is named. He traces among the continental Celts a multitude of beaver place names like Bibracte, Bebronne, Bievre. Macalister and MacNeill take up the tale for Ireland and find these beaver folk as Tuath Bibraige in Cork. Totemism is debated, but there are no beavers in Ireland and it is unlikely that their name had any meaning but a punning one.

Strabo says they were Thracians, others say Iberians, others Ligurians. Others again agree with Henri Hubert that they were Celts. Surely it is plain that they were everything in turn and ended up speaking English with a Cork accent.

Their ancestor, Bebryx or Bibrax, will have travelled with them, accepting, as they moved, appropriate modifications in his name, his life story, his language, his ancestry.

The Bibraige of Ireland had among their forebears two amalgamated ancestors in Munster, Araide Bibre, *ex quo* the Dal Araide [CGH 425], and Bebrae Fiachrach, an ancestor of the Ui Fiachrach [CGH 222]. In Roscommon there was Bibur, son of Tomanchenn, from whom the local Cenel Domangein must have descended. Patrick had found him fighting his brother Lochru (of what tribe was Lochru the ancestor?) and had paralysed the arm that held the sword. He had then cured him. Bibur and Lochru had become disciples and been given land for a church.

Iberians and Ligurians

It is usually thought that the Celts arrived in Ireland some three or four centuries BC. To reach it they must have pushed their way through earlier pre-Celtic tribes or brought them with them. We hear a good deal about these early tribes from classical authors. The most frequently mentioned are Iberians and Ligurians and, since there are Celtiberians in Spain and Celtoligyes in Provence, Celts must often have blended with them.

Greek and Roman writers believed that the Iberians were linked with a tribe of the same name in the Caucasus and had spread widely north and west. In the words of Avienus, a fourth-century Latin poet-geographer, the Iberians 'reach the icy waves of the northern ocean ... blond Germany and the thickets of the Hercynian forests'. Philippon, a more recent Iberian enthusiast, says they went up the Danube, held Germany as far as the North Sea and were represented by the Silures in Britain. Those who think the Silures of South Wales were Iberian, link them with Mons Silurus near Gibraltar, those who think them Ligurians, link them with the Salyes of Marseilles. There is the widest disagreement and a tendency, based on archaeology, to discount these immense wanderings and to argue that the Iberians were a Berber-like people from North Africa, who did not travel far beyond Spain.

There is the same disagreement about the Ligurians. They used to be identified with the Ligyes of the river Lycus on the coast of the Black Sea, who fought in the army of Xerxes [HDT VII 72], as well as the Ligyes, who lived to the north of Marseille, and the Ligurians, whose main focus was north Italy, south Germany and Switzerland, but others conjectured a vast heterogeneous

8. WHERE DID THE IRISH COME FROM?

Ligurian empire extending to the British Isles and Scandinavia. D'Arbois de Jubainville [Prem II 213] on philological grounds finds clear traces of them in Britain and Ireland. Nowadays such arguments are archaeologically questioned or discredited and, though Pierson Dixon, writing of the Iberians in 1940, says that they occupied the whole of Spain before the Iberians and Celts. Arribas, twenty years later in *The Iberians*, says they never crossed west of the Rhone. I mention these contradictory opinions merely to show that nobody knows.

To me the Ibar-Eber saints, heroes, tribes of Ireland and Gaul, the vast quantity of Lig-Lug-Ling proper names in Ireland, prove that both peoples visited us. I find it easier to connect the former with the Iberians than in the traditional way with yew trees and boars, and the latter with the Ligurians rather than with ravens and jumps and stones and spoons and heroes. And obviously we had many other invaders, who never registered their names in the visitors book.

The Veneti

Among the most mysterious of these westward-moving peoples were the Veneti. We hear of them first in Homer as Henetoi, breeding mules in Paphlagonia, which they left, it seems, soon after the Trojan War. Then, as Eneti or Veneti, they settled at the head of the Adriatic, giving their name to Venice and to Lake Venetus (now Constance). They here passed as Illyrians, but were connected with the people of the same name who lived in Brittany, giving their name to Vannes and considered to be Belgic Celts. The Celtic Veneti had the most powerful navy in Gaul; they offered strong resistance to Julius Caesar and must have been familiar with all our coasts. There are many places in Britain deriving their name from them. In Ireland we have Fenit and Fanad on the coasts of Kerry and Donegal and many others.

Henri Hubert and Bosch Gimpera include among those sharing this '*ancien nom de peuple*', the Venedi, the ancestors of those Slavs, who left their name with the Wends, round Berlin. Tacitus classes them as Germans [G 46], because, though primitive and plundering, they had settled houses. Beyond them across the Niemen, he placed a wilder people, the Fenni, who ate grass and slept on the ground. They are thought to be the forebears of the Finns. Were they an earlier wave of Veneti?

In Ireland too we read of nomadic people, the Ui Fenna [VSH I 182], who frightened St MoChuda's horses in the midlands. He set a curse on them that they and their descendants should be useless wanderers: *'Dispersi per diversas regiones ridiculosi et inutiles eritis.'* This is the moment for the rash and random suggestion that St MoChuda, who was hated and persecuted by the other saints, was himself the ancestor of the Chuds or Finns and that it was his own unchristianized race that he was cursing. Idiotic maybe but not so dull-witted as to take him for a real person and not to speculate about what he represented (see p. 106).

D'Arbois suggested that the Finns were once *'ou seuls ou avec les races similaires, maîtres incontestés de l'Europe'* [Prem I 13]. Maybe he was wrong, but it conforms perfectly to the pattern of pre-history that there should have been in various parts of the world Veneti speaking Paphlagonian, Illyrian, Celtic, Slavonic, Teutonic, Latin and Finno-Ugrian tongues. And no doubt there is some good reason why the Norwegians should call the Lapps Finns and give to the Finns themselves the name of Kvaens. 'Anything may happen in the course of time,' wrote Herodotus.

The Thracians

It was from Thrace that the principal invasions of Ireland are said to have come. Among the leading Thracian tribes were the Getae, the Briges, the Mygdones, the Thyni. And in Ireland we have ancestors, Get and Brig, Magdon and Tene, with many variants to their names and different pedigrees. And there is an abundance of corresponding saints.

The Getae

The Getae were Celto-Thracians, called by Herodotus 'the noblest of the Thracian tribes' [IV 94]. Ridgeway [I 519] argued their Celtic strain from their belief in human immortality and their four-yearly human sacrifice, a custom that Diodorus Siculus ascribes to the Celts. The Getae used to consult their gods on these occasions by tossing a human being on some upright spears. If he died it was a sign that the gods had received him graciously as a messenger. Ridgeway does not remark on the curious parallel in the life of St Canice [VSH I 164]. The saint, wandering in Wexford, found a crowd gathered round Cormac, their king, to watch a boy being thrown 'according to a foreign custom' on to some spears. St Canice prayed to God, who listened to him and the boy did not die. *'Nam projecto puero super hastas stantes sursum positas, nec*

8. WHERE DID THE IRISH COME FROM?

potuerunt jugulare vel lacerare eum. Hic est Dolue Lebderc, quern rex Cormacus sancto Cainnico obtulit, cujus civitas dicitur Cell Dolue.' Instead the king gave him as a present to Canice. He later became St MoLua of Killaloe and was called Lebderc or Squint-eye because of the effect on him of this horrible experience. St MacNisse of Connor (3 Sept.) similarly saved the baby saint Colman of Kilroot (16 Oct.) from this ordeal of being tossed on spears.

The Getae, despite such practices, were much-admired allies of the Romans. Ovid relates that they were indomitable farmers, who kept one hand on the plough, the other on their sword, to defend themselves against their northern neighbours. In classical times the focus of their domains was in Transylvania, but they had also settled Bohemia, Galicia, Silesia, the Ukraine. German historians used to claim that the Getae were the ancestors of the Goths, who ultimately displaced them and absorbed them; Jacob Grimm supported this view but it is not now widely held. More weight is given to the opinion that it was the Gothones, whom Tacitus places west of the Vistula, who were the kinsmen of the Getae and that they were later the Prussians and Lithuanians.

The Briges

The Briges or Phryges, more than any other Thracian tribe, may claim to have left clear traces in Ireland and later in this volume I write about them. How can they be dissociated from the Brigantes of Thrace [EA of G II 253], who reappear in Switzerland, Gaul, Spain, Yorkshire and the south of Ireland? It seems to me ridiculous to argue that the Brigantes were Celtic except under their most westerly appearances.

Brigantes, Veneti and Ligurians illustrate well the thesis that early tribes give their name to the territory through which they pass and almost never take their names from it. The first two both bordered on Lake Constance, so it is called both Lacus Venetus and Lacus Brigantinus. It owes its present name to a third early tribe the Consuanitae. To the north of them lay the Vindelici, who are supposed to be German and to have acquired their name from the two rivers Vindo and Licus, which unite at Augusta Vindelicorum (Augsburg). But we find Licati on the Licus (now the Lech) and Veneti and Ligurians only a short distance to the south. So I have argued that it is not the junction of the rivers but the junction of the tribes that gave the Vindelici their name. We have already met the Ligyes on a river Lycus on the Black Sea and it is not very rash to guess that the Licati of the Licus were akin to the western Ligyes and Ligurians and that they were not called after the western river Licus but rather gave their name to it. In Ireland I relate to the Vindelici the Sil Findloga of South Leinster [CGH 38].

It may have been some distant memory of a pre-Celtic past that brought to Ireland the Phrygian legend of the ass's ears of King Midas and of the barber who told the terrible secret to the reeds. In a sacred version of the story it is St Brigit herself, the Christian counterpart of Brigantia of the Brigantes, who punished an impious king of Leinster with a pair of ass's ears.

The Thyni

There are various more shadowy tribes of Thrace, which scattered far and wide. We cannot ignore the Thyni, who left their name on various promontories and islands. In Asia Minor they merged with the Bithyni and in Illyria formed with the Medes the Medobithyni. Compare these two kindred tribes with the mid-Munster neighbours, the Ui Thenaich and Ui Buithenaich [CGH 299]. We do not know of their westward extensions, though the names of rivers like the Tyne and saints like Thaneu, Tenna, Tinne can offer a clue.

The Mygdones

I can scarcely omit the famous Thracian tribe of the Mygdones, since Partholon was said to have come to Ireland from Mygdonia [LG III 39]. Their home was in Macedon, but they wandered also to Asia Minor and must have merged with the Bebryces and the Briges-Phryges, for Mygdon, as king of the Bebryces, encountered Hercules on the Black Sea. As brother of Hecuba, wife of Priam, he also figured in the Phrygian family tree and with Hercules battled against the Amazons. He must be Midgen in the following lines from *The Graves of the Leinstermen*, in the *The Book of Leinster* (translation by M.E. Dobbs):

> Aithbel, best of women, was mother of Ercol (Hercules) and wife of Midgen. She slew ten Fomore at the strand of Tonn Clidna ... She went with the Amazons, when raiding Syria. She was ruler of the Gaedils and for seven years ruled Eire.

Is this just a faint literary echo of something an Irish scholar had read in Strabo or Apollodorus, or were the Irish simply reshaping to their own needs, as did the Bebryces and the Phrygians, a story about the Mygdonic ancestor of them all?

8. WHERE DID THE IRISH COME FROM?

I do not think that distance would have stopped the Mygdones or any other Thracian tribe from reaching Ireland, for we find them on the river Mygdonius in Mesopotamia, led there by Alexander. Those who in early times travelled northward and westward, would have gone beyond the reach of Greek and Roman chroniclers and it would not be strange if history was silent about them. Strabo had written:

> As for all the nations that are barbarian and remote, as well as small in territory and split-up, their records are neither safe to go by nor numerous; and as for all the nations that are far off from the Greeks, our ignorance is still greater [XXX II 117].

Other Peoples

When Herodotus and Strabo were writing, the races of Europe seemed temporarily at rest. Celts, Ligurians, Iberians, Germans seemed to have fairly recognizable frontiers. Yet, maybe, if one knew the tribal genealogies and could analyse the composite tribal names one would guess that unity was recent and precarious.

Here and there the shadowy memories of earlier peoples survived. The Tartessii, a people of once-fabulous wealth and civilization, had lived near Cadiz and traded with the British Isles. For Herodotus their glory was still recent but in the time of Strabo they had been romanized and the Turduli and Turdetani, two races whom Strabo could not easily distinguish, had inherited their name in a battered twofold form, but neither their language nor their fame.

Beyond the Tartessii in Portugal, along the Atlantic coast, Herodotus was aware of the Cunesioi or 'Dog-folk'. Avienus places them on the south-western promontory, but Strabo does not recall them, saying only that this promontory was called 'Cuneus', because it was shaped like a wedge. But could not that name have come from the Cunesioi? Rhys (*Celtic Britain*) suggests that they came to Ireland and left traces of their presence in the many dog heroes of Ireland, Cu-Roi, Cu-Corb, Cu-Chullain and all the rest. Rhys believed the Cunesioi were Silures but there is the usual wide disagreement about this.

North of the Cunesioi an equally shadowy people, the Cempses, is recorded. Philippon relates them to the Camponi in Aquitaine. Rhys traces their name in Campsie Fells in Scotland and in a dedicatory inscription in Pictish country.

I omit here all mention of the many peoples of central and northern Europe, who, directly or through kindred tribes, may have left their mark on the peoples of Ireland and on the names of their ancestors, heroes and saints. I will write of them in their proper place in this volume or a later one.

Inevitably this is a scrappy summary of the races who lived in Europe, when Bith, son of Noah, perished on Slieve Beagh in Leitrim and other famous invaders from Dacia and Thrace left their names forever on our hills and lakes.

The Irish may have been unjustifiably precise when they said that Gaedel Glas had cut their language out of seventy-two different tongues, but they were not wrong in supposing that they and their speech were the creation of many different peoples. There were all those generations of men whom the Celts had neighboured, as they travelled the long road to Ireland; there were those that had preceded them there; those that had followed. For though Ireland is not, like the Troad, on a highway between two continents, it was the end of the habitable world. Those who fled there from oppression or overcrowding were likely to stay there. They were always aware of many predecessors and eager to know their names.

> 'Queen,' said Teigue, son of Cian, to Gothnia's daughter, fairest of the whole world's women, 'set me now forth, I pray thee, every colony that ever settled Ireland and the tongues that served them all.' [SG 390]

Early peoples always have an answer even to the most difficult questions and Gothnia's daughter gladly accepted the challenge. She must have given a satisfactory reply, but we are not told what it was.

CHAPTER 9

Tribal Maps

These maps are only skeletons. In the case of Gaul (Map 3, p. 65) I have used most of the tribal information available; the map of Germany and Central Europe (Map 2, p. 64) could, with the aid of Ptolemy and Pliny and others, be covered with such a dense web of tribal names as to be unreadable and unusable. The map of Spain (Map 1, p. 63) has been the hardest to make. I have used Garcia and Bellido's maps, with additions, where these seemed significant, from Schulten and Bosch Gimpera.

I have not attempted a consistent chronology, for I am primarily concerned not with the tribes but with their ancestors, whom one can sometimes deduce from the tribes even when history does not record them. I shall never believe, for example, that Tricoria was the 'goddess' of the Tricorii, and that they were named after her. It was surely the reverse: she was their ancestress and took her name from the tribe whose name did not mean 'three troops'. The same applies to Nemetona and the Nemet group of tribes. These ancestors have a species of immortality, in that they are revered, as happened to Esus of the Essuvii, long after the tribe that claimed descent from them had been forgotten. Thus, despite my map, I have no evidence that the Tartessii ever coexisted with their successors, the Turduli and Turdetani. Yet there would be nothing to prevent their ancestors appearing as cousins or brothers in the same family tree.

All over Europe we find tribes of slightly divergent names, sometimes side by side, sometimes far apart, sometimes simultaneously, sometimes successively. In Andalucia there were, on the south-east coast, Massieni, Mastieni, Basteiani, Bastuli, Bastetani and to the east of them Bastulopoeni. In the north there are Vascones and Vescitani, early forerunners of the Basques and Gascons. There are Lusi and Lusones and Lusitani, Carpi, Carpetani and Carpessii (Map 1). Can one dissociate the Helvii, north of Nîmes, from the Helvetii of Switzerland and the Helvecones of eastern Europe [GDC 284]? And surely the Taurini of Turin were akin to the Taurisci to the north-east of them, even if they were different from the Turones of Tourraine and Thuringia (Map 2). Why did tribes add -*uli* or -*isci* or -*ani* to their names? It is usually supposed that it was because they had absorbed or been absorbed by a different tribe, though there is no agreement as to what this different tribe was, or what was the relationship to each other of the major tribes, Iberians, Celts, Basques, Ligurians, Sicani, Siculi. Many of the tribes were so ancient and widespread that they may have taken successively different nationalities and even languages. For example Arribas, in his book *The Iberians* (p. 83), treats the Suessitani of the Pyrenees as Iberian, but Bosch Gimpera equates them with the Suessiones on the other side of the mountains and the Suessiones of Soissons, who were Belgae.

My maps illustrate also Bosch's belief that the Suardones of north Germany (Suarini to Tacitus) were akin to the Sordi and the Sordones of the Pyrenees, the Surdaones of Catalonia, and their suspected ancestors, the Sardi, who left their name to Sardinia and were descended from Sardus, son of Hercules (Maps 1 and 2).

He also connects the Lungones or Lugones of Asturias and the Lingones of Galicia, with the Lingones or Longones of Langres and of the right bank of the Po in Italy, and with the Lindones of Landes and Langon. There were also the Longo-staletes from Langonia and Tallet in Narbonne.

Others link the Artabri or Arotrebae of north-west Spain with the Atrebates of Artois and Berkshire (Map 1).

On my map of central Europe, there is a cluster of tribes that must surely be related. North of the Veneti, who left their name in Venice, we see in the Swiss Alps two little tribes, the Venonetes and Venostes, who must surely be their daughters and in Vindelicia, which is south Germany, we find the Vennones close to Lake Venetus, which is now Constance (Map 2).

Amalgamated Tribes

Vindelicia raises the question of amalgamated tribes. I find it hard not to consider the Vindelici a Veneto-Ligurian tribe. The Veneti were also called Eneti, so it is not hard to associate the Vennones with the rivers Vindo (the

9. TRIBAL MAPS

MAP 1: SPAIN

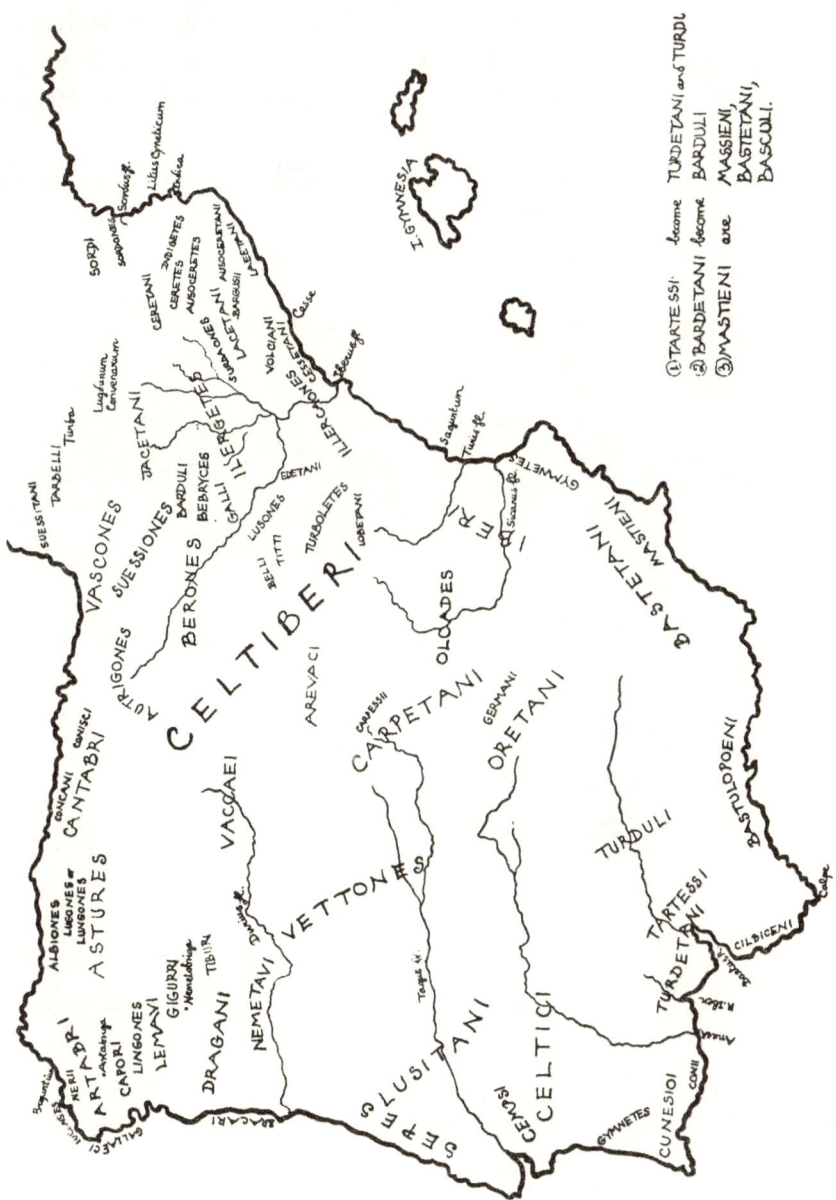

Wertach) and Aenus (the Inn). The tribe next door were the Licati, who lived upon the river Licus, now the Lech, and are stupidly supposed to have taken their name from it (Maps 2 & 3). Strabo's reference to the Vindelici shows that they were not a political term like the Austro-Hungarian; they probably had an ancestor, Vindelicus, to correspond to Celtiberus, ancestor of the the

Celtiberians, who were an amalgamation of Celts and Iberians. This Vindelicus would, in my view, be some sort of relation of the Irish Findlug, saint and ancestor.

In Germany note the Turones and the Chaemi, and between them the Teuriochaemi. Near the Turones too are the Hermiones and the Hermunduri (Map 2).

In Spain note the Ausetani, the Ceretes and the Ceretani, and near them observe the Ausoceretes and the Ausoceretani (Map 1). North of the Alps are the tribal twins: the Suanitae and the Consuanitae (Map 2).

MAP 2: CENTRAL EUROPE

In northern Gaul Bosch compares the Bellovaci with the Belli and Vaccaei of Central Spain (Maps 1 and 3). Indeed he appears to have found Bellovaci on the Douro (Map 1). Does Bosch guess too much? I think he merely opens up a new field of conjecture, the old fields – philological and ethnological – having been overgrazed. If the Belgian Bellovaci and the Iberian twins are to be compared, speculation about 'the meanings' of tribal names must be restricted. In northern France, south-west of the Bellovaci of Beauvais were the Bellocasses of Vexin (Map 3). Bello could not easily 'mean' anything because the Bellocasses also called themselves Veliocasses.

9. TRIBAL MAPS

MAP 3: GAUL

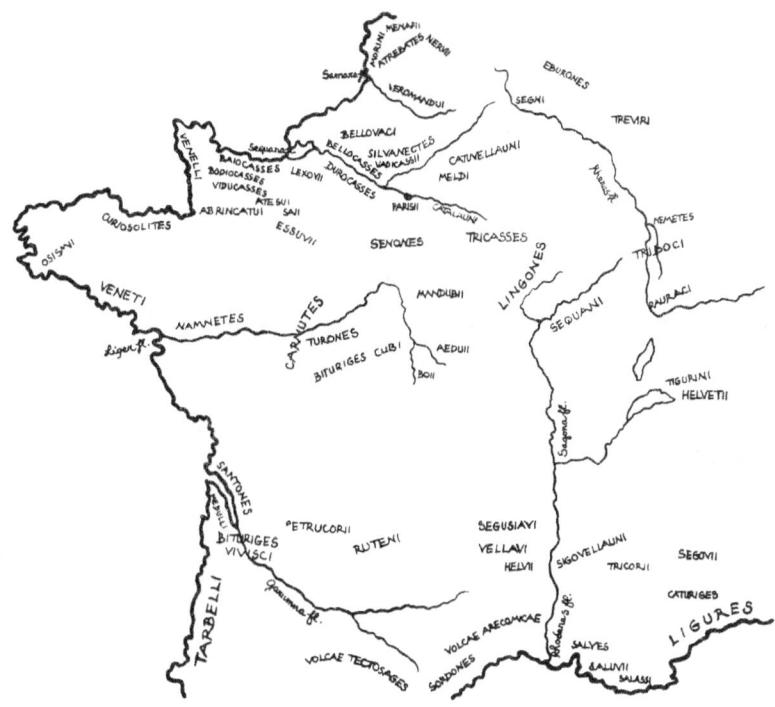

TABLE 3: TRIBES OF GAUL

TRIBE	HABITATION	TRIBE	HABITATION
Abrincatui	Avranches	Meldi	Meaux
Arverni	Auvergne	Namnetes	Nantes
Atrebates	Arras	Parisii	Paris
Baiocasses	Bayeux	Pictones	Poitiers
Bellocasses or Vellocasses	Vexin	Petrucorii	Perigueux
Bellovacci	Beauvais	Ruteni	Rodez & Rouerque
Bituriges	Bourges	Remi	Reims
Bodiocasses	Bessin	Sau Sagu	Sees
Carnutes	Chartres	Santones	Saintes
Caturiges	Chorges	Segovellauni	Valence
Catuvellauni	Chalons	Senones	Sens

Cenomani	Le Mans	Suessiones	Soissons
Curiosolites	Corseul	Sequani	The Seine
Durocasses	Dreux	Silvanectes	Senlis
Eburovices	Evreux	Tarbelli	Tarbes
Gabali	Galbaldunum, now Javols	Treveri	Treves
Helvii	Alba, now Aps	Tricasses	Troyes
Lepontii	Val Leventina	Tricastini	St Paul les Trois Chateaux
Lindones	Langon & Landes	Turones	Tours
Lingones	Langres	Vadicassii	Vez
Lixovii	Lisieux	Vellavi	Velay or Valentirois
Lemovices	Limoges	Veneti	Vannes
Lobetani	Lombey	Veromandui	Vermandois
Meduli	Medoc	Viducasses	Vieux

Irish Analogies

The main object of these maps is to suggest that the Irish tribes bore names that were very similar to those of the Continent and that as these could be Iberian, Gaulish, German, Ligurian or Illyrian, it is unlikely that these names had an Irish 'meaning', whether borne by the Irish tribe or its ancestor.

Below I have listed a few of the continental tribes, which I think had Irish kinsmen. I have left put those that are obvious and accepted, such as the Brigantes, Menapii and Cauci, and also, because they are too numerous to list, the Nem group, the Lig-Lug-Ling group, the Ven-En-Fin group. In fact this is only a sample.

Almost all these Irish tribes have recorded ancestors, for example the Artraige had Art and the Sortraige had Sord or Sort [CGH 152]; they were brothers, but apart from this there are indications that their tribes were akin. That is to say the Artraige had nothing to do with *art*, a bear, but would have had the same origins as the Sordraige (the Sardi?). We find also that very many of the continental tribes had ancestors, for example there was a 'king' Bebryx of the Pyrenees and an ancestor, Draganes or Dercennus for the Dragani, so it is fair to assume that these ancestors were more or less obligatory, such as surnames, Christian names, street numbers are now.

9. TRIBAL MAPS

TABLE 4: CONTINENTAL TRIBES WITH IRISH KINSMEN

CONTINENTAL TRIBE	LOCATION	IRISH KINSMEN
Albiones	North Spanish coast	Ui Ailbe – midlands
Artabri	North Spanish coast	Artraige – midlands
Bebryces	Pyrenees, Black Sea	Bibraige – Munster
Bracarii	North-east Spain	Ui Braccain – Kerry
Carpetani	Iberia	Clann Carbad
Chaemi and Chamavi	North Germany	Ui Caemain – Wexford
Dragani	North-west Spain	Ui Draignech – Connacht
Estiones	Switzerland, Baltic	Sil Eistich, with an ancestress, Estiu – South Ulster
Lacetani	Catalonia	Ui Lachtnain – Munster
Lemavi	North-west Spain	
Lemovii	Pomerania	
Lemovices	Limousin	Lamraige –Ulster, Munster
Olcades	Castile	Ui Olcain – Meath
Saii	Normandy	Cenel Sai – Louth
Segni	Rhine	
Segusiavi	Sagona (the Saône)	Ui Segain –Meath
Sordones	Pyrenees	Sordraige or Sortraige, Ulster
Suanitae	South Germany	Ui Suanaigh – midlands
Tartessi	South-west Spain	Dartraige, Ui Tuirtre, midlands

Fantastic interpretations were given to all these names, which indicate, I maintain, that they were all pre-Celtic and hence meaningless. Ailbe was found under a stone, *ail*, alive, *beo*, by a wolf; his grandfather was Olchu (Big Dog), ancestor of the neighbouring Clann Olchon. The Bibraige were connected with beavers, but there were not any in Ireland, the Clann Carbad with chariots, the Ui Caemain with *caem*, beautiful, the Ui Draigneach with *draigean*, blackthorn, and so on all the way through.

Certain areas, notably the Dessi district of Waterford or Conmaicne in Leitrim, seem to provide most of the tribal names; this is merely because most

MAP 4: BRITAIN

9. TRIBAL MAPS

records have survived from these places. The pattern is an all-Ireland one. Let me illustrate from one Waterford tribal group how the names of Iberian tribes were woven into the family trees [CGH 280, 285].

Mug Ruith and his Iberian Relations

Celtchair and Mug Ruith were two patriarchs of Fermoy. Altogether they had between them about a score of sons and some daughters who bore the names of the local tribes. Different genealogists arranged the matter differently. Thus while Sem, ancestor of the Seimne, and Fer Tlachtga, ancestor of the Ui Fir Tlachtga, were both sons of Celtchair, they have in other pedigrees a more complicated relationship. Fer Tlachtga becomes Tlachtga, daughter of Mug Ruith, and Sem becomes Simon Magus, who invented with Mug Ruith, Slave of the Wheel, a magical wheel. Simon had three sons, Nero, Carpent and Vetir, who all became lovers of Tlachtga [MD IV 187]. Mug Ruith was ancestor of the Fir Maige, who gave their name to Fermoy, and of the Rothraige, whom MacNeill curiously believes to have been a wheel-making folk [MacN 82]. He was also called Magus Rotarum and has all the marks of a compound ancestor, yet Canon Power, the splendid and dedicated historian of Fermoy, can write that 'it is just possible that he was a real person'. In fact he and his brother, Lug Roth, and all their kin only make sense tribally. One of his fathers, Cunisc [CGH 285], was surely ancestor of the Conisci of the Biscay coast of Spain, while his daughter's lovers, Nero, Carpent and Vetir, were surely ancestors of the Neri of Galicia, the Carpentani, as Pliny calls the Carpetani, and the Vettones of central Spain (Map 1).

I will not here discuss from what amalgamation of ancient tribes Celtchair and Mug Ruith derived but since the Semnones were a branch of the Suebi, who reached northern Spain (Map 1), it seems likely that as Seimne and Tuath Semon they reached Ireland and that Sem and Simon Magus were their regional representatives in Fermoy. Inevitably MacNeill, because *seim* means a rivet, believes, despite the much befamilied Sem, that they were smith folk [MacN 75].

Long after the tribal names were forgotten the ancestors' names will have hung on as vague memories to be woven into poetry and anecdote. Thus not only did Simon Magus have an Irish son called Nero, he also embroidered a cloak for the Emperor Nero, which Cuchullain later acquired [THU 179].

Part 2

CHAPTER 10

Tribal Charts and Tables of Name Variants

The best way to develop and to test my various hypotheses has been to organize the saints into charts, collating them with the tribes, the heroes, the place names that seem to correspond. I have made over 200 such charts, but owing to the vast numbers of the saints there should be twice as many. The charts are working tools or, better, observation trays, to which every now and then I have made a random addition in the appropriate column. If I could have printed several such charts and a table of variants in each chapter dealing with a particular group of saints, it would have liberated the text from many indigestible strings of names. But to prepare my charts for the printer is very laborious and I have only given one sample, the first of the fourteen Carpetani charts (see pp. 142–3) and three tables of variants: the Thracians (p. 97), the Brig-Bard folk, (p. 98), and the Carp folk, (p. 174).

My Carpetani chapter is the fullest and probably the most boring. I have not abridged it as I would wish, for I have to demonstrate in at least one chapter that the long lists of pun-elements in my Glossary are justified. They were all in use for the interpretation of proper names.

The Goban Saints and the Cruithne

In the other thirteen Carp charts I test my theory that the Goban saints and the Cruith saints also derive from the Carp folk of Iberia.

The argument flows, with one break, by biographical equation and no thought of any science of sound changes.

Corp	is Carp	is Garb	is Gob
Corp	is Crob	is Crub	is Craebh
Crech	is Cruith		

It will be noticed that there is a gap here between Craebh and Crech, which I cannot easily bridge. I cannot say, as Boucher de Perthes did, '*Ma science est la prévision*', but I can offer several weak arguments to bear the weight of one strong one.

Here is one of them. Iona is called Cruib Inis (Paw Island) and also Craebh Inis (Branch Island), and the Grecraige were there [H 311; SK III 489]. So was St MacCreiche (their saint-ancestor?), who came, as they did, from Co. Clare. Prevision and a few more such arguments tell me that the paws, the branches, the Grecraige and St MacCreiche, together betray the presence of the Cruithne and link them with the Carpi.

This is an unlearned way of arguing, but one we often use. When we meet a girl called Molly, caring nothing for dentals and liquids, we deduce from past encounters that she was christened Mary and we are usually right. It is the way of R.E. Matheson, the registrar of births, deaths and marriages, who pursued names like Alexander, Archibald and Quigley through Antrim, Derry and Armagh, noting their variants. It is my way. I know from my charts that St Crobnatan is St Corpnatan and that the Garbraige are the same as the Gabraige, the Gobraige, the Cupraige, and the Gubraige, whose ancestor was Gubbi, which is the same as Goban.

Obviously in the illiterate centuries the distortions of proper names must have been far more extravagant than in nineteenth-century Ulster and in my charts and tables I have explored only the inmost, most conservative circle of variants. In a later age St Maelrubha of Applecross had forty-six mispronunciations of his name.

But is 'mispronunciation' always the right word? When the English settler turned Droiched na gCarbad, the Bridge of Chariots, in Kilkenny, into Carabine Bridge, or when Lord Chesterfield erected a Phoenix in the middle of Phoenix (*fionn uisge* or clear water) Park, they certainly thought they were improving matters. In my charts I argue that Droiched na gCarbad was itself an 'improvement' and that the numerous Carbads in the names of places and people all hark back to the Iberian Carpetani and not to the legendary chariots.

10. TRIBAL CHARTS AND TABLES OF NAME VARIANTS

Kenneth Jackson and St MoChuda

Though I am envious of Celtic philologists, they themselves sometimes admit that ancient proper names are beyond the reach of their special science. Professor Jackson [EBC 301], puzzling over the nicknames of the saints and trying to explain why St Kentigern was also called Munghu and MoChoche or MoChua, both implies this and proves it. Arguing that Munghu and MoChua are both distortions based on the 'Cu' of Cunotegernos (Kentigern) he writes:

> These pet names usually distort the real name very greatly … It is nothing compared to what happened with the names of the Irish saints, Carthach and Cronan, whose nicknames were Mochuta and Mochua respectively.

Now, if Carthach could really be 'distorted' into Mochuta (MoChuda), plainly any name could be distorted into any other name and philology is helpless. But, in fact, these two nicknames are not distortions. Look up the life of St Carthach [LIS II 282] and you will see he was called Carthach because he was *dear carthanach*, to God and man, and MoChuda because the bishop who reared him, St Carthach the Elder, said to him, 'Thou art my portion, *mo chuidig*.' In fact two absurd explanations were being given for two alternative and quite different names. And you will see that it was principally in Kerry that he was called Carthach and that the old St Carthach lived there too, but was not nicknamed MoChuda.

Only the tribal explanation will help us here. St MoChuda, a Kerryman, had been expelled from his Westmeath cult centre of Rahan by a band of furious midland saints headed by the Abbot of Clonmacnois, who were jealous of his rich monastery and his 847 monks. This was surely a war between ancestors. The Chud folk, expelled by the other tribes from the midlands, had merged with the Clann Carthaich, later the dominant tribe of the south-west, the MacCarthys, and MoChuda himself had merged with their ancestor, Carthach, son of Cathbad [CGH 299], who had a dozen different family trees, according to the region in which his tribe was settled. He was also christianized as the venerable Bishop Carthach.

St Cronan and St MoChua

The same can be said of the Cronan-MoChua 'distortion'. There were fifty-nine St MoChuas and a large number of St Cronans, but only four or five of them were equated. There is no suggestion that one name is a sound-variant of the other and not rather an alternative. St Cronan of Ros Broc, Co. Carlow, had two alternative names. He was MoLing [LIS II 236] and Dairchell. This, I suggest, was simply because the Ui Linga, descended from Ling, son of Mal [CGH 309], were in the neighbourhood. And there may have been a branch of the Ui Dairchella of Tipperary there too [CGH 373].

As for an Ui Cronain tribe there were several in these parts and Cronn or Crann, brother of Ling, seems to have been an ancestor of one of them [SH 264; CGH 102, 105].

If sometimes a St Cronan is also called St MoChua, that is simply because of some regional overlapping of the vast and early Cu tribe with the Corn-Creon-Ceron group of north-west Scotland (the Carn-Cer group of the continent).

Terminations

I have included doubtfully in my charts names like Brecan, Coeman, Lugid, Draigen and Ailech. What was the meaning of *-an, -ech, -en, -id*? The moderns say that Coeman just means Little Coem and, since *ail* is stone, Ailech just means Stony and so on. But the ancients rejected such simplicity. Coeman, they said, was Coem-An or Handsome-Brightness, Lugid was Lug, son of Ith, Ailech meant either Stone-Horse, because a horse, *ech*, carried up the stones to that famous Donegal fort or Stone-Ach, because a man carried them and under their weight exclaimed 'Ach!'

It is unlikely, surely, that after nearly a thousand years we should hit on a simple explanation of these names the ancients had elaborately dodged. Were their puns just silly or did they indicate that these names were known to be composite, though the tribal meaning of *-an, -ech, -en* and *-id* had been forgotten? I give tribal explanations of these syllables in my Glossary. I do not claim that I am right but that I am looking in the right direction.

More reading and reflection could produce new affiliations and refute or confirm those that are now tentative. But I do not think anything is likely to shake my conviction that we shall never know better without an immense ebullience of that guessing and counter guessing, which characterized the early days of archaeology when it was country-based and its original purpose and powers were still understood.

CHAPTER 11

St Brigit and the Breac Folk

St Brigit of Kildare has for a very long time been regarded by many as a fabulous character. This is not only because of the three Brigits, daughters of the Dagda, who were patronesses of various arts and sciences, or because there are thirteen other St Brigits of Ireland and Scotland, whose lives are not easier to authenticate than hers. It is because she has been loosely but confidently associated with the Brigantes, the large tribe that inhabited Yorkshire in Roman times and which has been traced in the south-east of Ireland. Camden in his history of Yorkshire supposed that they had given their name to Breconshire and to Brigus or Birgus, the river Barrow in Leinster. Others have traced them at Brechin in Scotland, at Bargy in Wexford, in Bregia or the plain of Meath. She has been identified rather insecurely with Brigantia, the goddess to whom dedications have been discovered in the north of England and who is supposed to have given her name to at least two rivers, Brigantia or Brent, one a tributary of the Thames, the other at Glastonbury, where Brigit is culted.

None of this is very satisfactory; the Brigantes also had a male god, Brigans or Bergans, who must be compared to a giant called Brigio or Bergion, who fought with Hercules in southern Gaul. The ancestor or ancestress of the Brigantes was probably a genealogical fiction, who acquired supernatural powers only by degrees. If he or she had great divine importance, would not the worshippers have been certain of his or her sex? It is best to consider that rivers, plains, mountains were in the first place called after tribes and that it was the poets who later discovered fabulous beings, like the ox Breg, or Bregu, the son of Breoghan, rival eponyms for Bregia in Meath, or Braccan, son of Braca, the Irish-Scoto-Welsh hero, who left his name in Breconshire and Brechin.

But who were those Brig-Breg-Brac people? The Brigantes have laid their trail thickly across Europe to Ireland from Thrace, where Ridgeway discovered them [EA of G II 253]. On their western course we can trace Bregenz in Austria, Lake Brigantia, now Constance, Brigantium, now Briancon, in the Alps, Brigantium in north-west Spain, Brigantomagus near Toulon and so on. Henri Hubert introduces the Burgundiones to this catalogue of names.

Would it not be more satisfactory to consider that the Brigantes were a hybrid people and that their wanderings were begun by the Briges, an undoubtedly Thracian tribe, whose eastward incursions have been described by Strabo? He says that they crossed into Asia, changing from Briges to Phryges, and became the ancestors not only of the Phrygians but of many tribes upon the Black Sea. As Thracians themselves they can hardly have been unrelated to the Brigantes of Thrace and as they moved westward they would account for the many Brig tribes of Europe, the Segobriges and Nitiobriges of Gaul, the Lato-brigi of Switzerland and the Brigolati of Bessarabia, the Brigiani of the Alps, and, near Brigantium, the Brigiosi of north-west Spain. Among the rivers there was the Brigulus, now the Saône, and the Bargus of Thrace, to set beside Brigus, now the Barrow. And in Ireland we find scores of heroes and saints, both male and female, called Brig, Briga, Mo-Brig, Da-Brig and so on.

An examination of these people and places and their alternative names quickly shows that Brig-Berg-Brec are only the beginnings of a name corruption that must have extended untraceably far. Celtic scholarship, tied to the belief that almost all the names of early tribes of Gaul and the British Isles are Celtic, has to translate the word *brig*, wherever it occurs in a proper name, as 'strength' or 'height'; thus the Brigantes lived 'on high places', the Nitiobriges were, according to Holder, '*Kampfberuhmten*!' The fact that the Brigantes, like the Briges, were themselves of Thracian origin is ignored or dismissed. Yet surely the Brigolati, who are not known to be Celtic, must bear to the Lato-Brigi the same obscure but probable kinship that the Wallace-Smiths do to the Smith-Wallaces. Surely each half of these names is a proper name and neither an adjective.

If we associate the word *breac* with the Briges rather than with its Irish meaning 'speckled', Irish early history is straight away illuminated. It becomes clear why Simeon Breac, the leader of the Fir Bolgs, came from Thrace, as did Partholon, an earlier invader of Ireland, who had a son Brecan and a son-in-law, Brec. Has this question been seriously discussed, since nearly a century ago Skene, discovering that Scottish kings were called *breac* as well as Scottish churches, fields and rivers, suggested that the word must have some unknown

'Pictish' meaning? He did not refer to the hundreds of Irish heroes, heroines and saints nicknamed Breac. There were, for example, no less than three saints called St Caeman Breac, two ancestors called Eber Breac, two called Bressal Breac. Surely they did not all seven have freckles?

The Brig Folk in Scotland

Nor did Skene discern the connection of *breac* with Brigit, though it is obvious. King Nechtan Breac was a great admirer of Brigit, whom he had known in Ireland; he founded a church in her honour at Abernethy, which was built by his predecessor, the Pictish king Bruide or Bruigde, and she is supposed to have died there. There were holy ladies from Cornwall, Meath and Kildare, who were called Breac or Breaca and were disciples of Brigit. There were of course several Scotch Brigits. The parents of the Irish Brigit were said to have ruled over the Orkneys and lived in Caithness, so that the Hebrides were known as 'Brigit's Islands'. And in Caithness and elsewhere in the north we find many 'speckled' places, fields and rivers and mountains: Kirkmabrick in Wigtownshire is thought to mean the church of St Aed mac Breac, who founded Tech mic Bricc, the house of the son of Breac, in Westmeath [WJW 166]. It is curious that both in Wigtown and Westmeath, it is not he but Brigit who is culted in the church [OH II 214].

All this can be rescued from the domain of folklore and fabulous hagiography, if we assume the tribe of the Briges from Thrace merged with other tribes on its long journey and shaped and reshaped its name and its ancestor to changed conditions.

The Irish genealogies confirm that *breac* was a tribal word and did not in the first place mean 'speckled'. Bresal Breac, was ancestor of the Ossorians, among whom were the Breacraige tribe and several speckled (*breac*) lochs, heights and meadows, as well as churches dedicated to Brigit. And we find an abundance of 'speckled' place names, ancestors and saints such as St Caeman Breac and St Aed, son of Breac, among or near the Breacraige of Westmeath.

Dr MacNamee, in his valuable work on Ardagh, is so wedded to orthodoxy that he accepts MacNeill's theory that the Breacraige were a fishing tribe, since *breac* means trout. Yet there is no such thing as an early tribe with a professional or occupational name. They were none of them nameless parvenus, ready to describe themselves after some local and accidental craft. They all had immense pedigrees reaching back to the beginning of history.

MAP 5: DECIES IN WATERFORD

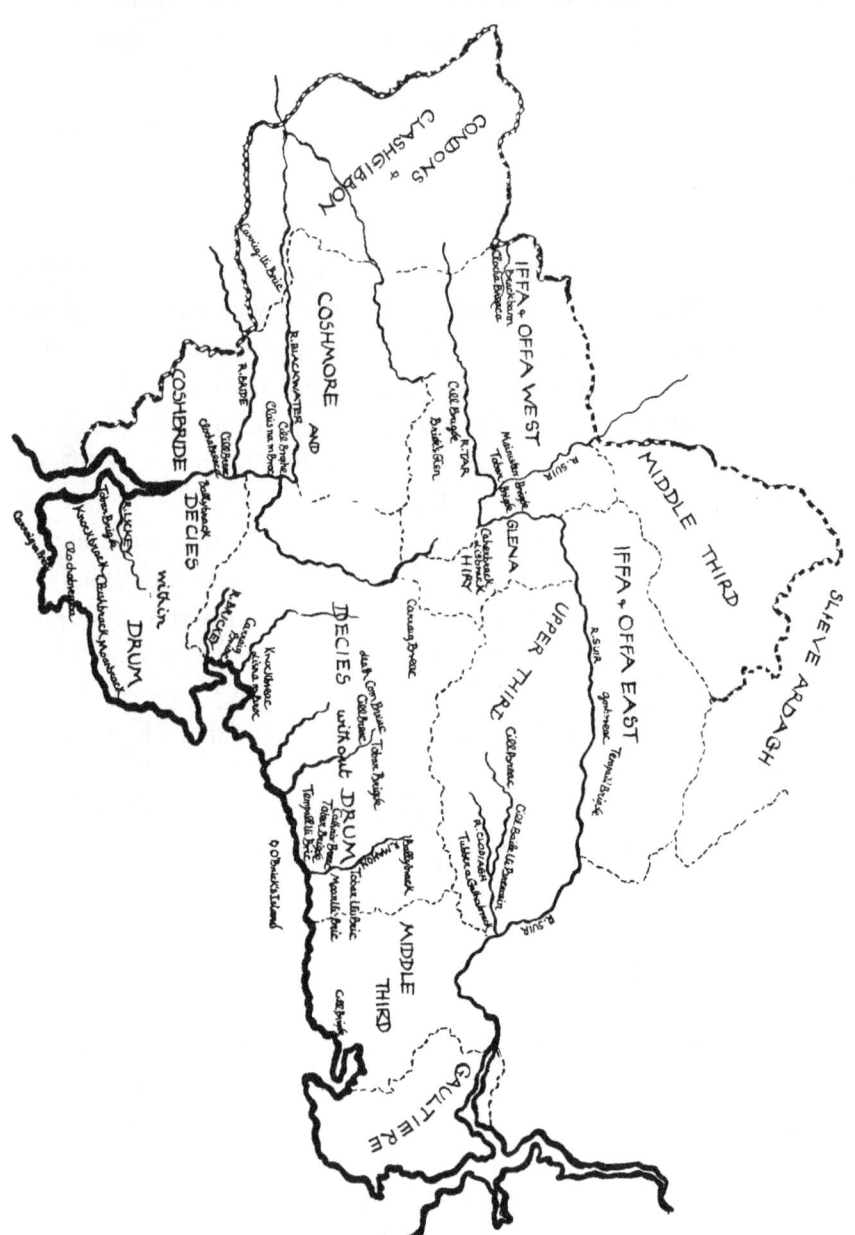

MacNeill, of course, is justified in so far as the delusion that the Breac folk were linked with trout or speckles is a very ancient one. The many hills called Knockbrack were often thought to be speckled,. Boswell and Johnson, meeting such names in the Hebrides, thought they referred to fields speckled with buttercups and daisies. Sometimes, as in Mayo, Knockbrack has been rechristened Trout Hill.

If we study O'Brien's *Corpus*, only in so far as it touches on the problem of St Brigit, the complex relationship of saints, tribes and genealogies becomes apparent.

There were, for example, two Brigits who were daughters of Dubhtach. One, Brigit of Leinster, was the saint of Kildare, the other, Brigit of Ulster, was ancestress of the Ui Brigte of Waterford. These Ui Brigte, later the O'Brics, were the ruling tribe in South Waterford and several Tipperary and Cork baronies. They had three separate founders: Eogan Breac, Brigit – who was sister to many local ancestors, including Sem, ancestor of the Semne tribe – and Breacdoilbh or Speckled Doilbh. His name was plainly composite, for his brother, Doilbh, was ancestor of the Ui Doilbh or Doyles.

The Breac Folk in Decies

Canon Power in *The Place Names of Decies* has studied very closely the territory of the Ui Brigte in Waterford, so that it is possible to make a map to illustrate my contention that St Brigit was associated with a very ancient Brig people, whose heroes and whose habitations survive in legend and topography as being *breac* or speckled (Map 5).

It will be seen from my map that the river Brigid, now the Bride, and the river Brickey both flow through the Ui Brigte territory. Canon Power sees no significance in this, but believes that the first river is called after a Celtic goddess, Brigit. He compares the Yorkshire Brigantes in whose name he finds the root *bri*, meaning strength. The second river he believes to have been speckled, *breac*. The fact that on the banks of these rivers there had lived a large tribe who traced its descent to Brigit, a mortal with a large family, and to two men who were 'speckled', Breacdolb and Eogan Breac, does not seem to him relevant. As is shown on my map there was, according to Canon Power, a third river to the north, the Breacban, or Speckled-field.

It will be noted that on my map there are four churches and four holy wells of St Brigit. There are also three speckled churches (Cill Breac), two speckled towns (Baile Breac), four speckled rocks (Clocha Breaca), two speckled crags (Carraig Breac), two speckled mountains (Cnoc Breac), three speckled forts (Lios and Cathair Breac), a speckled bog (Moin Breac), a speckled field (Gort

Breac), and the well of a speckled gate (Tobar a Geata Bric) and a speckled half-hollow (Leath comh breac). Well, maybe the gate was speckled and the rocks, mountains and bogs, but the churches, the forts, the towns, and all the men?

I think the Ui Bric accounted for many of them. Even now their name remains on several sites on the map, a church, a well, an island, a bog and two crags. One of these crags, Carraig Ui Bric, now Carrigabrack on the Blackwater, is already in danger of a speckled association for a local legend relates that a magical cow with speckles used to graze there.

North of the river Bride is Kilbree, Cell Brighe, and for its patroness Canon Power suggests a Welsh saint from St David's, St Brighe or Brigit, culted on 12 November. But would it not be strange if she had come so far and then established herself by a river of her own name, Brigit? Her two sisters, St Duthracht and St Tigern, do not sound Welsh but recall the names of local ancestors, Durthecht and Tigernach [CGH 401].

I have marked on the map some places called after badgers, *broc*, because the tribe name Ui Broc is a variant of Ui Bric.

Many odd problems arise out of all this. I believe that they will only be solved if we recognize that this region intensively, and the whole of Ireland sporadically, were once inhabited by the Briges of Thrace. They were also the Phrygians.

Among the more celebrated Brigit saints, we must not omit St Brigit of the Ui Ercain, who rescued Patrick from a vile conspiracy against him in Wicklow-Carlow. She was a cousin of Brigit of Kildare, to whom many of her miracles were transferred. Not only she but most of these Brig-Breac figures belonged, like Brigit of Kildare, to the Clann Artcorp, a not very prominent Wicklow tribe. Artcorb had a son called Conlead [CGH 82], the name of a very curious bishop, who succeeded Brigit at Kildare, and I am sure that the characters in her legend as well as in her pedigree were derived from the ancestors of the surrounding tribes. The pedigree had only symbolic truth, of great value, for the symbols recorded the meeting and blending of tribes, so no attempt has been made to synchronize them; thus in the same pedigree Brigit of the Ui Ercain, who rescued St Patrick, is four or five generations later than Brigit of Kildare, who herself was later than Patrick.

How are we to decipher these ancient symbols? I will describe a very recent attempt of mine in relation to Brigit. In *The Martyrology of Donegal* I read a poem about her in which she is described as a lover of 'early rising', *moch eirge*. This straight away struck me as a very prim everyday virtue to ascribe to so tremendous and ubiquitous a miracle worker. It must, I thought, be a tribal pun.

But were there any tribes with the improbable name 'Early Rising'? It was some weeks before I discovered them in *The Book of Fenagh*. The Ui Mael Mocheirge, or 'Servants of Early Rising', are descended from Mael Mocheirge, one of thirteen brothers, each of them ancestors of a Co. Leitrim tribe. The family still survives at Mohill and Drumshanbo in Leitrim as Earley and Early. One of Mael Mocheirge's brothers was Braici, ancestor of the Ui Braici, and he had a cousin called Brug or Brugaid. Brigit herself had been very active in the district. She was veiled at Ardagh by St Mael and had gone with him to St Aed Mac Bric (10 Nov.) to be cured of an illness. This Westmeath saint is surely a variant of the famous Cavan saint, St Maedoc (Mo-Aedoc), a son of Brig, who rode down from heaven in a chariot with Brigit as his sole companion. Each was a regional representative of the composite ancestor of Aed folk and Brig folk.

Obviously Maelmocheirge did not mean 'Servant of Early Rising', but was a tribal figure, since Mael, Moch and Eirg are the names of ancestors. Moch, for example, was ancestor of the O'Moghans of Sligo and he got up *moch*, early, we are told, to find a site for a church for St Attracta on Loch Gara. In my Glossary I have suggested the tribal meanings of *mael*, *moch* and *eirge*.

Maelmocheirge, of course, and all his relations never existed. I doubt whether those who manipulated these venerable figures in their pedigrees, believed in them as much as, say, Professor Bury, the Victorian rationalist, who wrote a life of St Patrick, believed in them. It would be a very disruptive belief. They had to be as bodiless as algebraic or geometrical symbols, because the equations they solved, and the history they demonstrated, would all collapse if a single creature of flesh and blood was intruded among them. He would be as damaging to the exposition of early history as a thick line or a bulky point would be to geometry.

Chapter 12

St Patrick: His Family and Household

It is 17 March and I am contemplating a picture of our national saint on the front page of a national daily. A bearded and mitred figure of great dignity, he seems to be about to deliver some message to our sad generation. From the letterpress we can guess what it is. He is telling us that the woollen blankets and undergarments manufactured by the Snowflake Fleece Company are staunch and absolutely reliable. Folds of snowy cloth hang from the arm, which holds the crozier, and it is plain that he too in his time knew that worth will tell and was the enemy of all that is mean and shoddy.

For 1500 years St Patrick has been obliged to endorse a variety of strange opinions. He is such a revered and unassailable figure that, if some dubious or unpopular cause has to be recommended, it is important to allege that St Patrick espoused it. We know so very little about St Patrick that few can contradict us. Apart from the *Confessions* and the *Letter to Coroticus*, we know nothing about his thoughts and activities that we can really believe. As for the *Confessions* and the *Letter*, the most we can say about them is that a fifth-century missionary might well have written them and that, if a later ecclesiastic invented them and attributed them to Patrick, he did it with skill and plausibility. The real force of the argument for believing in their authenticity is that most people in Ireland want to believe, and that anyone who opposed this strong current of opinion would be heading for trouble.

It is not really safe to question any detail of the Patrician tradition. When Professor Zimmer maintained that the *Confessions* were a forgery and that Patrick was an obscure missionary whose fame had been built up in order to assert

Roman orthodoxy, he was violently abused and a young student of his studying dialects in the west was advised by the police to leave Ireland. Professor Carney tells how after a lecture in a Dublin suburb, in which he had dealt critically with the story that St Patrick was in slavery to Milchu at the base of Slemish in Co. Antrim, he got a telegram from some pilgrims on the mountain repudiating 'Carney's base attempt to deprive Ulster of its Patrician heritage'.

It is useless to say that much very scholarly work has been done on Patrick and to claim, as Professor Bury did, that truth about him can be reached 'without any prepossession'. The real Patrick is buried under the religious prepossessions of the fifty generations that shaped his story.

Bury's own prepossessions were mountainous; his argument, which circles deviously round the foothills, defines their extent. He was a rationalist and as an historian he had a great reverence for the civilizing mission of the Roman Empire. He considered that this mission reached Ireland in a travel-stained form, sadly corrupted by Christianity, and that, if only Rome had annexed Ireland, the influence of a few colonial cities and small towns with municipal organizations would have done more to civilize the savage Iberians and Celts than all the little clerical communities that sprang up in the three centuries after Patrick's coming.

Yet Patrick, in Bury's view, though he came to Ireland encumbered by foolish superstitions from the capital of the world, could not all the same, as an emissary of Rome, fail to shake a little the self-centred provincialism in which the barbarous island was immersed. Patrick therefore was to be commended and Bury, though brought up as an Irish Protestant, tended to take the Roman view of him and to oppose the Irish Protestant argument that Patrick was the representative of an early non-Roman and Celtic Christianity, which was not subservient to the Papacy. This was the view of James Todd, the Regius Professor of Hebrew at Trinity College Dublin and the most eminent of Patrick's biographers previous to Bury. Todd held that the Irish Protestants were the legitimate heirs of Irish Christianity, which was distinguished from the Roman kind by so many details, by the form of tonsure, the date of Easter, the emphasis on monasticism and that it was only after the synod of Whitby in AD 664 that it succumbed to its powerful and domineering rival.

Bury chides Todd for his 'unmistakable ecclesiastical bias' and declares that in his view 'the Roman Catholic conception of St Patrick's work is generally nearer to historical fact than the views of some anti-Papal divines'. Bury was essentially a modern. The rise of folklore and the study of comparative religion have made many scholars incapable of seeing the fabrications of the devout except 'against the background of their age', where they seem appropriate and even pleasing. So it has come about that Ledwich, who had less 'historical perspective' and believed that lies were lies through all recorded time, is still lively and provocative, whereas Bury seems now evasive, tepidly credulous and very dull. Yet Bury, despite his rationalism, is held in esteem by Irish scholars, while Ledwich, the Christian, is universally scorned.

Patrician scholarship now principally turns upon dates. Chronology has always fascinated Irish scholars. It is as though they thought that the more indefinite personalities and events of history could be skewered into position by obits and floreats and synchronisms. Thus from the Irish annals we know the exact year in which the moon turned into blood and a woman ninety-four feet long was washed up in Strangford Loch. We know that it was precisely in AD 1118 that fishermen caught a mermaid in a Kilkenny weir. As for the Irish saints, we have such an abundance of dates that Canon O'Hanlon knew or could shrewdly guess the very day on which several thousand of them expired. Where there are discrepancies, from which it might appear that a man was older than his great grandfather or consorted with men who lived two centuries after him, there are many ingenious explanations as to how these misunderstandings occurred.

The argument is now focused on the date at which Patrick's mission in Ireland began. Was he before or after Palladius, who, according to the *Chronicles of Prosper*, was officially dispatched from Rome in order to be the first bishop 'to the Irish who believe in Christ'? Or was he perhaps the same as Palladius, who was also called Patricius? In this dispute I am attracted by the unorthodox common sense of Mario Esposito, who maintains that Patrick must have preceded Palladius, that is to say he must have come to Ireland before AD 431. How otherwise could he have failed to mention Palladius and those earlier pioneers, who had converted 'the Irish who believe in Christ'?

To me it appears that this problem has interest only because it concerns the Dark Ages and that the personality of Patrick, if it is genuinely revealed in the *Confessions* and the *Letter*, would not, translated to a later epoch, have aroused much interest. Centuries before Patrick, Greeks and Romans had said things and preached things far more in tune with the beliefs of our age, they had shown courage equal to Patrick's in propagating them, a greater lucidity in expounding them.

Bury thinks that the missionaries, Palladius and Patrick, both came to Ireland more to combat the Pelagian heresy, which had infected the Christians living there, than to make converts. If this is so, we are mostly in these islands, like Bury, more sympathetic to Pelagius than to those who were sent to extirpate his teaching. For like Pelagius we mostly believe in free will. We do not believe in Original Sin and that babies dying unbaptized are subject to the torments of hell. We do not consider that no one but a baptized Christian can be virtuous.

By being dexterous with dates, scholars now win praise for accurate and sober judgment. Yet scholarship becomes a game of tiddlywinks in a senior common room with counters instead of men, if we discard our 'prepossessions'. Bury, shedding his passionate rationalism in the interests of objectivity, became a very credulous person indeed. He grossly underestimated the capacity for intricate and ingenious invention possessed by men who consider that the truth has been supernaturally revealed to them. He thought that the greater part of the Patrician mythology must be founded on fact, because it is not without inner consistency. He tormented himself trying to reconcile the discrepancies of fable upon the plane of reality.

Possibly the problem is outside the scope of normal historical investigation; most of those who have tackled it show little insight into or interest in the workings of the primitive mind. They do not enquire whether early people, when they invent, erect their fabrications on the foundation of remembered things, or whether they dispense with memory altogether. To me it is obvious that the Patrician stories are not different from the stories of the other saints. They are not built on the fragments of a dimly remembered past, for the past is so much occluded by the engrossing present that it is more deduced than remembered. Bury and other hagiologists often seem to think of legend and folklore as a thick soup in which fragments of truth float about like meat and vegetables only partially dissolved. They do not reckon how everything gets ground to powder during the illiterate centuries and that, where books are few and negligible, only such memories survive as are linked by language to the things that meet the eye. It is only in the sophisticated centuries that history is based upon tradition, upon the pious handing down of truth. A primitive gets his history by rummaging in the debris of the past that surrounds him, in order to regulate his genealogies. It is on proper names of places and peoples, as he judges correctly, that the dust of history lies thickest and is least disturbed. Or is that a too modern metaphor? Let us rather say that a proper name speaks to him of the past in contemporary language. Squeeze it a little and a story, a choice of stories, will drop out of it. Pagan and Christian scribes were expert name squeezers.

Let us consider Patrick's numerous family and friends. He had thirty-one nieces and nephews, all of them saints, two hundred and fourteen other named saintly collaborators and a vast household of retainers, waiters, embroideresses, brewers and swineherds.

Let us start with his sisters. He had five of them and a brother, Deacon Sannan. The sisters were called Tigris, Darerca (22 Mar.), Liemania, Lupita (27 Sept.) and Ricella, and there is some dispute as to how St Patrick's thirty-one nephews and nieces, bishops and saints, were to be allotted among the five women. It is usually supposed that Liemania bore three bishops and four male saints to Restitutus the Lombard, her second husband, whereas St Lupita, being unmarried, bore none but illegitimate children, only one of whom, Aedan, was a saint. St Ricella seems to have been a virgin. Therefore the remaining twenty-three saints, some of them very illustrious in Irish history, were divided in various ways between Darerca and Tigris.

I will here deal only with Patrick's sister, St Lupita, his embroideress, St Erc, his brother-in-law, Restitutus, his uncle, St Martin, and Trenfer, his sainted Strong Man or Champion. I have put his chaplain, St Beschna, and his brewer, St Mescan, in my chapter on the Vascones, and the others will be allocated to whatever section they seem to suit. But first let us follow St Patrick for a short distance on his missionary journey round Ireland. I will end the chapter with St Erc, his embroideress, and Trenfer, his sainted Strong Man or Champion.

St Patrick's Missionary Journeys

My book is not about real people but fabulous ones, who for me are more interesting and historically illuminating, and so in this Patrick chapter I concentrate chiefly on *The Tripartite Life of St Patrick*. Many used to consider it a fanciful chronicle of real events, but their numbers are slowly shrinking. To me the book is full of carefully composed and meaningful inventions and I believe I value it more than those do to whom it is distorted history.

I first interested myself in Patrick's missionary journeys when I was in Co. Monaghan and read in the *Tripartite Life* that, when Patrick had visited the Monaghan parish of Donaghmoyne, a certain Victor hid himself from the light of the gospel behind some blackthorns. St Victor is thought to be a Latinized version of St Buaidh-beo (28 Feb.) – see the Budini in my Glossary. He was revealed to Patrick by a supernatural radiance, drawn out from behind the blackthorns and made a bishop. Canon O'Hanlon thinks the blackthorns were 'emblematic of his mental blindness'. But the oddity of the story points to some tribal pun. I reflected on the Draignean tribe, now O'Drynans or Drennans, who trace their name to blackthorns. But was this tribe ever in Donaghmoyne? Before I went there, I looked up Shirley's *History of County Monaghan* and found such a congestion of blackthorn place names in Donaghmoyne as I have never seen in any other parish. There was Drumdreeny, Aghadreeny, Rosdreenagh; the ridge, the field, the wood of the blackthorns. Primitive people are matter of fact, interested in man rather than landscape. They call places after their owners, not after the useless and ubiquitous scrub that grows there. Were there O'Drynans there? In Rushe's *Monaghan* I found a roll of the taxpayers of Monaghan parishes in 1663 after the Cromwellian settlement. There are twenty-four parishes in this little county; in Donaghmoyne parish and there only I found O'Drynans listed.

Could I still find traces of the Blackthorn tribe after a thousand years? In the graveyard, now closed, of the old Protestant church at Donaghmoyne, I found an old woman. No, she said, there were no O'Drynans. Then I remembered that Rushe had said that after Cromwell their name in Monaghan was often anglicized Thornton. 'Are there any Thorntons then?' It was a shot in the dark for, except from Rushe, I had never heard of Thorntons in Ireland. 'Not now,' she replied, 'the last of the Thorntons left Rosdreenagh a month ago.' I was satisfied now that I had found the blackthorns, among which St Victor had taken cover. The O'Drynans had been there from time immemorial. Later I learnt that, as Thorntons, they had been tenants of the Marquess of Bath and one of them had tried to murder his agent, W.S. Trench, the writer, who lies under a marble cross beside the church. There were other Blackthorn tribes, saints and heroes in early Irish history, in Galway, Mayo, Westmeath and Iona. Clearly they were a very early and widespread people. Among the familiar nomadic tribes of early Europe their name most resembles that of the tribe known to the Romans as the Draganum Proles, which lived on the Bay of Biscay before the Celts and traced their descent from Draganes. But I thought too of Draig, Traig or Trega, an Irish ancestor figure who might also be ancestor of the Thracians, from whom the Irish doggedly traced their descent.

Recently a Portuguese scholar has concluded that the Draganum Proles must be of Celtic origin, simply because *draighean* is blackthorn in Irish. Turn this argument upside down and it makes sense. The Draganum Proles were not Celtic but in all probability some kind of hybrid Thracians. When the Celtic pressure from the east and north became irresistible, they would leave for Ireland as many before and after them must have left from that shore. When in the course of time the Irish and their language had submerged them, their name would inevitably be connected with blackthorns.

The whole *Tripartite Life of St Patrick* could be interpreted tribally. Here I mention only a few passages. Patrick's missionary work in mid-Munster, that is to say Limerick and Tipperary, deserves the closest attention. When he came to the land of the Mennraige or Muinrige, he punished their chieftain, an evil dynast, and told him his people would not prosper. As Mennraige, their ancestor was Cuscraid Menn; as Muinrige, Muin Menn; as Moinrige, Moinne; as Ui Muindech, Muindech [CGH 366]. No doubt Mantan ancestored some further variant of the tribal name, which I have not been able to trace.

Patrick found one of his disciples loafing with a friend under a bush (*fo muiniu*) instead of attending an important farewell party on a hill, and he said his name henceforward should be Muin and that they were both doomed for the rest of their lives to be in charge of the church of Kilteely.

Another of his disciples, Deacon Mantan, figured discreditably in the same district. Some boors or buffoons, headed by a man called Derg, son of Scirire, had asked very insolently for some food from 'King' Lonan of the Ui Lonain, who with St Mantan's assistance had been preparing a banquet for Patrick. They had refused and Patrick had been gravely displeased. Shortly afterwards, as Patrick had foreseen, a little boy called Nessan arrived with a cooked wether or castrated ram, *molt*, in a basket. Patrick put things to rights immediately; he gave the cooked wether to the buffoons and immediately they all dropped down dead. Thereafter he predicted obscurity and dishonour for Lonan's tribe and a very dismal future for St Mantan and his church. He predicted that it would be 'the resort of the very dregs of the people' and that pigs and sheep should trample on his dead body. Others say that St Mantan landed with St Patrick at Kilmantan (Co. Wicklow) on his advent to Ireland and that a wicked man knocked out his teeth when he touched the shore, so that he was *manntach*, toothless. Colgan, the great hagiologist, visited Kilmantan graveyard and found it desecrated, exactly as Patrick had prophesied!

As for Nessan, the little boy, he was baptized, made a deacon and given a church and a monastery at Mungret, to the west of Limerick; his mother, who thought he ought not to let Patrick have the ram that the king had ordered for the feast, was punished by being buried outside Mungret graveyard 'beyond the reach of the church bells'. We do not know her name, but no doubt she was ancestress of some extinct or unimportant tribe. St Fintan of Dunblesc, who lived nearby, had a very similar adventure with some buffoons, who asked insolently for food, and had to be punished. That was at Loch Derg, north of Limerick, and I think these episodes concern the Derg tribes and the Lom-Lon tribes, who left their name together with some puns about *lumme*, cloaks, in Limerick

(Luimneach). *Loma* means a buffoon and *lon* means food or provisions. Nessan is the name of a Munster ancestor [CGH 298] and the wether, *molt*, undoubtedly recalls the Moltraige tribe, who lived in this barony, and whom I discuss in 'The Sons of Mil'. The sheep and pigs who desecrated St Mantan's church are probably meant to represent the Caer folk and the Mucc folk.

This St Nessan, like a dozen other saints, became a leper, *lobhar*, but I am sure he, like they, owed this misfortune to the presence of the Ui Labrada tribe. They were nearby in Orrery, north Cork. About six miles south-east of Mungret is Disert Labrain, now called Inch St Lawrence, for Labhras is anglicized Lawrence. I have no doubt that it is because of this combination of circumstances that, according to *The Martyrology of Donegal*, 'a very ancient old vellum book states that Nessan, the Deacon, was like to the Deacon Laurentius', that is to say, St Lawrence the Martyr in his habits and life. This St Lawrence was roasted on a grid iron and a pot of his melted fat given by Pope Gregory XIII to the king of Spain. Except that both lives are improbable, his life in no way resembled that of our St Nessan; it is evident that the old vellum book was endeavouring to substitute more illustrious and admired Roman saints for these obscure Irish ones. St Nessan had at Mungret, according to the *Psalter of Cashel*, 500 preachers, 500 psalmists and 500 young men devoted exclusively to spiritual exercises. If this is thought an exaggeration, we must not blame St Nessan, of whom we read in *The Martyrology of Donegal*:

> Nessan, the holy deacon, loves
> Angelic pure devotion;
> Never came outside his teeth
> What was untrue and guileful.

St Lupita, St Patrick's Sister

St Lupait or Lupita is the strangest of St Patrick's sisters. She was venerated at Armagh on 27 September. She and her sister Tigris were captured in Brittany by some pirates, called 'the seven exiled sons of Fectmagius', from the east coast of Scotland, and sold into slavery in Louth at the same time as Patrick was sold to Milchu in Antrim. Could Fectmagius have been the ancestor of the Vacomagi, who in Roman times lived in Aberdeenshire? For such guesswork there is fine precedent. J.B. Bury reads Sechtmaide and suggests that he was the Emperor Septimus Severus.

Perhaps because Lupita's name recalls *lupanar*, a brothel, and *lupanus*, lewd, in Latin or maybe because *lupait* means a little pig in Irish, she was very careless about her reputation. Three times she was implicated in scandal. Her first misadventure occurred at Ardagh in Co. Longford, where she shared a religious house with her nephew St Mel. Evil tongues began to wag about an incestuous relationship and Patrick himself was obliged to intervene. The two saints cleared themselves miraculously and St Mel fished some salmon out of a ploughed field. The Clann Bradain, later the Salmons, lived near here also. St Lupita carried live coals in her chasuble without burning herself or her clothes to a place called to this day Multinny, from *mael teine* or harmless fire. There is a Wicklow tribe the Meic Maeltine of the Ui Mael [CGH 356]. They must have had a branch in Longford. It had all been a misunderstanding. This is how it happened. St Mel was in the habit of rising at midnight to go to confession and his aunt, who was aged seventy at the time, used then to go to his empty bed. '*Sancta illa femina solebat se ad soporandum collocare, pellibusque cooperire in sancti praesulis lecto.*' She had wrapped herself in his bedclothes simply in order to acquire some of his sanctity by this indirect contagion. St Patrick, though fully persuaded of their innocence, advised that St Lupita should transfer her part of the religious establishment to Drumcheo, a few miles away under Slieve Golry.

St Lupita also had a liaison with St MacNisse of Connor, which could not be explained away so easily. St Patrick prayed that the lecherous hand, which St MacNisse had laid upon his sister, should fall off. It did so and Carn Lama, or the Carn of the Hand, is where the saint's hand was buried.

The tribal origin of the second story is obvious; the Lamraige, with an ancestor Lama, were constantly beset by puns about hands and they lived in that neighbourhood.

Her third misadventure was fatal. She sinned with Colman of the Clann Bressail and, deeply penitent, flung herself down in front of her brother's chariot. 'The chariot over her!' ordered St Patrick, and his chariot was driven over her three times. So she died and went to heaven and Patrick sang her requiem. One of her illegitimate children was St Aedan of Inis Lothair and he begged Patrick that her descendants, the children of his bastard brothers and sisters, the Ui Failain tribe and the Ui Dub Daire, should go to heaven. The Ui Dub Daire were a northern tribe with which the Ui Bressail were associated [CGH 417]. Patrick agreed but said they would always be sickly, *galraig*. I think they lost their health for one of two reasons. Perhaps it was because St Lupita's cult centre, Drum Cheo, was under Slieve Golry in Longford. This mountain is called after the Calraige, a great and widely dispersed tribe of the north west, who were descended from Lugaid Cal. On the other hand the Galraige of Iveagh bordered on the territory of the Clann Bressail in Armagh, to which her seducer belonged.

St Lupita's three haunts were Louth, where she was a slave, Armagh where she was a concubine, and Co. Longford where she was so gravely misunderstood and where, as I have related, she had a conventual establishment under Slieve Golry. Who did St Lupita represent? There is no obvious answer, as there is to Liemania, her sister, who appears to represent the Fir Leamna. The Cenel Lupae or Ui Lappae or Ui Lipi, descended from Lappan, son of Dimma, lived in Wicklow and Kerry. Possibly, as they were near the Liffey or Liphi, they gave their name to the river, but St Lupita's adventures were all farther north.

On the Continent the river Lupia became the west-German Lippe; Lupodunum is Lupf near the source of the Danube, and the Lepontii, a supposedly Celtic tribe, left their name on the Val Leventina, near St Gothard. The Lepontii behaved in an exemplary tribal way. They had an ancestor Lepontius, who had two brothers Tauriscus and Salassus, ancestors of the neighbouring tribes, Taurisci and Salassi. The history of the tribe was woven from puns. Its name came from *leipo*, Greek for leave, because they were left behind with frostbite when Hercules was leading them across the Alps.

But, if Lupita was, as I believe, an ancestress, none of these would come very near to her. More fitting descendants for her in her early continental career would be the Lobetani, whom Ptolemy places among the Celtiberians in Spain. They are said also to have left their name at Lombez south-west of Toulouse. They are an unimportant tribe, but then she was rather obscure herself.

St Erc, St Patrick's Embroideress

Apart from his kinsmen, St Patrick had a very large household, both clerical and secular. I shall have to pass over many and transfer others, like St Catan, his tailor, to a different chapter. A word here about his embroideresses. He had, in fact, three but let us take one of them, the daughter of Daire. I do not think anyone before me has spoken disrespectfully of her. Eugene O'Curry, one of the first and greatest of Irish scholars, writes of these ladies:

> No sooner did Christianity raise its heavenly banner in our island than the charming ingenuity of woman was put in requisition to adorn with befitting dignity and splendour the glorious and devoted soldiers of the Cross. St Patrick kept three embroideresses constantly at work, with, we may be sure, a sufficient staff of assistants.

The difficulty about St Erc is that St Columba also had an embroideress, called Ercnat, several generations later, who is culted the same day (8 Jan.) as a St Ercnat, who was daughter of that Daire, who gave the site of Armagh to Patrick. The latter Ercnat died of carnal love for St Benen, while he was singing psalms and was resuscitated by Patrick. These women look to me the same, since apart from their names there are four points at which one or other of them overlap:

1. Being daughters of Daire.
2. Being disciples of Patrick.
3. Dying on 8 January.
4. Embroidering.

Moreover St Oengus the Culdee tells us that St Columba's embroideress was called Ercnat, because *ercadh* is an old word for embroidery. That is to say two of them must have chosen their profession because of their names, like Mr Bun, the Baker, and Mr Chip, the Carpenter; indeed I believe that all St Patrick's attendants qualified for their jobs in some such way. For instance, according to St Aengus, St Ercnat, Columba's embroideress, was identical with St Cuach, virgin of Kilcock in Co. Kildare, who was St Columba's cook. St Cuach must have got this post either from a simple Nordic pun or because *cuach* means a bowl. The two saints were assimilated because the Ui Erca and the Ui Cuaich are contiguous tribes of Kildare and it would be natural for them to economize in ancestresses and in the Church feasts, which they later acquired.

There were very many Erc saints, male and female, merging with heroic figures of the same name in Scotland and Ireland. Erc also appears as an element in hundreds of compound proper names. With Erc, the daughter of Daire, I would group not only Erc, the father of Daire, ancestor of the widespread Daire tribe of Ulster, but also St Patrick's sister St Darerca (22 Mar.), a famous matriarch of tribes. If I am right in supposing that the names of ancient tribes were modified but never abandoned and that the founder assumed different disguises and pedigrees as his tribe divided and scattered, then the Erc tribe must have been among the greatest. St Patrick was never done cursing or consecrating the Ercs; they exercised dominion over large parts of Britain and Ireland and it is hard to see how so great a tribe could have covered our islands, if its name was unknown on the European mainland from which it must have come.

The oddest and perhaps most significant of all the Ercs is the blessed Erc, the daughter and mother of Scottish and Irish kings, for she gave her name to Ulster, Crich mac nErci. Her first husband Sarran 'had dominion over Picts and Saxons', but no doubt because of the numerous and scattered tribes to which she had to be ancestress, she left him in order to marry two other chieftains to whom she bore ten kings of Ireland. Canon O'Hanlon records with satisfaction that she did penance for these evil ways, for leaving Tory Island she did a fifty-mile walk to Drumlene where blood had oozed from her fingertips. Why was this district associated with blood? Not only did Erc's fingers bleed there but so did the patriarch Ith, son of Breogan (*Irish Nennius* 241), and there was a shower of blood 'Fros Fola' at Drumleene in the reign of Niall Frossach or the Showery. *Fola* must be a tribal word. I will show in my chapter on the Frisii, that *fros* must also have been a tribal word, since there were several celebrated showers and a place called Frosses and another called Drimfries all at or near Drumleene (see p. 229).

Erc had knelt at every second ridge on the way across the Donegal hills. Her nephew, St Cairneach, to whom Drumlene belonged, had told her she would go to heaven and that one out of every two kings of Ireland would be of her seed.

Erc is an interesting instance of a fictitious ancestress half-way towards sainthood. Cairneach blessed the spot where she died and, calling it Cell Erca, put it in charge of a bishop. The multitude of her illustrious descendants would have been an obstacle to more explicit canonization. Drumleene on Loch Foyle, bequeathed to St Cairneach by Erc, was his principal Irish church.

Cairneach had a sensational career also in Wales, Scotland and Cornwall, where he built an underground city (tin mines?) among the Cornavii as well as a large monastery, which a wicked brother turned into a fortress. The Cornavii are also marked in the Caithness area on Ptolemy's map and some scholars have suspected that they were not different from Ptolemy's three tribes, which reached south-westward to the Sound of Mull, the Caerini, Carnonaceae and Creones. It is therefore not at all surprising to find another Cairnech, not a saint, dominating in this area over Orcs and Cats. He was surely ancestor of a very widely dispersed tribe.

St Cairneach's cruel first cousin, MacErc, the son of St Erc, after capturing Ireland, also took sovereignty of Britain, Cat (the Catti of Caithness) and Orc (the Orkneys).

Who were St Erc and her powerful son, MacErc, and all the other Erc saints and ancestors? What race was so dominant that it could claim to hold a greater part of Britain and Ireland?

Orc, the Orkneys, which was held by MacErc, is a very unstable word (I believe it only punningly acquired the meaning 'boar'). It is sometimes written Forc and Porc and Proc and the ancestor of the Tuath Orc was Forc, son of Conall Cernach. Orc is surely the same as Erc also. We are told that the sons of

Ercal (Hercules), the Cruithne from Thrace, took the Islands of Orc. I believe the Erc tribe were the Thracians, who in Europe gave the shelter of their name to so many lesser tribes.

The Erc Folk and the Thracians

Traigia, which is Irish for Thrace [LG II 83], was also the name of one of the 'women of Bith', an early invader [LG II 209]. Traig, Thracian, is the same as Draig, which is the same as Derg, which is the same as Erc. Each of these equations occurs in many forms. I will give an instance of the first only. There are three lists of 'the servitors of Mil', who headed the Milesian invasion of Ireland. In the first list Traig figures, in the second his place is taken by Trega, in the third by Draig. The other stages of Traigs' transformation into Erc are illuminated by many similar equations; they occur so often that they can scarcely be accidental.

Since a chapter on the many hundreds of saints and heroes who I believe to derive from Traig the Thracian ancestor would be too long and complicated to undertake now, I have made a diagram to show how he changed his name in many different directions (Table 5).

Recently I observed in O'Brien's *Corpus* that several ancestors, whom I had not previously considered, fit appropriately into my argument.

[CGH]	p. 49	Fergus Tregbotha	is Fergus Dergbotha
	p. 260	Triccdromma	is Ercdroma
	p. 375	Tridene	is Draichdene

These lend support to my equation, based much earlier on very many names.

$$\text{Treg (Tricc, Tri)} = \text{Draich (or Draig)} = \text{Derg} = \text{Erc}$$

Below the Thracian Table of Variants I have set a Brig-Bard Table, for I believe Restitutus the Lombard, and the Irish St Martins, whom I treat next, belong to the Bard Group (Table 6, p. 98).

12. ST PATRICK: HIS FAMILY AND HOUSEHOLD

TABLE 5: THE THRACIANS AND THEIR VARIANTS

Tres		Tregen	Treg	Dreg	Dr(eg)en		Derg	Herc
Tret(h)		Tren		Reg			Der	Erc
Ret(h)		Tern	Treog					
		Ern						
Trad	Trib	Trigin	Trig	Drig	Dr(ig)in			
Trat			Tri	Rig				
Rat				Rioc	Dirn			
Tart								
				TRAG				
	Trab	Tragin		Dra(i)g	Draigin	Drat	Dai(g)re	Arg
	Tarb(h)	Tarn		Rag	Dran			
		Taran			Darn	Dart	Dar	
		Arn						
		Iarn						
Trot(h)	Trob	Tro(ge)n	Trog	Drog	Dro(ge)n			Orc
Roth	Torb	Torn		Rog	Dorn			
Tort		Toran	Torc	Dorc	Dor			
Rus	Turb	Tuiren	Trug	Drug	Durn	Drud		
		Tuir	Turc		Dur	Rud		
						Ruad		
						Druad		

Note that Tregen-Tren (col. 3) and Draigin-Dorn (col. 6) are perhaps forms of Traig-Finn.

TABLE 6: THE BRIG-BARD TRIBES AND THEIR VARIANTS

Bald	Blad	Brat	Brad	Frag	Brac	Bal	Bran	
Ball	Blat		Bard	Brag	Barc		Barn	Bar
	Blai		Mart	Barg				
		Bret		Breg	Fraech			
		Breth		Berg	Brec	Bec	Bren	Ber
					Berc		Bern	Breo
BRIG									
		Brit			Bric	Bic		Bior
		Brith		Brig / Frig			Birn	Bir
	Blot	Brot	Brod	Brog	Broc	Boc	Bron	Bro
	Blod				Broic		Boirn	
		Brut	Brud	Brug	Bruic		Bruin	
			Bruid	Burg				

Note that Bran-Bron (col. 8) are perhaps forms of Brig-Finn.

Restitutus, St Patrick's Brother-in-Law

I must go back to Restitutus the Lombard, who married St Patrick's sister, Liemania, and gave her a son, the Irish St Germanus. He got his name, as Father Shearman points out, because the father of St Germanus of Auxerre was Rusticus, and the father of St German of the Isle of Man was Ridicus or Redgitus of Brittany and it was only suitable that our St German, who converges on them both, should have a father with a similar name. Where the name came from originally I do not know, but, whether St Germanus of Auxerre was real or fictitious, one could believe anything of his father.

I think I know why Restitutus was a Lombard. The Lombards or Langobardi are oddly prominent in early Irish history. King Cormac is said to have entertained them at Tara and the very early King Ollmuccaid, or Big Pig-Man, fought with them several centuries before Tacitus recorded them in

12. ST PATRICK: HIS FAMILY AND HOUSEHOLD

northern Germany. In the days of St Patrick the nine daughters of the king of the Lombards came to Armagh and asked him where they should stay. He fixed them in three different cells near Armagh, two of which are named.

Finally there is an unexpected ancestor, called Longbardan, in a Munster Genealogy [CGH 378]. All these people and stories were surely not fabricated out of nothing at all.

Now if the Lombards or Langobardi have any claim to appear in such a context, it is surely as echoes from the remote period when the Lang or Long folk and the Bard folk were first amalgamating – that is to say long before their union had acquired that German character, which they had not to shed until they became Italians. There has always been philological guessing about the meaning of Langobardi. Some say it derives from the long river banks or Borde, which they cultivated, some say from the long swords, Barte, which they wore, and of course the possibility of long beards has not been overlooked. In fact there was a tribe, the Lacco-bardi, on the coast of the low countries, and in Spain we find Lacco-briga and Lango-briga as names for the same place. Obviously the component parts are tribal and change their meaning after every fresh corruption.

That Langobard was a composite word is clear from the names of St Patrick's nephews, the sons of the Lombard, St Nechtan mac Ua Baird and St Usaille (or Auxilius) mac Ua Baird, 'sons of the Bard'. Odder than this St Usaille was culted at Cell ua mBaird (now Killymard) in Co. Donegal, and there seems to have been a conviction that he or his father was a bard. This recalls the Clann Baird of Roscommon, who were alleged to be hereditary poets in Ui Maine. Note there is Bardomagus in Lombardy [PREM II 270]. But it seems to me very unlikely that a fictitious Langobard should disintegrate into a couple of bards. It is more likely that the Bard family should expand by amalgamation into Langobards. The two sons of the Bard, St Nechtan and St Usaille, themselves look fictitious. It is almost impossible to distinguish St Nechtan (22 Apr.), a Boyne saint, from Nechtan Nair of uncertain sex, who presided over the source of the Boyne, and from St Nechtan Nair of Co. Derry and Aberdeen (a sort of Neptune to the fishermen), and Nechtan Nar, an early invader from Thrace. Who were these people? Some time I must discuss their relationship to the Nechtraige, the Nemedes and the Nervii.

Who were the Long folk and the Bard folk? I think they were originally Ligurians and Briges and that the former left the Ligones, Lingones, Lungones and Longones as their heirs in Spain and Gaul, and the Ui Linga and their saint St Moling in Co. Carlow (see pp. 28–9). Significantly the Ui Longain lived near Armagh. To the Bard folk I can only allude here. Bard, as I show in my chapter on Martin, is clearly a tribal element in composite proper names. Columba had two uncles, Telbard and Teldub, Finbard was the son of Bardan and so on. That they evolved from the Briges is suggested by the fact that Tigernbard was the son of Brig and Rigbard was the son of Brige, and there is a well-tried equation between Brig and Brad and Bard.

St Martin, St Patrick's Uncle

How am I to deal with the Irish St Martins? There were five of them. In the first place I have to admit that St Patrick's uncle, St Martin of Tours, from whom our Martins were fantastic Irish offshoots, may really have existed. I make this admission with reluctance for Sulpicius Severus, the biographer of the famous Gaulish saint, made him as unpleasant and as incredible as lay within his power. Sulpicius was the worst sort of liar, an educated, smooth-tongued diplomatist. Everything that he tells us about Martin would be disgusting were it true. He and his monks reviled the scholars and poets of antiquity, so immeasurably their superiors in knowledge and truthfulness and in the perception of beauty.

'Of what profit to posterity,' writes Sulpicius, 'to read of Hector's battles and Socrates' philosophy? Not only is it folly to imitate these writers but not to attack them with the utmost fierceness is sheer madness.' Martin set fire to ancient and lovely temples and cut down sacred groves and pretended that angels assisted him. Of all this Gibbon once wrote: 'The prudent reader will judge whether Martin was supported by the aid of miraculous powers or of carnal weapons.'

That was an eighteenth-century view. For some curious reason the twentieth century is far more indulgent. For example, the eminent scholar Mrs Chadwick thinks of Sulpicius as 'a great biographer and the most delightful writer in Gaul of his day'. She is deeply moved by his story of an angel helping Martin to struggle with the emperor and she justifies all the lies by saying that the book would have had no sale had there been no 'marvels' in it. Posing the question whether Sulpicius really believed his own stories, she admits: 'It is difficult to feel any confidence that he did, despite his repeated and grave assurance of their genuineness ... We must not allow the miracles to discredit Sulpicius' narrative in its essential features.' She adds that the credibility of it all is 'essentially a question for experts'.

Here it seems to me that she is extending the authority of scholarship far beyond its legitimate limits. We normally judge liars by intuition as much as by inconsistency in their information, and this faculty does not desert us when the liar is not our contemporary but died long ago and we have to lean a little on grammarians and palaeographers. It is true that the community in which Sulpicius lived was favourable to self-deception, but he himself in any time or place would have been outstanding as an earnest and sophisticated self deceiver. He belongs to that great class of subtle men who do not themselves claim to have seen angels at Mons or visions at Fatima, but who thrive in the intellectual twilight in which these delusions are frequent, and find them beautiful and touching. Sulpicius was a lawyer, highly educated and cultured, and claims to have known Martin personally. Douglas Simpson in his life of St Martin's disciple St Ninian finds this credulity 'simply staggering' and sees in it evidence for 'the breakdown of the scientific mind with its capacity to judge tolerantly and objectively'.

All my sympathies, of course, are with Dr Simpson. Applauding Martin and Sulpicius, we are treacherous to those calm and truthful souls who must certainly have survived, unhonoured and unrecorded, in the waste places of Gaul; scholars who retained, like Mrs Chadwick herself, the power to judge between truth and falsity. We know that the official religion of the ancients still survived in the days of St Martin, for he professes to have been tempted by the devil in the guise of the gods and goddesses of Rome. If the memory of these gods survived, so too must that sceptical spirit, which for many generations had undermined their pretensions. The Greek philosophers, the Stoics and Epicureans, had long before, with logic rather than fanaticism and carnal weapons, destroyed the hold of the pagan gods upon the educated mind. The spirit of truth is imperishable. How can we doubt that it survived, though almost suffocated by the crudities of invaders, by the sly prevarications of men like Sulpicius, and the gross untruthfulness of Martin's votaries? Though their posterity has forgotten them, undoubtedly there were learned and truthful men, who struggled against the myths of the past and the myths of the future and said: 'None of these things happened. They are lies.'

Some say that St Martin of Tours never existed. It is more probable that Sulpicius had in his mind some half-real prototype or maybe several, which he amalgamated and dissected, stripping them of certain qualities and adorning them with others. Martin, as we know him, is Sulpicius' creation, but there must have been some reality behind the artefact. Yet the real Martin is so elusive that one would be doing no great injustice to the truth by declaring that he did not exist or had the historicity of Cinderella or of Ali Baba, to whose fictitious personalities without a doubt some real people must have contributed.

The story of Martin of Tours is woven very closely into Irish hagiography and legend. Let us examine a strand or two. He was, to begin with, it is said, St Patrick's uncle, a brother of his mother, Concessa, who must, therefore, have been, like himself, a Pannonian of Celtic stock from Hungary. St Martin is said to have conferred on St Patrick a monk's tonsure, when he visited him at Tours, and, in his gratitude to his uncle and mentor, the apostle decreed that at Martinmas a pig should be given to every monk and nun in Ireland.

In the story of the holy woman, Kentigerna, it is shown that it was possible to give alms in honour of St Martin at Martin's Cave in west Cork with the same spiritual efficacy as if they were given at Tours. And I suggest that, as Kentigerna had a husband and a son who were both authentic tribal figures, she too must have been one and that Martin had some tribal significance in west Cork (see p. 184).

St Columba (Columcille) was no less implicated than Patrick in the story of St Martin of Tours. We are told that he had at Derry a famous wonder-working gospel, which had once belonged to St Martin. It was stolen from Derry by the English in 1182. He had come by this in a strange way. St Martin had been buried with a gospel on his bosom, having predicted before his death that a holy stranger from Erin, whose name would be composed of the bird that lit on the head of Jesus and a church, i.e. Colum(ba)cille, would one day open his tomb and take away the gospel. And, in fact, a hundred years later Columba chanced to be in Tours, and, as a reward for finding the lost grave of Martin, he was allowed to take St Martin's gospel with him and invited to appoint the next bishop of Tours. He appointed St MoConna, son of Finncoem, who had, under Columba, christianized Aberdeen, cured seven lepers in Mull and turned a boar to stone. There were four MoConna saints, all connected indirectly with Columba, but I have not been able to find a reason for this story.

St Ciaran of Saigir, near Birr in Offaly, also found his way to Tours and extracted relics of Martin for his church. He even begged to be buried with St Martin at Saigir as though it was not just a limb or two but his whole body that he had taken away from Tours [LIS II 120].

In all, ten Irish saints visited Tours: Patrick, Columba, MoConna, Nathcaem, two Ciarans, Tigernach, Laserian, Maedoc and a Scottish one, Ninian. Father Shearman tries to deal with these complications by suggesting that some episodes really relate to an Irish St Martin, who had the same feast day (11 Nov.) as Martin of Tours [SH 449]. This Martin was a companion of St Patrick, who was left by him 'with a party of his people' at Martartech in Kilkenny. As there are several other places called after Martin or churches dedicated to him in this neighbourhood, Father Shearman thinks they belong to the Patrician saint rather than to the saint of Tours.

His boldest suggestion concerns Tory Island off the coast of Donegal, which was called Tor-inis Martain [SH 392] and confused with Tours of the Turones, where St Martin ministered. He suggests that the Patrician Martin died and was buried there and that it was from his tomb that St Columba extracted the Gospel, which he placed in Derry, appointing his cousin St Ernan as its first abbot.

If the Gallic Martin is a shadow, the Irish Martin is the shadow of a shadow. His importance is that he illustrates how fabulous saints could be constructed. Those who wrote of him had so little confidence in him that they had to prop up his authenticity by identifying him with the Gallic Martin. One must not waste time discussing whether an Irish Martin existed. He did not and could not. Why then were five invented?

I would offer my usual explanation. The Martini tribe was widespread in west Cork where Kentigerna of Rosscarbery gave alms in honour of St Martin, in Tipperary, Limerick, Roscommon, Tyrone, Leitrim. In Leitrim, at least, it produced the clear suggestion of a saint, for there was a tribe there, the Clann Martain, and a subtribe called the Mael Martain, which might in Christian times claim to be called after a disciple of the saint 'the tonsured one of Martin' [FEN 387]. But as I show in 'The Sons of Mil' Leitrim had many tribes in which 'Mael', being followed by unsaintly suffixes, plainly did not mean, as alleged, 'tonsured one of', and the Clann Martain was also there called Clann Bardain.

The Bard tribes are the same as the Mart tribes because of an m-prefix, which I will not attempt to explain. Thus the Dal mBairdine were the same as the Martini. The Clann Bardain or Clann Martain had two eponymous ancestors, Bardan and his great great grandfather Martan. Bardan had a so-called Finbard. The Martini were descended from Rigbardan.

So I would suggest that St Ciaran's attachment to St Martin derived from the proximity of the Muinter Rigbardan (now the O'Riordans), which must have represented a fusion of the Rig tribe and the Bard or Mart tribe. Martan and Bardan were the same and that is why St Ciaran had a clumsy clerk called Bardanus, who once let out the sacred fire at Saigir, so that Ciaran had to rekindle it by blessing a stone until it blazed. Bardanus also upset a cauldron of milk, which had to be magically refilled. Because he was always in the wrong, can one argue that his posterity was not much esteemed? I do not think one can, for there was also a much venerated bell called Bardan Ciarain or Kieran's little bard, which St Patrick had given him in Italy on his way to Rome.

The bell is also called the Bernan Ciarain, or Gapped Bell of Ciaran, but this must be because Ciaran was of the Dal Birn of Ossory. According to Patrick's prediction it had rung out for the first time at the spot where Ciaran had to build his monastery, that is to say at Saigir.

I have no space to refer to the other Irish Martins and the various churches, raths and rivers that appear to be called after them. Someday I shall write more of Tory Island and the odd succession of saints and heroes associated with it, for, as elsewhere, they wear for me the appearance of tribes rather than people but seem there to follow each other in layers that are tidier and more decipherable than elsewhere. But all this would take me too far away from the saints with whom the chapter opened.

How remote was the connection between the Bard-Mart folk of Ireland, with whom I include Restitutus the Lombard, and the Barduli-Bardyetani, south of the Pyrenees? St MacCarthain of Clochar was Patrick's 'Strong Man' or Trenfer, having carried him across a river, and since there was a Trenfer tribe with an ancestor, Trenfer, who left his name to this day with the Treniers and Traynors of Clogher, it is clear that St MacCarthain (15 Aug.) was assimilated to him as he was to Fer da Crich (Man of two Borders), ancestor of the Ui Fir da Crich. St MacCarthain was also 'Bind' from the Cenel Binnich of Tyrone and 'Aed' from the local Aed-Ech folk. Canon O'Hanlon said that his own tribe, now the McCarrons, still survived near Clogher in his time. St Tigernach of Clones, who took Clogher from St MacCarthain, was also called Fer da Crich. This odd title was explained as 'Man of two Dioceses'. There are a very large number of ancestors whose names begin or end with *fer*, a man; I have counted over 200 such names, some of them borne by many men, some by only one or two. It seems to me that the suffix is always tribal, even when the tribe is hard to identify. Here are twenty names, whose interpretation is easy, since they are linked with tribes to which I refer many times in these chapters.

TABLE 7: FER NAMES

Fer Aine	Fer Corb	Fer Garb	Fer Menn
	Fer Crom	Fer Gel	
Fer Baeth	Fer Cu	Fer Glas	Fer Sen
Fer Benn		Fer Goboc	
Fer Blai	Fer Det		Fer Tri
Fer Bolg	Fer Domnach	Fer Loga	
Fer Buidi	Fer Dub		

12. ST PATRICK: HIS FAMILY AND HOUSEHOLD

These names follow the usual pattern, and it is clear that *fer* did not mean man, and that the suffix did not bear the meaning ascribed to it.

(1) *Fer*, though usually at the beginning of the name, is sometimes at the end, thus Mathfer, Trenfer, Findfer; sometimes *fer* occurs in the epithet, as in Cairpre Niafer and Art Aenfer (Champion-Man and Single-Man).

(2) Sometimes the link with a tribe is explicit, thus Caelfer is ancestor of the Caelrige, Fer Ceite of the Dal Ceite, Fer Bolg of the Fir Bolg, and so on many times. At other times the link can fairly be deduced, thus Cobfir and Mathfer recall the Ui Cobain and the Dal Mathra.

(3) There are fanciful stories about these names, which show that they were inscrutable. Thus Fer Tri, ancestor of the Corcu Fir Tri, was so called because his wife gave three (*tri*) cries, when her son Nia Mor was killed. Fer Benn, who was the same as Fer da Benn and ancestor of the Benntraige, had two horns, *da benn*, on his head. Fer Ded or Vir Fumi, Son of Smoke, was a fireman and Fer Gair was a good shouter, because *de diadh* is smoke and *gair* is shout.

(4) These *fer* names tend to go in geneaological groups, and, as I have argued elsewhere, this suggests that they were genealogical fictions and they were classed together because of the acknowledged kinship of hybridized branches of a Fer tribe. Thus Fer Fi was brother of Fer Maise, Fer Cing of Fer Tlachtga, Fer Ruith of Fer Nuad, son of Fer Lugdach, and so on a score of times. But sometimes the ancestors are grouped by their suffix, thus Fer Corb was son of Mug Corb, Fer Demmain was the son of Daman.

(5) Fer Aine was husband of the great ancestress-goddess, Aine, and O'Rahilly [EIHM 289] deduces from this that *fer* here just meant husband but I have not found any other instance of this and I would argue as usual that Fer Aine was the amalgamated ancestor of the Fer and Aine tribes appropriately married to Aine, the ancestress of the latter. Otherwise it is difficult to explain another ancestor, Echach Fer Aine; there is no record that he too had a wife called Aine. The Fer-Aine link is sustained by the fact that the great Aine of Knockany, Co. Limerick, had two sons, Fer Fi

and Fer Maise. Also the famous invader Partholon had a son Fer and a daughter Ain, who were incestuously married. He also had a son Feron, who is perhaps an amalgamation of the two.

(6) Like other tribal words *fer* or *fir* occurs several times as a name in itself without suffix or prefix. Thus Fir and Fial were the twin sons, some say the son and the daughter, of Macha. They were born prematurely at Ard Macha (Armagh), when their vainglorious father, Crunnchu, boasted that his wife Macha could outrun the king's horses.

(7) *Fer* is sometimes of female sex or has a nonsensical meaning. Fercarthan, who died at Forcarthain in Kildare, was a princess. Fer Amhla, who was the mother of five or six midland saints, seems to be the same as Fer Blai, who was a man [CGH 243]. What is one to say of Finn's door-keeper, Mac da Fer, whose name means 'Son of two Men'? Why was the mouth of the Moy river in Mayo called Inber na Fer, the estuary of the men?

(8) These Fer ancestors had frequent aliases, because, I maintain, in the course of time, adjacent or kindred tribes assimilated their ancestors. Just as Fer Amhla is the same as Fer Blai, so Fer Ceite is the same as Fer Rein and Fer Domnach as Fer Gaile [CGH 244].

(9) These integrated ancestors can also disintegrate. Thus Fer Ceite Mac Deda becomes Fer mac Cedi mac Dedaid [CGH 377].

(10) Like other composite ancestors, they were sometimes associated with places whose names echoed their attributes. Thus Fer Dub, Black Man, lived at Dubatha or Black Ford, the Ui Fer Gair, descended from Fer Gair, lived at Loch nGair, now Loch Gur, Limerick.

These names correspond well to Gaulish names, for Holder and others have identified Fer tribes and Fer heroes in Gaul and use *fer*, a man, in the explanation of their names. The Veromandui, for instance, who left their name in Vermandois in northern France, are thought by Holder to be 'Those whose meditations are concerned with men.' Farther south in Narbonne we find the Veragri and the Vertacomacori. There are place names too in England such as Verulamium, St Albans, Vernemeton, Nottingham, and Verometum near Leicester.

Could the Verones, whose chief settlement was Varia in northern Spain, be Iberian representatives of this ancient Fer tribe? They are also called Berones and I have suggested that their ancestress was the Spanish-Irish lady Bera,

12. ST PATRICK: HIS FAMILY AND HOUSEHOLD

daughter of Eber, who left her name at Berehaven in Cork. But there are other tribes like the Viruni of Pomerania, who might be remotely implicated in this complex story.

There are several Gaulish heroes like Verudoctius and Vercingetorix. Verudoctius recalls Fer Dechet [CGH 285]. As for Vercingetorix, I have already mentioned Fer Cingit, son of Fer Maic, ancestor of the Cenel Fermaic [CGH 244], and suggested that, like his namesake, the female Cingit, he was probably the ancestor of a tribe. Fer Menn (Stammering Man) might be an Irish version of the ancestor of the Veromandui. Fer Corb would correspond to the Gaulish Viricorb [GPN 287].

CHAPTER 13

Saints of the Vascones

St Mescan, St Patrick's Brewer, and St Bescna, his Chaplain

An Irish scholar has said that the Corcu Baiscinn, who lived on the long projection of Co. Clare that skirts the north shore of the Shannon, were Basques, but he said this so diffidently and so long ago that I cannot trace his name. One need not, however, apologize for suggesting that the tribe that occupied Corcovaskin, as this promontory was called, were the Vascones, who left their name to the Basques and the Gascons, and who covered in classical times the same Pyrenean region where the Basques were later located. For it is the Basque language that rouses so much fiery argumentation and there is no indication that the Vascones spoke Basque. Their name may have become a *nom de peuple*, adopted by successive invaders. Strabo indeed says that the Vascones were indistinguishable from their other tribal neighbours, the Asturians, Cantabrians etc. He may, of course, have been wrong He was disdainful of barbarian distinctions and in the same paragraph he expresses his reluctance to mention a number of queer tribal names of Iberia, which were displeasing in sound and of no importance.

For once I must venture into the realm of phonetics with a few unpretentious observations. There are very few place and tribal names in ancient Spain that contain the 'sc' sound and they almost all occur in or near the Pyrenees – Osca, Menosca, Biscargis (Biscay), Muscara, Cascantium, Virovesca, and among tribes we find the Vascones, the Vescitani and the Conisci. The Vescitani are obviously a variant of their neighbours the Vascones, and Virovesca must be derived from an amalgamation between the Vescitani and their powerful Celtic neighbours the Verones or Berones.

This sound 'sc' seems equally rare in Irish proper names. Indeed among the tribes we only meet it amongst the Basc, Musc, Esc or Uisc peoples, and the evidence of kinship suggests that all these people belonged to the same tribe, whose name was differently pronounced. Cairbre Bascain, the ancestor of the Dal Bascind, was the brother of Cairbre Musc, the ancestor of the Muscraige, and the Dal Bascind are called Dal mBascind and equated with the Dal nOengus Muscae.

Among the saints the same picture is apparent. St Mescan (St Patrick's brewer) and St Bescna (St Patrick's chaplain) were both culted on the river Faughan in Co. Derry, and certain scholars have said they were the same. I have suggested already that St Mescan brewed for St Patrick because *measc* means drunk; possibly St Bescna was his chaplain because *bas* is death. The ancients had the same difficulty as the Christians in explaining these names. Cairbre Baschain was Cairbre of the smooth (*cain*) palm (*bas*), but there is a more ancient explanation that he had an easy (*cain*) death (*bas*), having died on a pillow. As for his brother Cairbre Musc, like other Corbs and Cairbres, he had committed incest, *corbadh*, with his daughter Duibfionn, the ancestress of the Corcu Duibne of Kerry. He was called Musc, because of this *mo-aisge* or inordinate desire. Alternatively it was his exclamation 'My shame!'

All the stories about the Musc and Basc ancestors suggest that they came from far away, that is to say that they are ancestors of ancient continental tribes or tribal amalgamations and not just of local communities. We are told in Cormac's glossary that at one time the tribes of Ireland and Britain each of them had property and friends on either side of the Irish Sea. 'Each knew the residence of his friend … such were the divisions of all the families, for each had a proportion in the eastern island.' Because of this, said Cormac, Cairbre Musc had two homes; and when he was visiting his family and friends in the east, he stole by a trick the first lap dog, *mes-chu*, that was ever brought to Ireland. Without a doubt the lap dog, *mes-chu*, is a further attempt to explain the name Musc. This very complicated story, the competition for its ownership by three kings of Ireland, is full of the detailed and deliberate absurdity that is inevitable when complex history has to be related in puns and parables.

None of the other Measc, Masc, Musc heroes were arbitrarily invented. On the lowest level there were actual place names to be explained, and the odd behaviour of these symbolic figures is fully accounted for, if we recognize that as individuals they are deputizing for tribes and, in their domestic adventures, are obliged to illustrate the movement of widely scattered kindred peoples over many lands and through several generations. Such a one was Mesc, the daughter of Bodb, a great chief in eastern Scotland. In my chapter on the Budini, I show that there is strong evidence for the existence of a Bodb-Bud tribe in eastern Scotland (see p. 209).

Mesc was carried away by Garman, who gave his name to Loch Garman, now Wexford harbour; she died of shame (*Mo Aisge*! My Shame! once more perhaps) and her name is borne by Mag Mesc, a plain nearby. A little later Garman was killed by four brothers, Mes Seda, Mes Roeda, Mes Ded, Mes Delmon. They are clearly themselves representatives of Mess-Mesc hybrid tribes, of whom there were some ten on the east coast of Ireland. And it would not be hard to say what tribal amalgamation each one represented. Mes Delmon, for example, would derive from the fusion of the Mess-Mesc folk with the Ui Dilmona, a south Leinster tribe [CGH 73]. The four brothers are related to Mescorb, son of Cucorb, son of Musc, of the Dal Mescorb, a Wicklow tribe. If an examination were made of the family tree of the Mess and the Corb heroes, who pass on to their sons and daughters detachable syllables of their names, only prejudice could deny their tribal significance.

I should not leave the Basc folk without recalling the old legend that Gurguntius, king of Britain, invited the Basclenses or Basques to settle in Ireland, though plainly it is fantastic the way it is told by Giraldus and Geoffrey of Monmouth. It was seriously believed all the same. Because of this supposed occupation, Giraldus claimed to have noticed certain Basque customs among the Irish and he says that Henry II, who owned the Basque capital of Bayonne, derived therefrom a claim to the ownership of Ireland too.

St Escon and the Fish

It is rather hard to connect the Esc-Uisc people with the Musc and the Basc. Nonetheless St Escon (20 Nov.) is also called St Mescon and Colgan suggests that they are the same, though St Escon's cult centres are to the east and south in Antrim and in Leix.

The Dal nUisce or Uiste and several kindred-sounding tribes cannot be located precisely but they could be the same as the Dal Muisge, since a Co. Louth tribe, the Ui Faelchon Conaille, is derived from both of them [H 336, 334]. Estiu, wife of Nar, was a legendary lady of Athlone. The Aes Iste were in Kerry. A number of place names in the west of Ireland, which

Joyce connects with *uisce*, water or *iasc*, fish, betray their traces, I believe. He says that Murrisk, a coastal region in Sligo, means 'sea-shore-marsh', yet so sensible an explanation cannot stand up to the persistent Irish desire to give complicated and absurd ones. They say the name comes from a huge sea fish (*muir iasc*), cast ashore by the sea, which destroyed Ireland, its earth, air and sea, with three mighty stinking 'evomitions' from its alternate ends, mouth and tail, in three successive years. Alternately the place was called after a woman named Muiresc.

A rather similar woman, Muiresc, was the daughter of the king of Scotland and herself had a daughter Muirinn (Mor-find), who ran messages for Finn. She was the ancestress of the Clann Morna of Clare, and, perhaps, therefore of the Morini. Her family relations, her sister, her lovers, her foster-brothers, sons of the king of the Catti of Caithness, are all very complicated and would, if carefully analyzed, yield, I believe, much information about the goings and the comings of the early tribes between Scotland and Ireland.

This Muiresc is also called Mata Muirsce and had seven children, all of them obviously tribal ancestors of Connacht. These children are also attributed to Magach, a male, but not Mata Muirsce's husband. They include En or Finn, Docha or Toiche, Annluan, Cet and Bascall and Mug Corb. Finn or En is obviously the ancestor of the local branch of the Veneti or Eneti. Cet is similarly related to the Getae, Magach and Mata, which I will later suggest to be forms of the Mygdonic ancestor. Bascall would appear to be a Vasconic hybrid; Mug-Corb is Carpo-Mygdonic. The Ui Annluan, a Mayo tribe, and Toiche or Docha, are puzzles that seem soluble.

I am sure, anyway, that Muiresc did not mean 'sea shore marsh' and since Mag Muiresc (Murrisk) in Sligo extends from the river Easky to Ballyeeskeen it is equally plain that the words concealed in these two new place names are not as alleged *iascagh*, fishy or *uisce*, water.

Continental Relations: Ulysses and Aesculapius

Except for what is indicated by their association with Finn, the grandson of Baiscne, the Basc-Musc people seem in Ireland to have been rather subordinate. In the story of the invasions, Baschon, the archetypal ancestor, figures as a mere servitor of Mil.

Where did the Basc-Musc-Isc people come from before they reached the Pyrenees as the Vascones? One thinks of the Iscaevones or Istaevones from the river Issel in Germany. They must have been a powerful people, because Iscaevo or Istio was one of the three sons of Mannus, the father of the German people. They called their city Asciburg, now Asburg, and declared that Ulysses had visited it. That is in the Rhineland but eastwards there is another Asciburg and Asciburgius Mons is in Saxony, so these places can only be associated with them, if they were a widely ranging people. Ulysses or Ulixes might have been a Roman attempt to reproduce the name of their ancestor, compounded perhaps with the ancestor of another tribe. Ulixes founded another city near Malaga in the country of the Basculi in southern Spain [S II 58, 83]. It bore his name, we are told. The nearest tribe were the Exitani, with a capital Sex or Hexi. To the north-west lay the Ileates, who may account for the multitude of Il settlements near the city of Ulysses. I do not believe Ulixes founded either Asciburg or the city near Malaga but Holder mentions, without being able to locate it, an Iberian proper name Ilixo. If, as seems probable, Il folk mixed with Ex-Esc folk near Malaga or in central Europe, the resultant ancestor might assume the features of Ulixes and account for some of his wanderings.

In looking for other Esc-Ex-Ist folk we should not ignore either the Aestii, ancestors of the Estonians, who Tacitus in his *Germania* (p. 45) noted upon the shores of the Baltic, or the Estiones, who lived beside the Brigantes on Lake Constance. Tacitus says they were akin to the Suebi but spoke a near-British tongue. The Brigantes came to Yorkshire and Ireland so what was there to prevent the Estiones or some of their distant kin from visiting us (Map 4, p. 68)? Were they related to the Ostiones of Brittany [GDC 130] and the Ostidamni, who lived among the Dumnonians of Devon and Cornwall?

Then there is Aesculapius. He was not a wanderer like Ulysses, but there is much about him to suggest that he was built on the Irish domestic pattern as the ancestor of a combined tribe, the Histiaeans and Lapiths of Thessaly, who from Strabo's account were much intermingled. Aesculapius was born at Tricca in Histiaeotis, where was his oldest shrine; his mother's lover was Ischu and she was a Lapith. Ixion and Ischomache, both Lapiths too, come into his complex story like the echoes and half echoes of an Irish origin tale. Of course by the time these stories were written in the form we know them, the Hellenes were no longer interested in tribes but in cities and individuals. The genealogical trees of earlier times had all flowered into luxuriant poetry and anecdote. It is only by accident that now and again the branching pattern of tribal ancestry can be seen in its nakedness. Can we guess that once upon a time Istio of the Iscaevones and the ancestors of the Histiaeans, the Aestii, the Estiones and the Aes Iste, all budded from the same branch?

13. SAINTS OF THE VASCONES

I am grateful to Robert Graves for suggesting that Asclepios, his Greek name, meant 'unceasingly gentle', while the Latin form, Aesculapius, 'which may well be the earlier of the two', meant 'that which hangs from the esculent oak, i.e. the mistletoe' [Graves I 176]. Mr Graves is something of a druid himself and these are druidic interpretations. The fact that he has found two different ones for what is obviously the same name suggests to me that, as with ancient Irish names, the originals, being tribal, had no meaning at all and hence were very flexible to fancy.

CHAPTER 14

Some Saints of the Cunesioi

St Finncu and the Dogs

A couple of generations ago Rhys remarked on the number of dog names deriving from *cu* or *con*, a dog, in early Irish history. Cuchullain, whose name means the Dog of Guillen, is the best known of them. He recalled the Cunesioi of western Iberia whom the ancients thought of as 'the dog tribe'. According to Herodotus they lived beyond the Celts upon the extreme western edge of Europe, on the Atlantic coast of Portugal and Galicia. They were also called Conioi and they had two towns, Conimbriga and Conistorgis. Rhys thought they were Silurians; other writers attach them to the great Ligurian race, but I do not think anyone denies that they were pre-Celtic. Did the Celts assimilate them when they came to dominate the Atlantic shore or did they push them into the sea? I do not know but it is natural to argue that those who lived by the sea were the first to cross it and that the Cunesioi had arrived in Ireland before the Celts.

How otherwise is one to explain the multitude of peculiar dogs that early Irish proper names recall, for in later days we have shown no particular tendency to call ourselves or our dwellings after dogs. Faced with the problem, most Irish scholars repeat the old notion that *cu* in proper names meant hero, because the Irish admired the noble qualities of dogs. Yet, if we investigate a little, we see that this explanation is late, false and sentimental.

The bishop of Ardagh, Dr MacNamee, who has written a valuable early history of his diocese, takes the traditional line. Resenting perhaps that St Maelcu, his first predecessor in the See, should have been called Bald Dog or

14. SOME SAINTS OF THE CUNESIOI

Crop-Eared Dog, he interprets this rude name as Comely Cleric (i.e. Tonsured Hero). But there is no evidence for this. The early Christian chroniclers insist that, in Maelcu, *cu* meant dog not hero, and *mael 'sine auribus'*, not 'tonsured'. They say that St Finncu's or Finnchua's name meant not flaxen-haired hero but white dog and that St Ailbe had given it to him, because he used his teeth when fighting. St Finncu (25 Nov.) lived near Mitchelstown among the Ui Finain and the Ui Cuain under Slieve Cua, the Knockmealdowns. He paid for his land with wine, *fion*. He was also known as St Mo Cua Finn. The Irish heroes accepted their dogginess as candidly as did the saints. Conall Cu's mother was like a dog [CGH 163]. Cucullain, the dog of Cullen, did in fact stand on Cullen's doorstep and attack strangers.

Other saints and heroes were St Onchu, Water-dog, and Dobarchu, Otter, also considered a kind of dog, St Caelcu, thin dog (20 Feb.), St Muircu, sea dog (12 Jun.), St Cudub, black dog. There were fifty-eight saints called MoChua.

There were tribes corresponding to all these notabilities. St Onchu, as I have related elsewhere, lived among the Ui Onchon in Carlow and Dobarchu, whose name can be written Cu Dobuir [CGH 68], was the ancestor of the Ui Dobarchon of Munster and was turned into an otter by St Brendan [LIS II 79]. His son, Cucuan, seems to have been ancestor of one of the Cucuan tribes of the south-west. I do not know any saint called Dobarcu, but St Maeldobarchon (19 Feb.) of Kildare more readily evokes a triple tribal amalgamation than 'an otter without any ears'. Most of the names of these dog heroes involve recognizable tribal elements. There are many, for instance, Cu Glas, Cu Ois, Cu Corb, Cu Buidhe, Cu Odor, Cu Gamna and Bladcu; that is to say Green Dog, Deer Dog, Chariot Dog, Yellow Dog, Dun Dog, Calf Dog and Strength Dog, and corresponding to them the tribes Glasraige, Osraige, Corbraige, Ui Buidhe, Odoraige, Gamanrige and Bladraige. At least five Munster ancestors were called Cu-cen-Mathair or Dog without a Mother. Could they have acquired this extraordinary name without reference to the Dal Cein and the Dal Mathra, which once at least in Munster we find associated [CGH 191]?

I do not know an early episode in which Cu or Con figures as anything but dog. It is noticeable too that the names are all obviously synthetic since the two parts are reversible. As well as Dobarchu and Cu Dobuir there is Cu Glas and Glascu, who, some think, gave his name to Glasgow, Maelcon and Conmael, Cu Odor and Odorcu, Conbel and Belcu, Cu Garb and Garbcu, Conlaeth (10 May) and Laethcu, Cu Finn and Finn Cu. The people as well as their names can divide into two. Thus the Bladraige are descended both from Bladcu and from Blad, the son of Cu.

Conn, the personal name, seems to have been as mysterious as Cu; it was not known whether Connacht meant 'Hound-slaughter' or 'the children of Conn'. The Ui Cuinn, descendants of Conn, are in the same barony as Loch Conn (in Latin Lacus Canis) and we have appropriate dog stories.

In insisting that ancient words must have a modern meaning, the Irish poets would stop at nothing. Lugaid mac Tri Conn, son of three dogs, for example, owed his birth (how is not quite clear) to three dogs emerging from the head of a buried skull. O'Curry tries to make this story more sensible by suggesting that Lugaid's mother had connection with three Cu heroes, Cucullain, CuRoi and Conall Cearnach. Tri Con to me is, of course, just another tribal amalgam to be analysed. My guess would be Thraco-Cynesian.

The clearest picture of compound tribes and ancestors comes from Scotland. There were three Cu brothers: Cu Sidhe, Dog of Peace, ancestor of the Clann Con Sithe of Fife; Cu Catha, Dog of War, ancestor of the Clann Concatha of Lennox; Cu Duilig, Canis Avidus, ancestor of the Clann Conduilig of Mull. There were many peace and war ancestors, and a glance at my Glossary would suggest that the first two were Cyneso-Siginnic and Cyneso-Getic. Who were the greedy dogs? I have put a couple of them among the Dal-Dul ancestors, whom I have set provisionally among the Silures, but it is an open question.

St Canice and the Head Folk

I believe that *ceann*, a head, in Irish proper names, also derives from the Conioi or Cunesioi. To prove this is hard, but to show that the 'head' meaning is deputizing for a more ancient one is easy. A vast number of Irish proper names contain the word *ceann* and it often produces so easy and respectable a meaning that modern scholars must often lose patience with the Irish poets, who insisted on a grotesque one.

Many Irish places could be called quite appropriately after a headland or head, but invariably some human's head is introduced. Kinnity in Co. Leix is Etig's Head, because the head of Etig, the nurse of Tethba, was buried there, but even in this explanation there can have been no confidence for we are told that Ceann Edig, ugly head, now Kennedy, was the father of St Fintan, the patron of Kinnity. A place similarly named Ceann Eitech in Roscommon was, we are told, called after people called Edig or Cinn-Eitigh. That is to say there must have been Cinn people and Edig people, whose descendants bore an amalgamated name. Surely *ceann* and *cind* are like *cu* and *con*; the heads and the

14. SOME SAINTS OF THE CUNESIOI

dogs are two different ways of modernizing an ancient tribal word. In fact head tribes often had dog ancestors. There were two tribes in Connacht, the Cindcnamha or Bone-heads, also called the Ui Cind or Heads and the Cindgamhna or Calf-heads. There were two heroes who look like their tribal ancestors: Cu Cnamha, Bone-dog, and Cu Gamna, Calf-dog. There were also in the west and north-west several Cnamh tribes (the source of many puns about bones) and in Mayo were the Gamanrige. In my pun Glossary I have suggested more distant origins for these Bone folk and Calf folk.

Negative arguments are always easiest and give least offence. So let me argue first that *ceann* did not mean head in proper names. This meaning was thrust upon it with a too exaggerated emphasis. A person with *ceann* in his name was doomed later in life to have an adventure with his own head or someone else's. One Ceannfaeladh was beheaded by Balor, a second had his head trepanned by St Briccin, the first Irish surgeon whose name is borne by our Irish military hospital, a third threw Suibne's head into the river Blathach. Fothad Canainne liked to have severed heads round him when he drank, and his own head, when cut off, spoke. Yet it is also said that he took his name from his dog, Canan. In the reign of Fiacha Ceannfinnan men had white heads and there was an Aran St Ceannfionnac (26 Mar.) who was beheaded. He and Moelgubi, 'Calvus Tristitiae', were our only two martyred saints, and both suffered because of their names.

There is much more I could say about heads and dogs, but I would prefer to write about our own St Canice of Kilkenny, who is widely celebrated as St Kenneth. In a variant of his name, Ceanneich, he is Horse's Head and he had enough magical horses and skulls in his life to justify this. He had some skill with heads too. When St Dagan (14 Sept.) was decapitated by raiders from Ossory, St Canice put his head back so perfectly that the only permanent trace of the accident was a circular scar round his neck [VSH II 178].

St Canice's pedigree is a palimpsest, which only a country scholar of the old type would have the patience to decipher. A county registrar like Matheson, for example, could do much more than an orthodox philologist to track this elusive and ubiquitous wonderworker to his source. For it is in regional caprice that we must look for the reason why Canice and his relations had so many aliases and such extravagantly interlocking kinships. A county registrar aware how the Alexanders of Ballymoney became the Elkinders of Cookstown might have the right sensitivity to guide him. When it was too dark to work in his garden, he would come in and arrange in a horizontal line all the sons of Fergus mac Roich from whom Canice's descent was traced and all their variations.

He would soon discover that Canice was hatched out of a cocoon woven from several intermingling tribes. He might begin with the Ui Dallain and the Ui Connaith, since Canice was of the Ui Dallain tribe. Dallan was one of Fergus' sons, Condad was another; but Dallan had at least four brothers, whose names, it would appear, were variants of his own. They are: Aulom, Corb Ulum or Aulom, Ulad and Aed Alain. These brothers reappear as their own nephews in parallel lines of descent and St Canice appears with a different pedigree at the end of four of them. And different tribes emerge in cousinship, the Ui Chonach, the Ui Connath, the Dal Condath and the Muinter Cinaith. It is obvious that nature intended Canice to be the ancestor of all the tribes but, in Christian stories, as a celibate and a saint, he had to be violently wrenched from the head of the pedigree and inserted in the lower reaches.

He was born among the Cianachta or Genus Connath of Derry. He spent a long time among the Cianachta of north Tipperary and also visited the Cianachta of Louth and had a very peculiar relationship with their patron, St Cianan. For, while among the Cianachta of Derry, St Patrick prophesied the future greatness of St Canice and also predicted St Cianan, at that time in the womb of a local chieftain's wife. But, in fact, though St Patrick later baptized him, St Cianan began as a very evil man, obviously a pagan ancestor. Before he reformed he sold St Patrick to some pirates for a cauldron. He is culted in Jura and Mull and may represent a combination of Ceann folk and Finn folk. I suspect that Canice was the ancestor of the Cianachta themselves, an amalgam of Ceann and Eth or Ech. A reputed ancestor was Eth Cen, but that is merely these syllables in reverse. The Ui Dallain were at Little Island in Waterford harbour as well as in Derry, so it was suitable that the southern Ui Dallain should have their share in the glory of Canice and that on his birth a cow should walk from Little Island to Derry to bring him milk.

I am sure it was because the Dal Condaich and Ui Maic Caindig are located in the south-west that later on St Canice went there and induced twelve bad men to throw off their wickedness and become monks. While there he dined with some nuns in the territory of the Ui Conchinn, Dog-heads, now barony of Magunihy or Mag Coinchinne, and resurrected the roast lamb, which they set before him. The Ui Maic Caindige are also called Ui Maic Cainne and there is an unlocated place Ros Mic Cain, the promontory of the Mic Cainne, with which a St Caindech is associated. Is it not likely that this too is in Kerry?

14. SOME SAINTS OF THE CUNESIOI

St Conchind and the Dog Heads

St Canice's visit to Kerry raises the question of the Conchinn or Dog-heads, a tribe which played a considerable part in Ireland and Scotland. For a brief period the Conchind ruled Ireland having driven out the first invaders [LG II 179]. Perhaps at that time they were dogs or semi-dogs, for the chronicler says that for thirty years afterwards there were no men left alive in Ireland. King Arthur encountered them in Edinburgh, Congal Claen fought them in Ulster and Finn fought them elsewhere in Ireland. Had they some connection with the Dog folk? I had supposed they might represent the amalgamation of two variants of the Dog folk, assuming that the Ceann folk and the Cu folk fundamentally are the same. I have toyed with the idea that they might be the Concani tribe, mentioned by Horace, who lived among the Cantabri in northern Spain. These Concani may have derived from the Conioi or Cunesioi. They must have been a fairly distinctive tribe, if Horace had heard of them [HOL I 1091].

Undoubtedly their principal settlement was in Kerry, where St Abban built his monastery of Cell Achaid Conchenn, which was later to be taken over by the Kerry saint St Finan, and it would appear that one St Conchind came from this monastery though she was a woman. And can it be different from the Kerry nunnery among the Ui Conchinn in which St Canice resurrected the roast lamb? Twelve holy men called Concinn were attached to St Sinchell's monastery in Killeigh.

There was also in Kerry a famous warrior, Concend mac Dedad. The Ui Deda, whom I have rashly called Dacians, were the great power in Kerry. He cherished in his house his friend, Fergus mac Roich, when marauders from Spain had wounded him. The principle of tribal amalgamation is seen clearly in Kerry; another of Dedad's forty sons was Iar, and the tribe the Ui Maic Iair Conchind, the sons of Iar Conchind of Kerry, show that the two brothers were amalgamated as well as their tribes. This Ui Deda connection is repeated in Rath Conchind in Femin, on or near Slievenaman in Tipperary. There Ceallach, the son of Dubh Dead, Black Tooth, who owned the rath, was so insolent to his guests that a companion of Finn declared, because of his snarling and biting, he must be christened Doghead. Another Rath Conchind in Antrim was called after a wolf-dog's head. At Ibar Cinnconn in Connacht Queen Maeve struck off the dog Ailbe's head and stuck it on a pole. Why was Ailbe a dog? I do not know but, as I have said, St Ailbe's father was Olcu or Big Dog and the saint was suckled by a wolf-dog. The head stuck to the chariot pole and fell off at Ath Cinnchon, Dog's Head Ford, in Westmeath.

Yet occasionally the writers permitted themselves to acknowledge that the Conchind were a forgotten race, for Conchind Cennfada, Long Head, was the warrior daughter of Concruth, the king of the Conchain. At the same time there was the usual head preoccupation, for, like Fothad Canainne, she had a palisade of stakes all round her, on each of which, except one, there was a head. Fothad Conchinn was the father of Dorn, an Ossory hero. Fothad has been (probably correctly) associated with the Votadini of east Scotland. The same names and attributes differently arranged occur in all these stories, so it is clear that both name and attribute were multiple tribal elements. Conchinn Cennfada is paralleled by Conchann, the daughter of Congal Ceannfada. Though Congal Claen fought against the Conchinn, his mother was called Conchinn; Finn similarly fought against them yet he was reared at Drumconchind in Ossory, where his aunt, Bodmall, lived with her father-in-law, Conchind. Ceallach son of Dubhdead, was, as we have seen, called Conchind, as an insult, yet St Conchind (20 Aug.), was daughter of Cellach, the ancestor of the Ui Cellach. Moreover there was a beautiful maiden, Conchinn daughter of Bodb, living on Slievenaman, obviously with the same claim to give her name to the Rath Conchind there as had Cellach with his 'doghead' snappings.

I have the impression that the Conchinds were considered more disreputable in the north than the south, where they seem to have been firmly entrenched in Kerry. On the Isle of Man Conchend was a repulsive giant sea monster, who pursued and killed a second sea monster. Another Conchinn was the father of the musician Cas Corach. It was no doubt because of the Latin word *concino*, make a harmonious sound, that he was connected with music. Even about the northern St Concinna of Killevy near Armagh (13 Mar.) there is something a little disreputable. She was the sister of St Fintan Munnu of Wexford (21 Oct.), and, coming south with her mother, begged to be allowed to visit him. He agreed and said he would join her in Louth near Dundalk, but she was not to come farther south. Though he only took a day to travel to Louth, she had died and been buried, when he got there. He prayed for a night at her tomb and resurrected her with a severe warning: 'See that you do not come to see me again, because if you do, I shall desert Ireland completely and sail away to distant lands.'

Can one argue from St Fintan's disapproval of his sister, St Conchind, that the Conchind people were in retreat from the Finn folk? It is paralleled by the story that St Abban's monastery at Cell Achaid Conchind in Kerry was taken over by the Kerry St Finan.

As for Ceannfada, the longheaded, it is also a nickname of Conall Cearnach's horse, as well as of several chieftains, and I do not believe therefore one can

14. SOME SAINTS OF THE CUNESIOI

infer any macrocephalic heroes. I would rather compare it to the Caninifates of the Batavi in Holland. Nechtan Cennfada was chief of the Ui Fidgenti of Limerick and Kerry. The Caenraige (barony Kenry) were beside the Ui Fidgenti. That he was a remote, ubiquitous and universal ancestor, whose nickname was improvised wherever the Cunesioi and the Fid folk amalgamated, is suggested by the fact that in Scotland he had an exact duplicate, Nechtan Cennfada. Skene deduces from Pictish nicknames like Cennfada that the Picts spoke Irish, but if Cennfada did not originally mean longhead, and, if the other Pictish nicknames were also tribal names to which an Irish shape and meaning had been given, this argument fails. In proper names it can happen that Fid is substituted for Fad and Gen for Cenn and Fidgenti would therefore be Cennfada in reverse. Fid I have placed among the Eth folk in my Glossary.

I must conclude with some oddities I cannot explain and which perhaps only illuminate the pun-loving mentality in its extreme form. We have noted some Scottish associations of the Dog folk. St Kentigern or Dog-prince was of Glasgow, which is Glas-cu or Green-dog. St Kentigerna (7 Jan.) or Dog-princess was a Scoto-Irish saint, of Leinster and Loch Lomond; she was sister of St Conchind or Dog-head and shared a feast day with her.

But the most arbitrary bit of nonsense concerns St Christopher of Kynoscephalae, or Dog Head, in Greece. He was also called Concinn and culted the same day (28 Apr.) as an Irish St Concinn. He also shared a death day with an obscure saint, St Cucephas, whose name also might be thought to be Dog Head.

CHAPTER 15

Saints of the Veneti

It has long been assumed that at some time or other the Gaulish tribe from Brittany, the Veneti, occupied some portion of the British Isles, but it has never excited much interest. Many years ago Rhys suggested that they had left their name in the Welsh province of Gwynedd or Gwent, where the Ordovices lived in Roman times. Canon O'Hanlon in his ten volumes refers to this once as a truism, other scholars connect them with the Vennicnioi, whom Ptolemy placed in Donegal, or with the Vennicones, a tribe that had spread up the east coast of Scotland from the Firth of Forth (see p. 158). Each of these remarks, if dropped not casually but with force and precision, would explode like a bomb, and surely have intellectual repercussions.

Goddard Orpen, for example, has suggested that the name of the river Finn in Donegal and of Loch Finn, into which it leads, may derive from the Vennicnioi, who once lived there. Others had said that it meant 'the white river', from *fionn*, white, but this has to be dismissed, because the river is noted for its inky blackness and so is the loch. Orpen also rejects a long complicated legend about a woman called Finna who was drowned in it while trying to save her brother, one of Finn's warriors, who had been attacked by a wild sow. She left her name on the lake and Loch Muck to the south of it was called after the sow.

Well, Orpen may be right but there are thousands of places all over Ireland, and Scotland, in whose name *finn* occurs and which are supposed to be white or associated with Finn, a legendary hero throughout the Celtic world, or with his multitudinous namesakes or half-namesakes. He is Gwynn in Wales. All these derivations seem equally improbable and, if we accept a tribal explanation for the Finn places of Donegal, we had better try it out everywhere. For example, the Blackwater river in Meath could scarcely be thought white, yet it used to be called the river Finn, until it met the Bo river, when it became the Bo-finn or the Boyne, the white cow river. The lady Bofinda of the Boyne was certainly, in the first place, invented to preside as ancestress of the two amalgamating tribes, the Bo tribe and the Finn tribe; she only became a river goddess in the days of their decay. Who were the Finn tribe? Assuredly the Veneti had something to do with them originally, though time and space and poetic fusion and fancy will have shaped their name in different ways in different places.

First the fact that dozens of Irish heroes and saints had the aftername Finn, white or fair, has led some writers like Macalister to talk of blond Celtic invaders, but in fact the biggest concentration of Finn proper names is in the south-west and the north-west where the people seem smaller and darker than in the rest of Ireland. Donegal is the land of the Vennicnioi

Secondly these Finn folk had the habit of coming from places whose names also include this same word for white or fair. This is perplexing. If dozens of people nicknamed Hearty came from Hertford, we would suspect that Hearty had not a personal but a collective significance and so it is with the Finn folk. To take three or four out of many:

St Finnian of Moville came from Drum Finn and was of the
   Dal Fiatach Finn.
St Dublitter Finn was of Finglass.
St Fintan was from Findrum.
St Finnian of Clonard was of the Ui Finechglas and Clonard
   was originally called Ros Findchuill.

And the secular heroes behave similarly. Fingin came from Finngabair. Finn himself was at Sliab Ban Finn (Slievenaman), which means 'the mountain of fair women' and died at Cill Finn in Perthshire, the white church.

Thirdly, there is the argument from pedigree. This starts with the early invaders. Agni Find was son of Glunfind (White-knee), who was the son of Lamfinn (White-hand). There are parallels in Scandinavia, where Finntuir was the same as Thor-finn and was the father of Dolfinn and went to Vinland, which is in America and has caused much controversy because it is said to mean Vineland.

Fourthly, the Finn folk clustered in groups, as though their chroniclers were thinking in terms of tribes rather than families or individuals. Finn Mac

Cool's tutor was Finegas, his son was Finbel, his salmon Fintan, his musicians were Finnchas, Finnbruinne, Finninghean.

He or some other Finn was one of the husbands of Cailleach Beirre, the famous nun of Bere, and she bore to him Fintan and Feindid. Then among the saints St Findlug (3 Jan.) and St Fintan (3 Jan.) were brothers and like St Finnian of Moville were of the race of Fiatach Finn. St Finnbar, Fair-top (4 Jul.) and St Barrfionn, Top-fair (8 Nov.) were also brothers.

Fifthly, there is the argument from ridiculous explanations. St Lon Coisfinn, White-leg, had long white hairs on his leg; St Finnchu, or White-dog, of Mitchelstown, Co. Cork, used his teeth like a dog when he fought. In the reign of King Fiacha Ceannfionnan all the cows had white (*finn*) heads (*ceann*). In the reign of Fionnscothach wine (*fion*) flowers (*scoth*) were first pressed.

This recalls St Fintan of Clonenagh (17 Feb.), who was called after wine (*vinum*) because he was nourished on it for seven years and later, when his diet was muddy water and unthreshed barley, poured the wine of sound religion and doctrine into his monks.

Sixthly there is the argument from tribal elements. It is easy to recognize the familiar tribal syllables in compound words and to accept also the evidence that a compound ancestor was formed by the synthesis of two simple ones. Thus we are told that St Finnchu was the son either of Findlug or of Find son of Lug. St Findlug of Dunblesc had an alternative name, Loga.

Among familiar tribal compounds we find Aedhfinn as well as Cu Finn, Eber Finn, Glunfinn, Lamfinn, Maelfinn, Finbel, Finnbeo, Finncaem, Finncas, Findlug, Finnech, Finnscoth. There are other names like Caerenn, Caelan, Brendan – alternatively Caerfinn, Caelfinn and Broinfind, in which the *finn* element is submerged. From what I have said, or will say later, it should be possible to recognize in all these names the abbreviated names of the Iberians, Cunesioi, Geloni, Getae, Ligurians, Scythians and many other tribes with whom the Veneti mixed.

St Fintan Munnu and Others

In the extent of their travels and the multitude of their monasteries the Finn saints rivalled all the others. St Finbar of Cork gave his name to an island off Campbelltown in Scotland and he travelled through Rosshire and Sutherland. St Finan Lobar, the leper, from Co. Dublin and Kerry, was a disciple of Columba, and very active in Scotland, being culted in Islay and Kintyre and Inverness. St

15. SAINTS OF THE VENETI

Finan Cam, the crooked, of Kerry and Leix, St Findlug of Dunblesc in Cork (5 Jan.) and many others travelled far through Scotland and Ireland.

One of the most curious of them is the famous St Fintan or MoFinnu (21 Oct.), who is often called Munnu. His complicated life was typical of a hundred other Finn saints. His chief cult centre was Tech Munnu, the house of Munnu, now Taghmon in Co. Wexford, but he was also culted in Inverary and at half a dozen places in the east and west of Scotland. He had an island, Eilean Mhunna on Loch Leven, which gave its name to the parish of Elanmunde. There used to be an annual fair of St Munnu in Forfarshire and he is said to have died at Kilmun in Argyllshire, where his grave was exhibited, and the custodians of his crozier enjoyed certain privileges for many generations.

But many seemed disinclined to allow that St Munnu travelled in Scotland at all. St Columba, according to his biographer St Adamnan, had in a vision heard the commandment of the Lord. If St Munnu came to Iona, he was to go straight back to Ireland, where he was destined to build a great monastery in Leinster. And Columba told his friend, Baithen, that when he succeeded him as abbot, St Munnu was on no account to come to Iona [JRSAI 79: see illustration of St Munnu at Kilbunny, Co. Waterford].

St Columba had tried to get rid of St Munnu once before. Munnu was the beloved son of one of his disciples, Tulchan, on Iona, and St Columba warned Tulchan that, as he loved Munnu more than God, he must throw the baby over a cliff. If St Canice had not sent two white birds to pick him out of the sea, Munnu would not have survived. But, in fact, it is said that St Munnu did get land on Iona itself from 'a rich man called Enan'. Since the Veneti were also the Eneti, En folk converge on Finn folk and this Enan was surely an unbaptized version of the ancestor of the Veneti.

Why did St Columba have such a grudge against Munnu? There is no evidence that he had any prejudice against Finn saints. Could it be that the Finn ancestor was less perfectly christianized in Scotland than in Ireland?

In Ireland St Munnu had many monasteries and, though his main one was in Co. Wexford, he was incessantly moving. He merged easily with other saints. At the synod of Leighlin (I have mentioned his lively proposal for settling the date of Easter) he became a leper (*labar* or *lobhar*) and punished a local chieftain, Suibne, for mocking at his affliction. Like other saints, he must have become a leper through merging with the ancestor of a local branch of the Ui Labrada. There was one in the Carlow-Wicklow neighbourhood [CGH 24]. Clearly he was identifying himself with St Finan Labar of Kerry and Scotland (16 Mar.).

At Clonenagh in Leix he seemed to impose himself on the very hard and ascetic abbot, St Fintan, who lived on bread made of straw. He became abbot himself and the two Fintans had a strange relationship with a third saint at Clonenagh, St Maeldub; out of mutual esteem they each added his name to theirs. The next abbot at Clonenagh was a fourth saint, St Fintan Maeldub, who seems to be different from the other three.

Much the same thing happened at Lann Maeldub on the Boyne, near to St Finnian's church of Rosnaree. St Fintan, St Maeldub and St Fintan Maeldub were all three culted there.

Their Relations with Other Saints

Like other 'Celtic' saints, the Finn saints were constantly moving, often handing over their monasteries to other saints, often taking over new ones. The incoming saint was in the habit of saying to the departing one: 'Not here, O blessed So and So is to be the place of thy resurrection,' and prophesying where it was to be. Usually the saints parted with mutual benedictions but occasionally with curses. The Goban saints, who seem to me to belong to the same group as the Corb and Cruith saints whom I have linked with the Carpetani, were a special target for contempt and ill-treatment. One of them was chased out of Aran and right across Ireland to Anglesey by a furious old St Fintan, sometimes called 'a wealthy landowner of Aran'. Another St Goban in Co. Wexford had his monastery borrowed by a second St Fintan for twelve years. It was then returned with a curse on it. A third Goban, a presbyter, was ejected with curses by the stern St Fintan of Clonenagh (17 Feb.) in County Leix and died miserably in sin. The only St Goban who really prospered, St Goban Finn, clearly owed his success and his thousand monks to his after-name (see p. 168).

To what extent can one judge the history of ancient tribes from the adventures of these saints? I find I can do very little about this now and yet I feel confident that one day some key to the complex pattern of ancient thinking will be discovered and we shall know. Can I make the guess that the Finn folk were later than the others and that, therefore, their heroes and saints were in the ascendant? Is that why their saints seem saintlier than other saints and richer in the number of their monks and in their confidence of heaven? There is conflicting evidence. But it seems clear that the Goban folk were despised, except for their craftsmanship, and that not only the Finn saints but all the saints ill-treated them.

15. SAINTS OF THE VENETI

The Dub folk, whom I equate with the Fir Domnaan of the west, the Dumnonii of Devon-Cornwall and the Damnonii of mid-Scotland (Map 4, p. 68), also look like an earlier and 'inferior' people, but the Finn folk seem to have brought off a more successfully paternal relationship with them.

In the dim confused light thrown by these stories one might try out the theory that it was the Veneti, who were more responsible than the other tribes for the celticizing of the early peoples of Ireland and Scotland. As evidence for this theory there is the magical transfiguration of another ruler called Aedh Dubh, king of Ui Briuin. He was changed by three different saints into Aedh Finn, the progenitor of the *sliocht* or tribe of Aed Finn of Breiffne in the north-west midlands. This miracle was done at greatest length by St Maedoc or Mo-Aedoc of Drumlane in Co. Cavan, to whom the dues of the Sliocht Aed Finn were to be paid. It was regarded as of great importance since two other saints, St Caillin of Fenagh, Co. Leitrim, and St Berach of Kilbarry and Kilcorp in Roscommon, are also credited with it. The lives of Berach and Mo-Aedoc and *The Book of Fenagh* are fascinating medieval documents. In each case Aed Dub was invited to put his head under the saint's cowl, and, when he extracted it, instead of being *dub*, black and hideous, it was *finn*, fair or white and beautiful. This certainly suggests that to be *dub* was to be inferior.

All three saints, who belonged to the adjoining counties of Leitrim, Cavan and Roscommon, in view of the part played in the transformation of Aed Dubh, claimed immense dues from the Sliocht Aeda Finn on behalf of their *coarbs*, that is the families, which controlled the churches after them. St Maedoc, for example, required a dowry, including cattle, for the *coarbs'* daughters. In return he bequeathed his relics to his churches, his crozier and St Martin's ankle and the Blessed Virgin's hair and an enormous quantity of holy bells and brooches and promises of heaven. Since St Caillin and St Berach claimed almost as much from the Aed Finn tribe and offered as many relics, there must have been difficulty in collecting their debts and some rivalry. So there are many stanzas of maledictions against those who withold their dues. Here are one or two, very much abridged.

'Let my bells be rung swiftly,' chanted St Maedoc,
'Against the O'Reillys!
I am the fire of the blood-red coal,
I am a treasury of the Canonical Scriptures.
Short-lived their race and their renown
The folk that provoke me to jealousy.
On those, whom I excommunicate or who outrage me,
Consumption, Cholera, Paralysis,

Sudden Death and Hell.
Sharper than any spear in its woundings
Are my clerks and my relics.'

If I am right in supposing that the transformation of Aed Dub into Aed Finn, which agitated in this way the saints of Roscommon, Cavan and Leitrim, concerned the assimilation by the Veneti of some earlier Dub tribe, there should be traces of the Dub tribes. If, as I believe, the Dubs were connected with the Dumnonians of the west of Ireland, it is not surprising that Dub forebears are evident in the lives of all three saints. For example, four generations before St Berach was born, St Patrick dined in Connacht with a chieftain called Dobtha, the ancestor of the Cenel Dobtha, who later lived around St Berach's church of Kilbarry, at a place called Achadh Grene, or Field of the Sun. It was called Field of the Sun, because, seeing that Dobtha had no candles to cook the supper by, St Patrick made the sun continue to shine until the game, which Dobtha had provided, was all cut up and dressed. This place must be Aghagranna on the Roscommon border of Co. Leitrim. The sun here must have been tribal, as is indicated by another story. When St Patrick was among the Aes Grene, a tribe of Clanwilliam barony, Co. Tipperary, he lost a tooth at Ath Fiacla or Ford of the Tooth, while washing his hands. It was recovered because it shone like the sun, *grian* or *greine*. A church was built at Kilfeacle (Cell Fiacail) nearby to house it and four ancestors of local tribes, members of his household, were left in charge. I discuss the Grene folk later.

As supper was preparing, Patrick prophesied to Dobtha: 'There shall not be one headship of thine own seed over thy race until doom.' But because of Dobtha's hospitality, he improved this, as he thought, by saying that they would never be under one ruler but under several. The following day Patrick did not baptize Dobtha himself but prophesied that Dobtha would live to be baptized by his own great-great-great-grandson, St Berach, who would fill all Erin and Alba with the fame of his mighty deeds and miracles.

Clearly, when the pious narrator told this story, the Cenel Dobtha were a respectably subordinate people, whose pieties and pedigrees had been assimilated by one or more dominating tribes. One of these tribes was surely the Finn folk, for St Berach's mother was Finmaith and he was baptized as Fintan, but acquired the name Berach (pointed) because of the 'acuteness and sharpness' of his miracles. More puzzling still he seems to have been a Protean character like St Fintan Maeldub, for at Kilbarry were three saints, St Fintan, St Berach and St Fintan Berach, who, some say, were all the same.

15. SAINTS OF THE VENETI

Whether or not Berach should be associated with the Berones of northern Spain, with whom I associated Caillech Bere or the nun of Bere, I do not know, but he and perhaps they too appear to me to have certain characteristics of the Brig folk. There is a reflection of this religious alliance, when on a secular plane a certain Berach Breac, the speckled, fell in love with a lady called Find.

The other two saints, who changed Aed Dub to Aed Finn, St Caillin and St MoAedoc, also have Finn and Dub antecedents. St Maedoc was 'fostered and nurtured by O'Duffy', i.e. Dubthac, son of Dub Da Crich, who was the nephew of Aed Finn. He was prophesied by Finn MacCool.

As for St Caillin of Fenagh, his grandfather was Dubhan, the ancestor of the Cenel Dubhan, and his tutor was Fintan the sage, who came to Ireland before the flood, and stayed there two hundred years, dying at the age of four hundred. I consider that St Caillin was Gelonic; we are told that he was very *cael*, thin, and it is possible that he had the same tribal significance as St Caelfionn, Thin-fair (3 Feb.), being like her descended from Fergus MacRosa. In certain respects too he corresponds to Lughaid Cal, the ancestor of the Calraige of Sligo, who had a branch at Slievegolry, not far from Fenagh.

Perhaps the Finn folk and the Dub folk really did become allies and fraternize. You will find in the genealogies that Aed Finn was brother of Aed Dub [CGH 74] and there were at least eight other pairs of brothers distinguishable from each other only by their afternames, Finn and Dub.

Possibly this Dub-Finn alliance was not everywhere popular. A powerful Aed Dub turns up in Scotland too, a very wicked chieftain from Ulster, and St Columba, who had been so severe to St Fintan Munnu was equally stern with a certain St Findchan (Cyneso-Venetic), who offered his protection to this Aed Dub on the island of Tyree, and even wished to ordain him. No bishop would lay his hands on Aed Dub's head unless St Findchan interposed his own. St Findchan did this and St Columba decreed that the hand that had helped to consecrate the son of perdition should rot. So St Findchan's hand fell off and was buried on an island. This island may be Lamh Odhar, or Dun-coloured Hand Island, off the east coast of Iona. There are other places called Lamh, where the hands of other saints or associates of saints fell off because of impiety. The meaning is clear since one or two of these hand stories have been explicitly linked with the Lamhraige, a tribe of Tipperary and Ulster.

In these stories I have used only a very small portion of the material available. A principal difficulty is that by the time our records were written, every group in Ireland seems to have been thoroughly 'veneticized', and the tribal conflicts and tensions that interest us are mostly already a thing of the past.

The Board-Faced Saints and the Birds

En, son of Miled, was one of the early invaders of Ireland, and I am tempted to say that he was the same as Finn, because one of the seven sons of Magach, queen of Connacht, was alternatively called En or Finn.

The Veneti were also called the Eneti, the Vennicnioi of Donegal were the Ennicnioi, St Finnian of Moville was also called St Ennio MacFiatach. The Ui Finechglas of Wicklow, among whom St Finnian was born, are also called the Ui Ainechglas descended from Bresal Ainechglas and, as *ainech* means face, and *glas* means green, Bresal had a green face, which derived from a birth mark. Other tribes and heroes are called Clarainech, Flat-face, Dergainech, Red-face, Cichainech, Breast-face, Brocainech, Badger-face, Cuainech, Dog-face, and Maelainech, Bald-face. That is to say, a Finnech or Ainech tribe merged with a Glas tribe to make the Ui Finechglas and there are tribes or heroes to correspond to all the other elements of the attributes: Broc-, Cu-, Cich-, Clar-, Derg-, Dub-, Gorm-, Mael-.

There were six board-faced saints, Clarainech, and as many heroes. This has been explained as 'lacking nose and eyes'. The most famous of them was St MoBi of Glasnevin (12 Oct.) who, at the celebrated school of Glasnevin, taught many Irish saints including St Columba, to whom he bequeathed his wonder-working girdle.

Canon O'Hanlon was perplexed by the three Clarainech saints, Cronan, Baithen and Segin, who were culted together on 29 January. To account for their affliction and their close association, he suggests that they were brothers or 'descended from some common progenitor' and victims of a hereditary disease.

However, the famous Ulster warrior, Congal Clarainech, had an alternative aftername, Claringnech, which means Flat-nailed. Is it not clear that their nickname was an inscrutable tribal word? It must derive from a Venetic association with the Ui Clare, who were descended from Clar, son of Brigit, ancestress of the Ui Brigte of Waterford. That might explain why St Brigit miraculously cured one of these board-faced people.

The way is now open for saying that the En saints and heroes are related to the Finn folk. We can now offer an explanation for the vast quantity of birds (*en*), who left their eccentric traces across the Irish landscape. They were seldom ordinary birds but went about in pairs and often had to be elaborately explained. The two birds of Snam da En on the Shannon were really two brothers disguised as birds to court a woman warrior, *fennid*. We are told that Druim da En (Ridge of two Birds), or Drum Enaigh near to Snam da En, was so called because the Fianna fowled there. The Fianna killed a monster at Ros Enaigh at Glendaloch and Finn had a fairy sweetheart there. Gleann Eanaigh is also known as Glendaloch [OH I 58].

There are several score of places called after two birds, most of them in the north-west and west of Ireland. In addition to Snamh da En, there are four others in the neighbourhood of Clonmacnois. Many Finn saints had adventures with birds. To mention only one, two birds came to the rescue of St Mo-Finnu or Munnu, as I have said, when St Columba wanted to drown him on his way to Iona.

In the *Book of Rights* we learn that it was taboo for the king of Ireland to listen to the birds on Loch Swilly. Could this concern the Cenel Enna, who lived in Tir Enna, which bordered on Loch Swilly and in classical times was peopled by the Vennicnioi?

St Aenboin and the Units

I do not know who St Aenboin was or whether the Cell Cuaich where he is culted is Kilcock in Kildare or Kilcoagh in Wicklow. If the latter, I think he may once have had a paternal interest in the people who lived at Rath Oinbo, the Rath of One Cow, in Wicklow.

I do not think that *aen* meant one, though there are many stories to suggest that it did. There were two places in Antrim and Limerick called after Fer Aen Darta, the Man of One Heifer, and it is said that this heifer was the solitary survivor of a great plague that destroyed all the cattle in Ireland. At Imblech Fir Aen Darta in Limerick, as well as the solitary heifer, *dart*, there lived an unfortunate lady called Dartaid, who was murdered by a wicked man on the Blackwater, called Corb Liath (the Grey), son of Tassach. There were on the Blackwater three tribes, the Ui Corb, the Ui Tassaich and the Ui Liathain, who had closely related ancestors Corb, Tassach and Liathan [CGH 225–229]. There are heifers and people called Dartad elsewhere, and this suggests that men, women and heifers all derive from the wandering Dartraige tribe and that Aen must be tribal too.

There is a tribe called the Ui Aoinfir, One Man, in Westmeath and an ancestor called Infir or Findfer mac Cuscraid and several people called One Man. Yet who could believe that Art Aenfer was called that because he was his father's 'single surviving son'? Who could believe that Aenfer Aeife was the 'single' son whom Cucullain begat on Aeife of Skye, complicating his life with various taboos about units, which were ultimately to kill him? Surely Aen is just another Venetic element. Otherwise how explain the hundreds of names in which it features always awkwardly as One. There is Oen Dub, Oen Gel, Oen Goban, Oen Lamgaba, Oen Beithe, Oen Sciath, Oengus, Oen Garb, that is to say One Black, One White, One Smith, One Hand Wail, One Birch Tree, One Shield, One Strength, One Rough (see p. 141). There was a great battle fought by men with one leg, *oencos*, one hand, *oenlam*, and one eye, *oensuil*, and Cucullain once cut a withy, using just these single members. *Cos*, a leg, is a very variable word in attributes and alternates with *cas*, curly. The one legged men, *oencos*, like the name Oengus, suggest to me a Veneto-Getic compound.

Observe how these names are built up. Lamgabaid or Hand-wail, his hand cut off by Cet, would represent the Lamraige and Gabraige (Liguro-Carpic). In Oengoban, father of St Oengus, I would guess that the Veneti were substituted for the Lamraige. In Oenlamgaba all three tribes are combined in the name of an Ulster hero.

Aine the Sun Goddess

Aine, meaning 'brightness', is the subject of a long discussion by O'Rahilly about the sun worship of the ancient Irish. He says that the goddess Aine, 'brightness', must be identified with her sister Grian, which means Sun, and who lived at Cnoc Grian seven miles away from Cnoc Aine or Knockainy in Limerick. In another context she was wife of Cruinn in the north of Ireland. *Cruinn* means round and therefore O'Rahilly infers that Aine, Grian and Cruinn were three different names for the sun god or goddess, and he notes that in east Clare there was a river, a lough and a graveyard called Grian. Yet what traces of sun worship are there in Irish mythology? Remarkably few. Early people, except maybe for the megalithic peoples, are not very interested in the sun but intensely interested in themselves. If there is a congestion of Grian place names in east Clare it is because a Grian or Grinn people lived there. There was a Limerick tribe, the Aes Grene, and I am sure that it was they who provided a name for the goddess Grian and have shaped her nature out of her name. She was married to Cruinn, probably because the Grian folk and the Crinn folk of Ulster are the same. Similarly Aine of Cnoc Aine acquired her name from the Ui Enna or Ui Enda, who lived at Cnoc Aine. There is a Fer Aine, a male too, but tribal ancestors change their sex very easily, more easily than sun goddesses do, and the multitude and variety of Aines seem to me further proof of their Venetic origin. I have already suggested that Fer did not mean man but was also a tribal element.

Aine's kinship with Finn recurs in many forms. Aine of Cnoc Aine, Co. Limerick, was called Aine Finn. Aine of Rath Aine, Co. Down, was a wife of Finn, another Aine was daughter of Finn, Aine of Lis Aine, Tyrone, was of the Ui Corra Finn.

There is a poem about Aine giving her name to Cnoc Aine. She behaves in it much more like a tribal ancestress than a sun goddess. 'Said Aine Finn, "Let the charming hill have its name from me ..." Thereupon Aine sallies forth and scatters wide the ancient tribes ... She and hers then sit down around the hill and quarter it: the brave and gentle men make of it four equal portions.' Ui Enna Aine came from Enna Aine [CGH 389].

One must assume Aine's portion is the largest and the best; what is left over is shared among the ancient tribes. But the poem was written centuries after she had sat down around the hill. It is democratic in sentiment. Very pleasant things are said of the ancestors of the other tribes, for by that time all of them are relations of Aine. 'Aine was at the eastern point and so the hill is shared among friends.'

St Enda

I have noted nine or ten saints called Enna or Enda, but no doubt there are many more; the most illustrious of them is St Enna of Aran, whose school was the most notable in Ireland next to that of St Finnian of Clonard. Many famous saints were his pupils. He was vigorous and worldly and even brutal and dissipated, before he became a saint; at the moment he enjoys considerable favour, and jet planes have been named after him. In spite of all this there is no denying that he is very odd. There is no mention of him in the annals, though many impossible people have been chronicled there. I think his early wickedness derived from the fact that his monastic biographers failed to distinguish him from a secular Enna, who must have been his prototype and bequeathed to him his pedigree. This secular Enna had the same father Conall Derg, king of Oriel, as St Enda of Aran, and with his two brothers, Lochan and Sylvester, was consecrated to the devil. They destroyed half the churches of Connacht, but then, repenting, on the advice of St Finnian of Clonard, reconstructed them and went to sea in a curragh. A bishop who accompanied them recounted to St Mo Cholmoc of Aran all the extraordinary adventures, comparable to those of

Maeldun and Brendan, which they endured. St Mo Cholmoc wrote them down in verse. These travels might be echoes of the voyages of the Veneti or Eneti, who in Brittany were famous seafarers.

Plummer and Kenney try to persuade us that, owing to the misreading of a pedigree, a real and saintly Enda has got confused with a wicked and fictitious one [Misc.]. Yet everything we know of both is equally fictitious and, though St Enda's wickedness is described in general terms and there is no mention of the churches burnt by his secular counterpart or the murderous designs he cherished against his father, the principal priest at Clogher in Oriel, yet St Enda's former wickedness is an obsession with all his biographers. In the Latin life he is compared to Saul, who became Paul and repented of his sins, and we are told how his sister St Fanchea begged him to reform. She was ancestress, perhaps, like Fuinche, of another Venetic tribe, the Corcu (F)uinche. When his evil companions sought to draw him away, she recalled to them the verse of St Matthew, 'Whatsoever thou shalt bind on earth shall be bound in heaven', and she then bound their feet to the earth, until they repented and could be set free. She told them that, if you fix your mind on earthly things, it is obvious that you will get fixed yourself in the earth. When Enda said he would repent, she gave her consent to his marrying one of her holy charges, but she first asked the young woman whether she would sooner have an earthly husband or be the bride of Christ. She chose the latter and died.

When Enda said that he must defend his father's inheritance she reminded him that their father was a warrior and that his inheritance was sin and crime. Then he built for St Fanchea the church of Cell Aine in Louth and was restrained by her from using a plank, which he held in his hand, upon the heads of his enemies. He went to St Ninian of Rosnat and from there to Italy and to Rome. Thither his sister and her maidens followed him, sailing the ocean on her cloak; but in Rome Enda would only consent to speak with her through a veil. On her return journey she died on the cloak; two churches claimed her body and their claims were adjusted in the usual way by harnessing some oxen to her coffin. In due course the oxen arrived at Cell Aine in Louth. The oxen who appeared to go to Baile Barrigh on the Liffey were only an hallucination. On arriving there the oxen urinated prodigiously and from their urine the place was called Cell Aine or 'church of the urine'. But we are also told that Aine, daughter of King Solmglas of Greece, lived at Cell Aine.

There was another Cell Aine, ascribed to St Enda, on Loch Corrib, and, since we find the Ui Enda Aine tribe settled at Cnoc Aine in Limerick and St Enda connected with two Cell Aines, is it not clear that Aine is neither an aspect of the sun goddess 'brightness' as O'Rahilly would maintain nor urine as it would seem to be to St Enda's biographer? Aine and Enda are ways of referring to the ancestor of the Veneti.

No modern scholar has questioned the existence of St Enda, and Father John Ryan traces to him the foundation of strict monasteries in Ireland, and attributes to him a certain originality of method. 'He followed a rule of astonishing severity.' This is to be inferred from the story that on Aran he used to send out his monks every evening in curraghs without any hide covering and that they all came back bone dry, except one, who had stolen some food that belonged to St Ciaran. Thought on such lines is 'corrupting to the mind'. Enda did not exist and his father Conall Dearg, the church burner, who belongs inextricably to the fabric of invention, cannot be excluded from his story, since he is the father of other notable people as well, of St Cairech Dergan (9 Feb.), of Clonboirenn and of Darina, wife of Oengus mac Nadfraech, who presented Enda with the island of Aran.

Writing of the Corb saints I show that Enda behaved on Aran much as Aine did at Knockany, when she shared out the hill with the ancestors of 'ancient tribes'. After routing Corban, an evil early landowner, Enda divided Aran between himself and nine fellow saints, and then, to their dismay but with heaven's blessing, he changed his mind and kept half for himself. Only St Brecan prospered at Kilmurvey, but he was perhaps half Venetic, Breac-finn.

I suggest that Enda's travels by sea, like those of St Finbar and St Barr Finn, might be echoes of the voyages of the Veneti of Brittany, who were the most famous sea travellers in Gaul. And maybe there were more distant echoes from the Eneti of Venice and Paphlagonia, from whom the Veneti were supposed to be descended, and whose travels were celebrated in Homeric legend. Some say that Aeneas was the ancestor of their tribe.

The Gwynn Saints

Corresponding to the Irish Finn, son of Nuada, we have the Welsh Gwynn, son of Nudd, and there are many similar parallels. Some will attribute these to a shared folklore. I find it easier to explain them in tribal terms.

I shall leave to a Welshman the Gwynn saints, who equal the Finn saints of Ireland in numbers and eccentricity. Gwynn, Gwynno and Gwynnoro were three of five saints all born at the one birth. Gwynnteirbron had three breasts to nourish her three holy children. St Gwynan, of Brychan's family, had his feast the same day as St Finian of Clonard, who is said to have spent twenty years in Wales and obviously had his Welsh counterpart. They persuaded Baring-Gould that they existed, but could they have survived a less indulgent scrutiny?

CHAPTER 16

The Carpic Saints

St Corba and the Chariots

(A) THE CHARIOT FOLK

The Carpi, who lived on the Danube, must have given their name to its tributary the Carpis, which some say is the Drava, others the Sava. From all accounts they were of Thracian stock and it is natural to suppose that like the other early tribes, they expanded far and wide. Surely they must have been akin to the Carpiani and the Carbones, whom Ptolemy locates in north Germany, and to the Carpesii and Carpetani, powerful tribes in Spain (Table 4, p. 67). As I have shown, these tribes with matching names tended to live near each other. Was the small difference of nomenclature a hazard of nomadic life, or was it the result of an actual blending of tribes? Sometimes there is a regular pattern of change, which suggests that an incoming tribe absorbed and rechristened the old tribes. For instance in Spain we get the Basculi or Bastuli near Gibraltar, the Bastertini in east Spain, and in the north the Vascones and the Vescitani (Map 1, p. 63); Ridgeway and others have tried to identify the intruding races to which such modifications are due.

In Ireland there was an abundance of ancestors, saints, tribes and place names, which recall this people (Table 5, p. 97). Corb, who is called by Rhys an Iberian god but is surely rather the ancestor of the Carpi-Carpetani group, has many namesakes in Ireland. There was Corb the Firbolg chief, whom we hear of at Loch Corrib or Corbes, which must have drawn its name from the same tribal source as he did. His head was buried, we are told, at Carn Cinn Corb near Corrib (allegedly the Cairn of Corb's head). The similar tribal sources of names were Corbbraige interchanged with Orbraige [CGH 294], and Orbsen Mor with Corpsen [*Genealogy of Irish Saints*, 1546].

There was Lugaid Corp, the ancestor of the Dal Mes Corb or Messincorb, and Corb Gailni who was Queen Medb's ambassador to Cor(b)mac. Corb occurs both on its own and as an element in other names. Thus Artcorb was son of Fid-corb, son of Corb: and Cucorb was father of Niacorb from whom the Dal Messincorb were descended. Another Artcorp is son of Mosscorp, son of Moscegrai or Messgegra, son of Corp, of the Deisi. There was a Gegrige tribe [H 437]. I have no doubt that Art, Fid, Cu, Nia, Messin and Moss all represent tribes with whom the Corb tribe allied itself.

There were many other tribes in which this tribal element occurs, the Dal mac Cuirp, and the Ui Corpain and Ui Corbmac. There were the Corbraighe or Corbetrighe, whom MacNeill, after the usual philological manner, believes to have been chariot makers because *carbad* means a chariot. But the Carbraige of Fanad in Donegal are also called Coirpraige, a tribal name, which figures widely without any but fantastic chariot associations. And Carbad, surely related to the Carpetani – the Spanish variant of the Carpi – occurs as an ancestor several times. Therefore the connection with chariots is a desperate Irish attempt to make sense from what was unintelligible. The attempt was, as we shall see, constantly made. But there were other suggestions for the interpretation of these names; *corbadh* means incest and *coirpthe* means corrupt. And when two or more fantastic interpretations are given of one name, it is my practice to believe that the origin of the name was completely unknown. Thus Cairbre is said to be Corb-ri or Chariot-king because he was brought dead in a chariot to St Ruadan, who revived him, but it is also said that he was so called because of the 'incestuous' murder of his father in law. It is also said to mean Corvi filius, Son of a crow. Cormac in his glossary (p. 29) suggests it means *coir-breo*, a just flame. Cor(b)mac, the child of Nessa and her son Conchobar, was 'son of incest', but St Cormac (11 May.) was 'son of chariot', because he was born in one. *Corbadh*, from incest, passes to mean infamy and hence the unbaptized state and we find that Cu Corb the father of Niacorb owed his name to the fact that he was for long unbaptized. He evidently passed on the reproach to his son. The same explanation was given in medieval times to 'a false fellow' in Co. Down, nicknamed 'Corbi', because he was unbaptized and destroyed forty churches.

If we turn to toponomy the same picture meets us. Patrick's chariot broke down twice at Ath na Charpaid on the river Daolin in Donegal and at Ath Carbaid at Boyle in Roscommon. There are many other names, such as Tulach na Carpit near Ard na Carpat in Co. Tyrone, where Cairbre fought a battle, and there is Oilean Carbaid or Chariot Island near Iona, and many improbable chariot stories.

(B) ST CORBA AND ST COBRAN

Among saints, St Corp, Corba or Gorba belongs to one of those migrant families of holy sisters and brothers to which I have earlier drawn attention; St Brig was her sister, St Setna her brother. If Brig was ancestress of the Briges, if Setna was ancestor of the Setantii of Louth and Lancashire, who was St Corp? Surely the ancestress of the Carpi. Another saintly trio similar to Corp, Brig and Setna were Corp, Lassar and Dare (see p. 151).

I believe that the Aran Islands were once a great stronghold of these Carp-Corp people (see Table 5, p. 97) and that in the life of St Enda, its principal saint, we have a picturesque account of their subjugation by the En-Fin folk and some other tribes. Corban was the very wicked king of the Island of Aran, in St Enda's day. When the saint approached it, Corban's subjects all fled in wonder and horror to the coast of Clare, 'for the sun cannot abide with darkness nor heathendom with the light of the Gospel'. Only Corban stood his ground, a second Pharoah *obduratus in malicia*, but finally even he was convinced by a miracle and Enda took over the island. Further quarrels about precedence were settled by two doves flying from Rome. One dropped a missal into St Enda's lap, the other flung a cape over his shoulders. Only St Brecan at the Kilmurvey end of the island resisted. Each of these saints and the wicked King Corban too followed the same pattern of behaviour. They had widely scattered cult centres all over Ireland and beyond it; they converged on other saints with similar names and different pedigrees. And often they figure not as saints at all but as evil men, destroyed by their own sins, or partially redeemed by the Gospel. Of course, when these stories were written, everything had been blurred by centuries of intermarriage between newcomers and natives, victors and vanquished. Were there any true Carpi left, any true Briges? I think that St Enda had already had his way with them and they were half En-Fin folk when the hagiographers took note of them. Just as Brendan is Broen-finn, and Caelan is Cael-finn, so Corban is perhaps Corp-finn and Brecan Brig-finn.

Anyway Corban is certainly not a random invention, but partially, at least, inherited the misshapen name of a forgotten race. In other parts of Ireland the Corb folk had their representatives in pious fiction; they were usually impious and unfortunate, but could sometimes, as I have said, be redeemed. St Ciaran of Saigir in the midlands also had trouble with a wicked king called Corban or Cobran, who had an evil eye. This St Ciaran and his mother, St Liadan, who lived nearby, also had two unfortunate disciples called respectively Gobran and Cerpan, who died miserably. St Ciaran dealt with them just as St Enda would have done. King Cobran was struck blind at Rathdowney, Co. Leix, where he gave himself and his property to Ciaran, Gobran was redeemed from hell and Cerpan was revived. Obviously Cobran or Corban, Gobran and Cerpan never lived and their names are four regional variations of the same name. Yet they were not idly invented, for there is today at Rathdowney a place called Kilcoran, which Canon Carrigan, our local historian, well-versed in the Irish of Leix, says is the church of St Cobran. There is a large rath around some ruins and a mound, removed a hundred years ago, which was found to contain a mass of human bones. Did a saint or a wicked king ever live there? Is it not more probable that it was the settlement of an ancient, widespread tribe, submerged by later tribes – the Corb tribe, in fact, or some derivative of it.

(c) CONTINENTAL SAINTS

There were, of course, many Corb saints outside Ireland. The continental ones are best studied in the lives of St Fursey and the twelve companions, whom he took with him from Ireland to Suffolk and to Gaul. There is a cluster of them still recalled in the north of France. They conform to the Irish pattern and Corb place names are in an odd way interwoven with their story. St Corbican (26 Jun.), for example, an ascetic saint who lived on roots and herbs, left Ireland with St Fursey and St Goban; they spent their first night in France at Corbie on the Somme, collecting property from sinners, on whom appalling punishment was visited.

Another odd Corb saint from this neighbourhood was St Corbinian (8 Sept.) of Chatres near Corbeil in the vicinity of St Fursey's oratory at Lagny. His mother was Corbiniana.

The Romans, in their day, encountered Corb puns. Scholars have remarked on the Celtic quality of Livy's story about Valerius Corvus, who was shielded from the Gallic foe by a large crow. But surely the anecdote just reveals the old habit of using ancient tribal words as if they had a modern meaning.

St Fuinche Garb and the Rough Folk

A famous invader called Garb is also called Carbad, and there are many other reasons for treating the Garb folk as allied to the Carpi and Carpetani (Table 5, p. 97). Or is it necessary to go on believing that Fergna Garb, the son of Salach,

16. THE CARPIC SAINTS

was *garb*, rough, and that his descendants were called the Garbraige after this failing of his? (This tribe also derived themselves from Fer da Gabar or 'Man of two Horses', so that we shall consider later as part of the group the tribes linked with *gabhar*, a goat or a horse.) Fergna Garb, the son of Salach, Fergna the Rough, son of Dirty, recalls townlands in Westmeath and many other places called Garbsalach, and the many saints and tribes and heroes and places who were given the often vastly inappropriate name of *salach* or dirty. Garb, the son of Salach, symbolized, I do not doubt, the amalgamation of two tribes and Garbsalach was a place where they lived.

Certainly the poets took trouble to explain why the Garbh or Garb folk were called rough. Five saints and innumerable chieftains bore this name. Let us take St Fuinche Garb (21 Jan.) of Loch Erne. To avoid a suitor she swam under water across the lake to Inis Clothrann, where St Diarmait, looking at the shells and weeds clinging to her skin, remarked 'That is rough.' Maelgarb equates with Oengarb, the uniquely rough (see p. 132). Tuathal Mael Garb (Bald-rough) had a hairless and dented skull because his mother gave birth to him on a stone; but, when it occurs in place names, Maelgarb is said to be a cattle disease.

There appear to be two saints called Senach Garb with mothers called Broin Finn, one of them a smith from Armagh (2 Nov.), the other (10 Sept.) from Clonfert, Co. Galway. Clonfert was the cult centre of the male Broin Finn, whom we know as St Brendan. A third Senach Garb, not a saint, gave his name to Slieve Senaig Garb or Slieve Mis in Kerry.

I do not believe these people named Senach can have been called rough because they were born on stones or because they were covered with shells or, even, as Canon O'Hanlon suggests of one of them, because they were 'somewhat rough in their manners'. I find several clues in Kerry. On Slieve Senach Garb itself there were three heroes called Garb and in the neighbourhood we find the heroes, Aed Garb and Garb, the son of Baedan, as local ancestors and the good 'son of Garb' [VSH II 90], who befriended St Finan, and the river Garbh Abhann, or the rough river, the same derivation given to the Garonne in France.

Let us follow the first St Senach Garb to the barony of Ui Neillan (Oneilland) in Armagh; its dominant tribe was the O'Garbheth, now Garveys, and we find there Domnach Maccu Garba. Is this 'the church of the sons of the rough one'? Maybe I am wrong in thinking the Garb folk were the Carpi but can anybody go on believing that they were rough?

TABLE 8: CHAR*

TRIBE	SAINT	CULT CENTRE	HERO or ANCESTOR
Moccu Carbad		Cluain Carpent, (1) Connacht (2) Ulster, where Medh's 100 chariots fell into the river.	Carbad, father of Ailill Miltenga
Moccu Rea, Leinster			Carbad, father of Goll Carbad Cennliath at Mag Coba [LG V 313]
Clann Carbad (Pender 22)			Carpent, brother of Nero [MD IV] Carbad, king of north Germany, father of Rig [THU 486] Cerb, son of Buan
Ui Cerb Mag Breg ex Daire Cerb	Birth place of Cearban	Feart Cearban, north-east of Tara	Daire Cerb *ex quo* Ui Cerb
			Art Cerb of Luighae [SG 512] Cerpus, father of St Brioc
Dal Corb (with Dal Buein) ex Fer Corb and Buan, Goddess of Capa [H 331]	Cerpanus, priest of Killyon, Laois		Cerb Gailni, ambassador of Medb to Cormac
			Corb, Fir Bolg chief at Loch Corrib Corb Ulad *ex quo* Dal n Uladh
Ui Corpain of Cairbre. Gabra, Longford	St Corp or Gorba (sister of St Lassar and Dara at Cell Ingonmeman)		Fer Corb (with Buan) married Moga Ruith of (1) Ui Causam, Cavan (2) Duncermna, Cork.

16. THE CARPIC SAINTS

F THE CARPETANI

IABITATION	AFFINITY	DISGUISE	COMMENTS
echt Maicc Carbad (Rea, Leinster)	Carpetani, Iberia		Carbad in proper names seldom meant chariot. (1) It is an odd name for so many men to wear. (2) It is an odd name for a tribe.
an na Carbad, Tara ulach Carbad, Monaghan	Carpessii, Iberia Carvetii, near Carlisle	Carbad = chariot	(3) There are several 'chariot' names and anecdotes in Donegal where were the Echcairbraiges, Echcarpad and Carbraige of Fanad.
Drum Carbit, Antrim ilnagarbet near tradone, at Corrib t Carbetagh enna tri Carpait, outh of Limerick	Carpi on the Danube	Corbadh = incest or corruption	
ethrama in arbaid, Mayo	River Carpis = Sava or Drava [Hdt IV, Grenier 122]		Anecdotes to explain the inexplicable: (1) The King of Cairbre (explained as Cairbre-ri, i.e. chariot king) is brought dead in a chariot to St Ruadan who revives him [OH IV 153]. (2) St Cormac (11 May) 'was son of chariot', i.e. born in one. (3) Why did Cobthach Cael sham death in a chariot? Echoes same idea as (1) above. See my Gob chart p. 174. (4) Cearb, owner of chariot yoke [EIS 40].
Ath na gCarbad, Lismore Ath na gCarbad, Dundalk		Cerb = lopped or maimed [SG 512]	
Olean Carbad, Iona	Carpentoracte, near Avignon	Carbad = jaw	
Athcarpait Fergusa, mid-Munster	Carbantorigum, Scotland		
Ard na Carpat, battle of Cairpre, and Fraech near Tulach, near Carpat [THU 298]	Note: Carbad father of Rig [Rhys]		
Rot na Carpat (St Fuad)	Corb		

TRIBE	SAINT	CULT CENTRE	HERO or ANCESTOR
Carbetraige Cerbraige (chariot folk) [MacN 82]	Priest Corban of Lugmad		
			Lugaid Corb *ex quo* Dal Cairpre, Cliach
Ui Corbmaic, Galway	St Cor(b)mac (11 May)		Artcorb, son of Fidcorb son of Corb
	St Corbmac (26 Mar.) or Aithgen, cook to Brigit of Bothdromnach.		Artcorb, son of Messcorb, son of Cucorb, father of Nia Corb *ex quo* Dal Messincorb
Carbraige, Corpraige, etc, *ex quo* Ethne, mother of Columba.	St Corban (12 Jun.)	Corrib and Corban	
Dal Mac Cuirb [GT 132]	St Corbman (8 Sept.)		Mug Corb, son of Conchobar
Ui Cuirb (Ui Mac Caille, Cork)	Birthplace of MacCuirb in Clin, pupil of Gregory [LIS 14]		Corbmac, son of Conchobar
Dal Mesin Corb, Wicklow	St Cuirbin Craebhdech of Ui Fidgenti of Cluain Cairpthi	Cluain Cairpthi	Ardcorp, son of Mess Corp, son of Moscegrai of Deisi [VSH II 35]

16. THE CARPIC SAINTS

HABITATION	AFFINITY	DISGUISE	COMMENTS
ae na Carpat ar Tlachtga [G 133, 190]	Iberian god	Carabine Bridge	
hcarpad = hcairpre, rth-west of aphoe, Donegal	Carpiani near Bastennas	Lugaid Corb ate deer's offal	Corb-Coradh in proper names seldom meant incest, corruption or impiety. (1) Cairbre so-called because he murdered his father-in-law incestuously.
och Corrib Corbes, Corbsen, c) where Carn inn Corb (Corb's ad) was buried.	Carbones, near Venedici		(2) Cormac was the incestuous son of Nessa and her son Conchobar (elsewhere explained as 'born in a chariot'). (3) Cucorb was so-called because he was so long unbaptized but he was the father of Nia Corti and ancestor of Dal Messin Corb.
atrick's Chariot eaks down at) all Carbinds on ver Boyne OH VI 266]) Ath Carpaid on ver Duol, Donegal OH 266]) also at Drum onchind [OH VI 6, SH 270]. Why?	Vercorf on coin of Coritani, AD 25 (see Fer Corb)	The Siaborcharpat or ghost chariot of Cuchullain [THU 356]	Note that the whole family and tribe had one Corb in their names. (4) O'Donovan [Bill of Rights 163] refers to a false fellow nicknamed Corbi of Co. Down because he was unbaptized and destroyed forty churches. This was AD 1407 yet I suspect that he was merely a member of Corb tribe of Mag Goba (see chart of Gob p. 174). (5) Cluam Coirpthe was so-called because St Berach revived a lot of 'corrupt' dead bodies there after a battle. He chose it for his monastery because the wild stag
		Cluann Coirpthi = meadow of corruption. Lugaid Corb ate bad bits of the deer [SG 538]	(*carvus*), which he harnessed to his chariot of books, lay down there. Compare St Cadoc's stag, which gave its name to Llancarvan (or Llangabran) (*cervus* or *carw*, which gave its name to the monastery). Note Cluain Coirpthi is also written Cluain Cairpre.

TRIBE	SAINT	CULT CENTRE	HERO or ANCESTOR
Cenel Cuirpn, Tipperary	Priest Corban or Curufin (20 Jul.)	Kilbarry of St Berach	Four bad Corb folk: Corbecan, bad landowner in Avranches, Normandy opposes St Severns (1 Feb.). He is also robber a Corbei against St Corbicar Corbanus, bad landowner of Aran, opposes St Enda. Keb opposes St Ronan in Brittany.
Ui Cairpre Lagin, Kildare	St Corban	Cell Corban, Cell Corbnatan, Cell Crobnatan, all at Kill near Naas.	
Ui Cairpre Diona Cliab, Sligo	St Corbnatan		
Ui Cairpre Aedha, Limerick	St Crobnatan		
Ui Cairpre Luachra, Kerry			
Clann Cairbre	Daughters of Cairbre	Kill, near Naas	Three brothers: Cairbre Riata *ex quo* Dal Riata, Cairbre Musc *ex quo* Muscraige, Cairbre Baschann *ex quo* Baiscinn.
(1) Cruin, Roscommon (2) Cruith, Limerick (3) Guill, Tipperary	Daughters of Cairbre (15 Jan.)	Crebec, Craebhach	Cairbre, enemy of Patrick at Tailteann

16. THE CARPIC SAINTS

HABITATION	AFFINITY	DISGUISE	COMMENTS
IBERIA: Corbate among Vaccaei, Corbite among Suebi			
FRANCE: Corbeil, Seine et Oise, Corbeng, Aisne, Corbre, Somme, Corbigny, Nievres, Corbion, Luxembourg, Corbières, Basses Alpes, La Corbie, Jersey.		St Corbban = Cerbban, surpassing in piety (*crabud*) rests under branches (*craeb*). [MD IV 341]	
		Cairbre = Corb-ri (chariot king)	Cairbre: At Kill in Co. Kildare recurrence in proper names of syllables Cairb-Corb-Cerb-Craeb-Crab-Crob-Creb convey different meanings with similar sounds. Are not the Carb tribes responsible? St Corban and the Daughters of Cairbre both came from Kill near Naas. This place was also called Craebh but is a different Craebh from that associated with the Craebhach, where the other Daughters of Cairbre were culted. Therefore Craebh is only a verbal development of Carbh, Cairbre, Cerbban, etc. (see Table 9 p. 174).

Hubert Butler's original handwritten Chart of Carpetani. (1972 edition)

16. THE CARPIC SAINTS

St Gabhran and the Goats

Now we can pass on to the horse or goat folks, the Gabraige, the Ui Gabra, the Cenel Gabran and the Fir Gabrae. Many of their names have alternative forms moving sharply away from horse or goat. The Ui Gabra are called Ui Gobla and Ui Gabla and Ui Gabalaig, Loch da Gabur is Loch Gobar, Magh da Gabhar is Mag da Gabhal, and so on. Llanngabrain in Wales is also Llangarbhan, now Llancarvan. There was a very ancient tribe called the Gaborchind (Goat-head), who may have been that midland tribe that St Patrick turned into goats. But Gabhran, who gave his name to Gabhran, now Gowran in Co. Kilkenny, was a hound, while four different men called Gabhran are also said to have given their name to this small village. There are also fictitious-looking kinships to confirm that Gabhr or Gabr was a variant of Garbh and Corp: for example the Gabraige of the river Suck were a branch of the Dal na Corp; Cana Garb was descended from Gabhran, and so on. Four or five saints, Gabhran (14 Nov.), Gabrian (24 Jun.), Gobran, a lay brother of St Ciaran, Cobran (19 Jul.) and Chebrien (23 Jan.), have Cornish and Gaulish colleagues, Chebran, Gobrian and Gibrian, as odd as themselves. In the lay genealogies Gab, Goib, Gabr and Garb are interchangeable (Table 9, p. 174). Gubbi was ancestor of the Garbraige or Cupraige or Gubraige, Gaban was ancestor of the Clann Garbain.

Naturally the many goat and horse names of Britain and the Continent fall under suspicion. There were the Gabrantivici in Yorkshire, Gabarus (the river Gave) in Bearn, Gabris or Gievres among the Bituriges Cubi, Gabromagus in upper Austria, Gabhrinis in Brittany and Gabreta Silva (the Bohmerwald).

In Italy I find a tendency of the Capr- or goat names to cluster together. The more real goats there are in any region the less likely are they to be used in place names, whose purpose is to distinguish one spot from another. Capracotta, Capriati and Capraro are all near Carpinone in the Abruzzi. Monte Caprea is over Carpineto near Rome. The odd St Cerbone, who went to Rome with a flock of geese and pulled Pope Vergilius out of bed, is from the region of Carboli and Capraia. The period of the first Carpic wanderings through classical lands must have been very early indeed, and perhaps there are legacies in Greek and Roman mythology. Cebren was the river of Troas and father of Oenone. Cebriones, the giant, was killed by Venus and Cerberus himself needs watching, for he was not only a dog but also a fabulous Cretan thief.

St Seighin Gabal and the Forks

One of the great ancestresses of mid-Leinster was Ethne Gabalfada or Long-legs. *Gabal* means a fork and this disrespectful term was applied to her legs. She had many relations in Connacht, being sister-in-law to Queen Maeve, but she herself was the ancestress of various tribes of the Ui Gabalaig in Leix, Kildare, and Carlow. The tribe was called after her legs, we are told, and there was a hill, Drum Gabhla (near Sletty) in Carlow [SH 195], and another in Leix, Duma Gabhle, called after her tribe. She was very close to the Corb family for her father was Corbmac and her grandfather Cucorb and her great-grandfather was Mug Corb and, through an enormous family tree, she was related to almost all the saints and ancestors of mid-Leinster. The Ui Gabalaig stretched, for the most part, along the Barrow so to my thinking the river Feegile or Fid Gaible, which flows into the upper Barrow, conceals their name. But modern scholars think it means Wood-fork and that a river with forks in it (*gabal*) flows through a wood (*fid*). This simple explanation did not interest ancient scholars, who say that a hero, Gabal Glass (the Green or Grey), son of Ethedon, threw a magical tub made by the Dagda's daughter into a wood and hence the wood was named after him. The poem is very obscure and is probably full of puns on the names of forgotten tribes. I certainly think that one of the many Glas tribes was responsible for Gabal being *glas* (green), for the Feegile river is also traced to a lady called Gabal, daughter of Goll Glas, who built a fort, Dun Gabail, in the neighbourhood and there is a local ancestor Glasgabal. Nor can we forget the famous green cow of Gabhlan, the smith of the Tuatha de Danaan, which left its tracks all over Ireland. It was Glas Gabhnen in Co. Donegal and Derry, Glas Gabhlen of Glen Gevlin in Cavan.

As for Ethne Gabal Fada and Fidgabal, I think they owe their names to a mingling of Fid-Fad tribes (see St Fid) and Gabal tribes. In the west, Aed Gabalfada (the father of St Sarnait, a virgin saint of Clare and Aran) must be explained similarly.

Gabal appears in compound names with reasonable frequency. In Waterford, Dargabal, a descendant of Dara, was ancestor of the Daurgabal tribe. His nephew Daurthecht was ancestor of the Daurthecht tribe. He had a son called Eogabal or Yew Fork, who lived in a yew tree and was grandfather of the famous ancestress Aine of Knockany in County Limerick. The Eoganacht Aine lived round Knockainey, so Eogabal, Aine's grandfather, is a suitable compound ancestor.

16. THE CARPIC SAINTS

I know nothing of St Seigin Gabal of Rathvilly, Co. Carlow, except that he was well within the range of the Gabal folk. I would suggest that the Sigyni had mixed with that section of the Gabal tribe, of which he was ancestor.

Who were the Ui Gabalaig? On the Continent we find the Gabali, north of the Cevennes. They left their name at Javols and Gévaudan in south-central and south-eastern France. The river Gabellus, now called Secchia, runs through Emilia-Romagna to the Po. No doubt it is said that this river also forked, but I would look for another explanation.

This Gabal group seems akin to the Carpic one. Gablan, a famous builder, was also called Garbhan. Ethne Gabal Fada's tribe, the Ui Gabla, were also called Ui Gabra. St Seigin Gabal's father was Senach Goibhnenn. The smiths, and the goats, the horses and the rough folk seem inseparable, and Ethne Gabalfada's close family ties with the Corb folk seem to confirm these affinities.

St Crebriu and the Branches

I need not apologize for leaping now to the Fir Craibi of Connaught, their namesakes of Co. Derry, the sons of Croeb from Cromarty, and a large group of homonymous peoples. They were concerned with branches (*craebh*, branch) and piety (*craibdech*, pious). The Fir na Craibhe in Derry seemingly took their name from the lady Craobh, daughter of Eogan, who was drowned at a fall of the river Bann, to which she also gave her name. There was a special congestion of these branch people in Westmeath, where we find Tir da Craobh or 'the land of the two branches' and the famous Lough Crew or 'branch lake', Craobh Uisnig and five other branch places. Not far off was Craebh Laisre, Lasar's branch, where according to a late legend, a two-month-old baby cried out 'Good God'. In my view the babe of Craebh Laisre is an echo of the two virgin saints [TRIP 135] of Mayo, Crebriu and Lesru, daughters of Gleru, who called out to Patrick from their mother's womb that he should come over from Britain to convert the Irish. (As for Gleru, I find that Gleran was an alias of St Grellan, a saint who was a tribal leader and who came from Craebh Grellain or Grellan's Branch near Boyle.)

These two ladies seem to occur in other large saintly families. Elsewhere there were Craebh, Lasar and Find, daughters of Erc, and we have already met Corp, Brig, Lassar and Dare as sisters in other large families in various places (see p. 139). St MoLaisse Craeb is a portmanteau saint in whom both virgins are assimilated.

The Ui Croibine, descended from Croibine, son of Suibne, lived in the midlands, and I have no doubt that they were one of the reasons why St Patrick visited a copse in Westmeath composed of Croib, Sciad and Draigen, or 'branches, hawthorn and blackthorn', where he founded a church. There were in Westmeath distinct traces of Sciath and Draigen tribes and in my view, for reasons related elsewhere, these shrubs represent Carpi, Scythians and Dragani.

Whether or not I am right about this there can be no doubt of the equation Corp = Corb = Cuirb = Cruib = Craeb (p. 74 and Table 9, p. 174). Colgan uses it in his suggestion that St Cruibin Craebdech, St Devout Pig's Trotter of Louth, is St Corban; Cell Corpnatan is also called Cell Crobnatan, and St Corpnata is St Craebhnat. St Corban, who was culted at Cell Crobnatan, now Kill, Co. Kildare, is also called Craeban and we are told of him that he was surpassing in piety (*crabud*) and rested under branches (*craeb*). There too were St Garban and the saintly daughters of Cairpre; Craebh Bancheda, where the nun Columnatan is culted, is also at or near Kill.

How did the famous Band of Red Branch Knights, Craebh-derg or Craebh-hruadh, at Armagh get its name? I have forgotten the official explanation but both forms are surely tribal. A king of Connacht was called Cathal Crobhderg (Red-claw), but we find him at Baile na Craibhe (the town of the branches) in Mayo. Is his name different from that of the virgin Saint of Kerry, St Crobh Derg, or Red-claw? Craebh and Crobh, branches and claws, are surely both fancies derived from the forgotten Carpi. Craebh Finn, Crob Finn or Crofinn was queen of Tara. Crob Criad was steward with St Colman of Lann in Westmeath. He was called Hand of Clay, Crob Criad, because, it seems, he was resurrected from the dead to wash the feet of visiting clergy, and he became the ancestor of the Ui Cruib Criad of Wexford. With the same group let us associate Cruife or Gruibo, the mother of Corb Olum, and in Wales Graban, the herald of Maelgwyn, who gave his name to the river Graban. The Ui Gruibni were a tribe of Munster [CGH 197].

Provisionally I have placed the Grec, Crich, Corc Saints and the saints of the Cruithne in my Carpic charts, but, while their links with each other are strong, the Carpic links are rather tenuous (Table 8, p. 142 and Table 9, p. 174). St MacCreiche is a key figure.

St Gregory and the Greeks

Probably the most famous of ecclesiastical puns was that of Gregory the Great, who, confronted with some handsome English captives, said: '*Non Angli sed angeli!*' The schoolbooks usually leave the pun there, but in fact Gregory had carried it two stages further. Learning that they came from the northern province of Deira, he remarked that it was fitting that they had been called from the wrath (*de ira*) to come to the Mercy of God. When he was told that their king's name was Aella, he wound up with a pun on Hallelujah.

Pope Gregory himself stimulated the Irish monks to a corresponding pun piety, for, like St Martin of Tours, St Hilary of Poitiers and Pope Sylvester, he had a Celtic equivalent who shared his feast day and some of his adventures. The Irish St Grigoir of Aran and the Blaskets (12 Mar.) was also made pope. Can one find out how this happened?

Thurneysen was greatly puzzled by an ancient prophecy that Pope Gregory the Great would be descended from CuRoi mac Daire, the famous chieftain of the Dingle peninsula in Kerry [THU 445]. '*Wie der Verfasser auf diesen Gedanken gekommen ist, ist unbekannt.*' It is not, however, at all unknown. Father Shearman, author of *Loca Patriciana*, knew a great deal about it and wrote at length in 1876 in the *Kilkenny Archaeological Journal*. He writes that there was an Irish St Grigoir or Gregory who was a native of the Blasket Islands opposite to the Dingle peninsula. It was said that he went with two other Irish saints, Faelcu and Pupaeus, to Rome and that, while they were there, the pontiff died. Then, after a dove had descended on St Pupaeus' head he was offered the papacy, but declined. Father Shearman dismisses this as idle talk but suggests that Faelcu and Grigoir no doubt went to Rome but afterwards settled in Aran.

He thinks it natural that, because of this visit to Rome, the Aran islanders should confound their St Grigoir with Gregory the Great and make him share a feast day (12 Mar.) with the great pope. And it was not surprising that they should call after him Gregory's Sound, the strait between Inishmore and Inishmaan, through which he passed on his return from Rome. In 1876 the fishermen, who voyaged down the sound on their way to Galway, still lowered their sails in homage to the Irish pope. To Father Shearman it also seemed natural that in Kerry, Grigoir's native land, the strait between the Blaskets and the mainland should also be called Gregory's Sound and that at Glenbeigh, on the opposite shore, his pattern should be celebrated on 12 March. *The Martyrology of Òengus* (12 Mar.) says the body of Pope Gregory, of the children of Dega (the Ui Dega of Kerry?), was sent by God in a case from the Tiber to Aran, where a strand is also named after him. So it is obvious enough why St Gregory the Great was given the Kerry pedigree of his Irish namesake.

But there was another reason why St Grigoir of Aran should have been called a pope, since it affected four or five of his fellow Aran saints, who also, we are told succeeded to the papacy. I think that all the Aran popes were tribal ancestors. There was a Papraige tribe with an ancestor, Pupaeus Papa, son of Mugdom Dubh of Oriel [H 562].

I think that Grigoir's own tribal origins are exceptionally clear. Opposite Aran on the Clare coast were the Grecraige or Crecraige tribe with an ancestor called Grecus and the territory of the Grecraige on Loch Gara in Sligo is still called 'the Gregories'. I cannot find the Grecraige in Dingle, though it is quite possible that Castle Gregory there is not, as alleged, called after an Elizabethan landlord Gregory Hoare. Beare Island less than fifty miles to the south-east is called Inis Grecraige, and since they were a widely dispersed people they are surely responsible for St Grigoir of the Blaskets as well as for St Grigoir of Aran. Grecus is said to have been the ancestor of the Greeks as well as of the Grecraige, and, by his cruelty, to have driven the ancestor of the Fir Bolgs ahead of him to Ireland. Plainly the sphere of his interests and his influence was by no means parochial. He represented some large and roving community, which dissolved into other tribes, demanding other ancestors. In the west there were the Grecraige, descended from Grec mac Arod, in the midlands and Munster were the Gracraige, descended from Grac; there were the Ui Creachain of Mayo, descended from Crecan; there were the Ui Moccu Grecci and many others. It is not surprising therefore that Achadh Greg (Greek-field) should be one of Ireland's many names. Can we guess what this large, widespread and important tribal group can have been?

In *Western Islands* (p. 33), Robin Flower quotes another explanation of Gregory's Sound from a medieval manuscript. A pilgrim from the Blaskets went to Rome and begot Gregory the Great. When the pope died, his coffin was put in the Tiber and the current swept it to Aran where he was buried in the edge of St Gregory's Sound.

In the meantime there are other saints to consider. There was St MacU Greca of Findchill (25 Jan.) and St Colman Grec of Fermoy and several others. St Colman has puzzled Canon Power, the historian of the decies of Co. Waterford. Could he possibly, he asks, have been a Greek? But he decides that he must have been one of the Grecraige. I think it would be more correct to say he was of the Gracraige, for we read of this tribe being transferred from the midlands, together with the Corcu Dula or Dala of the Decies.

And there were of course heroes too and beasts. I will only mention a bull called Grogin of Gortgrogin (Grogin's field) at St Colman mac Luachain's monastery in Westmeath. He was called Grogin because he used to cover mares (*graig*). I would connect him with the Ui Gruccain of Westmeath.

16. THE CARPIC SAINTS

Now we must pass over to Scotland and Wales. We are told of a famous King Grig of Scotland, AD 878–89, who was ancestor of the Macgregors and was also called Gerg, Giric, Curig, Grim and Gregory the Great, and was a sort of saint. We have located Pope Gregory the Great in Aran as an alias for the ancestor of the Grecraige, so surely this Gregory the Great must be of the same manufacture. His posterity did not really believe in him, for his church Egles Girig in Magh Girgin (the Mearns in Forfar and Kincardineshire) is dedicated to St Cyriacus (16 Jun.). St Cyriacus of Tarsus at the age of three was torn from his mother's arms as she was led to martyrdom. Crying out, 'Christ is king!' he had his brains dashed out by a brutal soldier upon a marble staircase. In Scotland this baby saint replaces King Grig, and, in Wales, St Curig (26 Jun.) of Llangarig and other places.

In France and England too this decorous and cosmopolitan St Cyriacus was often used by the Latin monks to replace the more uncouth members of the large Grig-Curig community. We find him also as St Kerec (17 Feb.) in Brittany and St Cyres in France and Exeter.

St MacCreiche and the Plunder

I have mentioned the Crecraige or Crec folk, who sometimes shared ancestors with the Grecraige. But they had ancestors of their own too. Crecan, for instance, was ancestor of a Mayo branch, and Dil mac da Creca or Dil son of two Plunders represented the Kilkenny-Tipperary Crecraige. He was a druid who must also have been ancestor to the Dilraige tribe of Munster; he was blind, *dall*, and was successful in recovering some booty or plunder, *creach*, on behalf of the Ossorians, when they were chased from Tipperary.

But could '*da creca*' really mean 'two plunders'? There was an ancestor called just Da Creca and there was a saint, St Fer da Crich (30 Aug.), descended from a famous Ulster ancestor, Colla da Crich. In the case of the saint, *crich* is supposed to mean boundary or territory and it is thought he was called Man of two Territories, because he had a parish in Ulster and a parish in Scotland.

There were several saints called MacCreiche. The most fascinating of them lived in the barony of Corcumroe, Co. Clare, where, opposite Aran, a branch of the Crecraige were established. I think he bore the same relation to them that St Grigoir of Aran did to the Grecraige. There is a life of him in Irish, which is full of detail and could tell us much of the early tribes of Clare. The writer could not decide whether MacCreiche meant the Son of Plunder or the Son of the Territories, so his story takes account of both possibilities. He had been a great friend of St Ailbe, visiting him at his cult centre of Emly in Tipperary and living there as a hermit and then going on with him to Aran. This intimacy was so close that he was originally called St MacCroide Ailbe or Son of the Heart of Ailbe. Writing of St Ailbe, I suggest that St MacCroide Ailbe was the shared ancestor of the Crec folk and the Ailbe folk. St MacCreiche's church of Kilmacrehy on Liscannor Bay is not far from Slieve Ellbe or Elva, familiar variants of Ailbe, in north Clare, and he had a fellow saint there called St Mac Aible. A similar friendly relationship with the Brig folk is suggested by the fact that his mother was Briga and that the well at Kilmacrehy is dedicated to Brigit.

This MacCreiche had land-owning relations in Kerry and was also active on Inishceltra Island in Shannon harbour. That is why he is 'Son of the Territories', but others say that it was because he was successful in causing restitution of some plunder, *creach*, to his nephews in Kerry that he changed his name from MacCroide to MacCreiche.

St MacCreiche of Lugmad or Louth (11 Aug.) is supposed to be different. He was cook to St Mochta of Louth, who was also called Mochta Lug, in deference, I suppose, to the Lug folk. MacCreiche had the same warm intimacy with him that his namesake in Clare had with St Ailbe and so he was called MacCroide Mochta or Son of the Heart of Mochta. In this way he would represent an east-coast intimacy between the Crec folk and the Mochta folk. The Tuath Mochtaine were a south Ulster tribe. Once, we are told, the two saints, Mochta and MacCreiche, went together to Iona and St MacCreiche, in his capacity of cook, I suppose, offered St Mochta some nuts. St Mochta refused them, replying that the real owner of the land with its nuts would not come for a hundred years. He referred to St Columba.

What is the meaning of this story? I can only suggest that somehow St MacCuill (25 Apr.) is involved in it. He was a saint of south County Down, a man of appalling wickedness, who was converted by St Patrick on Strangford Loch and became the first bishop of the Isle of Man. His name is said to mean Son of Nut Tree. He is called sometimes St MacCuill Moccu Greca and also Demana and I think that means that he was the amalgamated ancestor of the Ui Moccu Grecci, who were in the neighbourhood and also of the Cenel Demmain of Strangford Loch. That means that, in one of his aspects, St MacCreiche would be St MacCuill and it would be suitable for him to offer nuts. St MacCuill is an obvious christianization of Mac Cuill, an ancient ancestor of the Tuatha de Danaan, and his god, we are told, was the Nut Tree (*coll*, genitive *cuill*). For more about St Mac Cuill see the Gelonic saints.

But why Iona? Well there are indications of Cuill folk and Cuill saints in and around Iona. As for MacCreiche, we are told that the Grecraige were in Mull and also in Cruib-Inis. Now Iona is Craebh Inis, or the Island of Branches, and also Cruib Inis or Paw Island, and it lies just off the coast of Mull. To my thinking Cruib and Craebh are both Carpic echoes, and if the Grecraige were in Iona, it would not be strange to find St MacCreiche there too. Why was Mochta there? I do not know.

St Corcaria and the Purple Folk

It is to me barely credible that W.J. Watson should say that the king of Munster, Corc, son of Lugaidh, is 'of course a perfectly historical character', who went in the fourth century AD to the east coast of Scotland and settled the land between the Dee and the Tay with his Munster men. He is extravagantly fabulous. He had four wives, variously described as Scottish, Irish and British, and many uncles, aunts, brothers, sisters, sons and grandchildren, and a stepmother, and all of them are clearly related to the tribes and mixed tribes of Cork, Limerick, Tipperary, Kerry, Kincardine and Forfarshire, and to their more remote continental predecessors. And they have all left their names on the rivers and lakes and mountains of Ireland and Scotland. Many different pedigrees use the same names, but change their sex and kinship. As one varied genealogical pattern is imposed upon another, certain constants are to be detected in certain places. We have an algebraic problem of the greatest intricacy where the symbols all have human features that constantly change. Who will solve it? When?

One of Corc's wives, Leamhain, links up Lennox with the river Laune in Kerry; a son, Maine, links up another Kerry river, the Maine, with Clackmannan; another son, Daig, links the Ui Dega of Kerry with Dundee and the river Dee. Some of these links are explicit, some have been plausibly deduced by writers like Watson, who are impelled by a certain fantastic consistency in the many records into believing that these people once lived.

Here I will deal with the Corc folk only. Corc went to Scotland because his stepmother Dael, a Munster ancestress, having failed to seduce him, had him banished and there he begot Cairbre Cruithnechan, who was later the king of the Cruithne of Killarney, Co. Kerry. The region that Corc settled between the Dee and the Tay is called Mag Gergin (now the Mearns) and I have told how it is connected with Grig, Gregory the Great, St Cyriacus, St Cyrus and the Mac Gregors. The king of Alba's poet, who welcomed him to Mag Gergin, was called Gruibne, recalling the Ui Gruibne tribe of Munster. Long before the time of Corc and also before King Grig of Mag Gergin, an earlier ancestor Ciric son of Cruidne had given his name to the same place, Mag Circinn.

Corc's father-in-law, Feradach Find Fechtnach, king of Alba, whose territory lay between the Tay and the Dee, had a namesake who was king of Ireland and had the same long complicated nickname, Find Fechtnach, 'the fair righteous'. The two kings purport to be different, but how could they be? I can only explain the duplication tribally. In classical times the Venicones and the Vecturiones lived between the Tay and the Dee. But they must have got to Ireland too. So it happened that their combined ancestor, Find Fechtnach, turned into the epithet of a third Scoto-Irish tribal ancestor.

Meanwhile in Ireland Corc's sons and daughters were appropriating land or yielding it. Corc had a son who married a lady who looked like a saint, Cairce of Cell Cairce in Westmeath, and they had a son called Cuircne, who gave his name to a district Cuircne on Loch Ree. Corc himself took over half this territory, leaving the other half in the hands of the Ui Garbain.

King Corc of Munster was also in Caeraige Cuirche, now Kerrycurrihy by Cork city. A fiery ball, *caer*, fell on his wife and son and two chariot horses, *ech carpait*, and killed them. St MoChuda resurrected them.

There was another territory inhabited by Corc folk in the barony of Clanwilliam, Tipperary. The Ui Cuirc were the ruling family. When St Patrick visited them at Ath Fiacla one of his teeth, *fiacal*, dropped out in a ford (*ath*) so he built a church Kilfeacle, and left the tooth in charge of a disciple of his called Cuircne. I think that it was as the ancestor of these Ui Cuirc that Corc, son of Lugaid, took three hostages, Grac, Dula and Maine, from the midlands to Munster, where they became the ancestors of the Gracraige, the Corcu Dula and the Mennraige. Grac I have assumed to be, like Grec, a variant of Corc; Dula is, I think, a variant of his stepmother Dael; Maine of the Mennraige is surely just a west Munster variant of Corc's son, the Scottish Maine.

I've related these anecdotes to explain that Corc and his people were very widely scattered in Munster and the midlands, and that he was so constantly attending to them himself that it is impossible that he could simultaneously have been settling an Irish colony in the east of Scotland.

There were many other Corc saints with what is to me a Carpic appearance. St Curcagh (21 Jul.) lived in the region of the Grecraige of Roscommon; she was a descendant of Colla da Crich; St Curcagh (16 Nov.) was also of the Grecraige. There was also St Corcaria or Curcagh (8 Mar.), two saints called Corcan on 7 January, and others on 30 September and 4 April.

16. THE CARPIC SAINTS

From the north I should mention the Ui Cruimther Corcrain called after the priest (*cruimther*) Corcrain of Druim Crom among the Corcraige. He is a mystery. Could a tribe be called after a celibate priest? Cruimther is sometimes written Cruibther and perhaps *cruibther*, like Cruib and Crom, is a Carpic echo. (There was a virgin Crumtheris placed by St Patrick near Armagh [TRIP 232].) The Corcraige and the Ui Cruimther Corcrain lived in the barony of Iveagh, Co. Down [H 361].

In the adjoining barony of Oneilland lived St Corc of Kilmore (4 Apr.). In this barony, whose leading family was the Ui Gairbheth or Garveys, we find St Senach Garb at Cluain Ui Moccu Greci (2 Nov.) and, as I have mentioned earlier, Domnach Maccu Garba. These are all Carpic names and this is as I would suppose, for it is in the counties of Down and Antrim that the Cruithne, to whom I refer in the next section, had their main stronghold. Since the Corcraige lived in south Down it is clear why the purple (*corcra*) wind came from the east. (I refer here to an Irish treatise on 'The Colours of the Winds' [OC III 132], which is plainly based on tribal punning, see chapter 26.) I have mentioned also Dorn Corcra or Purple Fist, a nickname of Cucullain; he is associated with Slieve Gullion or Sliab Cuillind. You will remember he was the dog (*cu*) of Cuillen in Co. Down and that is also the region of the Ui Dornain and the Corcraige.

I will make a final guess. The prefix Corcu, which is thought to mean 'tribe of', is in fact a Carpic remnant. Corc Duibne was the ancestor of the Kerry tribe, the Corcu Duibne, from which we are told Pope Gregory the Great descended. If Corcu was a mere collective noun, Corc could never have deputized for the other ancestress, Duibne. There was also Corc Dul, ancestor of the Corcu Dula and Corc Losat of the Corcu Losat and one or two others.

St Cruithnechan and the Wheat

I have very little doubt that the Cruithne, which in historic times was the name of the Pictish people, owed their name to the Carpi, though there must have been many other ancient tribal names that the early people of Scotland and northern Ireland had an equal right to assume. Analogously the Romans called the entire Hellenic people after the Graeci, the small early tribe that the invaders encountered first on the Illyrian mainland.

We have seen that Magh Girgin, the Mearns in Kincardineshire, is associated with Grig and also with St Cyriacus, who is associated with St Curig.

But we are also told that it owed its name to Circin or Cirig, son of Cruidne, and that Gergin in Donegal was the land of the Cruithne. We know too that Cairpre Cruithnechan was the ancestor of the tribe that lived at Magh Gergin in Scotland. Two other places, Groth and Gart, are described as 'the land of the Cruithne', and this word an ancient writer informs us comes from *creachad* or plunder. We have seen the same improbable derivation given to St MacCreiche, who was also called MacCrithe. Everybody tried to translate Cruithne. Gibbon was mocked by Bishop Reeves for saying that they were called this because they ate wheat (*cruithnecht*), yet I think the word early on had this pun meaning. There were many places improbably called after wheat, and there was an odd saint who was carried to his burial under a load of wheat (see p. 260); others said Cruithne came from *cruith*, a pattern; and that meaning is discovered in the names of certain ancestor figures, in which the syllable *cruith* can be found. A famous lady was called Noichruthach or Noichride because either she had 'nine shapes' or always had 'new shapes'. I do not think that my guess that she was Nemedo-Carpic is more improbable.

If Groth is the land of the Cruithne, we can surely take the Gruthraige (MacNeill's 'cheese-manufacturing' tribe, for *gruth* means cheese), the Sil Creide and the Cerdraige (MacNeill's 'tribe of craftsmen' for *ceard* means craft), as variants on the tribal name [MacN 82]. The Cerdraige were near the Crothrage of the Galtees, Slieve Crott, and Cruithne, the wife of Finn, daughter of Lochan the smith, lived among them. Lochan also had a son called Cruithnechan. Of course there were plenty of puns connecting Cruithne and Cerdraige with 'crafts', and also with *cruit*, harp, *crodh*, flesh, *croide*, heart, *gruad*, cheek, *cruit*, hump, and so on. Creidne or Cruithne, for example, was craftsman, *ceard*, to the Tuatha da Danaan. Equally fabulous was the lady Ailbe Gruadbrec. Did she really have a speckled cheek or was she concocted tribally? There were Ailbe tribes, Cruadh tribes (the Cruadhluinde of Co. Down, for example), and Brec tribes.

There are some thirty Critan, Croidan, Cruithnechan saints, not one of whom can ever have lived. One of them was associated with Caislen Credi or Mons Credulitatis, the Hill of Faith, at Scone, but a similarly named mount in Ireland is derived from a heroine Credni. Let us note Crutbolc, the king of the Picts, as an amalgam of Cruithne and Bolgraige and carefully collate Cridenbel, the satirist, who had his mouth in his heart, with all the other heroes and saints with extraordinary mouths.

16. THE CARPIC SAINTS

St Mac da Cerda and the Craftsmen

Ceard or *cerd* means craftsman. I have written elsewhere about St Mac da Cerda, the Son of two Arts, who was sometimes a lunatic, sometimes extremely wise. There was also St Daigcerd or 'Good-artificer', who made ecclesiastical furniture for St Ciaran, and, still in church circles, there was Laidcen Lethcerd, or Half-craftsman, the father of St Canice. O'Curry and MacNeill are convinced that the Cerdraige of Munster were craftsmen, as we are told in *The Book of Leinster*.

O'Curry associates them with the great hoard of ancient gold found at Cullen in Tipperary, but the pedigree of the tribe makes it unlikely that their craftsmanship was more than a pun on their name. They were descended from Carban or Corban, the son of Cerdan, the son of Cerd Beg, the son of Cerdraige and there were other Cerdraige, at Beare in west Cork and Kerry. The west Cork branch were descended from Dairfine Cerd, which links them with the tribe of the south-west, the Dairfine, or Dairini, who are also said to be descended from Daire son of Dega. St Daig or Daigcerd (18 Aug.) was pre-eminent as a craftsman saint, making 150 bells, 100 croziers and 60 cases for gospels, but when he settled at Inish Cain mic Dega in Co. Monaghan, now Inishkeen, two of his brothers who lived there, were jealous of him. They would have killed him had it not been for the cleverness of a disciple, Naindech, son of Maine, who dressed himself up in the Abbot's vestments. When St Daig's brothers rushed at him their spears glanced off the holy vestments. St Daig then banished them both to Beare in west Cork. As I have related, there was a branch of the Cerdraige in Beare. MacNeill thinks that because of the copper mines there it was a suitable place for them to be. This seems to be unlikely. Encerd, or One Craftsman, one of the half dozen heroes with *cerd* in their names, came from Beare and behaved like a composite tribal ancestor rather than a coppersmith. One of his three sons, Glass, married the daughter of the king of Norway, but the son looks as though he himself was also the king's swineherd.

I would try to explain all this as follows. The Daig folk dominated or were amalgamated with the Cerd folk in St Daigcerd's part of Monaghan. Observe that Daig's cult centre, Inishkeen, is also called Inish Cain mic Dega, which turns Daig into an ancestor, and that Daig Dorn, a famous ancestor of the neighbourhood, was brother to Mugdorn Dub, who gave his name to the adjoining barony of Cremorne (Crich Mugdorna). Did the Daig folk really chase some of the Cerd folk to Beare, or is the story only meant to recall some half-forgotten kinship between the tribes of Beare and the tribes of Inishkeen?

The latter I suspect. (Maybe there is some significance in the fact that the famous Old Woman of Beare, the nun ancestress of so many tribes, was also known as Digde. But the Daig folk must be considered elsewhere.)

St Criotan Certronnach (17 Sept.) was probably a compound Cerd. He was nephew to St Ronan and, as cellarer, doled out St Comgall of Bangor's wines. He divided them fairly and hence was called Certronnach, for *cert* is right and *roinn* is division.

With the Cerd folk I would also link the Criad or Clay folk. Crob-Criad or Hand of Clay was steward of St Colman mac Luachain and ancestor of the Ui Crob Criad of Wexford. He washed the dirty feet of some midland saints with his hands.

Colla da Crich (Colla of the two Territories) was a great Ulster patriarch, the grandfather of Daig Dorn. He was thought to be really Colla of Criad or Colla under Clay. The reason for this name was that he was the bastard son of another famous Ulster ancestor and not, as his mother claimed, the son of Crinna Cerd, the goldsmith. So to make him look dark and dirty like a *cerd*, she rubbed clay (*cre*, genitive *criad*) into his limbs. It seems that Cerd is just a form of Cred and Cruith, because the Cred-Cruith people also had a punning relationship with 'craft'. Cruithne, who was one of Finn's many wives, was daughter of a craft worker at Cullen, where the Cerdraige lived. Creidne, the Cerd, was the first worker in precious metals and an artificer at Tara. Cruithne, son of Cind, was the artificer (*cerd*) to the great invader, Cathluan.

The fact that Corban was the son of Cerdan confirms me in my guess that the Cerd-Cruithne folk were related to the Carp-Carpad group, the Carpi and Carpetani (Table 4, p. 67).

St Cairbre Crom and the Crooked Folk

Who were the Crom folk? I believe that they link up by a roundabout route, which is hard to explore, with the Carpi. One strand of the argument is that the Scottish Grim is the same as Grig and Gerg (Table 9, p. 174). Here I will merely argue that Crom is a tribal word and did not, in proper names, mean 'crooked'. There is an anecdote about St Cairbre Crom that obviously hinges on tribal puns. A wicked king came up from hell to the saint as he was praying. He was coal-black and begged Cairbre Crom to intercede for him. The saint agreed and six months later the king reappeared, half speckled; after another six months of the saint's prayers, the wicked king was 'white'. There are so many overt puns that it is necessary to suspect covert ones here, involving *dub*, black, *leth*, half, *breac*, speckled, *finn*, white, and possibly a parable, not very easy to read, of tribal displacements. Analogous to this is the tale of Cairbre Crom, king of Munster, who was made into Cairbre Caem (the beautiful) instead of being Crom (the crooked) by the local saint St Finchua (the Ui Caem, now O'Keeffe, lived in the vicinity). He died of shock when St Cranat, to avoid his importunate advances, pulled out his eyes. He was buried at Cell Cromglaisi, where his namesake, St Cairbre Crom, had been educated. Were they called crooked after the cell, or was the Cell called crooked after them? This question has been answered in both ways. There were two other Cairbre Croms, a king and a wicked steward, who stole St Ciaran's cow, and a Cairbre Crom-cinn (Crooked-head). There was a Crom Derg (Crooked-red), with a brother, Derg, sons of Connra in Roscommon. There were also St Cromm, St Cramsech, St Cruimine, St Crom Dithruib and several others. There was an Ui Crommine tribe in Leinster [CGH 351] and a Clann Cromain in the midlands [FEN ex Croman].

Enna Crom was ancestor of the Ui Enna Crom tribe of Mayo. Called 'the bowed', he was the first of the fifteen sons of Amalghaid to 'bow' before St Patrick. You would have thought that his brother, Crom Dub, had bowed too, but, in fact, he was wicked. Crom Dub (Crooked Black) sometimes figures as a pagan, sometimes a Christian. His feast day, the last Sunday in July, is still kept. He is in fact the ancestor of the combined Crom tribe and Dub tribe of the west.

St Gnavan and the Bones

St Gnavan is the only Bone saint I know and I know little about him except that he was Irish and came back to Britain from Gaul with St Cadoc and two other saints. There is no reason to suppose he is not fabulous.

Perhaps St Fechin would be a more suitable representative of the Bone tribe (the Cnamhraige of the west of Ireland) but his relationship with them is rather complex. The Cnamhraige seem to have been a sub-tribe of the Ui Fiachra of Tireragh barony (Tir Fiachra), Co. Sligo, and there is a significant number of Bone places and people in Sligo and in particular Tireragh. There is, for example, in that barony Cul Cnamha, the recess of the bones, and Cnamhcoill or Bonewood (now Craughwell). There is also a tribe the Ui Cindcnamha, the Headbones, and a hero Cu Cnamha or Dog Bone. Nobody seems to have connected the bone places of Sligo with the Cnamhraige and Ui Cind-cnamha.

For example, Cul Cnamha in Ballysadare Bay, Co. Sligo, is said to be called after a hero, Cnama, who was killed in the Battle of Moytura; others say it is called after the bones of Eochaid, son of Erc, king of the Fir Bolgs. He was killed in the same battle by the three sons of Nemed who accompanied the invading army of the Tuatha de Danaan.

Yet plainly Cnamh is a tribal word, for the Ui Fiachra of Sligo and Mayo, in whose territory lived the tribe of the Cind-cnamha, were a focus of puns about ravens (*fiac*) and bones (*cnamha*). In my account of the Fiac saints I relate how a chieftain of Tireragh, Co. Sligo, where lived both Cnam folk and Fiac folk, was called Cnamhfiac or Bone-raven, allegedly because he was either devoured by ravens or very warlike. In the same place I have related a Bone-raven anecdote about St Fechin of Fore (20 Jan.), who, in Tireragh, was also neighboured and presumably culted by both Cnam folk and Fiac folk. This saint of Westmeath was specially associated with the Fech and Fiac tribes; he was born in Tireragh and built a church, we are told, at Ballysadare. He got his name Fechin because his mother saw him eating a bone and said, 'That is my little raven (*fiachan*).'

There are many places called Cnam but they are mostly in or near the region of the Cnam folk and, when the place names are explained, the explanation is always so odd that a tribal origin is obvious. Cnamross, now Camross, is explained as Cnam Fross or Bone Shower because the bones of a little boy who was carried from a battle in a shield melted in a Bone-Shower.

The Clann Cnaimsighe, whom I would reckon to be a mixture of Cnamh folk and Sig folk (see St Seigin Gabal), seemed to have lived on the Derry coast. They derived from Conla Cerd, who lived, as Cerd folk well might, at Dun Cruithne near Magilligan strand (see St Daigcerd and St Cruithneacht). Conla was a superb artist in precious metals and he was engaged in making a splendid shrine when he died. It remained unfinished in Dun Cruithne until St Columba arrived. Seeing that no living artist was capable of completing the shrine, St Columba opened Conla's tomb and, saying 'In the name of Our Lord Jesus Christ, arise!', he resurrected his bones. After completing the shrine, Conla lived on to have a family, hence the Clann Cnaim-sighe or 'the posterity of the bones'. The shrine was kept at Magilligan until the sixteenth century, and to this day their descendants the Kneafseys, Crampseys and by translation Bonars, live principally in the north-east corner of Ireland.

The Ui Cindcnamha of the west are an interesting tribe for they illustrate well my theories. Firstly they are also called Ui Cind, proving that tribal names are composite. Secondly there was in the Mayo-Sligo region, where they lived, a hero Cu Cnamha or Dog Bone, the charioteer of Amalghaid of Tir Amalghaid (Tirawley). How can he be anything but the ancestor of the Ui Cindcnamha, and as such is he not evidence that *cind* or *ceann*, head, and *cu*, dog (genitive *con*), are, in proper names, interchangeable?

Who were the Cnam folk? Cnamchaill, Bonewood, in Tireragh, which must be related to the Cnam folk of Tireragh, is now Crawhill and places called Creamcaill or Garlic-wood are also anglicized Crawhill. And Joyce in his *Irish Names of Places* says Cneam and Cream are interchangeable.

I do not believe in bones or garlic, but I think the Cnam folk were variants of the Crim-Crom folk (see Table 5, p. 97).

Apart from those I have mentioned, the principal representatives of the Bone folk are the MacCnaimhin, that is to say the MacNevins.

St Cearc and the Hens

I have found three saints called Cearc, one in Mayo, one unlocated, one in Leinster. The Leinster St Cearc, also called Corc, was one of the three virgin saints of the Ui Loscain Cruaich. Her name means hen and my opinion is that she had some connection with a very famous Irish bird called Cearc Bairrche or Bairrche's Hen. For the Ui Bairrche tribe came from the same area of east Leinster, as did St Cearc and a sub-tribe, the Cenel Croicni, lived among them. If one was going to make a sensible word out of shapeless tribal names like Cruaich and Croicni, *cearc*, a hen, would be one of a dozen possibilities. Bairrche was a giant cow-herd who gave his name to the Benna Boirche or the Mourne Mountains in Co. Down, and one of their peaks is called Hen Mountain. This famous hen was said to have been brought to Ireland by poets, but otherwise the only thing they recorded of it is that it sent a famous hero, Fothad Airgthech, to sleep with its clucking (*fodord*, murmuring) in south-west Donegal on a hill called Ard Fothaid.

Now there was a disciple of St Columba called Cearc, who left his name on the Circe river (Sruth na Circe) at Glencolumcille, also in south-west Donegal to the west of the Corker river and the Cruachgorm or Blue Stack Mountains. When St Columba came to this wild spot, it was infested with the demons that St Patrick had driven from Cruach or Croagh Patrick in Mayo. They poisoned the rivers and dwelt in clouds of dense fog. One of the demons slew Cearc with a spear before St Columba had time to rout them by hurling his bell, the Dubhduibseach, at them and to dispel the darkness.

The Glen of the Circe river is also called Glen Gairge after a hero Gerg, son of Eber, who owned a bronze pot that was stolen by Conchobar mac Nessa, and begat a Donegal tribe the Ferann Geirg. This suggests to me that the Gerg folk and the Cerc folk are the same (see Table 9, p. 174).

There are some hen places on Loch Corrib near another river Gairge, that flows into Loch Mask. Hen's Castle, Caislean na Circe, opposite Kirk Island, is under Kirkogue and Corkogue mountains. And the stories that account for the hen are not very plausible. We are told, for example, that the Lady Flaherty defended the castle, when her lord (the cock), was away. Nor, looking farther afield, can one believe in the toponymical hens. In Co. Waterford we have Tobar na Circe and Lis na gcearc. One could believe in a well being called after a hen, but not a fort.

St Goban and the Smiths

I think the Goban saints belong to the Carpic group or a related tribe, the Cubi. I had better give such evidence as I can find and hope that others will investigate further.

Why were they Carpi (see Table 9, p. 174)?

Firstly, the Gobans were all smiths or builders because of their names (*goba* is smith), and there seems to have been a vast number of celebrated men attached to these two professions among the Carpic group. Cruithne's father was a smith, and Senach Garb was a smith, Garban and Gabal were builders and so on. Secondly, Gub, who once held power in all Ireland, and Capa, grandson of Corb, who was one of Ireland's first invaders, seem to correspond to Gorbonianus and Gurguntius, who did the same in England. Finally, Gob names and Corb names are often oddly associated. St Goban of Laon (20 Jun.) had, as one of St Fursey's twelve companions, left Loch Corrib (Corbes) in Ireland for Crobheresburgh in Suffolk and then, accompanied by the Irish St Corbican, had gone through France, pausing on the way at Corbie on the Somme. On the third day they reached Corbeny near Laon. St Goban's brother Etho (10 Jul.) then settled on the little river Corbriol, east of Cambrai, while Goban pressed on to Laon and being, like all Goban saints, a good builder made himself with his own hands a cell at the village near Laon, now called Saint Gobain.

When the Vandals arrived on the spot, a couple of centuries after their time, and cut off his head, it was enclosed in a silver case but it has disappeared. Canon O'Hanlon thinks that the Calvinists are to blame.

16. THE CARPIC SAINTS

There is a special concentration of Gob and Corb names, sacred and profane, in the Aran Islands: St Goban, St Gobnait, St Caradoc Garb, as well as Corban and Goban. But St Cybi or Cubius, the Cornish-Welsh saint, is the most famous of them, so it is remarkable that neither of the two historians of Aran, Father Scantlebury and Mr O'Siochain, refer to him. He was the cousin of King Arthur and St David and better than any other saint he illustrates my contention that saints were tribal ancestors, whose adventures were a convenient way of recording the complex history of the tribes they represented.

St Cybi arrived in Aran with his ailing old uncle, St Cyngar, and his cousin, St Maelog, and spent four years there as Enda's disciple. As was suitable for christianized tribal ancestors, all three had churches in Cornwall, Wales and Brittany. St Cybi, for example, apart from his Welsh foundation, had two churches in Cornwall, next to the churches of his aunt St Non, his father St Selyf and his uncle Jestyn, all of whom had been in Brittany converting the Veneti. Yet Cybi's visit to Aran ended in disaster. An irascible old saint called Fintan chased them off the island and pursued them right across Ireland. Cybi, in his flight, stopped at three places to found churches, but Fintan was on his heels and finally said, 'Cybi, go across the sea!' Cybi replied by cursing all Fintan's churches, saying that in all Ireland only three would survive. Then he sailed away in a skinless curragh and founded Llangybbi in Anglesey.

Another version of the story describes St Fintan as a rich landowner of Aran. But even the richest landowner would not have properties all over Ireland from which to exclude intruders. A tribe would. In fact St Fintan must have been the ancestor of the Eneti-Veneti once more; throwing out St Cybi, he was only doing the same thing as St Enda had earlier done when he threw out Corban, the wicked native proprietor.

As for Cybi, he turns unmistakably into the Irish Goban when in his flight from Fintan he builds Kil Mo Cop at Artane near Dublin with his own hands. For Mo Cop is a name for Goban; there was a Goban culted in Aran, a kinsman like Cybi of St David of Wales, for his mother was St David's sister, Magna, who lived in the Galtees. St Goban and the virgin Gobnait of Aran and Ballyvourney are culted the same day (11 Feb.).

Though St Goban behaves exactly as all the other saints do, because of some caprice of scholarship he is usually regarded as more fabulous than they are. The critics of his sanctity connect him with Goibniu, the Celtic god of smithcraft. This god had a Welsh counterpart, Goibnenn or Gwydion, who was responsible for Abergavenny; he became St Govan in Pembroke and Sir Gawain of the round table. The critics believe that god and saint and knight all developed out of the Irish word *goba*, a smith. There must be about twenty of these Goban saints, whom the hagiographers have tried to distinguish from each other. There were many of them craftsmen and builders and Petrie, who reacted strongly against the scepticism of his day, has fused a cluster of them into one real architect, who built the round towers of Antrim, Ferns, Kilmacduagh, Killala, St Mullins, and was born at Turvey Strand north of Dublin of a dark-haired father called Tuirbi, a carpenter. 'This artisan was, if not a foreigner, at least very probably of foreign extraction and thus enabled to introduce arts not generally known in the country.' [RT 386] And Petrie suggests that he acquired his Co. Dublin property, which for a foreigner would otherwise have been difficult, as a reward for his craftsmanship. The ancient verse, which Petrie quotes, says:

> Though Tuirbi was southwards in his district mighty,
> It is not known of what stock he was.

Goban with his multiple personality and Tuirbi, his father, who was very important and powerful in the south and who performed some magical punful feats with a hatchet at Turvey Strand, can only be explained tribally. The poem as good as says so. There was a Tuath Tuirbe in north Co. Dublin and they must have neighboured a Goban tribe. The genealogists say that the Tuath Turbi were descended from Eber Finn of Clann Ebir, which means they were Iberian. They could have been the Tarbelli, who left their name at Turba, now Tarbes, north of the Pyrenees; they were probably the same stock as the Turboleti, on the southern side of the mountains. Clontarf, Cluain Tarbh, or Bull Meadow, is very close to Turvey and must derive from the same people and there are many Tarb-Torb ancestors.

But none of this helps to identify the Goban-Cybi folk. Was there a tribe whose name suggested smithcraft? As I have said my candidates are the Cubi of the upper Loire, a primitive tribe that was overrun by the Bituriges, the only Celtic tribe in Aquitaine. Gorgobina, an ancient settlement in that region, has for me a thoroughly Carpic and Goban look. Maybe it is just an accident that their chief town, Avaricum, to which the Biturges gave their name, Bourges, was the best built in Gaul and that they had celebrated ironmines, or is it possible that the Cubi gave their name to smithcraft, as the Cypriots gave theirs to copper?

Otherwise one must accept the current explanation, which seems to me absurd. The Biturges Cubi, it is argued, were a harmonious (*cubi*) people, who did not, like the other half of their tribe, the Bituriges Vivisci, huff off to the Atlantic coast but settled down where they were.

16. THE CARPIC SAINTS

I cannot accept this. Long ago I surmised that St Bite and his mother St Cobba or Copia, whom St Patrick left at Elphin in Co. Roscommon, were joint ancestors of the Bituriges Cubi. She was also St Coppa or Cipia (see *A Dictionary of Saintly Women*, A.B.C. Dunbar, Vol. 1, pp. 182, 206). I may well be wrong but certainly it is in such a way that related tribes survive in history as family parties. The context of the story is fabulous. The two saints were invented. What were they invented for?

Anyway I suggest that in Ireland the Cubi were hard-pressed by the Veneti, as in Gaul they were pressed by the Bituriges. That is why St Fintan chased St Cybi. That is why, in general, Fintan saints evicted Goban saints. St Fintan of Clonenagh, for example, a very stern disciplinarian, exposed one of his monks, presbyter Goban, as an appalling sinner at the very moment when he was celebrating mass. He was ejected and died miserably and wickedly.

Another Goban saint lent his monastery in Wexford to a third St Fintan. Fintan gave it back to him after twelve years but left a curse upon it.

Indeed the Gobans, despite their craftsmanship, always got the worst of it from all the saints. St Abban blinded Goban his church builder, for overcharging. Another Goban was such an ignorant man that he had to have his hands blessed by St Mo-Aedoc before he could build. And I think Canon O'Hanlon was describing a further reverse for the Cubi when he wrote:

> Entertaining a very high estimate of St Lassar's merits, St Goban resigned to him the monastery of Old Leighlin, and, through love of greater retirement, moved southwards over the mountains.

The canon was a good man, who always thought the best of everyone except for the celebrated antiquarian and critic of the saints, Dr Ledwich, who was 'a barefaced quack with the effrontery to substitute lies for history'. But about St Goban he was just inventing.

Most of the Gob saints were treated to more than their share of that elaborate pun piety, which borders on levity. St Gobnait, the virgin of Ballyvourney in Co. Cork (11 Feb.), was, because *gob* means a bill, known as 'the sharp-beaked nun'! She repelled a haughty chief by letting some bees out of a special beehive. She did this, surely, because of the neighbouring Ui Beice tribe, whose name means 'bees'.

There were one or two particularly illustrious Gobans, but I think the reason for this is that, where tribes compete and the more powerful one absorbs the weaker one, its ancestor is able to assimilate and exalt the weaker ancestor. I've mentioned the infamous presbyter Goban, whom the stern and austere St Fintan of Clonenagh expelled from his monastery. Well, there was an extraordinarily good saint, St Goban Finn (11 Feb.), also associated with Clonenagh; in fact his relics were preserved there. He was, I suggest, Cubo-Venetic, a conciliatory fabrication like the black Madonnas, which are exported to the Congo. St Goban Finn had many cult centres, which means that the same process of assimilation was happening all over Ireland. His main cult centre seems to have been at Tech da Goba, 'the house of the two smiths', now Seagoe on the Bann, in whose erection he was helped by a band of angels. He is also called St Mo Goppoc Artifex, the grandson of Lama, and another cult centre of his was at Killamery (Cell Lamraighe) in Kilkenny. The Lamhraige were descended from Lama, but others say their founder's hands (*lamh* is a hand) had been blessed by a saint who varies with the location of the tribe. I do not know anyone whose hands were blessed and who was not connected with the Lamraige. So the ignorant artisan Goban, whose hands were blessed by St Mo-Aedoc, converges on the great St Goban Finn Moccu Lama, who had a thousand monks and conversed with angels.

There was in Munster a lay Gobban Finn also, who reveals very clearly his composite tribal ancestry, for the genealogists link him both with the Ui Gubain and the Ui Finnia [CGH 227]. There were other hybrid Gobans too. Moelgubi lived among the Ui Mael, as did the Ui Gobbain tribe. *Moel* means bald and *gubi* means wailing, so the unfortunate Bald-wailing, being hostile to St Kevin of Glendalough, was crucified. I should compare him to Lamgabaid (Hand-wailing), whose hand was cut off by Cet. He would be ancestor to the Lamraige and Gabraige. He is also called Oenlam Gabaid, One-Hand-Wail, This makes him ancestor of the En folk also.

There is an Oengoba (or One-smith), whose son Aengus, the martyrologist, was a monk at Clonenagh like St Goban and St Goban Finn. Another Oengoba came from Iruath or Norway and in Norway too we find Rig Goban or the Royal Smith but Rig, I think, like Trig, meant Thracian [LG IV 137]. This Rig Goban had a dog, *cu*, who turned into a sheep Caera by night and converted water into wine, *fin*, when poured on its skin. *Rig, cu, caera* and *fin* are familiar tribal puns. If these Goban names had a meaning in the Irish language it would be very strange to find them attached to Norse heroes, but if they too derived from continental tribes, the oddity disappears. (I should mention in postscript, Snedgoba [CGH 354], an obviously composite ancestor, derives from the same Carlow-Wicklow region as the Clann Sneiden [CGH 351] and the Ui Gobbain [CGH 356].)

16. THE CARPIC SAINTS

A Greek Epilogue

Why did the Irish keep saying that they were related to the Greeks? There should be, and sometimes there has been, a continental epilogue to all my chapters, for I am as obsessed as the Irish poets were with speculations about our distant origins. But I am more self-conscious than they are and can only hint at possible equations and affinities, which they boldly asserted.

For example, they said that Cicol Grigairglun, an ancestral invader, came from the Caucasus with his warrior mother, Lot Luath, who had lips between her breasts and four eyes in the middle of her back. They brought to Ireland an army of men with one leg and one hand and fought a battle at a place called Mag Itha. We read elsewhere that the tribes of Ithier of the Caucasus all had lips between their breasts and four eyes in the middle of their backs.

Professor Macalister says, as usual, that we must dismiss all this as 'a weird monument of human folly'. But, if it is folly, it is well coordinated; for example, there were in fact three places called Mag Itha, two of them in Wexford and in Donegal, associated with an invader called Ith, and the odd names and strange anatomy could all derive from tribal combinations, colourfully interpreted. Did not Cridenbel, the satirist, have his heart in his mouth? And was Cridenbel a real name? It must be compared to Cruinbel, Round-mouth, who was the ancestor of the Ui Cruinbel of Co. Louth. Cicol Grigairglun occurs several times. He was the father of the lady Da Caech, who gave her name to Loch Da Caech or Waterford harbour.

Separately, Cicol, Grig and Glun occur as the names of fabulous invaders and heroes. Eber Glunfinn, who had white marks on his knee, and his cousin Eber Glundub, a very travelled pair, also derived from this region on the borders of Europe and Asia, so Cicol Grigairglun with his 'clapper-knee' would be a fit associate for the White Knees and Black Knees of the neighbourhood. I have suggested elsewhere that the Knee folk were the Geloni from whom the Irish claim to be descended. Their ancestor Gelon was also called Gleon; and Glun, also called Galu, was an ancient invader of Ireland.

As for the one-legged (*aen-cos*) and one-handed (*aen-lam*) people, Aen Lam, anyway, figures in Irish legend several times as a wounded hero. There were plenty of Aen folk and En folk in Ireland. What about the Caucasus? I cannot disregard the Aenianes, a tribe who lived to the north of Colchis. They also were a fit subject for puns, since Strabo says they had many bronze vessels, but did not that story originate in the fact that Aeneus means bronze?

But why had Cicol a clapper (*grigair*) knee? Were there Grig folk in the Caucasus too? I had better confine myself to showing that heroes and heroines behaved with an odd similarity at the opposite ends of Europe, and that the clues are there, if we had the courage and the knowledge to interpret them. I have told how Grig and Ciric gave their names to Mag Circin. Well, Circe, the enchantress, behaved like that in the Caucasus. She gave her name to the Circaean plain at Colchis, before she set out on her immense travels (see Apollonius, *Rhodius*, Vol. III, p.200). No Greek scholar has ever hinted to me that Circe was the ancestress of a wandering tribe. Yet surely this is obvious. Her brother, Aeetes, himself plainly tribal, was king of Aea in Colchis and north of Colchis along the Black Sea coast the first tribe were the Cercitae. The Sarmatians used Dioscurias, in the territory of the Cercitae, as their port, and Circe, before she started on her other adventures, was wedded to the Sarmatian king. Like all ancestresses, she married and gave birth wherever she paused. In Latium, she became the mother of Latinus and left her name on Monte Cerceo, and the town of Cercei and Ulysses seems to have found her at Circe's Island off Istria at the north of the Adriatic (see Cicero, *De Natura Deorum*, Vol. III, p.48). This island is supposed to have been Cherso, formerly Krepsa and Krexa, but the neighbouring island, Curicta, now Krk, would have suited her as well. For surely she was brought there as an ancestress by the Cercitae themselves. The Colchi are said to have landed there in pursuit of Jason and Medea and to have founded the city of Pola, now Pula, in Istria. If the Colchi went, the Cercitae, their closest neighbours, surely went too. And did Circe go with them to the river Krka, once the Corcora, which flows into the Sava, which some say was the Carpis? Or to the Kerka river, which flows out at Zara in Dalmatia? Nobody said she did. But we do know that she went to Athens, because her tomb near Salamis was well known. Did she go there to be somebody's mother or aunt? Was she displaced by Cercyon, the terrible wrestler of Eleusis, or by Cecrops, king of Athens, who is also Cercops? Strabo says that the Cecropides were barbarians and probably Thracians, so Circe would have fitted in with them.

But it is her journey along the Adriatic coast that interests me; I feel sure that that colourless nymph, Cercyra, daughter of Asopus, who gave her name to Corcyra, now Corfu, and also the nymph, Cerceis, were only deputizing for Circe. Genealogically, certainly, they were all related, for Circe and Cercyra were first cousins and Cerceis was aunt to both of them.

Inland from Corcyra, to the east of Dodona, lay Cerceitus mountain. Now, like the other Cerceitus mountain in Samos, it must have taken its name from the Cercitae, Circe's tribe. Had Circe some more distinguished descendants round Dodona? It was there, between Corcyra and Cerceitus, that the Romans first encountered the Graeci, a small undistinguished tribe, who perhaps still counted themselves Thracian or Illyrian and were not yet Hellenes. It is possible that the Irish were not being inaccurate or immodest in claiming so confidently to have come from Greece and to be kinsmen of the Greeks. There were several routes by which the memory might have travelled, for the Irish had different traditions about it.

There was firstly the Celtic route, which does not properly belong to this Carpic chapter. Celtos was brother of Gelonus, the ancestor of the Geloni of Scythia and also of the Fir Galeoin, an early tribe of Connacht. Celtos' other brother, according to Greek legend, was Scythes, ancestor of the Scythians, and the Geloni were said to be a half-Greek people living in Scythia, worshipping the Greek gods and observing Greek customs [HDT IV 108].

Then there was a pre-Celtic route. Grecus, ancestor of the Greeks, had driven the ancestors of the Fir Bolgs to Mayo and seems to have merged himself in Grec, the ancestor of the Grecraige of Connacht. The Greeks, to whom he was ancestor, might have been pre-Hellenic Graeci from the Adriatic coast.

There was a third slightly different route. A certain ancestor, Nemed, had lived among the Greeks of Scythia, i.e. the Geloni, but gone westward with thirty-four ships and travelled from the Caspian Sea to Ireland. This voyage might have the same pictorial truth that can be read in the voyage of the Argonauts. For the Argonauts too, some say, in quest of Circe's Island had dragged the *Argo* from the Caspian Sea to the Baltic. They had gone by an impossible route, using the Don, the Danube and the Elbe. Finally they had travelled round the coast of Ireland and through the Pillars of Hercules. It has never become quite clear where Circe's island was, though they reached it eventually. And why should it be clear? Circe, ex-queen of Sarmatians and Latins, was a Scytho-Greco-Romano-Caucasian ancestress and left her traces almost everywhere. Had she something to do with the Circe river in Donegal, now Stranakirk, and all those hens, *cearc*, to whom I have referred? By the time recorded history began, all the ancestors and ancestresses of Europe were related to each other. It was the task of the poet, the historian, the genealogist, to present this complex web of kinship in a contemporary form. He must make it arresting, encouraging, entertaining. He must try to make an intelligible pattern out of what must often have seemed mere chaos. The Irish and the Greeks had learnt from their common ancestors to do this task in a very similar way.

TABLE 9: THE CARP FOLK AND THEIR VARIANTS

	Gurg	Gub		Cuirp	Cuirb	Cruib	Crum	
	Cuirc	Cub		Cupr		Crub		
		Cup						
Cerc	Gerg				Cerb	Creb	Crem	
Gert	Greg	Ceb			Cebr			
Cerd	Creg	Keb						
Cred	Crec(h)				Cairb			
Gart		Gab(l)	Garb(h)		Carb	Crab(h)	Cram	
			CARP					
Grad	Garg	Cap	Gabr		Cabr	Craeb(h)		
Garad		Gam(h)			Capr			Cnam(h)
			Goba					
Gort	Gorg	Gob(l)	Gorb	Corp	Corb		Crom	
Groth	Corc	Cob(h)	Gobr		Coirp			
		Cop						
Crit(h)	Grig	Cip	Gibr		Cirb		Crim	
Cruith	Cric(h)	Cyb						

This chart is derived from the equations of personal and place names. It is based entirely on actual, not on assumed philological identifications. For example, Loch Corrib is called Orb-Sen as well as Corb-Es. Gulban is also called Bulbar. In most cases there are a number of instances of this identification. The weakest links are those with the Gorg, Greg and Gort groups in the first two left columns. I attach them to this group largely on the strength of geographical distribution.

Chapter 17

The Sons of Mil

St Maelcu and the Bald Folk

Odd as this may be, the Irish seem to have believed that the most exalted of their ancestors, the Milesians, were actually akin to those Milesians who founded Miletus in Caria and Crete. The Irish Mil or Miled, son of Bregon, had, like Miletus, son of Apollo, gone from Crete to 'Carenia in Asia Minor'. Mil had gone to Iberia, where he had begotten the Iberian ancestor, Eber. As son of Bregon, and husband of Scota, he also symbolized the kinship of Brigantes and Scythians. On their way to Ireland the Sons of Mil had travelled through Scythia and past Brigantia, now Braganza, in Spain, which Bregon had built.

Though the Sons of Mil were said to have landed in Kerry, that was perhaps because an ancient tribe, the Sil Mogad mic Miled, was established there. They must also have been strongly connected with the estuary at Waterford for the Barrow, the Suir and the Nore meet at Miledach, and Miledan was a comrade-in-arms of Finn and Molling at St Mullins, a short way up the Barrow.

The Bald Folk

But this chapter is principally about the thousands of tribes, saints, heroes and features of the landscape. *Mael* means bald or 'the tonsured disciple of', but in nine cases out of ten, the bald or tonsured meaning depends on a fantastic anecdote. Muirenn Mael, the queen of Ireland, sat in the royal stand at the famous Taillten Games, concealing under a golden crown her terrible secret, that she was bald. Beside her sat the king's second wife, Mugain. Mugain was barren and jealous of her fruitful rival, so she bribed a female satirist to pull the crown from Muirenn's hairless pate and shame her before her subjects. But the plot failed for, at the first tug, the queen offered a swift prayer to God and to St Ciaran, and at the very moment that the crown fell from her head a mass of golden hair rippled down to her shoulders.

I do not think that Muirenn Mael or any of the other 'bald folk' was really bald. What was she then? I suggest that like Muirne Muincaem (Pretty Neck) and a couple of heroes called Morna, she was co-ancestor of the Clann Morna or Morini of Co. Clare, and also a part-time ancestress of the numerous Mael tribes of the west of Ireland. The fact that *mael* is a tribal word, not meaning bald or dedicated, is proved by the strange concentration of Mael tribes in three districts in Ireland. Firstly there is Conmaicne Rein of Leitrim and Longford, secondly there is Mayo and Sligo, and thirdly the Ui Mail region of Wicklow, and there is evidence too from Wexford and the midlands.

Leitrim and Longford

For example, there were fully twenty Mael tribes in Leitrim and Longford, but most of them, like the Ui Maelmiadaig and the Ui Maelmochergi, had no corresponding saint to which the tribe could be dedicated. The Ui Maelciarain, or the tonsured disciples of St Ciaran, are the exception; but, as I have said earlier, St Ciaran Mael behaved like a tribal ancestor and gave the show away by being bald. The two principal saints of this region, St Mael or Mel and his brother, St Maelcu of Ardagh (6 Feb.), were very famous men. They were St Patrick's nephews, sons of his sister Darerca (22 Mar.) and had blessed Bridget while still in her mother's womb. Later Mel had veiled her. But he had been 'so intoxicated with the grace of God' that by mistake he had consecrated her a bishop. 'This virgin,' he then said, 'alone in Ireland will have episcopal ordination.'

One hundred and fifty years ago Ledwich said that Mel was a fictitious character of doubtful sex, to be identified with St Canice's mother, Mella. But since then the climate has changed. The large cathedral of St Mel at Longford was completed in 1891 and Ledwich had been denounced by Canon O'Hanlon as 'a thoroughly ignorant and presumptuous antiquarian'. In his oddly druidic way, Canon O'Hanlon, like the author of the *Tripartite* who calls St Mel *homo vere melleus*, a truly honeyed man, deduces his character from his name. 'It was typical,' he says, 'of those honeyed stores of Divine Wisdom and saintly qualities, which had been hived in his heart.'

Yet Ledwich was, as often, on the right lines. St Maul's parish in Kilkenny is, on ancient evidence, attributed both to St Canice's mother, Mella, and to St Patrick's nephew, Mel. This Mella is hard to distinguish from St Mella of Doire Mell on Loch Meilgi, now Melvin, in Leitrim, who was the mother of another St Canice and shared Doire Mell with a male saint called St Mell, and a pagan hero, Mel. I cannot doubt that St Maelcu of Co. Longford was a variant of Milcu, St Patrick's employer in Co. Antrim.

Who was his brother Mel? Dr MacNamee, the bishop of Ardagh, the diocese of which St Mel and St Maelcu were the first bishops, thinks that they were both the same. He is otherwise unable to explain why two brothers of roughly similar name should be made simultaneous bishops of the same see and should die on the same day of the year, 6 February. 'This,' he writes, 'is surely a combination of coincidences to tax the credulity of the most determined traditionalists.'

Maelcu means Bald-dog, or, as an early commentator wrote, *Molossus sine auribus*, i.e. dog without any ears. His name can be compared with the townland of Clashmilcon in Kerry, where a story is told about a spectral crop-eared hound. Dr MacNamee's translation, Comely-cleric, which I have referred to already, is not possible. A king of the Picts, Maelcu, grandson of Milcu, was certainly no comely cleric, but so wicked that St Columba cursed him to death. If his name was simply tribal and neither Irish nor Pictish, we have once more bypassed the problem of the language of the Picts.

The celebrated Milcu, to whom Patrick was enslaved on Slemish Mountain in Co. Antrim, had close and curious links with this Mael region of Longford-Leitrim. When Milcu heard, many years after Patrick had left him, that the apostle, now a free man and bishop, was returning to visit him, he destroyed himself on a pyre, leaving behind him four children, who all became saints. St Patrick placed three of them in Co. Longford near his nephews, Mel and Maelcu; the son, Guasacht (24 Jan.) was made a bishop in Granard and two daughters, both of them called Emer, were settled nearby at Clonbrony, which means the meadow of Bronach. The third daughter was Bronach and it has been thought odd that her two sisters should go and live in a meadow called after her, while she herself never went to Longford, but instead became the mother of two saints in Co. Down. Pruning these people of absurdities, Bury, in his life of St Patrick, does not reject them as impossible, and certainly, in the various tales about them, one has to acknowledge an inner consistency, which suggests that they cannot have been fabricated out of nothing. Yet the reality behind them must have been not individual but tribal. For example two out of three Bronach virgin saints operated in Co. Down, not far off from a Bronach tribe in Louth, and it is reasonable to conjecture that a branch of the same people also existed at one time near Clonbrony in Longford.

Milchu's family was no doubt transferred so easily to the north midlands, because of some affinity between the tribes, whose shadowy ancestors were venerated in Antrim and in Longford. When St Maelcu became a saint, the tribal ancestors, whom he had once fathered in his pagan days, were perhaps transferred to Milcu of Antrim. Otherwise it is strange indeed to find the children of the wicked chieftain of Antrim all grouped as nuns and priests around his remote and saintly namesake, whose uncle he had held in slavery.

Was there a Milcu tribe? The only one that I can find, the Muinter Milchon, was not in Longford but near enough. It was across the Shannon in the adjoining county of Roscommon. Farther down the Shannon on the east bank is Kilmeelchon (Cell mic Miolchon) or the church of the son of Milcu. If there are other Milcus or Maelcus in Ireland, heroes, tribes, saints, I have not been able to trace them.

Sligo and Mayo

In Sligo and in Mayo, the land of the Ui Maille or O'Malleys, we get the same tribal pattern. There was a tribe there in Tirawley, the Ui Mael Ruad, or the Bald Red, and in the barony of Tireragh, Co. Sligo, we meet both Mael and Ruad names in profusion. There is a hill there, the Red Hill, which had four Irish names: Mullach Ruad, Telach na Maele, Telach na Molt and Cnoc na Druad. *Molt* means a wether or castrated ram and it was called the Hill of the Wether and the Hill of Ruad, because a queen called Ruad, heavy with the hero Ailill Molt, had a pregnant woman's craving for this delicacy, which was later to become her son's nickname. Another story relates how it acquired its third name, Cnoc na Maili, when a hero, Mael Flidhisi, rested on it. There is of course another story to explain the druids. But Molt was a tribal word, because in the Mael district of Conmaicne Rein, we find the tribe Ui Muilt, descended from Molt. There was also the Moltraige tribe, oddly said to be descended from Moltraige. Totemism will not help here, for what tribe could choose a castrated ram for a totem, and could any real Irish hero be given such a name?

Is it not more probable that Molt is the same as Miled and Mael the same as

17. THE SONS OF MIL

Mil? That is to say we can sort the four names for Red Hill into two groups; it was called Mael and Molt because of the Milesians and Ruad and Druad, as I will argue later, because of the Thracians. The neighbouring tribe, the Maelruad, now Mulroys, owes its name to their amalgamation.

Yet the belief that *mael* always meant bald or tonsured is very ancient and persistent. Several clerics and druids were called Mael and also jesters. Were jesters tonsured too? One druid, Mael, had a god called Milthous, and three jesters of the king of Ireland were called Mael, Milith and Admilithi. As for clerics, in the same Sligo barony (Tireragh) as Cnoc na Maili (Red Hill), four wicked clerics, called the Four Maels, were deservedly hanged. They lived the other side of the Moy at Ard na Mael, 'the height of the tonsured', and were treacherous disciples of their first cousin, St Cellach of Killala, the great grandson of Ailill Molt. Their names were Maelcroin, Maeldalua, Maelsenaigh and the son of Maelibair, and I assume they were the ancestors of local tribes that had disappeared and could safely, therefore, be discredited. King Guaire of Kiltartan had bribed them to kill St Cellach, offering them four chosen spinsters 'with their complement of horses and kine' and also the whole barony of Tirawley in Mayo. All this time St Cellach was reading the psalms on an island on Loch Conn. He had been fasting for Lent and, when the boatload of clerics arrived, he was so feeble he could not run away from them. Also he thought that running away might be contrary to God's plan for him. Yet he managed to avert the first plunge of their four swords by holding his psalter against his bosom. The four Maels then shut him up in a hollow oak at Drum mic Dair (the ridge of the sons of oak) and killed him. They then became lords of all Tirawley and lived in a fort with four doors, a door for each Mael. But vengeance was at hand. St Cellach had a brother, who was called Cu Congeilt, because he slew a terrible monster called Congeilt that lived between Loch Conn and Loch Cullen. If you read my chapters on the Cunesioi and the Geloni you will see that this was a suitable place for it to live. There was a tribe too, the Ui Cucongeilt in the west. Cu Congeilt, disguised as a swineherd, insinuated himself into the fort of the Maels and had them hanged at Ard na Riag or Height of the Hanging, in Tireragh. Off the Mayo coast is Inis da Mael, now Inisdaweel, and south of Ard na Riag on the Moy is Rath Mael. The first is said to be 'the island of the two hornless (cows)'.

Yes, emphatically, a Mael folk once lived in Ireland and tonsures and cropped ears, baldness and honey, St Mel and St Maelcu, are merely devices (and there were hundreds of others) by which the ancients tried to explain the fading traces of this forgotten race and its hybrids. Finally, did *mael* mean bald? Many anecdotes suggest it did. Applied to an animal it is said to mean hornless. Applied to a holy man, it is supposed to mean 'the tonsured disciple of' someone. There are difficulties about all these interpretations and stories to justify them. And here to conclude are three pious anecdotes that show clearly in terms of the Mael folk how the ancients wrote history. One is from Wicklow, one from Wexford and one from Westmeath.

Wicklow

The first story comes from a Latin life of St Kevin of Glendalough in Wicklow where there are some thirty Mael tribes. The Glen of Imaal (Ui Mael) bears their name. A soldier, *miles*, by name Ruadanus (in Latin) or Ruadan, had very beautiful hair (red, *ruad*, no doubt) that he loved and cherished, 'thinking nothing of his soul'. This greatly distressed St Kevin, so he blessed some water and sent it to Ruadan Miles, ordering him to anoint his hair with it, *'quasi pro benedictione'*. The soldier gladly did his bidding and, when his hair all fell out, he meekly recognized that it was a punishment for his sins. He promised to mend his ways. Kevin blessed his head and new hair (this time of only moderate quality) grew on it. Now this is the kind of story that one writes to explain a word; it is not the kind of story that later monks wrote to commend virtue. It is based on two puns, Latin and Irish, for all this happened in the territory of the Ui Mail or *'nepotes Moel'* who might be called 'the bald people'. It seems to me also that Miles Ruadanus is a Latin pun on the name Maelruan. There was a tribe, the Muinter Maelruain or Maelruadain, farther north in Co. Wicklow. Their name might be supposed to mean 'bald red', and they had a famous saint, St Maelruain, who is as credible as the others and no more so [VSH I 254].

Wexford

The second story comes from the life of St Maedoc of Ferns in Wexford. There was a wicked king of Leinster, who gave a dun, hornless (ox), *mael odhar*, to a leper monk of St Maedoc. Camping on the banks of the Slaney, the king had a hideous vision in which he was carried to hell and a monster advanced to devour him with a gaping mouth. All at once a cleric came and thrust a dun hornless ox, just like the one the king had given the leper, into the monster's mouth to close it. Then St Maedoc, for he it was, struck the monster on the head with his crozier and, as a reward for his kindness to the leper, the king was liberated from hell. Neither C.H. Plummer, the editor of the life, nor anyone else has observed that the Sil Maelodhar, 'the dun hornless tribe', lived along the banks of the Slaney, giving their name to the present barony of Shelmalier [LIS II 210].

Westmeath

The significance of the third anecdote is equally plain. It comes from the life of St Colman mac Luachain (see *Life of Colman, Son of Luachain*, Kuno Meyer (ed.) 1911, p.85). The saint had brought many loads of soil from the tombs of the apostles in Rome to his church at Lann in Co. Westmeath. His mother, Lassar, came in the night and stole a bagful for her own church. Colman detected this and scolded her, and in an involved simile compared the monks of her church to dun hornless cattle. Now, from other sources we find that the Ui Maeluidhir lived at Cell Laisre, the church of Lassar [H 196]. It was natural that they should be compared to dun, hornless cattle, for that would be a fanciful interpretation of their name. In all these anecdotes the monks plainly did not take seriously the view that *mael* in a proper name meant 'the servant of'.

I have elsewhere written of Maine Mal, a typical composite ancestor from whom both the Ui Maine and the Ui Mail were descended. Mal is thought to mean prince, and Mall, another common aftername, is thought to mean slow. Mael, Mil, Mal, Mall, Meld, Molt are all akin and there may be a hundred other disguises under which the descendants of the Sons of Mil are concealed. We cannot overestimate our human capacity to adapt and distort. St Maelruba of Applecross in Scotland had forty-seven variants to his name, every vowel and every consonant of which is changeable, for example Malrou, Melriga, Milruby, Mulroy.

I would like to have written of Meld, an element in Irish proper names that is thought to mean thunder, also the Meldi of Gaul, who left their name at Meaux. I could write of St Meldan, the Irish-Gaulish saint and many other motivated fantasies. But there is too much material. If the vast hagiographical and mythological corpus of Celtic literature were examined in the light of such evidence, the pattern of the primitive tribes, their geographical distribution and remote affinities would gradually become clear. To do this, the first step has not yet been taken. Who were the Sons of Mil? I know no more than I have said, but I hope I have proved that they were a real people and not a fantasy of Irish historians.

CHAPTER 18

The Tigurini

This chapter is about the Tigern saints; Kentigern, Faeltigern, Lugtigern, Caeltigern and many more. It is also about the Tigern ancestors. *Tigern* in Irish proper names is said to mean prince. Who were they? Considering the known tribes of Europe and eliminating the more improbable, I have arrived at the Tigurini, the most enterprising of the Helvetians, who gave their name to a fourth part of the canton of Zurich, Tigurinus Pagus, and to Tegernsee in Bavaria. They had invaded Provence in 107 BC, had defeated a Roman army at Agen in the country of the Nitiobriges and appear to have escaped to the Atlantic coast down the Garonne. What happened to them then no one knows. Yet these invaders can only have been a relatively small group of the Tigurini, for a few years later we find the tribe battling with Marius in north Italy and just escaping complete annihilation. Fifty years later Caesar met them trying to cross the Saône, with a great deal of baggage. Most of them were slaughtered, but some escaped into the woods. We cannot infer, of course, that the Tigurini, who were driven to the Atlantic coast, drifted across the sea to the British Isles. But of these three vigorous enterprises we should have known nothing had they not been in contact with the Romans.

Ireland had been populated centuries before this; many tribes must have travelled, unnoticed by historians, across Europe to the islands. No doubt they ought to have left behind them coins, pots and bits of horse harness and beads, but perhaps they were careful or propertyless, or such property as they lost was borrowed or simply like everybody else's. I cannot press very hard the claim of the Tigurini to be relatively late settlers in Ireland or the claim of the proto-Tigurini to be early ones but, if we are agreed that the Tigern folk drew their name not from their princeliness but from an ancient tribe, what else can that tribe have been?

St Kentigern and the Princes

St Kentigern (13 Jan.) is one of the most famous Scottish saints. He is the evangelist of Strathclyde and like St Munghu was the founder of the church in Glasgow; he is said to have founded other churches in Lothian, where he was born, and to have converted the Picts of Galloway to Christianity. He died in AD 612 and the first life of him that we know was written five centuries later. Kenneth Jackson has written a close and careful analysis of the sources of our knowledge about Kentigern and the principal episodes in his life. His conclusion is that the saint's various biographers know more or less nothing about him or of the ecclesiastical history of Scotland in the time he lived. All their information is fictitious. Yet Jackson considers, curiously, that he really lived and was founder of the church in Glasgow and missionary in Cumbria.

Kentigern's life is in fact more fabulous than most, and to almost every fable there is a counter fable. Some say he was immaculately conceived, others say his mother was raped by the king of Scotland who shared her bed disguised as a maiden. Mostly they agree that his mother was the daughter of the Pictish King Loth of Lothian, who hurled her off a cliff for sins she had never committed. Some say that he then launched her on the ocean in an oarless boat and all agree that St Servan found her on the shore at Culross with her baby and reared the little saint as his pupil. When his cruel schoolmates decapitated a robin, it is uncertain whether he revived it by putting back its head, or by making the sign of the cross over it.

Everything else is equally disputable. Did Lailoken, the Wild Man of the Woods, actually interrupt the saint's preaching in Glasgow with his prophecies or were they not uttered until Kentigern was actually dead? Did King Morken of Cumbria lose all his crops through the flooding of the Clyde and die of gout because he oppressed Kentigern? Did he kick him? Did Kentigern then escape, via Carlisle, where he made some converts, to St David's in Pembrokeshire? Was he then led north by a white boar to Deganwy Clwyd in Denbighshire and did he found there a monastery for his monk St Asaph? Did he strike blind the local king Maelcun who interfered with the building? Did he then return to Strathclyde and help the new king Rederech, who had been baptized in Ireland, to restore Christianity there? And did Rederech's son Cu-Santin become a St Constantine?

Really what it all amounts to is: was Kentigern a real person? I think he must stand or fall with the other Kentigerns, mostly female, who behaved as extravagantly as he did.

First, there is Caintigern of Roscarbery, Co. Cork, wife of Badamna. She was a holy woman who mingled tribal realities with lively fantasy in the accepted way. Her son, Dangal, saw her distributing milk to the poor in Tours in honour of St Martin at the very same moment that she was doing the same thing at St Martin's cave in Cork. Dangal proved this by stealing the lid of her milk can in Tours, and finding that it fitted her milk can in Roscarbery. Now the story is built round a real Ui Badamna tribe in west Cork [CGH 259] and a real Clann Donngal [CGH 290, 298], though in the pedigree Donngal is ten generations away from Badamna. There was also a real Martini tribe in Cork (see p. 102) [CGH 306, 377].

Then let us take St Kentigerna (7 Jan.), the Irish widow of a Scottish prince. She was the daughter of Cellach, the ancestor of the O'Kellys of Wicklow, and was culted on an island in Loch Lomond and with her brother, St Comgan, in Ross-shire. She was sister of St Conchinn (20 Aug.) and of the lady Muirenn and mother of St Faelan, a Scoto-Irish saint with cult centres in both islands, and of St Mundus or Mo Finnu and several other saints. Cellach's descent can be traced for twenty generations and if we reason, as we must, that each generation represents a tribe, it is highly instructive. As for the two sisters Conchenn and Muirenn, I have shown, while writing about the Cunesioi, that there is a sure link between the Conchenn saints and the Ui Conchinn tribe of Kerry, Ulster and Edinburgh. Writing of the Morini I tell of the various Muirenns of Wicklow and I suggest their connection with the Ui Muirenaig who lived there.

A third Caintigern was married to Fiachna, son of Baedan Mac Cairill – whom W.J. Watson strangely accepts as a historic character – who died in AD 581 on Arran Island. He was the father of St MoLaisse of Leighlin, Co. Carlow, and of Arran, and his son Baedan was said to be king of Ireland and Scotland. Though they all behaved in a fairly fabulous way, it is Caintigern's son, Mongan, who drags the whole family after him beyond recall to fairyland. Like several others who had the syllable *mon* or trick in their names, he had the gift of changing his shape, and, as well as various animals, he became *monach*, a monk. He fought many sea battles and he did this, it is said, because his name Mong Find or White Hair suggested the waves of the sea. He was also thought to be a reincarnation of Manannan, god of the sea, and of Finn. He is to me the Menapo-Venetic ancestor, and by his marriage to the beautiful Findtigern, who is also called Breotigern (Breactigern), he involves himself further in one of those Tigern tangles, which can only be unravelled by recognizing that the Tigurini came to Ireland from Gaul and mingled with Veneti, Briges and Cunesioi and many others.

There were one or two male Caintigerns as well, a Welsh one, St Cyndeyrn (Kentigern) of Carmarthen, is culted the same day (25 Jul.) as St Mordeyrn (Mortigern) of Denbighshire. If Kentigern of Glasgow really went to Denbigh too, as did St Tigernach of Clones, it was because there was a Tigern family party there. Dr Jackson tries hard to make Kentigern plausible. Treating of his name, which some said meant Head Prince or *Capitalis Dominus* and others said was Cunotigernos or Dog-prince (the old confusion between dog and head to which I refer in my chapter on the Cunesioi), he explains the second title in the usual way. *Cu* meant hero, because of the noble qualities of the dog. But the female St Kentigerna could hardly be a hero and no one tried to gloss over the dogginess of her sister, St Conchinn or Doghead, because they gave her the same feast day (28 Apr.) as St Christopher Conchend of Cynoscephali which is Greek for Dog-head.

I do not see how it is possible to disentangle the truth from this maze of tribal puns and tribal fictions in which the male Kentigern is just as much involved as his female counterparts, if we consider that any of these people were real. If on the other hand we treat them as algebraic symbols, simple and multiple, to be used in the demonstration of the relationship of tribes, they are no longer nonsensical. The fantastic stories are no longer silly; they are a legitimate ornament like the grotesque capitals by which a serious text is illuminated.

A recognition of the dominant part played by fabricated tribal ancestors could clear up many other mysteries in the life of Kentigern. Surely the wild man, Lailoken, must have been Lulaig, ancestor of the Clann Lulaig of Morayshire. This tribe must have been known in Ireland, where there was an ancestor Lulaig and an Ui Lulaich or Liliuc tribe in Roscommon and Cork. They might have been akin to the Leleges, who wandered round the eastern Mediterranean after their ancestor, Lelex.

I would treat in the same way Kentigern's pet name, Munghu, and his cult centre, Glaschu or Glasgow. It is true, as Jackson suggests, that Munghu may have been adjusted by the Cumbrians or the Welsh to mean 'my dear' and Glaschu, which Baring-Gould takes to mean 'green dog', may have been adjusted to sound like 'dear community'. And there are other alternatives which the learned have suggested. But in fact there were Mong tribes, Glas tribes and Cu tribes in plenty. These would only become irrelevant if convincing proof were offered that St Kentigern himself ever lived. Can this be done?

St Luchtigern and the Mice

The Lugtigern-Luchtigern saints and heroes – and there are quite a few of them – would be on my reckoning Liguro-Tigurinic. St Ibar baptized Lugtigern, one of the twelve sons of Barr, ancestor of the Sil Barr, at Morett in Co. Leix; eighteen miles to the south was a monster, Luchtigern, the Mouse-prince (for *luch* is mouse), who was slain by Aithbel, mother of Hercules, in the cave of Derg Ferna, Dunmore, Co. Kilkenny. We may compare a twofold mouse story from the life of St Comgall of Bangor [VSH II 10]. A wicked landlord, Croidh, had a mother called Luch (*quod sonat Latine mus*) or Mouse. He refused some grain to St Comgall's monks, so it was all eaten by mice.

The Luchtigern saints are away to the west in Clare and Galway but so fabulous that no one could object to my seeing them as tribal fictions. St Luchtigern (28 Mar.) was brother of St Ciaran of Clonmacnois, of three other male saints, two holy virgins and a holy widow. For a time he lived near Clonmacnois with his brothers, Ciaran and Odran. They were disturbed by some riotous folk who lived on an island in a lake, until, in answer to Ciaran's prayers, island and lake were moved far away. Finally Ciaran left the cell, Isel Ciarain, to his brothers, who had been affronted by the lavish way he had given their substance, including a chariot and a pair of horses, to beggars.

Another St Luchtigern (28 Apr.) was culted in Clare and befriended by St MacCreiche. Both saints had a mother called Brig. He accompanied St Mac-Creiche, then an old man of 167, on a cattle-driving expedition from Kerry to Roscommon. The cattle followed meekly after the saints, who in the daytime would carry the gospels round the herd. When night fell, St Mainchin carried St Luchtigern's staff and St MacCreiche's bell around them and the cattle would lie down from vespers until matins. Baring-Gould has identified this Luchtigern with St Louthiern (17 Oct.) whose relics were deposited in Brittany and translated to Paris in AD 965. He is also St Luchern of Kilcasey in Ossory [SH 316].

Is this just country folklore? I think it is, on the contrary, the gay adornment of a serious and scholarly text. Look at the pedigree of St Luchtigern's maternal grandfather Forannan [CGH 145] and you will see how ingeniously the saint is fitted on to the immense and spreading family tree of the tribes of south Ulster. He was possibly once there by rights, as an ancestor on a fruitful branch of the tree that was adroitly pruned off, and he was put back as a saint.

St Foirtchern

St Foirtchern (17 Feb.), son of Fedelmid, son of Loegaire, king of Ireland, AD 428–63, is, as I shall show, a Tigern saint and one of the most famous figures in the Patrick story. When St Patrick had landed at the mouth of the Boyne, he himself went on to see King Loegaire at Tara and left his nephew St Lomman (11 Oct.), son of his sister Darerca, with the ship. After the prescribed interval, Lomman went up the river to Trim, where lived Fedelmid, the king's son. As dawn broke, the young prince Foirtchern came down to the Boyne to bathe and there met St Lomman reciting the gospels. Mystified and fascinated, he straight away believed and was baptized in a nearby fountain. Foirtchern's mother and grandmother (Scothnoe or New-flower, wife of Loegaire) were Britons like Lomman, so there was an immediate mutual understanding and 'Straight away Fedelmid believed with all his family and he devoted to him and to holy Patrick his territory with his possessions and with all his substance and with all his race. All these he devoted to Patrick and Lomman and to Foirtchern, his son, unto the day of judgment.' Foirtchern became a priest and later for a short time was bishop of Trim.

While Fedelmid and his family played their part in this gentle idyll by the Boyne, appalling things were happening to his parents only a few miles away. At this, the first of Irish Easters, King Loegaire, his household and his druids were putting up the most passionate resistance to Patrick and his new faith. The new creed only prevailed after the two chief druids were magically destroyed, one by an ordeal by fire, the other by flying up into the air under Patrick's baleful glance and then dashing his brains out on a stone. Patrick intoned the psalm, 'Let God arise, let His enemies be scattered!' And immediately there was thick darkness, an earthquake and confusion, in which the heathen massacred each other. The king and queen and all their courtiers fled, while Patrick and his companions, transformed into deer, trotted away.

The interesting difficulty in this story is the usual one. Most of the Irish who took part in it, except the saints, were the ancestors of one-man tribes called after themselves. Loegaire's grandfather, Eochaid [CGH 131], had five sons, all of them eponymous ancestors of tribes. Much the same could be said of his father Niall [CGH 133], with his fourteen sons, and of Loegaire [CGH 165] himself with twelve, and of his brother Eogan, with ten [CGH 134]. Fedelmid devoted 'all his race' to Patrick. What can this race have been? Surely not his two sons Foirtchern and Fergus? That would have been a very meagre offering, seeing that Foirtchern was a celibate and had 'devoted' himself anyway and that Fergus, after begetting two bishops of Trim [Todd 154], seems to me to have retained the chieftainship of his race for himself. We know his descendants for eight generations [Todd 152, 260].

None of this makes sense unless we think of these men not as living individuals but as fabulous ancestors, each of whom represented an entire tribe, whose kinship with other tribes could be illustrated pictorially by a genealogical chart.

How does St Foirtchern fare? His name is said to correspond to the British Vortigern. There is an ogam inscription in Co. Cork, 'Maqui Vorrtigerni', and he has always been thought a historical character.

Yet, though he was the second bishop of Trim, his cult centres are in Carlow at Tullach Ui Fedelmeda, now Tullow, and Cell Foirtchern, now Killoughternan. But the Fedelmid from whom the Carlow tribe was descended was not his father, but one of the countless tribal children of Enna Ceinselach, the ancestor of the great Carlow family, the Kinsellas. If Foirtchern was a real person, why did he leave all the responsibilities that he had inherited from the Fedelmid of Meath and establish himself among the race of a different Fedelmid in Carlow? If he was not real, if he and Fedelmid were ancestors of related tribes, there would be nothing odd in their movements. They could wander about Ireland separately or together, establishing themselves in different family trees, collecting different brothers, uncles, nephews.

So, though I cannot find a Foirtchern tribe, I am convinced that one existed, compounded, as I will show, of two ancient races that were widely established and very powerful.

I have only found three Foirtchern ancestors in the genealogies, but they are all illuminating. The first of the Foirtcherns, the son of Maelruba, is more obviously than the others a secular variant of the saint himself, for he occurs in the pedigree of the Deisi of Meath, who lived close to Foirtchern's church of Trim. His father Maelruba was ancestor of the Ui Maelruba, his grandfather Dicuill was ancestor of the Ui Dicolla, and he had a son Segan, who looks to me like the ancestor of the Ui Segain, who also lived near Trim.

The second Foirtchern, who is of Oriel, shows a tribal and Tigern origin more clearly still. Oriel embraces Armagh and parts of surrounding counties. He was a great Tigern centre and his father was Tigernach, one of the twelve sons of MacCarthind, a great dynast of Oriel and pre-Christian counterpart of St MacCarthain of Clogher. Foirtchern's brother was Catchern (British Catigern), the ancestor of the Cenel Catcheirn [CGH 144]. He had another brother with the extraordinary name of Cairpre Dercc Oirce, which, we are told, means Cairpre of the Lap Dog's Eye, for *orc* is a lap dog and *derc* is eye. He also had a first cousin called Foirc. This curious name is sometimes written Orc (or Forggo). I think it is obvious that Foirtchern and Vortigern are combinations of Foirc and Tigern tribes and that the former tribe explains the lap dog and his eye. My Glossary will show that Orc, Forc and Derc are all variants of Traig.

The third Foirtchern occurs in a very similar genealogical pattern in mid-Munster, where the tribes and people with Tigern in their names seem to congregate as elsewhere without being in anyway more 'princely' than others. I give several instances of this later on. Here it is only relevant to say that we find once more as in Oriel a Foirtchern or rather Fuirtgern, son of another Tigernach [CGH 398]. We find an Ui Forcc tribe, descended from Foirc, and three or four composite Tigern tribes. All this conforms too closely to the pattern to be fortuitous. It is explicable only if we think of Foirc tribes and Tigern tribes associating in mid-Munster and Oriel, in Carlow and the Boyne valley.

Who were the Forc tribes? This is not the right place to discuss them but it is plain that they were no small local group. Forc, son of Conall Cearnach, the Scoto-Irish hero, was ancestor of the Tuath Forc, which, according to Skene, gave its name to the river Forth. Forc, Orc, Porc, or Proc, the king of Orkney, who surely derived his name from the same tribe, was grandfather of St Servan, who looked after Kentigern in Fife. If the genealogies are closely studied, I believe that most would come to the same conclusion as I do, that the Forc-Orc tribe was a local manifestation of the great Erc tribe of Scotland and Ireland. In my Glossary I place them among the Thracians so that Foirtchern would be the Thraco-Tigurinic ancestor.

The Saintly Sons of Vortigern

What about St Foirtchern's British counterpart Vortigern? Does his historicity depend on Bede and Nennius and Geoffrey of Monmouth or are there other sources of truth? Is he more authentic than his great-grandfather Glou of Gloucester or his three holy Tigern sons, St Edeyrn, St Aerdeyrn and St Elldeyrn (1 Feb.) (Teyrn-Deyrn is the British form of Tigern), or St Faustus, the child he bore to his daughter? Vortigern may for all I know be a genealogical fabrication but men must have names and sooner or later real people will wear, more or less at random, the titles that were coined very purposefully for imaginary ones. Even if Vortigern was a real person that does not make it less probable that his sons were tribal fictions. Edeyrn (6 Jan.), for example, who comes closest to Eotigern or Echtigern, had a monastery at Llanedeyrn in Monmouth and another at Llanedern in Leon, Brittany. And it has been suggested that he was the same as St Eternus (30 Aug.), bishop of Domnach Mor in Ireland.

Yet to me the most interesting of Vortigern's sons is not a saint but a warrior, Catigern, who slew Horsa, the Saxon invader at Episford. His name is said to mean Battle-prince, but it is also borne, as I have shown, by Catchern, the brother of Foirtchern and son of Tigernach of Oriel. This Catchern was the ancestor of the Cenel Catchern, and few would deny that he was fabulous. It is certainly odd to find two peculiar names worn by a father and son in Britain and by two brothers in Ireland. Yet if my tribal explanation is correct, it would not be odd but normal. If Vortigern-Foirtchern was the Thraco-Tigurinic ancestor, and Catigern-Catchern was the Geto-Tigurinic ancestor, what could be more natural than that they should everywhere be near relations?

Since I wrote this, I have read H.M. and N.K. Chadwick's essay on Vortigern. They link him, as I have done, with St Foirtchern of Trim. H.M. Chadwick even suggests that Foirtchern might have been Vortigern's grandson and namesake, since we are told that his mother's father was a British king. Into this circle of affinities they also bring Foirtgirn, a rich 'plebeian', who, in Adamnan's *Life of St Columba*, is associated with miraculous events on the west coast of Scotland or the east coast of Ireland, and thirdly St Gurthiern, a Welsh-Breton saint, who, as grandson of Glou, was Vortigern's cousin. His name is a variant of Vortigern and his title was Rex Anglorum. Mrs Chadwick notes some striking similarities in the adventures of these four, Vortigern, Foirtchern, Foirtgirn and Gurthiern. She says that 'it is unlikely that several men of that name should have passed into tradition' and she suggests that 'versions of the saga or sagas of Vortigern were current in Ireland, Scotland and Wales and it was thought worthwhile in all three countries to record them and interweave them with hagiographical narrative'.

This conclusion seems to me three-quarters correct. It converts Foirtchern, Foirtgirn and Gurthiern into fable and leaves Vortigern the only reality. But the Chadwicks' arguments for the historicity of Vortigern convince me that he too was fabulous and derived, like his territory Gwrtheyrnion between the Wye and the Severn, from a hybrid tribe, known in Wales, Scotland, Brittany and Ireland.

18. THE TIGURINI

For example, Mrs Chadwick argues that the name Vortigern 'is not Irish but British'. I do not think she would have said this if she had had the opportunity of studying the Irish genealogies. I have mentioned three other Irish Foirtcherns in Meath, Oriel and mid-Munster, all three of them deeply implicated in Irish tribal kinships. The first was a neighbour of St Foirtchern of Meath, the other two were sons of different Tigernachs and neighbours of the Tigern tribes of Ulster and of Munster. Did these three also derive 'from versions of the sagas of Vortigern'? Though I agree that the genealogies are all artificial, they are built up from local Forc and Tigern realities and are independent of, though analogous to, the Vortigern saga.

Vortigern, the wicked king who slept with his daughter, and had saintly counterparts, St Gurthiern and St Foirtchern, conforms absolutely to the type of tribal ancestor whom we have met so frequently in Ireland.

Some Miscellaneous Tigern Saints

If *tigern* really means prince, it is curious that many of the Tigern notabilities were, as I have already shown, women and not men.

About St Faeltigern I know nothing except that she was culted on 17 March. Caeltigern, on the other hand, has some Scottish interest, for Watson thinks that it was her son, St Mo-Liba, who is culted at Kilmalieu at Inverary. She was the sister of St Coemgen of Glendaloch (3 Jun.) and the mother of St Dagan of Ennereilly (13 Sept.), so her associations are, like Foirtchern's and Kentigerna's, with the Wicklow-Carlow region in which there were no less than three Tigern tribes.

I have mentioned Vortigern's three sons and some other British Tigern saints and heroes, all of them wearing the familiar tribal prefixes, but there are many others. Catigern, son of Vortigern, had a well-known brother, Vortimer or Gortimer, who was also called Goirmthigern. There is also Rhydeyrn and Mechdeyrn and Maeltiern and an obvious tendency in Wales and in Scotland to present Edeyrn as Eternus. All these people have a look to me of tribal compounds not impossible to decipher. But the way to disprove this is either to demonstrate that they were real people or to show some other reason for their fabrication.

I would be interested to see an attempt to prove that St Siltiern (25 Jun.) was real, or, if fabricated, had nothing to do with the ancestor of the Silures and Tigurini. He was the son of Geraint, King Arthur's friend, and married St Gwen, the aunt of St David and by her was father of that St Cybi, who went with his uncle St Cyngar to visit St Enda in Aran, but was driven out of it by an angry saint called Fintan. He was known as Selyf and Solomon and as such was king of Cornwall and also of Leon in Brittany, where he imposed Christianity forcibly upon the Bretons. The Bretons say he was father of St Constantine or CuSantin (24 Mar.) for whom we have already found a father in Strathclyde, and St Illtud, but at Lansallos his cult centre is disputed by the virgin saint, Ildierna, who looks like a female version of himself.

Obviously one must associate with him (that is to say if he was not a real person and, of course, he was not) Selyf or Solomon, a holy man of Glendaloch, who wrote St Kevin (Coemgen)'s life.

> 'I am Solomon, pupil of Coemgen,' he sang,
> 'I was in danger in the eastern land,
> when my tutor came to my help,
> 'tis a large part of the world that he searched.'

East of Wicklow could only be Britain and we are not told that Coemgen, as a saint, was ever there but as ancestors he and Siltiern may well have travelled Europe. What brought Sil-tiern to Wicklow? I do not know but it is worth remarking that there are more Sil-tribes in Wicklow and Wexford than anywhere else in Ireland, as befitted the corner of Ireland that lay opposite the Silures, and more Tigerntribes too.

I should also mention the Virgin Digern or Tigern, who was culted with her two sisters, Brig and Duthracht, at Cell Muni, which Hogan places in Kildare. But I believe it was really in Waterford for among the Dessi we find a tribe, the Ui Diugurnach, with ancestor Digernach [CGH 310], and several ancestors Brig and Durthacht, an obvious variant of Duthracht.

St Tigernach of Clones

The greatest of the Tigern saints was St Tigernach (4 Apr.) of Clones, Co. Monaghan. He was at school in Clones and then kidnapped by pirates and taken to Strathclyde in the diocese of St Kentigern. He studied under St Ninian at Rosnat in Galloway until more pirates took him to Brittany, and then he returned to Ireland and founded a church in Clones. It is obvious that St Tigernach's visit to Galloway, like his various visitations of Munster, Kildare, the west of Ireland, Wales, Cornwall and Brittany, were intended to associate him with remote branches of the Tigern flock.

18. THE TIGURINI

There were many Ech folk in Galloway and among them were the MacEchtigerns or Horse-princes near Rosnat; W.J. Watson thinks they must have bred horses, but we find Ui Echtigern all over Ireland, as Ahernes in Co. Clare and as McCagherons in Antrim. In mid-Munster Eochtigern and Eotigern are kinsmen of Guithigern and Fintigern.

In Wales, Baring-Gould has found St Tigernach as St Teyrnog of Llandyrnog at Clwyd in Denbighshire, where we have already found St Mordeyrn (25 Jul.) and, on a brief visit, St Kentigern himself. In Cornwall Tigernach was, according to Baring-Gould, culted as St Torney at Northill. As for his captivity in Brittany, the presence of the fabulous St Gurthiern indicates that Tigern saints were at home there.

The tribal character of St Tigernach is betrayed in every line that is written about him and they are many. As a compound Ech-Ach ancestor he was the grandson of King Eochaid of Clochar, who, in order to make him bishop of Clochar, turned out the previous bishop St MacCarthenn. St Tigernach and St MacCarthenn were both also called St Fer da Crich, or Man of two Borders. This, it was said, was because St Tigernach administered the churches of Clones and Clochar, and St MacCarthenn had Clochar and Dairinis in Co. Waterford. In fact the Ui Fer da Crich were a local tribe, whose ancestor Fer da Crich was brother of Tigernach (married Muiredach), ancestor of the Cenel Tigernach [CGH 180, 301]. As I explain elsewhere, *fer* did not mean man, nor *da* two, nor *crich* border. I could not work out connections I sensed among Fer da Crich (married Suibne) [CGH 183, 420], Fer da Crich (married Onchon) [CGH 93], Clann (Ui) Fir (Fer) da Crich and Tigernach Garb [CGH 140, 414].

In handling the Tigern saints one must be, as elsewhere, totalitarian. One reaches the truth by a series of disembodied equations and, if even one out of fifty ancestors and saints proved to be real, the whole system would collapse.

Most hagiologists still argue like Baring-Gould did over seventy years ago. He had a breezy scepticism that could easily dispose of everything that is recorded about the lives of the saints, but he could not bring himself to demolish the saints themselves. Out of what he took to be nonsense he manufactured an ingenious sort of sense. And that is still the habit of all hagiologists.

Watch him at work on the story of St Tigernach. When Tigernach was a boy, he breathed as he slept three alternating breaths, one white, one red, one yellow. When he was with St Ninian his supernatural radiance so much impressed the king of Britain that he made him share the bed of his two little sons.

But the shock of so much sanctity was too much for them and in the morning they were both found dead. St Ninian was consulted and he persuaded the little saint to sleep with the boys a second time. This time the shock revived the two princes, but one of them remained blind, the other bald. They both then went to study with St Ninian too. Of this story Baring-Gould remarks: 'This nonsense may be reduced to a simple matter. The children made such a racket in the nursery playing with pillows that the good natured king and queen packed them off to school.'

Baring-Gould tried in this way to reshape St Tigernach in the image of a Victorian clergyman, developing from a high-spirited public-school boy to a scrupulous, much-travelled missionary bishop. These hagiological methods are not yet dead.

I believe that the stories concern tribal associations and that St Tigernach did nothing for which there was not a good reason. If you look up *fionn*, white, *ruad*, red, *buidhe*, yellow, *caech*, blind, and *mael*, bald, in my Glossary you may get a clue as to why he behaved as he did.

I list below nineteen Tigern prefixes and it will be recognized that they are the same as those which in other chapters I show to be tribal. I suggest in my Glossary the tribal connotation and the pun meaning attached to them.

Breactigern or Breotigern	Faeltigern	Lugtigern
Caeltigern	Findtigern	Maeltigern
Caintigern	Foirctigern	Mochtigern
Cattigern	Guithtigern	Mugtigern
Echtigern	Goirmtigern	Sentigern
Eotigern	Luchtigern	Siltigern

There is also Tigern, bard son of Brig, and one or two other names where Tigern itself is a prefix. A closer study of these names could tell us much about the travels and settlements of the Tigurini in Ireland and Britain. For example a number of relations of Mugtigern, Echtigern, Findtigern and other Tigerns appear in O'Brien's *Corpus*: Mugtigern = Mochthigern = Muchtigern [CGH 209]; Ui Felmeda (Lagin) [CGH 353, 430]; Fintigern of Ui Findtigern ex Duithennach; Eothigern married Guithtigern ex Duithennach [CGH 308]; Echtigern *ab quo* Ui Echtigern [CGH 237]. Are the names Tiernmael, Iartiern, Sultiern, Juntiern, Gurtiern and Gonotigernus [HOL II 1555] also somehow related?

CHAPTER 19

Saints of the Daii

There must be several thousand ancient places and ancient heroes in Ireland and Scotland named after a pair of animals, attributes or other objects. It puzzled P. W. Joyce and many others, some seventy years ago, but no one is particularly puzzled by it now. We assume, as we drive our car from the Loch of the two Blind People, Loch da Caech, which is at Waterford, to the Mound of the two Shoulders, Tuaim da Gualann, which is at Tuam, that the experts have it all in hand and that it would be presumptuous of us to speculate about these odd names. In fact the matter rests exactly where Joyce left it. It is still a vast enigma.

It is true that some learned people now believe that *da* in these names did not mean two but that it is an ancient genitive plural meaning 'of the', so ancient that a thousand years ago the Irish had already forgotten what it meant. Thus, it is argued, Loch da En, the Lake of the two Birds, in Monaghan is the same as Loch na nEn, the Lake of the Birds, in Roscommon. This explanation seems to me totally inadequate. Let us suppose that *da* meant not two but 'of the'. Does Dubh da Det, the Black Man of the Teeth, sound more sensible than the Black Man of the two Teeth? Are the Fort of the Hands, the Oak Grove of the Fools, the Fort of the Daughters, the Mound of the Dun-coloured Persons, more reasonable-sounding when there are several of these things, not just two?

The genitive plural hardly helps at all. And how could its meaning be so widely and universally forgotten? Even the learned people, who knew Latin, ignored this 'old form of the genitive plural' as though it had never existed, for they wrote *Vadum duarum Furcarum* for Ath da Gabal, the Ford of the two Forks, and *Boscus duarum Merularum* for Lis da Lon, the Fort of the two Blackbirds.

A magical interpretation was already accepted by those who wrote the lives of the saints and by their predecessors, who composed the vast epics of Irish mythology. Ath da Corr, the Ford of the two Cranes, is so-called, say the hagiographers, because Columba turned into two cranes a queen and her handmaid who insulted him at the synod of Drumceat. They have stayed at the ford ever since. Snamh da En on the Shannon, the Swimming place of two Birds, was so-called, as I have related (see p. 131), because two foster brothers, Buide and Luan, turned themselves into birds so that Buide could sleep with a married woman called Estiu. There are at least three other explanatory anecdotes about this spot on the Shannon. The two birds occur in all of them although the characters behave quite differently. They vary only slightly in their names; for example in one story Eitsen, a female warrior, replaced Estiu, and the two birds were just her pets. Were they all fabricated simply from the place names or was there, as I believe, some memory of tribes from which the place names derived?

On the next two pages I have made a list of fifty sample *da* words.

TABLE 10: SAINTS OF THE DAII

TRIBE NAME	DA WORD FOR PLACE OR PERSON	ALLEGED MEANING
Corcu Arad	Lathrac(h) da Arad	Resort of two charioteers
Benntraige	Fer da Benn	Man with two horns on head
Bolgraige	Sidh da Bolg	Fairy mound of two bellows
Ui Broc	Dun da Broc	Fort of two badgers
Ui Bronuigh	Fid da Bron	Wood of two millstones or sorrows
Ui Buidhe	Inis da Buidhe	Island of two yellows
Cenel Baeth	Daire da Baeth	Oak grove of two fools
Bodaraighe	Tuaim da Bodar	Mound of two deaf men
Tuath Caech	Loch da Caech	Lake of the two blind
Ui Conain	Sliabh da Conn	Hill of two dogs
Cairige	Inis da Cairech	Island of two sheep
Ui Corra	Ath da Corr	Ford of two cranes
Cerdraige	St Comgan Mac da Cherda	Son of two arts
Clann Caba	Baile atha da Cab	Town of ford of two mouths

19. SAINTS OF THE DAII

TRIBE NAME	DA WORD FOR PLACE OR PERSON	ALLEGED MEANING
Ui Dallain	Loch da Dall	Lake of two blind people
Ui Damain	Cluain da Dam	Mead of two oxen
Dartraige	Druim da Dart	Ridge of two heifers
Clann Dedad	Dubh da Det	Black one of two teeth
Ui Derga	Bruiden da Derga	Hostel of the two reds
Ui Draignen	Da Draighean	Two blackthorns
Ui Dubhda	Glenn da Dub	Glen of two black men
Dal Echach	Achadh da Ech	Field of two horses
Cenel Enna	Snamh da En	Swimming place of two birds
Ui Fiachra	Cluain da Fiach	Mead of two ravens
Ui Gabalaig	Mag da Gabal	Plain of two forks
Gabraige	Mag da Gabra	Plain of two goats
Ui Gamnain	Cluain da Gamhna	Mead of two calves
Glasraige	Sliabh da Glass	Hill of two streams
Ui Gobbain	Tech da Goban	House of two Smiths
Muinter Gualan	Tuaim da Gualann	Mound of two shoulders
Ingeanraige	Dun da Ingean	Fort of two daughters
Lamraige	Dun da Lamh	Fort of two hands
Ui Liagan	Druim da Liag	Ridge of two stones
Ui Liathain	Coa da Liath	Hill of two grey persons
Ui Liga	Loch da Lig	Lake of two colours
Ui Lochain	Cell da Loch	Cell of two lakes
Ui Lonain	Lis da Lon	Fort of two blackbirds
Fir Luirg	Ath da Lorg	Ford of two forks
UiMail	Cluain da Mael	Mead of the two bald-headed cattle
Dal Meidhe	Tech da Meadar	House of two mead vessels
Odraige	Tuaim da Odhar	Mound of two dun people
Ui Rathach	Cluain da Rath	Mead of two raths
Clann Rig	Cell da Righ	Cell of two kings
Rothraige	Druim da Roth	Ridge of two wheels
Ui Ruadhain	Glenn da Ruad	Glen of two red spots

TRIBE NAME	DA WORD FOR PLACE OR PERSON	ALLEGED MEANING
Cenel Salach	Cluain da Saileach	Meadow of two willows
Tuath Toi	Mac da Tho	Son of two silent ones
Torcraide	Cluain da Torc	Meadow of two boars
Cenel Treisi	Turlach da Tres	Lake of two conflicts
Ui Trena	Druim da Tren	Ridge of two strong men

Note that each *da* word I have given may recur in many different forms. There are, for example, twenty or more forts, lakes, hills, ridges and towns called after two birds; the same applies to the two dogs, the two ravens, the two oxen.

There are three forts called Dun da Benn, the Fort of two Peaks or Horns, and there is Fid da Benn, the Wood of two Peaks, as well as the man, Fer da Benn, who had two horns on his helmet. So altogether, there are many hundreds of names of people and places in which the number two figures.

Before we consider what *da* meant, I wish to urge that the last part of the word, at least, had a tribal character. In this list I do not assert any connection other than similarity of sound between the *da* word and the tribe with which I associate it. Tribes move about or fail to be recorded and I have not always found evidence of it in the appropriate place. Yet there is so clear an affinity between almost every *da* word and a tribe, that one is justified in arguing from the particular to the general and saying that all *da* words were tribal.

A good example is Fer da Bend, the Man of two Horns, who was ancestor of the Benntraige; or observe that place in the barony of Tirawley, Co. Mayo, called Turlach da Tres. It is thought to mean the Lake of the two Conflicts, for *treas* is a conflict, but it is obviously tribal for it is in the land of the Cenel Treisi, now the Tracys, in Tir Amalgaid. They were descended from Tressi, wife of Amalghad, who gave her name to a ford, Fersat Tresi, near Killala, in which she was drowned. Other poets with less reverence for the Cenel Treisi wrote of Tresi as an unfortunate lady-in-waiting who with two colleagues called Mel and Treg were turned into pigs. Mayo was a great stronghold of the Mucc (pig) folk.

19. SAINTS OF THE DAII

Da Saints

There were many *da* saints. St Fer da Crich, the Man of two Borders, ruled two dioceses. There was St Dub da Locha, the Black Man of two Lakes, the Abbot Dub da Thuile, the Black Man of two Holes, St Berchan Fer da Leithe, the Man of two Sides, who had two parishes. The oddest of this group of saints was perhaps St Mac da Cerda, the brother of the remarkable St Cuimin Fada, who was born incestuously in a basket, *cuimin*. St Mac da Cerda, the Son of two Crafts, got his name because he was sometimes a lunatic, sometimes extremely wise. He and St Cuimin had lively discussions in verse on religious and moral issues.

The druid Dil Mac da Creca helps us to understand St Fer da Crich and through him throws light on all the others. Dil was the ancestor of the Crecraige and engaged on two plundering expeditions (*da creachad*). He was also called Da Creca. He was also, I believe, ancestor of the Dilraige of Knockainey, Co. Limerick [SG 575].

The tribal significance of Creca and Crich is obvious. What about *da*? In the name Da Creca it could not mean 'two' or 'of the'. Could *da* mean god, another interpretation offered by O'Rahilly? I do not think so. He was an ordinary wonder-working druid with a large posterity and no pretensions to immortality. He was the grandfather of Fiachu Fer da Liach, or Man of two Sorrows, also called Muillethan or Broad-crown. Dil had predicted that, if Fiachu was born on a certain day, he would rule all Ireland, and, when his daughter showed signs of giving birth a day too early, on his advice, she sat astride a stone in the middle of the river Suir and held back the baby a full day. Then she died and, because of the pressure, the baby's head had a broad crown. His father died the same day and these were his two sorrows, *da liach*. Tuathal Maelgarb (Bald-rough) had a deformed skull for a similar reason.

What did *da* mean? I offer my usual tribal explanation. Strabo thought the Dacians must originally have been called Daii, because the Athenians used to name their slaves after their tribes, thus Lydus from Lydia, Syrus from Syria and so on, and Daius or Davus was a frequent slave name. A nomadic tribe of Daii lived around the Caspian Sea and farther east gave their name to Daghestan. The Daii have already been used by an Irish scholar to solve this mystery. Recalling the slave names in Plautus and other Latin authors, Whitley Stokes [*Revue Celtique* XXII 12n] suggested that *da* in Da Derga of Bruiden da Derga, the Hostelry of the two Reds, was 'cognate with Davus'.

And in fact there was an Irish tribe, the Clann Duach, descended from Dai or Dau or from Tigernach Dai [CGH 163]. *Duach* is the genitive of *dai* but is sometimes used as the nominative, and it must have been in compliment to this family that St Tigernach of Clones drove in a chariot drawn by angels to resurrect Archbishop Duach from the dead at Moyglass in Connacht.

In the pedigree of the Ui Dedad or Ui Degad of Kerry, Ded, their ancestor, and Dau or Da, ancestor of the Ui Duach, were brothers. Da Det, two Teeth, would be their shared ancestor. In this pedigree Fer da Liach, the Man of two Sorrows, is confused with Datluath or Degloth or Deccluaid. That is to say these names would be different ways of amalgamating the ancestors of the Luath-Liach folk and the Ded folk of Kerry.

The kinship between the Ded folk and the Dai folk is expressed in another way: a certain Duach Donn was the fosterling of Dedad and he gave shelter to him in Kerry, when he and his tribe were expelled from Ulster. Who were the Dedad or Degad folk and what significance is there in this affinity of Dau and Ded? Is it an Irish echo of that kinship between Daii and Daci that Strabo detected? The Degaid appear to have been the principal users of ogam writing in Kerry, Anglesea, Pembroke and north-east Scotland. St David of Pembroke, who had a saint-ancestress sister in Tipperary, is Daui.

Who was St Da Goban?

Da is, of course, like *mo* only not quite so usual, a prefix to the names of saints. Thus we have saints Da Goban, Da Celloc, Da Chua, Da Rioc. It has always been held to mean 'thy' and to be a title of respect brought from Britain by the Patrician missionaries. Thus St Lua would reverently be called St Dalua or Thy Lua as an alternative to MoLua, which means My Lua. Grammarians find this form of address possible. I do not. It often is indistinguishable from *da*, two, for Father Shearman says that Killaloe (Cell da Lua) is the church of the two saints Lua, while others say it was the church of St Dalua.

There is trouble too about Lann da Cholmoc, where St Colman or Colmoc lived in Ulster. He was called St Da Cholmoc, but he also had a brother of the same name. The two brothers, though saints, were not friends; St Colman (26 Sept.) struck his brother (30 Mar.) blind because he stained his eyelids with blackberry juice. Why did he do this? Had it something to do with the Smertae, a tribe of Rossshire? *Smer* means blackberry.

St Da Goban (6 Dec.), also called St Gobban Fionn, came from Tech da Gobha, the House of the two Smiths, in Ulster, where he had a thousand monks, but his relics were preserved in Clonenagh in Leix. But in Clonenagh there was only one Goban recorded [VSH II 102], a priest of such appalling wickedness that St Fintan of Clonenagh trembled when he heard him celebrate mass.

I have suggested elsewhere that this Goban was the as yet imperfectly christianized ancestor and that *da*, when applied to him, was not a reverential prefix, nor did it turn him into two blacksmiths. It made him the amalgamated ancestor of Da folk and Gob folk.

A further indication that the *da* words were tribal and therefore untranslatable is that the *da* ancestors were so frequently related to each other. Thus Dub da Boireann was son of Dub da Crich, who was the son of Dub da Inber. Similarly Fer da Benn, Man of two Peaks because he was king of Cnoc Aigle and Beann Boirne in Connacht, was great-grandson of Fer da Tonn, the Man of two (named) Waves of Co. Clare and Co. Mayo, who was the son of Fer da Mag, called after two Plains (named) in Connacht.

The most peculiar explanation of the *da* problem was contributed by Algernon Herbert in 1848. He thought that the clergy called Dub da Leithe (there were three of them helping Patrick at Armagh), which he interpreted Black two Sides, must have been black on both sides, i.e. tattooed all over. He disapproved of an earlier explanation of a fort in Co. Down called Dun de Lethglas. Jocelyn of Furness, who wrote a life of St Patrick, had said that an angel had released a captive and dropped his broken fetters on the dun, which was therefore called the Fort of the two (*da*) Half (*Leath*) Fetters (*Glas*). Herbert said that the real meaning was the Fort of the two Halves Green, that is to say the fort of people who were wholly painted green (*glas*).

I believe my explanation that these names come from the Leth folk, Glas folk, Dub folk and Da folk is closer to the truth. And yet I read writers such as Herbert with the greatest enjoyment. For in these lively interpretations, they showed that they had inherited some element of audacity and fantasy, which we have now lost. Country curiosity is almost dead. One might assume that these ancient problems had long ago been solved. Quite the contrary. They are still mysteries, but a civil servant has put them in a filing cabinet and locked the door.

CHAPTER 20

St Brendan

Recently two Canadians set off in a curragh from Ireland to America. They were anxious to prove that St Brendan's famous voyage to America was a practical proposition. The curragh soon upset and so will all attempts to prove that Brendan was a real person.

He was so inextricably interwoven with the ancestor system of south-western Ireland, that, if we accept Brendan, we have to accept all his relations too. One of his recent biographers, Brendan Lehane, tries to do just that (see *The Quest of Three Abbots*, John Murray). He says, for example, of his sister Briga, Abbess of Annaghdown in Galway: 'Nothing is told of her, it can safely be assumed that she was both placid and pleasing.' This assumption is safe only because no evidence is available that she was snappy and unattractive. There were several famous Brigs in the families of the south-western saints. An aunt of Brendan, called Brig, seems to have been actually married to St Ailbe of Corcumroe, Co. Clare, and to have been mother to St MacCreiche of the same district. St Enda, and to the north-east, St Comgall of Bangor, also had mothers called Brig.

Clearly Brendan, a composite saint, was shaped by the genealogists of two great seafaring peoples: the Veneti and the Brigantes. I do not know what tribe gave the termination '-antes' that we find in the Brigantes and also in the Novantes of Galloway, the Trinovantes of Kent and perhaps the Decantae of Moray, the Setantii of Lancashire and Louth. He was the son of Findlug and born at Fenit on the west Kerry coast. His first name was Mo Bi but then 'a fair drop', *broen find,* fell on Fenit and he was christened Broend-Finn or Brendan.

20. ST BRENDAN

Before him the pagan, Bran, had been a great voyager. Was Bran possibly shaped by an earlier combination of the Briges and Veneti? Did the name Brennus, the Celtic invader of Italy, have some similar origin?

West Cork and Kerry, where Brendan was born, is a great Finn area and one of its great saints was St Finan Cam, the Crooked (7 Apr.), the only person who could look on the radiance of Brendan. Derrynane, Daniel O'Connell's home, is Doire Finain, Finan's Oak; Caillech Bere, the nun of Bere, at Berehaven, had three sons, Find, Fintan and Feindid, who settled near Killarney at Crom Glenn na Fian. Ventry on Dingle is Finn Traig or Fair Shore.

St Brendan stood in the usual oblique relationship to the Brendan tribe of Co. Clare and its ancestor Brendan, son of Blat, *ex quo* the Ui Blait, son of Cass, *ex quo* the Dal Cass [CGH 235]. And many of his oddest adventures happened in Co. Clare with this Brendan's relations. There is a lively and intriguing poem about his cousin Dobarchu, ancestor of the Clare Ui Dobarchon, who was turned into an otter, *dobarchu*, by St Brendan, because he had killed some of Brendan's oxen that trespassed on his meadows.

Some of St Brendan's travels seem to be inspired by those tribal relations. Why did Brendan light a fire on the back of a whale (*bled*) and found a monastery called Bledach? Surely because his pre-Christian namesake had a father, Blat. Writing about St Blaan or Bledenus, I mention the link that the Bled-Blad folk had with whales.

I would give a tribal explanation too of his visit to the Island of Bridles (Srian). There was a saint called Srian and that he was a tribal conception is suggested by St Columba's uncle, Setna na Srian (of the Bridles), who must be linked with the Saithne na Srian. These again are to be equated with the Setantii of Louth and Lancashire.

Why did a bad monk on the island hide a bridle from St Brendan under his armpit? You will remember that St Molua Mac Oiche was hidden under St Comgall's armpit, *oiche*. Clearly we are up against the Co. Clare branch of the Corcu Oiche, descended from Fergus Oiche [CGH 393]. I equate Srian and Trian in my Glossary with the Tren folk, a Thraco-Venetic group.

Much more could be said about St Brendan, his intimacy with St Brigit, St Finnian, St Barr-find and St Enda, much too about his British and continental associations.

CHAPTER 21

St Ailbe and the Apples

No book on the Irish saints can be completed without reference to St Ailbe. He was even more venerable than St Ibar, who was struck blind for attempting to precede him in paying homage to St Patrick. He had been preaching the gospel in Munster, even before St Patrick. Therefore, many of the most orthodox scholars believe that he never existed. His father was Olchu or Big-dog and he was suckled by a wolf, who found him under a stone, *ail*, alive, *beo*, hence he was Ail-beo or Ailbe. In Latin he was Albeus or Helveus or Alveus, and it is natural enough to connect him with that Alb group of proper names, which stretches across Europe from Rome (Rome was Alba Longa, on the river Albula, the Tiber, and was ruled by a King Alba) to Alpis, the river Drava, to Albis, the Elbe, to Albion and to Ireland, where a number of places and of mythical people bear echoes of this ancient name.

Some say it was an Iberian word, others Ligurian; some connect it with *alp* and *alb* and say that the Alps and *albus*, white, both derive from it. The Irish, on the other hand, treat Ailbe as if it was a compound word and other words beginning with *ail* are treated as if they concerned stones. Thus Ailech, the famous stone fort in Donegal is Ail-ach! or Stone-alas!, because a certain hero was buried under a stone there, or Ail-ech, because a horse drew the stones to it. No doubt they were wrong about the stones, but had reason for avoiding more sensible translations. A broken-down tribal name is in fact meaningless and, therefore the best explanation is the most entertaining one.

In the sixth century BC, Himilco, the Carthaginian, travelled to the British Isles and long afterwards a Roman poet wrote a verse translation of Himilco's narrative. He had found a race called Albiones occupying the southern part of Britain at a time when the Ligurians held the northern shores of France and Spain. Pliny later noted the same people in Asturias on the north coast of Spain.

Their tribal ancestor seems to have been Alebion, who fought Hercules in Gaul, but he appears to have lost every battle, for mythology, which once placed him in Liguria, later confined him to the British Isles. Even Albion at last shrunk to Alba, which means sometimes Wales, sometimes Scotland. The last significant traces of these people survive in the Drumalban mountain chain, which runs down the centre of Scotland.

Was St Ailbe linked in any way with this race? To the ancients he was certainly a symbol of distant lands and forgotten peoples. He was not one of the sailor-saints like Brendan or Finnbarr. Voyaging to Rome, he preferred to spread out his cowl upon the waves, trusting to the blessed trinity to waft him to harbour. Yet he is associated with the far north. Once, in order to avoid mankind and the distasteful honours they lavished on him, he decided to sail to the island of Tile or Tele, which is thought to be Ultima Thule or Iceland. But the king of Cashel, deeming that Ailbe should not avoid his responsibility to all the souls he had saved in Ireland, had all the ports watched to prevent Ailbe escaping. Ailbe was obliged to send twenty-two men across the sea, magically without a ship, in place of himself.

But other stories suggest that Ailbe or someone very like him did escape, for we hear of Ailbiu, a monk of Thule. Moreover, when Brendan had sailed far out into the ocean for six months, he came to an island called the Island of the Family of Ailbe or Insula Albei. There was an abbot there and twenty-three monks (one more than Ailbe had sent into the ocean according to his biographer) and the abbot told them that eighty years had passed since the death of Ailbe, who had been a wealthy man, owning a great territory, which he had given up for the love of their island. Since his death God had cared for them, providing them, without any effort of theirs, with two meals a day and four on feast days, and they had had forewarning of Brendan's visit because a specially big supply had come. There were two fountains, one containing cold drinking water, the other hot water for washing. This looks to me like Iceland. The lamps lit themselves without oil when dusk fell and extinguished themselves at the right time.

Needless to say, Ailbe, whether he got to Iceland or not, found plenty of time to found monasteries all over our islands and Brittany. At Dol in Brittany he magically repaired a broken chalice for St Samson, and revived a married couple who had been executed for slandering him. Ailbe brought up St David and baptized him and left his name at Llanelfyw or St Elvie's near St David's in Pembrokeshire. It is clear that he concerned himself with St David's because of the tradition that Ailbe folk once lived there. But in Ireland why did he circulate principally in Munster and in north-east Ulster? It is true that he made a rather sketchy tour of the whole of Ireland, baptizing heathens but leaving some unconverted, because it was God's will that the honour of converting all of Ireland should belong to St Patrick alone. He does not seem to have paused among the Ui Ailbe of Co. Leitrim, the only Irish tribe bearing his name. They had an ancestor, Ailbe, who was obviously fictitious; he had a long and distinguished pedigree, but he is not our Ailbe [FEN 391].

St Ailbe secured Aran Island for St Enda, who held it '*sub sancto Albeo*', and he was active on the coast of Clare opposite, as the bosom friend of St MacCreiche. Indeed they were so close to each other that St MacCreiche's original name had been Mac Croide Ailbe or Son of the Heart of Ailbe, and he only became MacCreiche after he had secured the restitution of some plunder, *crech*, stolen from his uncles in Kerry. The meaning of this story is fairly clear. St MacCreiche's people, the Ui Moccu Crecci or Crecraige were, in north Clare, allied to the Ailbe folk. There is a local saint called Mac Aiblen, an ally of MacCreiche in the destruction of a monster, and a mountain called Slieve Ellbe or Elva just to the north of Kilmacrehy in the barony of Corcumroe, so the presence of the Ailbe folk in the district is evident.

St Ailbe's miracles were the usual tribal ones. For example, when he was in the Ui Fidgente in Limerick he converted a very wicked man by turning his enemies into trees, so that the decapitated heads that he brought back proved to be just logs of wood. *Fid* means wood and *cenn* means head, and the ancestor of the Ui Fidgenti, Fiachra Fidgennid, was so called because he planted a wood. So it is plain why Ailbe acted as he did in the Ui Fidgente.

He performed two obscure miracles in Carlow and Kildare and paid a brief visit to St Brigit to give her some sheep. Yet on the whole the Ailbes whom we meet in this part of Leinster are mainly heroic figures or dogs. Even more than Munster, where Ailbe died and ministered, it was an Ailbe region. Mag Ailbe, the Plain of Ailbe, now Moyalvey in Kildare, is very famous. It is called after a dog, *ailbe*, about whose possession all Ireland fought. Its severed head fell from a chariot at Cenn Ailbe. The old notion that Ailbe had something to do with *albus*, white, is kept up by the English name for the plain 'White Field'. This subject is complicated by a metathesis that brings Ailbe close to Abhall, which means an apple tree. St Ailbe's own island of Aran was called *ablach*, apple tree-like [THU 516], and when Hilary, the pope of Rome, was short of apples, Ailbe made heaven shower them down on him. Ailbe was the lap dog of a famous lady called Aillen and it was surely because of that that an apple tree grew through her body. Achad Ailbe (Field of Ailbe) is Achad Aible and among the apple tree-like places of Ailbe one might include the famous Romanesque church of Aghowle (Achad Abhall or Applefield) in Co. Wicklow. Mull and the Isle of Man were also called apple tree-like. Avalon too was an apple tree-like place. What should one make of its local saint, St Elvan (1 Jan.)?

Apples

Why are so many Ailbes dogs? I have mentioned two. I suppose St Ailbe's father was Olchu, because of some Cynesic kinship. Another Ailbe, sometimes confused with the saint, was the father of St MacCreiche and was called the 'War Dog of Sliab Crott', near St Ailbe's cult centre of Emly.

I had better be done now with Ailbe. I cannot see very far beyond the Albiones of Spain but it seems possible that the great group to which he and they belonged includes the Helvetii, whose wanderings precipitated Caesar's conquest of Gaul. Henri Hubert suggests that the Helvetii were kinsmen of the Helvii who lived in Provence, west of the Rhône.

He is guessing, of course, but as good a guess would be to say that they were related to the Helvecones, whom Tacitus places among the Lugii in eastern Germany. Believing as I do that the original tribes of Europe were as limited in number as the races of Europe today and equally tenacious of their ancient traditions, I think their names blurred at the edges, as did their peoples, and that it is more hazardous to suggest that vaguely similar tribal names are distinct than to admit that they are the same. The multitude of apparently distinctive names is an illusion. One can very safely guess that St Ailbe or Helveus was a distant cousin of the ancestor of the Helvii, whose chief town was Alba Helviorum (now Viviers), and also of the Helvetii and of the remote and unknown Helvecones of the far north.

CHAPTER 22

St Sciath and the Shields

I've mentioned that our great-grandfathers used to believe, on the authority of the ancient Irish, that the Scythians came to our islands and left their names in Scotia, but our grandfathers and fathers decided for us that this legend was ridiculous. To me it would appear more ridiculous to suppose that the Scythians, in some blended form, did not come here. They had in Europe mixed extensively with the Celts, so that Strabo tells us that Greek historians called all the northerns Celto-Scythians. Seneca reports them in Spain, where also was a tribe called Scoti, and modern historians say that they had reached central Europe by the seventh century, spreading from northern Hungary to Silesia and Lusatian Brandenburg. A decorated Scythian horse collar has been found as far west as Amiens. It has a curious pattern on it: two beasts on their hind legs appear to be whispering into the ears of a human figure between. And there are curious echoes of this pattern across Europe to Ireland. A scriptural interpretation is given to it usually; it is suggested that two lions are sniffing expectantly at Daniel or two demons with animal heads are whispering temptations into the ears of St Anthony. The illustrations will show that the original meaning of the encounter must have been different.

About the third and second centuries BC the Scythians seem to have almost disappeared. They were wandering bowmen, raising cattle and easily losing their nationality; they were less civilized than the Getae, but the incredible survivals of their garments and furniture and harness, which have been excavated by Russians in recent years in the Altai Mountains and which are on exhibit in the Hermitage Museum, show that although nomads they were

22. ST SCIATH AND THE SHIELDS

capable of much ingenious and beautiful ornamentation. There is confirmation that Herodotus had described with considerable fidelity how their kings had been sumptuously buried in a vast circle of stuffed warriors pinioned to stuffed horses. Legend and pedigrees fostered the belief in the kinship of Celts and Scyths, for Scythes and Celtos, the two ancestors, were brothers and both children of Hercules.

Our fathers and grandfathers were sceptical about the wrong things. While they dismissed with superior laughter the legend of the Scythian invasion, they accepted as real many travelled Christian missionaries, who, in fact, must have been shadows of shadows of the ancestral Scythes. Watson [WJW 331, 336], believes, for example, that the relics of a certain sixth-century virgin, St Sciath of Ardskeagh in Munster, arrived at St Skay's in Forfarshire at the same time that St Buite of Monasterboice, Co. Louth, was establishing himself at Kirkbuddo nearby. Watson, a distinguished philologist, is bothered by a discrepancy between the saints' names and their cult centres. There is confusion, he suggests, with *sciath*, a wing or shield, and *sce-sciach*, a hawthorn. Kirkbuddo must be formed from a diminutive 'Little Buite' and so on. Fussing over tiny philological difficulties, he hides from the gigantic biographical ones. St Sciath's history in Ireland and St Buite's manifold travellings through Scotland, Ireland, Wales and the Continent make this Irish church mission to Scotland a preposterous impossibility. Light dawns, if we suppose that the Scythians and their neighbours, the Budini, established themselves on the Scottish and Irish mainland and never completely lost touch with each other and their elaborate interlocking pedigrees.

As Watson suggests the word *sciath* brought to mind several words: shield, wing, hawthorn. If we note also *scath*, meaning shadow or phantom, and *scoth* meaning flower, and a similar word meaning haste, we are equipped for tracking down the passage of the Scythians through Ireland.

The same imagery accompanies the Scythians themselves, when the Irish related how they were descended from them. In the *Book of Invasions* Scythia is known as *sciath-gloin* or shield-bright, *sciath-brec*, speckled like a shield, and also the land of hawthorns, and *sciathaig*, shieldlike. The same images are used for the island of Skye, Skid or Scath. It was wing-shaped and Scathach, a female warrior, who derived her name from *scath*, a shadow, was queen there at Dunscait. She had two sons, Cuar and Cett, and Skye itself lay in the territory of the Caerones. Cuar, Caer and Ciar are frequently encountered alternatives, so Cuar would be ancestor to the Caerones. Cett is surely the ancestor of the Getae and the meaning of this kinship does not require further exposition.

ILLUSTRATION 1

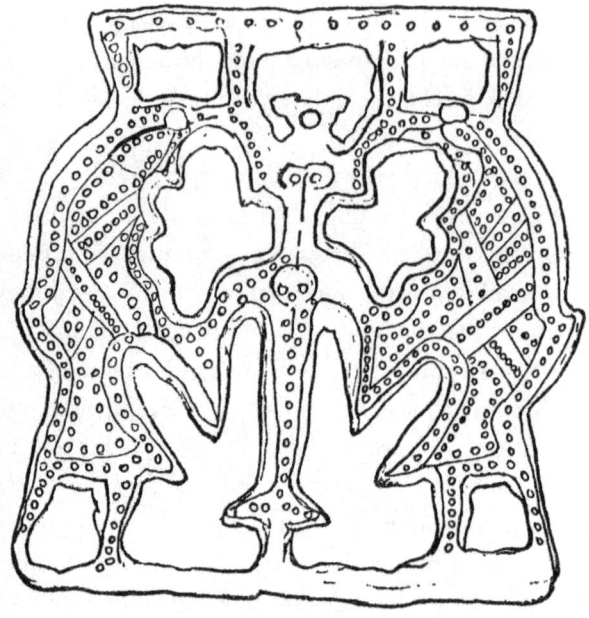

Scythian bronze horse-trapping from near Amiens, Ashmolean Museum

ILLUSTRATION 2

From a cross at Moone, Co. Kildare

22. ST SCIATH AND THE SHIELDS

ILLUSTRATION 3

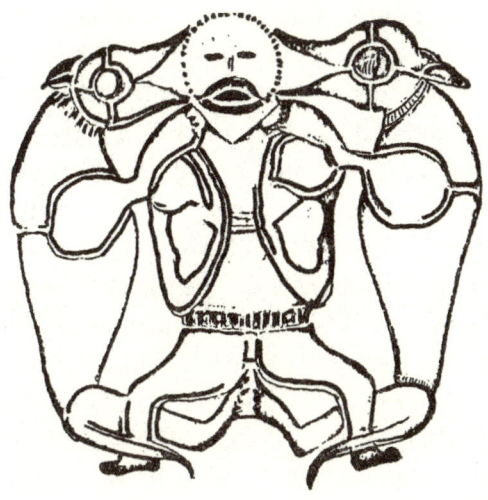

From a purse in a ship burial, Sutton Hoo, Suffolk

ILLUSTRATION 4

From south cross, Castledermot, Co. Kildare

ILLUSTRATION 5

From a cross at Kells, Co. Meath

We do, in fact, find the Sciathraige in Ireland, a tribe that MacNeill, ignoring the character of ancient tribes, believes to have an occupational name derived from the manufacture of shields. On the contrary it is certainly akin to another Irish tribe, the Scotraige, and the traces of these tribes are evident in the Tipperary-Waterford region from which the St Sciath, commemorated in Forfar, derived. We find in this region four saints, a St Sciath, granddaughter of Ciar (1 Jan. and 7 Sept.), St Ciara, whose sex is uncertain, of Cell Cere in Mag Ascad, and the composite St Ciarascadh of Cell Ciarascadh (16 Oct.), and near these last two, St Sciath of Port. I have taken these overlapping saints to be evidence of two overlapping tribes of the Ciar folk and Sciath folk. Where did this overlapping occur: in Ireland, Scotland or far earlier on the Continent?

It is significant that a majority of the Sciath place names are in this Waterford-Tipperary neighbourhood. On the Munster Blackwater, near to where St Sciath presided at Ardskeagh, we find Mag Sciath, Carraig na Sciath, and to the north in the region of the composite Ciarascad, we find Lis na Sciath, Donoskeigh, and Barnalascaw, all related by scholars, ancient and modern, to shields and shadows and hawthorns. The last *leath sciath* is the 'pass of half shadow' [INP II 482]! What can that possibly mean?

There is an abundance of lay heroes and heroines of this Scoth-Scath group. Scota, who married Fenius (a Venetic ancestor?) in Scythia, also married Mil, ancestor of the Milesians, and is buried at Glenn Scoithin in the Dingle peninsula. Eibhear Scot, who died in Scythia, is obviously a composite Scythian-Iberian ancestor. What is gained by saying that these ancestors are fictitious? Of course they are but, if we place them on a level with the equally fictitious saints, we get so complicated and consistent a pattern that we cannot believe in unmotivated invention; we see that fancy is weaving her fabric out of elements that were once real.

When the Sons of Mil first landed from Spain on Dingle, they found Slieve Mis full of demons under shields, '*demnaib fo sciathaib*'. If we recall Scota's grave on Slieve Mis, we can guess what the shields were. As for the demons, they constantly occurred wherever there were Dumnonians. In the life of St MoChuda we read that a certain 'jealous bishop', called Domangen, occupied Slieve Mis and would not give it up to him.

It was in Dingle too that Cu Chullain had his battle with the enormous and terrible shadow, *scath*, at Cahirconree, when Cu Roi mac Daire, the owner of the fort, was away in Scythia. Thurneysen, who tells this story from Bricriu's Feast, merely says that the Scythians played such a large part in Irish legend, because of the supposed descent of the Scoti, the Irish, from the Scythians.

22. ST SCIATH AND THE SHIELDS

But in this case was it not Dingle in particular that the writer was associating with the Scythians? With magical shields, magical shadows and Scota's grave, it had all the appropriate images. And the story is obviously tribal, for the shadow carried great oak trees in its hand. The oaks (*dair* is an oak), like Cu Roi's father, Daire, point unmistakably to the Dairine, the ancient tribe, whose ancestor is woven into all the genealogies of the south-west.

In this Sciath-Scoth group there are the usual number of heroes with preposterous names and curious anecdotes to explain them. Patently they are composed of tribal elements, twisted to give a meaning of sorts. Crimthann Sciathbel (Shield-mouth), had a mouth like a shield. As for Conall Sciath Bachall, Shield-crozier, St Patrick made the sign of the cross with his crozier on his shield. Bachall is also a tribal word.

Fionnscothach was a king in whose reign 'wine flowers' were pressed into goblets (*fionn* and *scoth* are taken to be wine and flowers instead of Venetic and Scythian ancestors). St Scuithin (Scoth-Fionn? Or St Sculthinus, Swithin, Scolanus; 2 July [OC III 26]) is perhaps the same. Walking with speed (*scothadh*) across the ocean with St Barr-Finn he plucked a flower (*scoth*) from the waves. At Scathderc on the black water St Cranat saw a red (*derg*) shadow, when she replaced the eye that she had torn out in order to repel an importunate suitor. But Scathderc, as daughter of Celtchair, is also a lady of the Blackwater as well as a place on its banks. She was the sister of many famous tribal ancestors of Munster, Seim of the Semonraige, Brigit of the Ui Brigte, and so on.

In fact all these curious compound names, differently shaped and attached to different people, places and adventures, occur all over Ireland. They are given so many different meanings that it is clear they had none. These names existed before the Irish language had shaped itself. Fianscoth (Wine-flower?) is also called Findsciath (White-shield). Scathderg is a hero of Leix but no story about red shadows and injured eyeballs is thought necessary to explain his name. *Sciath brec*, speckled shield, an epithet for Scythia, which Macalister translates 'checkered like a shield', is the name of two heroes. One of them, it is true, was the shield-bearer of Finn. This explains the shield but not the speckles. But there are as many women called Sciath as men, and, if Sciath really meant shield, it would surely not be a suitable name for a woman. Nor, if it was Irish for shield, is it very likely that a Norse warrior, Sciath Amlach, would bear it. Despite the long Norse-Irish intercourse very few Irish heroes have Scandinavian names.

If these people were, as I believe, Scythians, they seem, on my evidence, to have been early and few, and mainly in south-west Ireland and sparsely in

Scotland. What deductions can we make from the following proper names, as to the tribes they mingled with?

Sciathbacha	Sciathnechtan	Milscothach
Sciathbel	Scothniam	Minscothach
Sciathbreac	Ciarascad	Triscoth
Scathderg	Eber Scot	Urscothach
Sciathgabra	Fianscoth	
Sciathglan	Findsciath	

CHAPTER 23

St Tartinna and the Heifers

The Tartessii

The Roman poetical geographer, Avienus, writing in the fourth century AD, declared that the Tartessii, who lived at Gades outside the Pillars of Hercules, were among the early colonists of the British Isles. Philipon describes them as 'an Aegean people of superior culture, who came from North Africa to Spain and dispersed'[A XV].

They occupied Aquitaine and Languedoc, and he quotes a Greek writer, Phileas, as saying that the Rhône was at one time the border between Libya and Europe. There is a Silurus Mons and a number of Sil-Sal names in the land of the Tartessii as in the British Isles and, on the strength of these and other topographical affinities, Philipon suggests that they were the precursors of the Silurians. One of their 'gods' was Netos, whose name is familiar in Ireland.

Whether Philipon is correct or not in his deductions, it would have been extremely strange if the Tartessii had not visited Ireland as well as Britain, since we know that there was contact between southern Spain and Ireland from megalithic times, and the Tartessii, on the Atlantic sea board, were by far the most prosperous and adventurous of the early inhabitants of the Iberian peninsula. When the Phocaeans in Asia Minor were menaced by the Persians, Arganthonios, the king of the Tartessii, offered to receive them as emigrants in his territory. They refused the invitation but gratefully accepted the offer of money for the strengthening of their fortifications. It was a shorter voyage to Ireland from south-west Spain than to Asia Minor and it would be remarkable if there was no intercourse between the Tartessii and Ireland. Can we find any traces?

In County Louth

In the first place they seem to have left their mark in Co. Louth, where, in Conaille Muirthemne, Hogan records Ath Tarteisc and Tir Mor Tarteisc and the river Taurtesc, north of the Nith. It is impossible not to connect these sites with the Tuath Tartaisi of the same region. We might lose the trail here if it was not for a place in this neighbourhood called Tortgabail and a legend that Fiachra Tort, the ancestor of the Ui Tuirtre or the Tuath Tort, received his name *tort*, seizure, from his seizure of Conaille Muirthemne (*Book of Rights* 123. Reeves' 'Ecclesiastical Antiquities', 292–3). The Ui Tuirtre lived round Loch Neagh. South of them in Co. Meath, at Bile Tortain and Domnach Tortain, lived the Ui Tortain, whom it is impossible not to regard as a related people.

In Meath and Wicklow

These Ui Tortain lived round Ardbraccan in Meath and are also called the Ui Dortain, Ui Dothrain and Ui Dorethain; their kinship with the Tuatha Tort, or Ui Tuirtre, is made more probable by the existence of an Ui Dorthaind tribe near the south side of Loch Neagh.

These new aliases help us to extend the range of the Tort folk, whom I believe to be the Tartessii, southwards. The Ui Dothrain guide us to the river Dothrain, the Dodder, and to Dubh Dothra, chief of the Ui Briuin Cualann, through whom the river flowed. And in this north Wicklow region the tracks of the Tartessii become clearer. At Druimard, which O'Hanlon places near Donard, we find St Tartinna (3 Jul.). Her other name Dartinna recalls Cluain Dartada, also in this region, and a mythical personage Dartad, grandson of the king of the Britons, whom we find among the raiders of Da Derga's hostel nearby at Bohernabreena. We have not to strain much at probabilities to believe that Dartad is the pagan predecessor of his neighbour, St Dartinna, and it is impossible not to connect them both with Doigre Dart, the tribal ancestor of the Dartraige.

The Dartraige

The Dartraige were among the most noted of Irish tribes, their migrations being almost as celebrated as those of the Deisi. They are said to have been expelled from Munster, because of injuries done to the Ui Conall Gabra south of Limerick. They had to leave Munster for the west and, wandering in Connacht, they killed the kings of Partraige and Umall. They were driven across the Shannon at Athlone after forty years of plunder. Then they settled in the midlands in Delvin and in Fer Cell.

In later days it is in Sligo, Leitrim and Monaghan that the surviving tribes of the Dartraige are located. In Monaghan they gave their name to the barony of Dartry; in south-east Sligo we find Tir Tortaighe. How are we to explain the existence in Leitrim and Monaghan of townlands Drumdart and in Leitrim of Druimdartan also? Their location would connect them with the Dartraige rather than with *dart*, a heifer, as is the orthodox explanation given by Joyce [INP II 306]. And what are we to make of Drum da Dart, a sacred spot of uncertain location? It is normally interpreted 'The Ridge of two Heifers', but I believe that my view that it concerned the Daii and the Tartessii is more plausible.

Other Traces

If we accept the theory that in place names *dart* is as likely to refer to the Dartraige as to heifers, Imlech Fir Aen Darta in Limerick and Aenach Fir Aen Darta in Antrim are suitably placed. Yet Irish scholars ancient and modern believe that these names mean 'the meeting place of the single heifer'. This interpretation gave rise to the legend that there was a cattle plague in Ireland in the reign of Bresal Breac and only three heifers were left in the whole of Ireland, in Limerick and Antrim (those two we know) and in Conaille Muirthemne. But as I show in my chapter on the Veneti there were En folk as well as Dart folk, and Aendarta derives from their mingling. In the same chapter I refer to the lady Dartaid, who was murdered at Imblech Fer Aendarta by a triply amalgamated Munster ancestor, Corb Liath mac Tassaich [THU 305].

There are other Tort-Dart place names in the midlands, the south-east and Tyrone. *Dart*, which occurs in place names in the south-west of England, may admit of a similar interpretation. In the genealogies we find some ancestors with suitable compound names like Tortlugaid [CGH 228], Tortchis [222] and Tortbuillech [SG 397].

CHAPTER 24

St Fursa and the Frisians

It is surely very audacious to suggest that the famous St Fursey or Fursa of Loch Corrib and Suffolk and northern France had no reality except as the ancestor of the Frisians. He is among the most respected of Irish saints and is honoured in three countries. The venerable Bede devoted a chapter to St Fursa's activities in Suffolk, based on material furnished him by a very old fellow monk, who had met 'a very sincere and religious man', who had actually heard Fursa describe his visions in East Anglia fifty years before. When the religious man related this, he sweated from horror at the visions or from 'spiritual consolation'; Bede did not consider whether he had sweated from the effort of imaginative invention. Scores of biographies of St Fursa and comments on his life and his miracles have been written by other sincere and religious men in Irish, English, Latin, French and German. Many chapters have been devoted to his miracles and his famous visions, and Canon O'Hanlon says that these visions inspired Dante to write *The Divine Comedy*. How can one say that he never lived!

St Fursa's Irish Family

My reasons are the usual ones. In Ireland there are four St Fursas; for Irish saints this is a very moderate number of homonyms, and we can straight away set aside the Roscommon St Fursa and the Meath St Fursa, not because they have some independent reality but because they can be easily disentangled from the other two. The two that remain, the Ulster Fursa and the Munster-

24. ST FURSA AND THE FRISIANS

Connacht Fursa, are hopelessly embroiled, because, though they have the same feast day, 16 January, and the same adventures outside Ireland and share a number of ancestors with identical names, the Ulster Fursa is as closely tied to the region round Dundalk, where he founded Cell Fursa or Killursa, as the other Fursa is to Connacht, where he is linked with another Cell Fursa or Killursa, an ancient church on Loch Corrib.

The Ulster Fursa's mother was Bronach, the daughter of Milcu the farmer, whom St Patrick served on Slemish Mountain in Antrim. All Milcu's other sons and daughters became saints and moved, as I have related, to the diocese of St Maelcu at Ardagh in Longford, that is to say a son called St Guasacht and two daughters both called St Emer. The third sister, Bronach, herself a mother of five saints, gave her name to Clonbroney near Ardagh, where her two sisters were culted. All this looks to me a tribal affair. As I have explained in 'The Sons of Mil', the Muinter Milchon of the west midlands are probably the clue to Milcu and to St Maelcu, who was St Patrick's nephew. St Fursa's Ulster mother, St Bronach (1 Jan.), most of whose saintly sons were culted in the Mourne region of Down and Louth, herself had another church there at Kilbroney. There was a Bronach tribe in this region and St Fursa would scarcely fit into this family group, if he was not a tribal ancestor himself. Certainly, as a saint, he retains some of the immortality that the tribal ancestor often acquired, since, if his mother knew St Patrick in the fifth century, he could not as a mortal have evangelized Picardy in the seventh century.

The Connacht St Fursa was son of Findlug, king of Munster, and a lady called Gelgeis or White-swan, daughter of king Aed Find of the Aed Finn tribe. It will be remembered that he was Aed Dub (the black) until he put his head under the cowls of various saints and became Aed Finn (the fair). She came from the same Sligo region as a famous sow called Caelceis, or Thin Young Sow. The sow was charmed by the exquisite playing of a harper called Corran to a hill in Sligo. It was called after them both Ceis Corran and lies in the barony of Corran. Cael tribes and Cass tribes abound in Sligo, so Caelceis and Gelgeis are suitable tribal eponyms. An ancestor of the south-west, Aed Caelcos or Thin Leg [CGH 258] could belong to the same group.

On Loch Corrib itself St Fursa has a different pedigree; there are three churches on the eastern shore, Kill Fursa, Kill Cuana, where there is the stump of a round tower, and Kill Aine. The other two patrons, St Cuana and St Enda, are also well known, of course, and I have connected them with the Cunesioi and the Veneti, but only here are they all three said to be brothers, sons of Meda or Coirmeda [OH II 559] or Finmeda, a famous lady who had fifty-two children, all saints. In a fourth pedigree St Fursa and his two other brothers, Faelan and Ultan, are sons of Maelsnechta.

Searching for evidence that the Frisians had been in Connacht, I found a Fris tribe, the Tuath Fris, in the Curlew Mountains in Corran, where was Caelceis of Ceis Corran, and also on an island off the Sligo coast, Inis Tuath Frais. There was also a saint called St Mo-Frisius of Sligo, who attended a vast congress of saints assembled at Ballysadare south of Sligo town to meet St Columba [OH II 559]. I had been looking for just such a saint, and, though it is his solitary appearance in history, it seemed to me a very important one, because he is in exactly the right place. Four or five hagiographers say he is the same as St Frosius or Fraech, who was culted on 21 December at Cloone near Clonbroney, where Fursa's two saintly aunts Emer dwelt in a monastery called after his mother. But he might also be identified with St Frossach, 4 April, whom *The Martyrology of Donegal* associates with Cill Frasuigh, also in the barony of Corran.

Irish Stories of Fursa

I believe that Fursa, like other Irish saints, had an intelligible tribal reason for all the extravagances of his behaviour. For those who like guessing, I record the following stories, even though others may not find them as entertaining and stimulating to their curiosity as I do.

Only for the first of them, which seems intended to bridge the gulf between the Fursa of Louth and the Fursa of Corrib, can I find an explanation. When the two dead children of King Brendan of Louth arrived in a boat from Louth, St Fursa of Corrib revived them and threw a ruler, *regula*, from his scriptorium into the sea, to guide them back to Louth. There was a saint called St Riagal or St Rule on the Munster Loch Derg and at St Andrews in Fife, and a tribe, the Ui Riaglachain of Leitrim.

St Fursa probably used his ruler to guide the children because of Ros Riagla, or, as it is called in Latin, Collis Regulae, where now the ruins of the Franciscan abbey, Roserrilly, can be seen. It is in the parish of Cill Fursa.

St Fursa, in contrast to other Irish saints, had a very restricted missionfield in Ireland. He is not much talked of except near Corrib and in Louth and even less in Scotland, though Scottish hagiographers have said that he was the son of a king of Scotland and that his mother was St Kentigerna. Yet he makes an odd appearance in the Galtee Mountains in Cork and also in Co. Westmeath. In the Galtees he confined in a lake called Beldracon, a dragon, which St Ternoc's nurse had mistaken for a salmon.

In Westmeath he had the closest friendship with St Colman mac Luachain at Lann. He assisted at a great feast, which Colman held at the foundation of his monastery and he was given a third of St Colman's cemetery there and a tomb. Fursa, in gratitude, said that any monk who was buried in his cemetery would have as much credit as if he had made a pilgrimage. You will object that he was buried in Picardy and not Westmeath and that this must therefore be the Meath Fursa. I do not think that this can be so, for he is called, like Fursa of Peronne, St Fursa the Devout (Craibdech). A great deal was always made of his devotion. He wrote An Abgitur Crabaid, or 'Alphabet of Devotion', and there were some significant poems. One starts: 'Be Devout on the Feast of Fursey.' Another runs:

> Fursey the Devout loved
> In a well as cold as snow
> Accurately to sing the psalms.

The life of St Colman mac Luachain abounds even more than other lives with puns about proper names. Perhaps here St Fursa Craebdech was the Carpic Fursa revered among the Craebh folk of Westmeath; I refer to Fursa's Carpic associations elsewhere (see p. 226).

St Fursa paid an even stranger visit to Lann three years after St Colman's death. He was invited to dig up Colman's remains and put them in a shrine. He sat down first at Fursey's Cross at Lann and looked at the Wry Mill of Mullingar (*muillen cearr*) and started to curse. He left hell and disgrace of speech on the steward of Lann and his successor and some mysterious maledictions on the bell ringer. It was not until the caretaker came out with 'seven breaths of God' on his back and his wife brought a jug of milk and a jug of ale and laid it on Lic Fursa, or Fursey's flagstone, that Fursa relented and left various blessings on the cowherd and others. These blessings were conditional on prayers and fastings at his tomb, and he speaks as though the tomb was already there.

St Oengus the Culdee and his commentator, writing of St Fursa as though he were the Ulsterman, tells us that he was thrown out of the monastery of Louth and succeeded by St Ultan. This east coast Fursa paid a visit to St Maignen of Kilmainham near Dublin and in token of their union they agreed to exchange their diseases. St Fursa gave his headache and his piles and received in return from St Maignen the beast that was devouring him internally. It was necessary to pacify it every morning with three bits of bacon. Later, when he went across the sea to a great city, the local bishop reproved him for what looked like greedy behaviour.

> 'Not good devotion is thy life,' quoth the bishop.
> 'Thou art permitted, O Cleric,' quoth Fursa, 'to try that, which inflicts this on me.'
> Forthwith then leaps the beast into the bishop's throat. Now when everyone knew that, Fursa calls the beast back to him again and God's name and Fursa's are magnified through the miracle and all the city with its service land is conveyed to God and to Fursa.

No doubt many obscure tribal puns have shaped this story. If Fursa himself represented a tribe that appropriated the land of another tribe, his victory over the censorious bishop, who had to give up his land, would explain it all in Christian terms.

The Irish say St Fursa had his famous vision on his way from Corrib to Munster when he went to collect his brothers, St Faelan and St Ultan, for the pilgrimage to England, but Bede says he had this apocalyptic trance when he reached Suffolk. These visions of angels and demons battling for souls in the other world do not seem very interesting now, but they had a powerful influence in the Middle Ages. For a time, we are told, Pope Martin refused to be convinced but when St Fursa came to Rome with all his company of saints and showed him the ulcer on his neck, which he acquired from contact with the body of a blazing sinner, even the pope believed and flinging himself on the floor begged Fursa to become a cardinal and to intercede for him in heaven. The visions are informed by an ingenious morality. Fursa was afflicted with the ulcer on his neck, because he had accepted a legacy of clothes from a sinner. Thereafter he was vulnerable to the Evil One, though an angel stood beside him as his advocate. Sharing the sinner's goods, he had to share his punishment too. When a demon flung the roasting body at him, even though an angel caught it immediately and flung it back into hell, Fursa had been severely scorched. The moral of this story is a sound one. Priests ought not to receive presents from dying sinners. Their property should be divided up and given to the poor.

Fursa's Companions

When St Fursa set off from his home on Loch Corrib, he took with him some of the twelve pious young neighbours whom he had just ordained. These twelve are differently named. Some of them accompanied him to Suffolk, some

24. ST FURSA AND THE FRISIANS

went on with him to Picardy. The most important were his brothers St Ultan (1 May) and St Faelan (31 Oct.), St Goban (20 Jun.) and his pupil, St Guillebrod (17 Nov.), and Goban's brothers, St Etto (10 Jul.) and St Algisus (2 Jun.) and Algisus' godson, St Corbican (26 Jun.). I think I should add St Meldan (7 Feb.), his spiritual director from Inchiquin Island on Loch Corrib, and Meldan's brother, St Beodan, from north-east Ulster, for though it was only their bones, which he took with him to East Anglia and then to Picardy, where he finally buried them, they appeared to him in visions. As spiritual presences they always accompanied him.

St Guillebrod, who is Willibrord, the apostle to the Frisians, must also have been more a spiritual presence than a physical one, for he had not been born when the expedition set out. Although some say his birthplace was Galway, while others say he only went there to be baptized by Fursa, his English biographers, who included the famous Alcuin, all agreed he was English and came from Northumbria.

St Willibrord is the only one of the twelve, who was definitely not fabulous, yet his presence in this company of Corrib friends is very remarkable. The others all made their converts without violence by miraculous blessings and cursings, while Willibrord was a man after Alcuin's heart. What was his link with Fursa?

If one knows Willibrord's story, it is possible to guess. I have already told some of it. When he sailed for Friesland, which his friend, Pepin the Frank, was busy subduing, he selected pious companions, as Fursa had done. He landed in Denmark and collected thirty boys to train as missionaries and then send back home. Baring-Gould says with approval that these methods were later used successfully by the Central African Mission.

Then, as I have related, he sailed to Heligoland at that time called Forsetesland, after Forseti, son of Balder, the 'God' of the Frisians. He killed Forseti's sacred cattle to feed his crew and baptized three comrades in Forseti's sacred well and announced to Radbod, king of the Frisians, that Forseti was not a god but a demon.

Radbod was impressed by all this; he felt that his gods (but I believe that Forseti was, in the first place, an ancestor) had deserted him and he was inclined to give in, but, when he was about to be baptized by St Willibrord's assistant, St Wulfram (20 Mar.), he asked Wulfram if his ancestors were going to heaven too. 'No,' replied Wulfram, 'they are all damned.' Radbod straightway leapt out of the water, exclaiming, 'I'd sooner be in hell with my ancestors than in heaven without them!' Willibrord continued to chop up idols and hew down sacred trees and, with the Frankish armies behind him, he made hundreds of thousands of converts. Radbod died unbaptized, but after his death Frisian resistance totally collapsed.

But for the time being only. Forseti was more powerful than the soldiers and the missionaries supposed and very soon, as we learn from Alcuin's letter (see 'How Ancestors and Saints Were Made' p. 34). Charlemagne had to reconquer and reconvert the Frisians. Roughly the same methods seem to have been used, the same combination of brutality and diplomacy (see Ellis Davidson, *Gods and Myths of Northern Europe*, p. 171).

We are told, for example, that Charlemagne commanded twelve leading Frisians to set down their laws or else be put adrift in a rudderless boat. They chose the boat and had given themselves up for lost, when a thirteenth man appeared and steered them ashore with a golden axe and told them the laws that they needed to know. The story has a Christian colouring but the stranger is thought to be not Christ but Forseti himself.

Fursa and his Companions in Ireland and Gaul

Who were these twelve apostles in triplicate chosen successively by Fursa, Willibrord and Charlemagne? And why had Fursa, regardless of chronology, chosen St Willibrord for his group?

In his wanderings through East Anglia and northern Gaul St Fursa visited many places where the Frisians would have been. So I have not hesitated to suggest that it was as Forseti that he first made those journeys. If Forseti, alias Fursa, were the thirteenth man in that boat, how influential his testimony would have been! And if St Willibrord, the evangelist to the Frisians, were shown to be one of his disciples, Forseti, as Fursa, would go to heaven in glory, as King Radbod had wished.

But could Forseti have become Fursa? Forseti was also called Foseti and Fosta and even Vesta. The Germans called him Vorsitzer or President. Since Fursa himself was called Fro and Fros and Frosius, and in German, Forsee, he might easily have resulted from a Christian reconditioning of the Frisian ancestor. Fursa is supposedly akin to *fearta*, meaning virtues [OH I 236n], and there is in Louth a place Ath da Feartha, the Ford of two Virtues.

In Irish genealogies there were ancient ancestors called Forsaid [CGH 318] and Farsad and Fossan. And one of the four survivors of the Flood, besides those in the Ark, was called Fors. He landed on the east coast of Ireland.

And who were the twelve companions? Is it not likely that some of them were tribal ancestors, colleagues of Forseti, who, like him, lent their venerable authority to the new religion? Four or five of them adapt themselves readily to such a suggestion.

St Meldan

Take first St Meldan Mac Ui Cuinn (7 Feb.) of Inis Ui Cuinn, now Inchiquin Island in Loch Corrib. He and Beoan were among the closest of Fursa's friends, though it was their bones and not themselves that Fursa took with him to Picardy. They appeared to him in his celebrated vision, and Canon O'Hanlon thinks that Melden or Meaux, which is near Lagny, Fursa's principle cult centre in Picardy, may have taken its name from this dead saint of Loch Corrib. I find this difficult to believe. Lagny is in the territory of the ancient tribe, the Meldi, and it is to them that the name of Melden or Meaux is usually attributed. They must have had an ancestor called Mel or Meld or Meldan, who was culted also by distant relatives in Galway. O'Rahilly [EIHM 52] characteristically argues on philological grounds that the Meldi were called after their thunder god 'Meldos' who had an Irish counterpart Sigmall (Segu-meldos) on Loch Ree.

Indeed Mella was one of the leaders of the Fir Bolg at the great battle of Moytura, near Corrib [Wilde's *Loch Corrib*, 226]. As I have mentioned, when these ancestors were christianized, their simultaneous appearances in remote parts of Europe had to be explained by long pilgrimages. I link the Mel-Meld saints with the Sons of Mil or Miled.

What is one to make of St Beoan or Beodan, Meldan's brother, whose bones travelled with his to Peronne and who was culted with him (25 Oct.) in Co. Down? He has many equally fabulous namesakes, particularly in Ulster. It was a St Beoan, who resurrected a mermaid, St Muirgen, from Loch Neagh and baptized her, and he might well be connected with the Dal Buain of Ulster, to which belonged Milchu maccu Booin, St Fursa's grandfather and Patrick's employer on Slemish Mountain. And there is a Buan mentioned at the battle of Moytura [hence in Wilde *op. cit.* 220, Beoan and Mellan occur together also as father and grandfather of St Mo Chaemog (VSH II 164)].

But what was Beoan or Beodan's link with northern Gaul? There is nothing sure, but there may well have been Bod folk closer to Picardy than Normandy, where the Bodiocasses or Baiocasses lived in classical times. I have treated them as Budino-Getae and suggested that Catubodua, the war goddess, allegedly 'Raven of War', was their ancestor.

St Faelan

What is one to say of St Faelan and St Ultan, St Fursa's brothers? Why did they travel so far from Corrib? There were Faelan tribes all over Ireland and I have treated their saints, and for various reasons the Ultan saints too, with the Vellauni. In Britain the Catuvellauni stretched from Hertfordshire to East Anglia and also are recorded to the east of Lagny, St Fursa's cult centre. To the south, at Beaune, was Vellaunodunum. But through the centuries tribes wander far and exact geographical coincidence cannot be expected. I have assembled the Faelan names under 'The Vellauni' in my Glossary.

St Goban

Finally there was St Goban and his brother, St Algisus. St Goban of Corrib and Laon has all the marks of a tribal ancestor. He is probably connected with the Gubraige or Cupraige of east Galway, descended from Gubbi. Corrib itself is Carpic, for Corb, like Meld or Mella, was a great Fir Bolg leader at the battle of Moytura on the shores of Corrib, and the lake itself is also called Corbo. If it were not for the Cupraige, would St Cyprian, a Carthaginian saint, have had a well on the shores of Corrib [Wilde 76]? Note the similar St Cuppa of Corrib [H 124].

Why did St Goban go with St Fursa to Suffolk and to Picardy? I have treated him and Corbican as Carpic saints and already discussed their travels. I have noted that the name of St Fursa's Suffolk monastery was Crobheresburgh or Cnobheresburg and Crobh is a Carpic tribal element. Possibly there were memories of Carp folk in East Anglia and the Girvii of Lincoln and Huntingdon and Carvetii might be their distant kinsmen. In Gaul St Goban, as I have narrated, had many 'Carpic' adventures, which he shared in part with St Corbican.

St Algisus

St Algisus (2 Jun.), who was St Goban's brother and St Corbican's godfather, is more complicated. After leaving Ireland he built himself an oratory in Picardy on the river Oise but in order to complete it he decided to sell his Irish property, so he sent Corbican to bring back the purchase price. But Corbican, who lived on roots and suffered from ague, died in Ireland after collecting the payment. Then Algisus' parents carried out a plan which the two saints had agreed on in Picardy. They wrapped up the money, together with St Corbican's corpse, in waxed linen cloth and bound it with two hides and entrusted it to the sea. It floated up the Seine and up the Oise to the oratory where St Algisus awaited it. He took out the money and buried the body with psalms and hymns. I believe that Algisus is Faelgus, ancestor of the Clann Faelgus in the Irish midlands [FEN 387]. The Fael saints dropped the 'F' freely, Faelan being also Aelan [CGH 310] (see Ailgiusa of Clonmacnois [H 124]; D. L. Gougaud, *Gaelic Pioneers of Christianity*, 1923, p. 135, the well of St Algise at Vervins (Aisne); Ailgesach, etc, original manuscript). I think the idea of the anecdote is to link this Irish tribe with the Vellocasses who left their name at Vexin on the Oise. And I suggest that Algisus and Faelgus were forms of the Vellauno-Getic ancestor who had been inherited by both the Gaulish and the Irish tribe.

Fursa in East Anglia

We still have to consider Fursa's own travels through England and his journey through Gaul to Peronne. Scottish writers say he went first to Scotland, and Irish writers put his arrival in Suffolk about twenty years before the English do. Christianity had already come to East Anglia but in an odd form. King Redwald had been converted but, from deference to his piously pagan wife, he had compromised. He had erected a temple in which there was one altar to Christ and one to 'some demons'. Were these demons ancestors and comparable to those sinners, who became saints, Cianan, MacCuill, MacCarthenn, whom we have met in Ireland? If so, Fursa, Faelan, Goban and Ultan might have found a place among them and when the new very Christian King Sigebert succeeded, he would have agreed that the christianization of the various tribal ancestors, the Frisian one included, was a necessary preliminary to the conversion of East Anglia. When he built the monastery at Cnobheresburg, now Burgh Castle, near Yarmouth, the stories of the saints would have taken shape. And when one considers what trouble Forseti, whose worship may indeed have been barbarous, had given, the adjustments would have seemed a reasonable approximation to what Pope Gregory I had decreed in AD 601.

> The temples of the idols in Britain ought not to be destroyed, but let the idols that are in them be destroyed. Let Holy Water be made and sprinkled in the said temples; let altars be created and relics replaced.

It was well known that Gregory himself had a great appetite for pious legends.

But in East Anglia, as in Frisia, there was a serious setback. In 642 King Penda of Mercia arrived, defeated the good King Sigebert, who had become a monk, and began to restore paganism. Perhaps even Sigebert's work had been half-hearted for we are told that the heathen altar that Redwald had made could be seen a generation after his death and it was during this period that the pagan boat burial at Sutton Hoo, which is attributed to an East Anglian king, occurred.

When Penda arrived, St Fursa, his two brothers and a large company of saints set off for Gaul and on the way had some of those adventures that I have recorded and many more. Fursa bequeathed to his monks in East Anglia a belt, which they covered with gold. Those who wore it found themselves relieved of unchaste desires. The monks had also treasured and preserved his nail parings and some of his hair.

St Fursa in Gaul

A very significant halting place on his travels was a village called Macerias, now Mazières, where Fursa resurrected the dead son of a count and to which he was later to return to die, so that it was called after him Frochaeus. At the next town, when a rich woman called Erminfinde refused his meek request for a night's lodging, Fursa ordered her to be possessed of demons. When she was truly penitent, Fursa cured her and she 'gave herself and her vast possessions to the Lord'. The wealthy Erminfinde looks tribal and as if she had important relations. Who could they have been? The Hermiones were west of the Elbe, but the Veneti could be anywhere.

After some further adventures Fursa went to Lorraine, which at that time stretched to Frisia, and there once more he received the patronage of a king called Sigebert and further duplications are evident. Faelan and Ultan were established in a monastery at Fossey near Liège, Goban at St Gobain near Laon and St Algisus at Thierache. Fursa himself went to Lagny on the Marne, six miles from Paris. From there he was invited to Peronne and at last found a resting place for the relics of St Beodan and Meldan in a newly built church nearby. Here he did many very dreary miracles and at last died at Mazières when he was making a pilgrimage back to Suffolk.

At Mazières, or Frochaeus, where he had previously performed a miracle, a church was built for him called Froheim or Frosheim, for in Flemish Fursa was called Fros or Fro.

Could the Frisians Have Reached Ireland?

But were the Frisians ever in Sligo and Galway and Louth and Suffolk and Picardy? King Cormac is said to have entertained them at Tara [OC III 7] and Procopius wrote that the Frissones once held Brittia with the Angles and Britons. Who can, at this stage, say where they were and when? Tacitus records them in northern Europe in the first century AD and they may have been there long before. The sea was all around them. Did they never cross it without notifying the historians? The Firth of Forth was called the Frisian Sea. So was the sea north of Ireland Muir Frisegda [H 550] and Dumfries, which was held to be the Fort of the Frisians, lay on its shores. The Somme valley is full of places like Frise and Froissy and Froisse, and in East Anglia some say that such place names as Frissen-field and Frostenden, Friston and Friskney betray the Frisians. In Ireland they are to be conjectured not only from the Fris tribe in Sligo but also from many curious stories about showers, for *fras* is a shower. A king of Ireland, Niall Frossach, the showery, was so called because in his reign three showers of honey or blood and wheat and silver (all these are tribal words, *mil, fuil, cruithneacht, airgead*), fell in Inishowen, Co. Donegal. In the reign of another chieftain, Fergal, three similar showers fell at the same spot. It is not far from Lifford, where we find Drimfries and Frosses (see p. 95).

There was a shower of bones at Rath Cnamross (Cnamfros) in Leinster after a hero had dissolved on a shield and a shower of blood, *fros fola*, fell in great clots at Ard Ciannach, Duma Dessa, near Duleek, Co. Meath in AD 875 [Ir Nenn 209]. This was the territory of the Ulster Fursa, and it was only a repetition of a disaster that had befallen the same neighbourhood two centuries earlier. Man and beast had died after a disease-bearing shower. St Columba was obliged to send St Silnan to stem the plague with a piece of consecrated bread [Reeves, Adamnan II 4].

Patrick prophesied that the assemblies of King Ferchar of the Deisi would always be showery and there were several other showery Irish heroes [TRIP 208]. Certainly these heroes were not concerned with our normal Irish rain. What therefore was it that obsessed them? Till someone suggests a more likely source of concern, I shall stick to my theory of the Frisians.

CHAPTER 25

The Cicones

There were a number of Irish saints and heroes with remarkable breasts. There was St Mochua Ciceach, the breasty, who was also called Da Luanus of Craoibheach (4 Jun.). There is no record that he used his breasts for feeding babies of future eminence, but we must assume he did, for Lugaid Cichech fed the ancestor of the O'Mahonys from one breast and the ancestor of the O'Donoghues from the other. St Colman Ela had a pap of honey and a pap of milk for two other such ancestors, Baithen and Ultan, but he is not called Cicech and, without more evidence, I hesitate to equate him with that St Colman, who ministered at Cell Ciche (Breast Cell). There were other breasty heroes: among the males, Didil Cicech had three paps, Codal Corr-Chichech had round paps, and Fer Cichech, son of Fergus, is perhaps the same as Fer Cechech, who was ancestor of the Orbraige. Among the women, Admaer Trechichech had, as her name implies, three breasts. So did Fainche Tre-Chichech; Derinell Cetharchichech, the mother of St Mura, had four breasts. We are not told that Coinne Chichech, the ancestress of the Cinel Coinne, had breasts that were in any way remarkable.

One ought perhaps to mention Inber Cichmaine, a bay in Co. Down, which took its name, we are told, either from Cichmaine, son of Ailill Find, who was killed there, or from the breasts of Maine Tai. Inber Cichmaine was named after Cichban (White-breast), wife of Slanga [LG III 7]. This word as Cichmine occurs in ogam in the Dingle peninsula in Kerry. It suggests to me that there may have been a Kerry Cic tribe, whose name survives in the Da Chich Danainne, 'the Paps', just because the name describes so perfectly the two Kerry mountains, which are so called. I do not know if the Da Cic na Morrigna, in Co. Meath, the two Paps of Morrigna, are so appropriately named.

Was there an ancient tribe, whose name stimulated the poets to invent all these breasty ancestors? I can find none except the Ui Cichearain, who left their name at Lis Cicherain in Galway, and the Ui Cichainech or Breast-faced tribe of Muskerry and the legendary Muinter Ciogal that invaded Ireland. Cicol Grigairglun, their leader, was the son of Lot from the Caucasus. There were two other legendary Cicals and Cicols. One of them, a woman, was a grotesque, like Cicol Grigairglun, and wife of Fer Caille. In Gaul Mars was worshipped as Cicolui or Mars Cicinus in the Côte d'Or. Holder translates this the 'breasty' one.

There is Ciochmag, Breast-plain, and Duma Chich, as well as Cell Chich, but since I do not believe that early place names are ever descriptive, I am forced to suggest a pre-Celtic tribe. The most probable tribe seems to me the Cicones, known to us on the river Hebrus in Thrace. Perhaps their name, even in classical times, suggested – in a current tongue from which Irish descended – something 'breasty' and female, because it was the women of the Cicones who tore Orpheus to pieces. The Amazons were called in Irish Cich Loiscthe or 'burnt breasts', which is presumed to be a translation of *amazoi*, breastless, but was there a story that the Amazons burnt their breasts off? Or is there a possibility that the legend of the breastless women arose from a Greek translation of some ancient pun, an adaptation of a tribal compound word? That the Greeks were given to tribal puns is well known. Ligurians were connected with *ligys*, shrill, Dorians with *doron*, a gift, etc. In Ireland it is just possible that the Chich folk, who lived in Kerry, if they lived anywhere, provoked the Irish form of the Amazon legends, for we are told that the famous Kerry hero, Cu Roi mac Daire, battled against the Cichloiscthe or the Amazons.

CHAPTER 26

The Colours of the Winds

My study of the colours of the winds needs a page or two of introduction. Many early peoples wrote their histories in terms of tribal puns and of geneaologies in which eponymous ancestors of tribes took the place of real men and women. Stories of these ancestors were woven fancifully out of the names of tribes of whose real meaning the storyteller, who possibly spoke a different language from theirs, can have had no idea.

It has long been thought that Perseus and Medea, the ancestors of the Persians and the Medes, were given, when adopted by the Greeks, adventures that accorded with the sound-equivalent in Greek of their inscrutable oriental names.[1] To a Greek, Perseus suggested *perthein*, which means to destroy. Medea suggests the Greek word for devising or planning, so Perseus slew dragons and Medea plotted.

Similarly, biblical scholars hold that the twelve sons of Jacob took their names eponymously from the tribes they are supposed to have fathered.[2] From these names that may have belonged to non-Hebrew tribes assimilated by the Israelites, the writer of Genesis deduced a Hebrew meaning. Thus Issachar suggests 'hire' or 'shoulder' so various 'hirings' of a concubine for Jacob and some mandrakes for Rachel to promote conception were arranged by Leah when she bore him.[3] Later he bore burdens on his shoulder.[4] Victorian scholars were worried by the implications of the genealogies that we find in Genesis. How could Esau's grandson, Amelek, be the ancestor of the Amelekits since they are mentioned several generations before he was born? How could Heth, ancestor of the Hittites, be of father Canaan, ancestor of the Canaanites, when there is no evidence of racial affinity? These difficulties vanish if we grasp that

233

one of the purposes of the genealogies was to promote a sense of brotherhood between tribes that possibly shared neither race nor language.

Has anyone looked to early Ireland for traces of this ancient practice of writing history by means of anecdotes, by punning tribal names, by genealogies and eponymous ancestors? The evidence is surely there. Let us consider first the scores of very odd afternames worn by hundreds of heroes, ancestors, saints. I prefer 'afternames' to 'nicknames' since they are more like tribal attributes from which a word-juggler has extracted a Gaelic meaning. There are, for example, countless notables called *breac*, speckled, *cael*: thin, *garb*, rough, *mael*, bald, *menn*, dumb or stammering, *salach*, dirty. There are also compound names like *mennbricc*, dumb-speckled, *maelgarb*, bald-rough, *maelruad*, bald-red. And there are others too with strange coloured afternames, *buidhe*, yellow, *glas*, green, *odhar*, dun, and many more.

And to all these afternames there are corresponding tribes and compound tribes. Remembering that Irish tribal names had the suffix '-raige' or prefixes such as Ui (modern O') and Sil and Cenel, we find the Breacraige, the Caelraige, the Garbraige, the Ui Mael, the Mennraige, the Rudraige and the Cenel Salach and compound tribes like the Sil Mennbric and the Ui Maelgarba.

And often, as with the sons of Jacob, tribes took their names, we are told, from some peculiarity or episode conveyed by their ancestor's aftername. I do not know why Fergus Salach, the ancestor of the Cenel Salach of Argyll, was dirty, but Cuscraid Menn, the ancestor of the Mennraige, was dumb because the Connacht hero, Cet, had slit his windpipe.[5] Tuathal Maelgarb of the Ui Maelgarba was 'bald-rough' because his mother, when the birth pains came, had pressed against a stone so that his head was all 'hills and hollows'.[6] Yet surely the chroniclers of these strange stories were merely giving entertaining explanations of names that were foreign and meaningless to them. Surely, like Issachar, Fergus Salach took his name from his tribe and was dirty because that was the Irish sound equivalent of his name. *Menn*, *mael*, *garb* and *salach* were among the most frequent of the elements from which Irish tribal names were composed.

I have suggested that these elements of names and afternames derive, in various worn-down forms, from the names of the continental tribes that first invaded Ireland and intermarried with those who were there before them.[7] Through the Greeks and Romans we know of many of the tribes that ranged over Europe in these early centuries. Can we identify any of those who came to Ireland? Who for example were the speckled (*breac*) folk, a very large group that included Nectan Breac, an ancient king of Scotland, four speckled saints and many of the earliest invaders and chieftains of Ireland?

26. THE COLOURS OF THE WINDS

I think we get a clue in south Co. Waterford where the Ui Bricc or Ui Brigte tribe had two alternative ancestors, Brigit[8] and Eogan Breac or Bricc[9] and a third variant, Bregdolb[10] or Brecdolb[11] who had a brother, Dolb, ancestor of the Ui Dolb. Surely Bregdolb belongs to an earlier genealogical system when the artist did not try to conceal his art and the amalgamated tribes had amalgamated ancestors.

No one would deny, I believe, that the Ui Brigte were the appropriately placed representatives of the Brigantes of Thrace whom Ptolemy located among the earliest invaders of Yorkshire and south-east Ireland. In Yorkshire they worshipped the goddess ancestor Brigantia, and she has been frequently linked with St Brigit of Kildare who had various disciples called Breac and Breaca.

I believe the other 'coloured' tribes had similar origins. While I was wondering about this, I came across a mysterious passage that might have some bearing on my problem. It is in the *Seanchas Mor*, the great Irish law compilation, which is reported to have been put together in St Patrick's time. It is about the colours of the winds, and it is wild and inscrutable until we recall the early Irish tribal custom of recording history by anecdotes punning tribal names, geneaolgies and eponymous ancestors. It then emerges as a successful poetic attempt to convey ethnographical information.

The passage runs:

> He, the Lord, then created the colours of the winds so that the colour of each differs from the other; namely the white, *gel*, and the crimson, *corcra*; the blue-green, *glas*, and the green, *uaine*; the yellow, *buidhe*, and the red, *derg*; the black, *dub*, and the grey, *liath*; the mottled, *alad*, and the dark, *temin*; the dull-black, *ciar*, and the dun, *odur*. From the east comes the crimson, *corcra*, wind, from the south the white, *gel*, from the north the black, *dub*, from the west the dun, *odur*.
>
> The red (*derg*) and the yellow (*buidhe*) are produced between the white (*gel*) wind and the crimson (*corcra*); the green (*uaine*) and the blue-green (*glas*) are produced between the dun (*odur*) and the white (*glegil*); the grey (*liath*) and the dull-black (*ciar*) are produced between the dun (*odur*) and the jet-black (*cir-dub*); the dark (*temin*) and the mottled (*alad*) are produced between the black (*dub*) and the crimson (*corcra*), and these are all the subwinds contained in each and all the cardinal winds.

Eugene O'Curry, whose translation I use, comments on this: 'This theory of coloured winds apparently refers to the more characteristic colours which the clouds assume about the rising and the setting sun and which to a certain extent depend on the wind which blows at the time. It contains at least evidence of a distinct theory of the relations and combinations of colours.'[12]

Would any modern meteorologist be able to detect some Dark Age science behind these observations of colours and winds or any validity in O'Curry's comments on them? Surely it is significant that eleven of these fourteen winds have tribal names precisely corresponding to them and that the remaining three, *alad*, *gel* and *glegil*, are on the verge of a correspondence. Moreover most of these tribes are to be found at an appropriate point of the compass.

Perhaps I attach too much importance to these correct locations. I contend that early proper names containing, for example, the word *liath*, grey, marked the passage of a people of whom the Ui Liathain were the historic representatives, and that other tribes left their traces analogously. Though most early tribes were more densely concentrated in one region than another, they had all ranged widely over Ireland so the author of the wind chart may have selected such locations of early tribes as best accorded with his colour sense. He is only inconsistent with this twice when he suggests that the green and grey could be produced between the dun and white and the red and yellow between the crimson and white.

On the whole the tribes – if you accept them as tribes – are nearly all correctly placed. In the chart below I have noted those colours where the position of the corresponding tribe is precisely right.

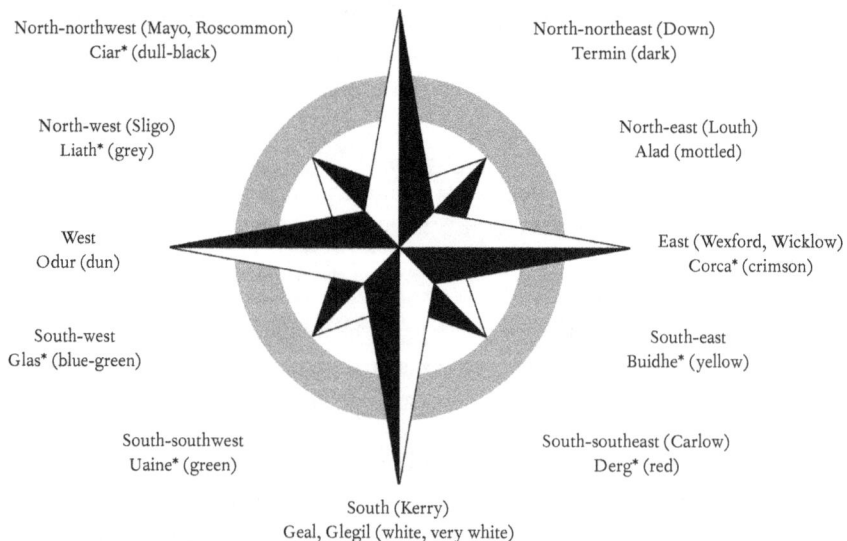

TRIBAL DISTRIBUTION BY THE COLOURS OF THE WINDS

North (Ulster)
Cir-Dub, Dub (jet-black, black)

North-northwest (Mayo, Roscommon)
Ciar* (dull-black)

North-northeast (Down)
Termin (dark)

North-west (Sligo)
Liath* (grey)

North-east (Louth)
Alad (mottled)

West
Odur (dun)

East (Wexford, Wicklow)
Corca* (crimson)

South-west
Glas* (blue-green)

South-east
Buidhe* (yellow)

South-southwest
Uaine* (green)

South-southeast (Carlow)
Derg* (red)

South (Kerry)
Geal, Glegil (white, very white)

*Colours where the position of the corresponding tribe is precisely correct.

26. THE COLOURS OF THE WINDS

North north-west: the Ciarraige of Mayo and Roscommon fit the Ciarwind well.[13] North-west: the Ui Liathain are better known in west Cork, but were great wanderers.[14] O'Donovan locates them in the north-east of Sligo and this accords.[15] West: the Odraige and Odorige are unlocated. The Ui Mac Uidir (the Maguires) are from the north-west midlands. The Clann Odorain are in the west but seem too far south.[16] South-west: the Glasraige are very widespread. The Glasraigi Arad fit just right.[17] South south-west: the Glasraigi Arad's neighbours and kinsmen, the Uaithne, also fit.[18] If this word also meaning 'green' is not close enough to Uaine, we have the Muinter Uainidi of Co. Clare equally well placed.[19] South: the Geal and Glegil winds are difficult. I suspect that Tempall Geal, Uisce Geal and Cathair Geal, all in Kerry, derive from tribes and not from whiteness [ed. note: One of Butler's linguistic markers, the 'sc' sound from Iberia, in the Uisce Gael tribal name matches the genetic DNA analysis of the most prevalent male Atlantic Irish y-chromosome in Kerry]. South south-east: the Ui Derggain and Clann Deirg (Carlow region) are rightly placed.[20] South-east: the Ui Buidhe suit.[21] East: The Clann Corcrain of Wexford-Wicklow are consistent.[22] North-east: the Alad wind is difficult. For the Ulaid of Ulster they would conform. There is a tribe, the Corcu Aland of Ulster, which seems to be the same as the Ulaid. There were place names, Cluain Alad and Ath Aladh, in the midlands and Louth. North north-east: the Temin wind must be linked with the Clann Temin but I can only trace it in Co. Sligo.[23] There is also the Ui Timin of Leinster, descended from Eocho Timin who on a certain occasion showed himself as *timin*, a weakling.[24] In north north-east Ireland the nearest likely tribe was the Sil Demain who once ruled Ulster or a large portion thereof, or a later more historical people, the Cenel Demmain of Strangford Lough. They were linked with demons. St Comgal of Bangor, Co. Down, had to expel a demon from a nearby rath called Rath Temmayn or Demmayn.[25] North: the Dubraige of Imlech Corcu Duib in Ulster, descended from Dubad, son of Mugdorn Dub, are rightly placed.[26]

We are left with the two alternate winds, the Cir-Dub or jet-black to the north, and the Glegil or very-white to the south. I cannot trace the Clann Cirdubain, the jet-black, in the north, but it is recorded in the west midlands where three tribes, the Clann Cirand, the Cenel Dubhain and the Clann Cirdubain, belong to the Conmaicne group.[27] Ciru, the ancestor of the first, was uncle of Dubhan, the ancestor of the second. Cirdubain figures to the west where he is grandfather of St Iarlath of Tuam and a member of the Clann Cirand.[28] The original

Cirdubain must have been like Bregdolb an amalgamated ancestor. The fact that the Clann Cirdubain existed with such an extraordinary name confirms me in my belief that the winds were tribal.

Only the Glasgil wind of the south has no discoverable tribe, yet there are two heroes, Sgoith Glegeal, son of Manannan, and Gleigal Garb, who figure in the story of the children of Tuirean.[29] To me that suggests there was a Glegeal-Gleigal tribe.

There were other tribes that recall other colours, *finn*, white, *ruad*, red, *gorm*, blue, *breac*, speckled, which the poet geographer did not need. There is such a rich variety that one might suppose that Irish tribes had a special liking for colour names. This is not so. I believe that all these tribal names are immensely old and developed out of other names with different meanings. In human speech there is a natural drift from the obscure to the appropriate, or at least the intelligible, and these names are the result. Take Fergus Dergbotha for example.[30] You will see that after his name is also Tregbotha and Threagbotha. If you are ingenious enough to find a meaning for the first variant, it will not apply to the second or the third.

In conclusion I have tried to explain this mysterious passage about the colours of the winds in the *Seanchas Mor* by attributing it to the familiar tribal practice of the early Irish of writing history by anecdotes, punning tribal names, genealogies and eponymous ancestors. I am conscious I may be wrong. *Hominum est errare et nescire.*

NOTES AND REFERENCES

1. Herodotus, Vol. VII, pp. 61–2.
2. M. Noth, *History of Israel: Biblical History* (Adam & Charles Black, London, 1958), p. 125.
3. Genesis, 30; 18.
4. Genesis, 49; 14.
5. R. Thurneysen, *Die Irischen Helden und Konigssage bis Zumsiebzehnten Jahihundert* (Salle, Halle, 1921), p. 94.
6. S.H. O'Grady, *Silva Gadelica* (Williams & Norgate, Edinburgh, 1892), Vol. II, p. 514.
7. H. Butler, *Ten Thousand Saints, A Study in Irish and European Origins* (The Wellbrook Press, Kilkenny, 1972), pp. 28–108.
8. M.A. O'Brien, *Corpus Genealogiarum Hiberniae* (Institute for Advanced Studies, Dublin, 1962), p. 116.

9. *ibid.* p. 397.
10. *ibid.* p. 394.
11. J. O'Hart, *Irish Pedigrees* (MH Gill, Dublin, 1881), p. 236.
12. E. O'Curry, *Manners and Customs of the Ancient Irish* (Williams & Norgate, Edinburgh, 1873), Vol. II, p. 133.
13. O'Brien, *op. cit.*, p. 279.
14. *ibid.* p. 195.
15. J. O'Donovan, *Genealogies, Tribes and Customs of Hy-Fiachrach* (University Press, MH Gill, Dublin, 1844), p. 2.
16. O'Brien, *op. cit.*, p. 299.
17. *ibid.* p. 321.
18. *ibid.* p. 321.
19. *ibid.* p. 245.
20. *ibid.* p 77.
21. *ibid.* pp. 29–30.
22. ibid. p. 348.
23. E.S.J. Hogan, *Onomasticon Goedelicum* (Hodges & Figgis, Dublin, 1910), p. 245.
24. O'Brien, *op. cit.* p. 65.
25. O'Grady, *op. cit.* p. 542.
26. C.H. Plummer, *Vitae Sanctorum Hiberniae* (Clarendon Press, Oxford, 1910) Vol. II, p. 167.
27. O'Brien, *op. cit.* p. 152.
28. W.M. Hennessy & D.H. Kelly (eds), *The Book of Fenagh* (Alexander Thom, Dublin, 1875) pp. 383, 387.
29. O'Donovan, Todd & Reeves (eds), *The Martyrology of Donegal* (Thom, Dublin, 1864) p. 349.
30. O'Brien, *op. cit.* p. 49.

Chapter 27
The Saints Leave Ireland
A Poem

The hagiographical details of this poem are accurate. St Odran, the hero, was a famous saint of Iona. It is said that St Columba, finding that demons were infesting a site where he wished to build, discovered that only by burying a holy man alive could they be exorcized. St Odran volunteered, but after three days Columba decided to dig him up again for news of heaven. St Odran, on being uncovered, instead of giving suitable information said: 'There is no wonder in Death, and Hell is not as it is reported.' Thereupon Columba cried out furiously: 'Earth, earth upon the mouth of Odran that he may blab no more!' And he was covered up again.

Odran, in this poem, talks of rejoining 'the gods'; he had not, at the time, read O'Brien's *Corpus Genealogiarum*, or he would have said 'our ancestors'.

> 'How can we stop men sinning?' wailed the monks.
> 'We've filled a thousand gilded shrines with bones,
> rekindled many an undying fire that died,
> renewed St Colman's thumb, St Lactan's arm;
> we've edited the lives of ninety saints
> and placed among St Patrick's next-of-kin
> the forebears of the just who pay their dues;
> we've put such curses in St Findlug's mouth
> that ulcers budded in the king of Creeve.

27. THE SAINTS LEAVE IRELAND — A POEM

And many a time, our chronicles relate,
arms withered, tongues dropped out, eyes lost their sight,
when evil men infringed our grazing rights
or made foul jests about our private lives.
But still men sin, they fornicate, they lie,
they dodge, they quibble, and distort the truth.
Ah, saints of Ireland, serve us, who have served!'

The saints said nothing and a hundred years
went by before it all began again.
'How can we stop men sinning?' wailed the monks,
'We've christened all the temperance clubs and guilds
with names of saints. We've built St Moling's School,
St Flann's Infirmary, St Ronan's Bank.
We've edited the saints for boys and girls,
omitting all that's coarse, grotesque, unclean.
And now at last in eighteen fifty-six,
through five years raffles, carnivals, appeals,
we've reared St Findlug's splendid church at Creeve
(it cost us all of forty thousand pounds),
copied from one the bishop saw at Rome.
But up-to-date, with scenes from Findlug's life
in washable Durescin in the nave
and angels holding lacquered gasoliers.
Nearby to mask the hot-water pipes a screen
of costliest malachite and porphyry,
donated by the Mayor of Boston's niece.
And in the sacristy the vestment press
even for the altar-boys is richly scrolled
by boarders of St Findlug's orphanage.
Upon the tympanum mid rich mosaic,
by Messers Meyer of Munich, Patrick stands,
enthroning Findlug in the See of Creeve
(he's in Carrara by Maguires of Cork),
while St Lugitha holds the title-deeds.
But still men sin, they fornicate, they lie,
they dodge, they quibble, and distort the truth.
Ah, saints of Ireland, serve us, who have served!'

The saints said nothing and a hundred years
went by before it all began again.
'How can we stop men sinning?' wailed the monks.
'We've taken the lead in sacred scholarship;
we've edited the lives with copious notes
and saints that even the Bollandists accept,
we've sometimes queried and ourselves condemned
the passages where solar myth has farced
the text. Why, Canon Keefe, page ninety-four,
note eight, declares St Findlug never lived
and that St Patrick never went to Creeve.
The episode (see ZCP Vol. V), is based
on faulty reading of defective texts.
We do not hide the truth from those, who read
the learned monthlies for the Honours Course.
But why confuse the simple or offend
the kinsmen of the Mayor of Boston's niece,
who lavished masses for her soul's repose?
Henceforward, though, our bishop is averse
from dedications to the obscurer saints.
He recommends the Roman Calendar.
Though Roman saints are often odd, like ours,
they're better known than our poor Findlug is
and have good standing with the Bollandists.
While much more up-to-date for nursing homes
are names like Bernadette and Fatima.
But still men sin, they fornicate, they lie,
they dodge, they quibble and distort the truth.
Ah, saints of Ireland, serve us, who have served!'

They moaned like this from habit. All supposed
the saints would take no notice, as before.
But Odran, always tactless and sincere,
poked up his head above the sod and said;
'You don't believe in us. It's just pretence!
Look at the footnotes, never mind the text!
When scholars hint, the vulgar show their hands.
They do not honour us. It's time to leave.

27. THE SAINTS LEAVE IRELAND — A POEM

Because I was St Patrick's charioteer,
a bookie used my name to mask his frauds.
St Lachtan's Dairy waters all the milk;
St Ita's Laundry tears the sheets to shreds.
Does Brendan care a rap for Training Ships
or Seamens' Missions? Does the Fire Brigade
need Lassar's patronage? It's all pretence!
You're using us to gild the status quo,
to lend a fake romance to platitude,
to clothe some prelate's lust for consequence,
some builder's greed in pitchpine and cement.'
Then bawled the fiercest of the saints, Fecheen;
'I'm patron of some Convalescent Home,
I, who once seized de Lacy by the leg,
bending to steal the head-stone from my grave.
He ran to Multyfarnham raving mad.
And Bridget said: 'When Strongbow lay abed,
I flogged him with my crozier until he died.
Ask Canice how de Peipo's archers fared,
who cut his grove at Finglas. Let us go!'

Then all around the coast the sacred rocks
began to float, Cuanna's, Declan's, Mogue's.
St Farnan launched his mighty oaken cross,
posting four saints at each extremity
to chant the psalms. Caldrons and altar-stones
and floating dolmens teemed in every bay,
St Gobban's anvil, St Molua's tub.
And for the saints that had no private craft
St Brendan brought his fleet to Dingle Bay,
skippered by Ternoc, Malo and Finbarr.
From every townland, lis and rath the saints
drifted and stowed their sacred gear aboard.
And Caeman, Patrick's chamberlain, took charge
and listed all the items in the hold;
St Finnchu's meat-hook and St Gobnait's bees,
the relics Onnchu carried from Clonmore,
two flying croziers and one jaundiced bell,

ten thousand casks of water turned to wine,
great bales of meat made fish and fish made meat.
And meanwhile Ailbe, swineherd of the pope,
marshalled the sacred livestock on the deck,
the stags that carried bibles on their horns,
the wolves that suckled saints, the dogs that preached,
the lambs that bleated hymns in thieves' insides,
Molaisse's badger, St Columba's crane,
three cocks that crowed for Matins, fourteen birds
that made their nests in cowls. Then fleas,
one case (St Nannan's), and St Finan's lice.
And while they listed, St Molua wept;
'We've lived beside them fifteen hundred years,
bearing the burden that their gods had borne.
We've cheered their loneliness and eased their pain
and veiled with poetry many an ugly deed.
How can we leave with all these precious things?
How will they fare?' St Dubhlitter, the clerk,
replied; 'There's less than you'd suppose down there.
That bale of curses that St Ruan brought
was put near Patrick's blessings in the hold.
They cancelled out precisely. Even the saints
are much reduced. That double bang you heard
was Ternoc meeting Naile on the deck.
Talking of Invernaile's rights and dues,
in mutual malediction both dissolved.
Those little puffs of smoke were homonyms,
meeting and merging. Fifteen Colmans fused,
ten Lassars, six misprints jumped overboard.
And fifty, badly mauled by Canon Keefe,
as late interpolations, all expired.
Let us be sailing now e'er worse befall.'
And Odran, peering down into the hold,
declared: 'There's nothing much in all this junk
they need regret. The lazy ones, of course,
will always want their cheeses made from stones.
But those with minds and hearts, by reason's light,
in brotherhood ...' but all the saints began

27. THE SAINTS LEAVE IRELAND — A POEM

to yawn affectedly: 'Why Mrs Humphrey Ward
said all of that in eighteen eighty-eight.
It's old hat now. Professor E.O. James
has plucked the Golden Bough.' And Findlug said:
'In his last Lenten Pastoral at Creeve,
our bishop showed how modernism is dead.'
But Odran, barely listening, bumbled on:
'I think we saints, in general, symbolize
those inner conflicts, tribal, personal,
the conscious mind has failed to reconcile
and hence externalized. And we survive
through muddled sentiment and failing nerve.'
He whispered absently in Findlug's ear:
'Look up that reference in Canon Keefe!'
St Findlug flinched, turned pale, began to quote
more Lenten Pastoral, abruptly stopped,
then sullenly said: 'Right! But where'll we go?'
And Odran answered: 'To rejoin the gods,
flesh of our flesh, conceived from nothingness,
our kinsmen, whom we routed and replaced,
and now, replaced ourselves, rejoin as friends.
There Lug will take Molua by the hand,
and Bran will welcome Brendan as his mate.
Sardus will call me brother, Hercules
will greet St Erc and from their golden thrones
the Phrygian gods in reverence will rise
to meet the Holy Virgin of Kildare.'
Then Findlug muttered gruffly; 'Let's be gone!'
And soon the great Armada sailed away,
skirting the Dingle coast through Blasket Sound.
And were they bangs or murmurs of the sea?
And was it mist that veiled the fleet from sight
beyond Kilshannig Point? And did they reach,
with saints and stock and sacred gear intact,
the haven of the gods? I do not know.

2 February 1956

Afterword
Irish Saints, Heroes and Tribes:
Bio-Archaeology and Hubert Butler

RICHARD S. CRAMPTON

Introduction

Since the centennial tribute *Unfinished Ireland, Essays on Hubert Butler* was published in 2000, Irish historical, archaeological and genetic research has verified more of his genealogical investigation in *Ten Thousand Saints, a Study in Irish and European Origins*. Alan Harrison, the late Irish-language scholar, confirmed Butler's linguistic approach to analysis of Ireland's tribal prehistory, indicating where and how to delve further into Butler's voluminous database. New discoveries, reports and books integrating Irish and European natural history, genes and bio-archaeology have also corroborated Butler's compilations of the wanderings of Irish ancestors, tribes, saints and heroes. Bio-archaeological evidence from Daniel Bradley, Barry Cunliffe, Stephen Oppenheimer, Brian Sykes, their research teams and many other genetic detectives, combined with bio-geographic data from Marion Newbigin, David Webb and Michael Viney, have provided hitherto unavailable science-based opportunities to evaluate Butler's premises and proofs of prehistoric Irish origins. In *The Atlantean Irish, Ireland's Oriental and Maritime Heritage*, Bob Quinn, a forthright amateur scrutinizer of history like Butler, traced many of the Irish tribal cultural threads identified by Butler. This essay collates Butler's canvassing of many Irish tales and linguistic remnants in *Ten Thousand Saints*, 'The Colours of the Winds' (published here for the first time) and 'Charts of Irish Tribes, Saints and Heroes' (Manuscript Library, Trinity College Dublin) with recently discovered, fascinating natural history and living archaeology of Irish and European genes. His largely overlooked work gives new investigative opportunities to bio-archaeologists since he indicated where to look for more genomic bits of Irish and European tribal prehistory.

AFTERWORD

The Country Scholar's Database

As an acclaimed leading twentieth-century essayist, Butler often said that his investigation of ten thousand saints, fifteen thousand ancestors and heroes, fifty tribes and the first invaders of Ireland was his most important work. He showed how Irish druids, poets and hagiographers used puncraft to keep prehistoric genealogical chronicles up to date. The druidic pre-surname Irish family tree, possibly begun before the last great glacial melt 7000 years ago, incorporated Irish tribal ancestors from Europe's Stone Age onward. Ten years after Butler's death in 1991, the science of human, animal, vegetable and bacterial molecular archaeogenetics gave new insights into Irish and European prehistory. He would have been pleasantly surprised that cumulative analyses of Irish, Breton, Basque, British, Cornish, Galician, Scottish, Welsh and other European male and female genes, ancient linguistics, legends, surnames, biogeography and archaeology fortuitously substantiated his prescient diachronic research. He clearly foresaw genetic connections among Irish, Basque and many other European tribes. With his legendary country scholar's skepticism of science and academics, Butler would have relished geneticist Ewan Birney's caveat: 'The genome is a bit like *War and Peace*: very long, quite boring and written in a language you don't want to learn.' Cultural anthropologists and archaeologists continue to examine and coordinate new findings from bio-anthropology, bio-archaeology and bio-geography, linking them to the history of the pre-Celtic and Celtic world of Ireland, Britain, Scotland, Wales, Cornwall, the Isle of Man, Brittany, France, Italy, Spain and the Near East. We will discuss the relevant genes later.

In 1941 Butler returned to his birthplace, Maidenhall, in the Nore valley near Bennettsbridge, Co. Kilkenny. A classically educated, gifted linguist, he proceeded to immerse himself in local prehistory and archaeology. He taught himself '*ad hoc* Irish', borrowed and collected books and journals, and read widely in Irish and European anthropological and archaeological texts. He revived the defunct Kilkenny Archaeological Society in 1944. For the next thirty-one years, before the information technology revolution, he explored many Irish archaeological sites. He assembled an onomastic, diachronic database, made tables, indices, glossaries, charts and maps. He published two reports, four essays, a dozen relevant newspaper articles and book reviews, and *Ten Thousand Saints*, a book about the origins of Irish and European heroes, ancestors, tribes and saints. He broadcast his concepts. The 1972 original edition's archaeological and anthropological linguistic Index and Glossary included 392 saints, 736 ancestors and heroes, 334 Irish tribes and their ancestors, 265 continental tribes and their ancestors, 124 historians and historic figures, and 616 commonly used tribal pun elements. In his 1971 catalogue, 'Charts of Irish Tribes, Saints and Heroes', he correlated the god, the '*da*' word for place or person, the saint, cult centre, hero, habitation and affinities to other tribes, 635 druidic 'disguise' words by pun-element, cultural variant or meme, and relevant explanatory notes. For example, the Briges tribe had 74 druidic variants, the Carpetani 80, the Mygdones 42 and the Thracians 126. The Daci had 120 '*da*' word variants for place or person. What appealed to Alan Harrison was Butler's clear indication of where to mine further rich lodes of Irish and European genomes. Butler's assembled variants, if datable, will provide geneticists with new opportunities to make more accurate assessments of Irish and European tribal prehistory.

From apparently messy, blurry, haphazard and random language, Butler systematically sought unexplained recurring peculiarities in names, beforenames and afternames and in idiosyncratic legends of Irish and European tribes, heroes and saints. His scrupulous methods and rational empiricism were resolutely inductive, like those of Alexander von Humboldt's. His evidence from assembled observations made so often is remarkably consistent. Indeed it greatly reduces chances of accepting contrarian hypotheses and surmises not based upon bio-archaeology. He accepted his work was not immutable. He sought new knowledge of discoveries, criticism and research from others. He never asked that his methodology, investigations or conclusions be taken on faith. In fact he longed for challenges to his work. Many of his qualitative and quantitative observations of linguistic combinations and patterns in the hundreds of Irish and European tribal, heroic and hagiographic names and legends have since been corroborated by ancestral bio-archaeology.

The Ancestral Irish Archetype

From his abundant compilation in *Ten Thousand Saints* and in 'Charts of Irish Tribes, Saints and Heroes', illuminated in Alan Harrison's introduction, Butler suggested early Irish saints and their allied ancestors fit an archetype. As he put it:

> We must look to the ancient pre-Celtic tribes of Europe to learn the origins of the Irish people, their tribal and ancestral names. The Irish repeatedly insisted their ancestors had come from Thrace, Spain, northern Europe and

the Caucasus. The origins of their race were heterogeneous, and they cited seventy-two peoples from whose different tongues the Irish tongue had been composed. They used the same punful picture language, in which the lives of the saints were written, and it requires to be interpreted in the same way. [TTS pp. 36–7; 'Charts of Irish Tribes, Saints and Heroes' p. 263]

A Christian by-product of the dying art of ancestor-making, Irish saints were composite ancestors of composite tribes. Well-established ancient druidic genealogical practice melded ancestors. Like the Greeks and Hebrews, Irish druids punned stories to keep tribal genealogy intact. Thousands of Irish ancestors, heroes, tribes and saints usually came punned from Irish or Latin and, rarely, English.

Thanks to the Daniel Bradley gene team's work in 2000, we now know the male Atlantic gene connects Basques to Irish, and we can examine Butler's then-unknown antecedent serendipitous discovery of it. How did Butler ever link the Irish with Basques? He asked crucial questions. Why were there ten speckled saints, eleven leper saints, and fifty saints called Mo Chua? Why did St Fintan of Aran in a rage chase the humble St Goban right across Ireland to Anglesey? Why did St Tigernach of Clones breathe alternately white, red and yellow? Why were there holy men and women nicknamed *Brocainechbindcorach* – Badger-face-sweet-tuneful, and *Derbindbelfada* – Sweet-tear-longmouth? Were these real men and women or were they, as antiquarians of 150 years previously insisted, 'monkish fictions'?

From his questions and savouring of mythological stories, Butler recognized that 'from Scythia to Gibraltar, the Celts mingled with all the people they met. Each tribe that reached Ireland carried portmanteau-wise fragments of other tribes and knew that fragments of itself coexisted in other tribal portmanteaus.'

Ironically these variant tribal word fragments he identified parallel today's molecular deoxyribonucleic acid (DNA) fragments of male and female genes with their archaeogenetic labels of 'short tandem repeat sequence, single nucleotide, restriction-fragment-length and insertion-deletion polymorphisms'. These molecular bits of genes tracked the Atlantic male's and European clan mothers' contributions to Irish and European genomes.

> There were Thracian, Iberian, German and Scythian portmanteaus with Celts in all of them, and the Celtic portmanteaus will have been as capacious and well-stocked as any. Fighting and merging its way across Europe, each tribe will have lost most of its cultural distinctiveness, as a Finn or a Bulgar does in Massachusetts. Only through their ancestral pedigrees will they have hung on to their identities. So, if we study seriously those long lists of obviously

invented beings, the tribal ancestors, every genealogy becomes a table of ingredients in a cookery book. We know how each tribal dish was composed and there are no limits to what we can learn about our past. [TTS p. 53]

Butler was well aware that language drifted although he did not describe it as the cultural equivalent of stochastic or random genetic drift as linguists and scientists do today [TTS pp. 27–30, 43–4, 53–60]. When bits of cultural imitation or inheritance replicate in languages, they are now called 'memes' or 'cultural variants'. They are thought analogous to replicator biological DNA genes but obviously less powerful. He used the term 'variants', not memes, to describe linguistic bits in names of Irish tribes, ancestors, saints and heroes that he meticulously identified, catalogued and inter-related. He recognized the importance of these cultural language variants in a myriad of druidic prefixes and suffixes. He preferred the terms 'before-' and 'afternames'. He found 'disguise' words and variants in 'pun-elements' and in the singular 'sc' sound of Basqueland. Druids and hagiologists often changed sequences of one or more prefixes and suffixes, added new syllables, made new mixtures of names for heroes, ancestors, saints and tribes with puncraft, and finally invented marvellous new bardic histories.

Early Irish Ancestors: Celtos, Scythes and Grecus

Early Irish antiquarians 'had mostly seen the saints not as objects of superstition but as numinous beings, who linked their neighbourhood and their neighbours with a Mediterranean world more ancient than Greece or Rome'. Three important ancestral memories connected the Irish to the Greeks. First, the Celtic link came from Celtos, brother of Gelonus, ancestor of the Geloni of Connacht. Celtos' other brother was Scythes, ancestor of the Scythians. Celtos and Scythes, both sons of Hercules, united the Irish and Greeks. Second, the pre-Celtic tie was Grecus, ancestor of the Greeks, who drove the ancestors of the Fir Bolgs to Mayo and merged into Grec, ancestor of the Grecraige tribe of Connacht. Third, the ancestor Nemed lived among the Greeks of Scythia whom Herodotus called Gelonians. He went west with thirty-four ships from the Caspian Sea to Ireland. 'This voyage might have the same pictorial truth that can be read in the voyage of the Argonauts.' In search of Circe's Island the Argonauts dragged the Argo from the Caspian to the Baltic using the Don, the Danube and the Elbe, an impossible route.

AFTERWORD

Finally they travelled around the coast of Ireland and through the Pillars of Hercules. They never made clear where Circe's Island was, but Butler saw important connections. Had Circe:

> Had she something to do with the Circe river in Donegal, now Stranakirk, and all those hens, *cearc*, to whom I have referred? Circe, ex-queen of Sarmatians and Latins, was a Scytho-Greco-Romano-Caucasian ancestress and left her traces almost everywhere. By the time recorded history began all the ancestors and ancestresses of Europe were related to each other. It was the task of the poet, the historian, the genealogist, to present this complex web of kinship in a contemporary form. He must make it arresting, encouraging, entertaining: he must try to make an intelligible pattern out of what must often have seemed mere chaos. The Irish and the Greeks had learnt from their common ancestors to do this task in a very similar way. [TTS p. 176]

As we shall see, bio-archaeologists lately uncovered a genetic connection among the Irish, Scythians and Caucasians that confirmed Irish antiquarians and Butler.

Puns

Butler formulated how to move from a pun-biography-anecdote about a hero, an ancestor or a saint to identify the ancient tribe whose name was attached but hidden. He indicated how the ancient writer tries:

> ... to communicate something too complicated for current speech. It has to be pickled against oblivion in pun language, the precursor of poetry. The puns preserve it safely but the dictionary for pun-language has not yet been written. We have to grope behind the phantoms, the saint, the hero, the ancestor, for the reality, the ancient tribe that once lived here ... The art of the genealogist-punster (or is it a science?) is intensely introverted. He buries the truth, where it is safe but almost indiscoverable. Is it absurd to see in this the first symptoms of the Irish obsession with words? When Joyce in *Finnegans Wake*, with sick and sterile nostalgia, buried the names of Dublin streets, shops, suburbs in polyglot puns, did he anticipate that one day foreign students, in pursuit of PhDs, would work out that Lucalizod certainly meant Lucan plus Chapelizod and that Cabinhogan probably meant Cabinteely plus Sallynoggin? [TTS pp. 21–2]

To understand Butler's method one starts with puns and punsters. The *Oxford English Dictionary* defines pun as a play on words that uses a word for two or more meanings or uses two or more words of the same sound with different meanings. Eminent Irish punners include Jonathan Swift (*A Modest Defence of Punning*, 1716), Thomas Sheridan *(Ars Punica,* 1719), James Joyce and Paul Muldoon. Swift and Sheridan communicated in puns like their druidic predecessors detected by Butler.

At the *Finnegans Wake* reading of New York's PEN Congress in 1966, Butler and Padraic Colum shared an epiphany with Joyce's pun of 'moyles and moyles' of river Liffey on 'Silent, O Moyle, be the roar of thy waters.' Likewise the place name Norluns, a Louisiana pronunciation of New Orleans, mimics Norelands, a placename on the river Nore below Maidenhall. Benjamin Franklin's antanaclastic wit famously demolished many: 'Your argument is sound, nothing but sound.' Wordsmith William Safire indicated how 'laid him on the green' slid into 'mondegreen' from misheard poetry and how American school children transformed 'I pledge allegiance to the flag' into 'I led the pigeons to the flag.' In his poem 'Hedge School', Paul Muldoon '... sheltered in a doorway on Church Street in St Andrews (where, in 637, another Maelduin was bishop)'. Here Butler would note how the druidic puncraft connects Muldoon and Maelduin to Irish-Gaulish St Meldan and the Milesians [see TTS p. 181].

Homonyms and Conundrums

Homonyms sound alike but spell differently: pare, pear and pair, not unlike the before- and afternames Butler dissected from druidic manipulation of the names of Irish tribes, heroes, ancestors and future saints. The *Encyclopaedia Britannica*'s 'homonymble' puns and games show what kinds of problematic polyglot interpretations faced Butler. The French *'pas de leur eaune que nous'* puns the American admonition 'paddle your own canoe'. In *Irish Eccentrics* Somerville-Large specifies Archbishop Whateley's ancestral conundrum: 'Why can a man never starve in the desert? Because he can eat all the sand which is there. But what brought the sandwiches there? Noah sent Ham, and his descendants mustered and bred.' A labyrinthine *Britannica* 'homonymble' pun poses this puzzler:

> How can a man escape from a solid, sealed room, containing only him and a table, in a dense forest? He rubs his hands until they are sore [saw]. Then he saws the table in half. Two halves make a whole. He crawls through the hole. Then he shouts until he is hoarse, and gallops away [Puns, *Encyclopaedia Britannica Macropaedia* (Benton, Chicago, 1974) V 19, 927].

In their bardic riddles, druids wove analogous puns, homonyms and conundrums that tracked tribal genealogy.

Butler extracted Irish tribal puns from:

> ... an enormous quantity of pun-elements. Every conceivable colour for example has a corresponding tribe, every member of the body, every beast and plant and physical attribute. This does not mean that there was an enormous number of tribes and tongues. It only means that in pre-literate days when strangers pronounced a tribal name in a new way, there were no dictionaries to correct them. Such consistency as existed came from the fixed belief that all proper names had a meaning, so the [cultural] variants [or memes] all varied in the direction of a familiar word [TTS p. 24].

He astutely unravelled mixed language puns, conundrums, glossographical palimpsests and bizarre biographies of heroes, ancestors and saints and thereby unearthed Irish prehistoric tribes and their roots, amalgamations and wanderings in Ireland and Europe. He recorded one of many examples of puncraft from a Latin life of St Kevin of Glendalough, Co. Wicklow, where thirty Mael tribes lived. St Kevin blessed the soldier (*miles*) Ruadanus. Miles Ruadanus is a pun on Maelruan. St Maelruain is the corresponding famous Wicklow tribal saint and the analogous tribe the Muinter Maelruain or Maelruadain in Co. Wicklow. An ancient walnut tree named for St Maelruain survives today in St Mary's priory, Tallaght.

Genes

Mindful of geneticist Ewan Birney's admonition, we will appraise how bio-archaeology works since it verified Butler's country-based exploration of Irish origins. Let's start with genders and chromosomes.

Men and women each have forty-six chromosomes that carry thousands of genes in the nuclei of all the cells in their bodies. These chromosomes come in forty-four pairs with twenty-two inherited from each parent. The other two nuclear chromosomes make gender. One is the female X and the other the male Y chromosome. If female we inherited two female X chromosomes, one from each parent. If male we inherited the female X from our mother and the male Y from our father. The completely male DNA of the Y chromosome passes only from father to son.

Because the iconic double helix of DNA is very chemically trackable, its history and age into prehistory are determinable by unique shapes of its attached lumps and bumps of molecules and the distances between them. Now contrast the cell's nucleus with its body substance, plasm, full of mitochondrial (mt) DNA. Unlike the X and Y chromosomes of the nucleus, all cell plasm only comes from the mother and never the father. Thus mtDNA only tells women's history. The unique shapes of mtDNA's attached lumps and bumps of molecules and the distances between them, just like the Y chromosome in men's DNA, track female remote past with age of line of descent into prehistory.

Thus geneticists have sets of male and female DNA tools to trace ancestral lines and their distribution in families, tribes, and regional and national populations, including molecular clocks to detect the ages of prehistoric events. Butler's perceptions follow European ancestral marker genes for people, animals and bacteria.

In *The Origins of the British* (2006) and in *Blood of the Isles* (2006), Stephen Oppenheimer and Brian Sykes summarized the work of many geneticists, linguists and archaeologists about the origins of the maternal and paternal clans of England, Ireland, Scotland and Wales. How then does Butler's linguistic archaeology correlate with bio-archaeology? We shall look where Irish maternal and paternal clans wandered with their marker genes and relate their distribution to the druidic cultural variants or memes and bardic historical accounts uncovered by him.

The paternal marker gene, the male Atlantic, progressed to Ireland from the ancient Near East. People spread west and north two ways, one by a Mediterranean and Atlantic coastal route, and another by a parallel route from the Black Sea up the Danube to central Europe, thence to the Paris basin, Low Countries and Baltic region.

First came hunter-gatherers, then agri-pastoral tribes. Ancestral Irish tribal spread involved wanderings into, stays in and very probably wanderings back into pre-Celtic and Celtic Liguria, Gaul and Spain, Galicia, Pays Basque, Gascony, France, Belgium, the Netherlands, Denmark, Germany, Ossetia (Scythia), Thrace, Greece, Crete, Ireland, Scotland, Wales and England. The last Ice Age pushed tribes to south Europe from their northern early Stone Age habitats. When the globe warmed, hunter-gatherers and primitive farmers moved west and north again.

Female gene markers tracked Irish maternal clans from the antediluvian Near East to Europe and Ireland. The distribution of the female clans matched the dispersion indicated by Butler's linguistic archaeology. Bacterial genes showed that *Helicobacter pylori*, the cause of human stomach ulcers, had accompanied these maternal and paternal clans.

Animal bio-archaeology disclosed confirmatory spread of domesticated cattle, pigs and sheep from the Near East to Atlantic Europe. Iberian and western French fauna also arrived in Ireland in a similar pattern. Mascheretti reported the pigmy shrew's genetic Andorran-Irish voyage and cited evidence of similar Lusitanian-Hibernian travels for the Kerry slug and the Irish pine marten.

Flora tracked by Marion Newbigin, David Webb and Michael Viney connected Irish heather and over seventy other plants found in Portugal, northern Asturias, north-east Galicia, the borders of the Bay of Biscay, the upper Pyrenees and western France to those found in Cork, Kerry, Mayo, Connemara and Galway. Did heathers and other florae sail to western Ireland from Basqueland, or did they couple with Neolithic settlers and cross land bridges from Pyrenean and Galician habitats? Heather's unique coastal Iberian-Irish distribution favours maritime arrival with the Basques or their seafaring cousins or tribal ancestors recorded by Butler.

The Linguistic Search for Irish Origins Begins

A gifted linguist and classics scholar with '*ad hoc* Irish', Butler studied the lives of saints in the original Latin, in the many historical and philological interpretations of them, and in translations of Irish. He chose Irish names, puns and stories because he felt Ireland's westernmost European site made a good base for geo-linguistic, historic, geographic, archaeological, toponymic and topographic inquiries, and correlations of prehistoric tribal wanderings.

Twenty-eight years later, with Butler's work unknown, but potentially available, to molecular archaeogeneticists, Daniel Bradley's gene team from Trinity College Dublin found that 'Ireland's position on the western edge of Europe' facilitated the auspicious genetic analysis of Basque-Irish links that by chance confirmed Butler's research. Bradley's group tracked the inherited male Basque-Irish-Atlantic gene down families' surnamed paternal lines, including those of prehistoric Gaelic origin. Their molecular data showed that the pre-Neolithic male Atlantic gene ascended from the Near East and peaked in the west of Ireland.

Today Butler's hermeneutical archaeological and anthropological data compare well with the many genetic markers of communal ancestry within the Atlantic region, from northern Iberia to western Scandinavia, that dated to the last Ice Age. Similarly, the female gene lines of European clan mothers, annotated by Brian Sykes in *Blood of the Isles*, disclosed several prominent Irish clan mothers. Like Bradley's considerations, Sykes' reflections validate how Butler explored prehistory: 'In my research around the world I have more than once found that oral myths are closer to the genetic conclusions than the often more ambiguous scientific evidence of archaeology.' Here one may imagine cheers from Jacques Boucher de Perthes and Hubert Butler. Sykes continues: 'Only when I began my research in the *Isles* did I come to appreciate that we are just as entangled in our own origin myths as everybody else. They are still very powerful and, as in other parts of the world, they may contain grains of truth that we can test by genetics.'

Butler summarized the premise whence began his investigation. 'The Irish had very definite ideas as to who the first invaders of Ireland were and where they came from. First before the flood [possibly the last great glacial melt 7000 years ago] came Cessair, daughter of Bith, son of Noah, with her fifty maidens.'

Today we may speculate: were these tribes present in Ireland before those land bridges from the Continent to Scotland to Ireland disappeared as glacial ice melted, sea waters rose and the great Doggerland plain settled beneath the North Sea? 'Then came Partholon from Mygdonia and northern Greece, via Sicily and Spain. After him were the Conchind or Dog-heads, who killed all men living in Ireland.'

We may wonder if this massacre created what geneticists term a hereditary bottleneck or a founder effect favouring the Basque-Irish male gene that came to Ireland by an Atlantic coastal route? 'Then came Nemed of the Greeks of Scythia. He and his people died of plague at Ard Nemed, which is Little Island in Cork, and only three of his following, Simeon Breac, Iobath, son of Beothach, and Briotan Mael survived.'

Butler documented the Scythian presence of tribes, ancestors and saints in Kerry, Tipperary and Waterford, and a strong Scythian connection with Scotland. Perhaps the legendary death of all from plague may have been exaggerated or the male Atlantic gene returned from Spain or Ossetia. The ancient territory of the Scythians included today's Ossetia (a disputed region between the Russian Federation and modern-day Georgia) where the male Atlantic gene that matches Ireland's is found in 43 per cent of men. The Scythian tribes, heroes and ancestors predated the shaping of the Irish language. We learn that: 'Beothach went to Boeotia or else to the 'north of the world' (Bothnia). Simeon Breac went to Thrace and Briotan Mael went to Britain and became the ancestor of all the Britons.' [TTS p. 39]

The Briotan Mael tribe indeed made its genetic footprint, for today we know 64 per cent of Englishmen and 83 per cent of Welshmen have that same Basque-Atlantic male gene found in 87 per cent of Irishmen.

The next invaders were the Fir Bolg, descendants of Simeon Breac in Thrace. They included two other peoples, the Fir Domnann and the Gaileoin. They covered the whole of Ireland, but were eventually driven to the islands of the west by the next invaders, the Tuatha De Danann. The Tuatha De Danann, who came after the Fir Bolg, are the descendants of Beothach from Boeotia and came from Athens and Achaea to Fionn Lochlann, which is Norway, and thence to Alba, which is Scotland. They were a magical people landing from the clouds in the mountains of Connaught. They were succeeded by the Gaedel or Sons of Mil, who came from Scythia via Spain and remained the dominant aristocracy of Ireland.

One possible trail of the male Atlantic gene closely follows Butler's assembled tribal stories. The Atlantic male gene rises in frequency from Ossetia 43 per cent, to Spanish Basqueland 89 per cent, to Leinster 73 per cent, Ulster 82 per cent, Munster 94 per cent and Connacht 98 per cent.

Irish Pagan and Holy Family Trees and Genes

Butler points out that Irish saints 'travelled far and wide, in Scotland, Wales, Cornwall, Gaul, Italy, and always came home to Ireland, leaving their names behind them for centuries in the places they visited'. He continues:

> And we know the pedigrees of their father and mother often for twenty generations [500 year time-frames for geneticists to explore if these epochs are datable] and the names of all their sisters, brothers, nephews, nieces, both religious and secular. St Paan was the uncle of St David of Wales, and was one of the forty-eight children of Braccan, a buccaneering Irishman, who gave his name to Breconshire, and though he was a very worldly man, gave it also to Kilbricken Church on Hook Head, thirty miles from Maidenhall. All forty-eight children were saints, twenty-four of either sex, and many of them have cult centres both in Ireland and Wales [TTS p. 4].

Butler observes: 'Irish saints, it must be noted, are supposed to have founded or ruled the monasteries and churches that bear their names. The idea of an honorary dedication is a late one.' [TTS p. 4]

Genetic confirmation of Butler's Irish-Welsh connection is robust. The identical paternal Irish Atlantic gene occurs in 86 per cent of men in mid-Wales, 84 per cent in the south and 83 per cent in all Wales. The maternal Irish clan's gene occurs in 11 per cent of women in mid-Wales, in 19 per cent in the south and in 10 per cent in all Wales.

AFTERWORD

Ireland's Diverse Antique Family Tree

Butler connected to the ancient world:

> There is an elaborate genealogical background to the invasion stories. The family tree, which started before the Flood [possibly the last great glacial melt 7000 years ago], had the ancestors of all the ancient tribes of Europe in its branches, some of them early medieval fantasies, some of them far older. There was Eber of the Iberians, Assur of the Assyrians, Longbardus of the Lombards, Perseus, Grecus, Saxus and cohorts of the Irish ancestors, whom we shall meet in the lives of the saints or have already met. After their distant travels and freqent minglings, many of the Irish ancestors, being amalgamated, were hard to identify. Such a one was Lugaid, son of Ith who was uncle of Mil and led the Sons of Mil to Ireland [TTS p. 40].

Butler noted Lugaid, which means Lug Ith, was as Lug a compound ancestor of dozens of tribes in many genealogies. Lug tribes in Gaul, Gascony, Liguria, Switzerland, north Italy, Tuscany, Iberia and Galicia wandered to Ireland, north Scotland, Wales and England. The tribal ancestor, Lug Mac Eithenn's great-great-grandfather, Miled, came from Spain. Thus Miled's tribe is a likely candidate to have made the ancestral connection of the male Atlantic gene found today in northern Spain, Ireland, Scotland, Wales and England. The male Atlantic gene followed Lug tribal paths from Celtic Liguria to Spain to Ireland, Scotland, Wales and England. Likewise Ireland's maternal clan mother's gene came from Tuscany.

The travels of these genes confirmed Butler's documentation of tribal wayfarings. As Butler and the geneticists agree, saints, heroes and ancestors did not necessarily father their tribes biologically. Butler recognized ancestors were created for tribal amalgamations by druidic genealogists. Then heroes, saints, ancestors and names of tribes went forth with their newly acquired druidic labels and extraordinary tales to remember them by.

The Bradley team contrasted their genetic proof of the singular dominant Ui Neill clan of Ulster with genetic diversity in the Eoganacht of Munster. The diffuse genetic origin identified in the latter tribe corresponds to Butler's elucidated cultural elements of tribal amalgamations, invention of ancestors and druidic legends about geneaology.

AFTERWORD

Names and Genes

Butler proceeds:

> There was a vast pool of such names, timeless and ageless as all ancestors were. [Many thought] the long catalogues of peculiar names that fill the pages of *The Book of Invasions* were senselessly invented. But the names recur again and again dealt out to different people like cards in a pack. Mil was not only father of the Sons of Mil, the last recorded invaders, he was also a female attendant of Cessair, the first invader; Mil's uncle, the mighty Ith, son of Bregon, was not only a leader of the Sons of Mil, he was also a servitor to Partholon. Servitors, wives, oxen, they mostly have names that are familiar even when they are odd, Milchu, Dorcha, Carthenn, Liger, Aine, and afternames, Breac, Mael, Liath, Lethderg, Echruad, Lamfin, Glunfind and there were the same impossible explanations for them, for example Lamfind or White-hand had luminous hands (so that he steered by night), his son Eber Glunfind, White Knee, had white spots on his knees, Cridenbel, Heart Mouth, had his mouth in his breast, names for which my Glossary will give tribal explanations. [TTS p. 41]

The prehistoric Irish sun goddess Aine, cited by Butler, has tribal descendants traced down to the family surname of the O'Kirbys of Munster thanks to work by the McEvoy-Simms-Bradley genetics team. Butler also relates how St Carthac the Elder, a bishop, brought up St MoChuda, a Kerryman. St MoChuda's tribe, the Chud folk, merged with the Clann Carthaic. Later the Clann Carthaic became the McCarthy surname in south-west Ireland. St Cairbre Caem lived near Fermoy close to his tribe, the Ui Caem, from which came the surname O'Keefe.

The Bradley genetic team also confirmed these saints, tribes and surnames. They also clarified that the powerful patrilineal Ui Neill genetic kinship was exceptional and did not apply to all Irish tribes.

Other surnames merit genetic exploration for the male Irish Atlantic gene. Butler connected the O'Malleys of Sligo and Mayo, the land of the Ui Maille tribe, to the Sons of Mil. The Mulroy surname descends from the Maelruad tribe when they lived in the barony of Tireragh, Co Sligo.

How this story unravels is intriguing. In Tirawley and in the barony of Tireragh, Co. Sligo, the Ui Mael Ruad (Irish for Bald Red) tribe left many place names. Red Hill had four Irish names: Mullach Ruad, Telach na Maele, Telach na Molt and Cnoc na Druad. He carefully traced the Mael and Molt to the Milesians and the Ruad and Druad to the Thracians. Opportunities for genetic inquiry also include the Kinsellas in Carlow with their ancestor Enna Ceinselach, and the Ahernes in Co. Clare and McCagherons in Antrim, who descend from the widespread Ui Echtigern tribe. Two Kinsellas entered The Leinster Modal (B9NW4 on Ysearch, http://clanmaclochlain.com/leinster.htm).

Making Ancestors and Saints

How did Butler decipher invented punned stories of tribal ancestors or heroes used to fortify druidic memories of tribal genealogical narrators? To illustrate his method, let's invent two neighbouring prehistoric Irish tribes named Cramps and Tons. When they merged, they concocted their ancestor, Crampton. The newly named Crampton tribe settled by a river bend (cramp, crimp, crump; *criom* in Irish) where they built a fort (town, *dun*) for protection. Tribal narrators punned a bizarre story to remember their genealogy. They described ancestor Crampton as very cramped, crimped or crumped hiding under a ton of wheat. The puns translated non-Gaelic words (Crampton) and syllables (cramp and ton) as if they were Gaelic. The Irish *criom* came later. The ancestor Crampton thus gaelicized to Dunlop, a fortified palace, and their habitat became Dunlop village at the river's bend.

Butler would ask, was that Irish village also in Ayrshire? Had a Crampton tribal branch gaelicized to Dunlop wandered across the Irish Sea into Scottish Gaelic territory? Yes, we know it had. Dunlop is in Ayrshire and contemporary Scottish biological anthropology and molecular archaeogenetics unavailable to Butler linked Ireland to Scotland. Centuries later Irish monks revised and wrote this invented oral traditional druidic story of the ancestry of the prehistoric Crampton tribe in a book. Butler cited 'there was an odd saint who was carried to his burial under a load of wheat' [TTS p. 160]. The tale ended with celibate St Dunlop martyred by suffocating beneath a huge mound of grain near Dunlop village where today a shrine, a holy well, a rath, a field, a loch or a hilltop still bears the saint's or the tribe's name.

Now back to the put aside Irish word *criom*. He would speculate that the druidic genealogical cultural variants or memes of the Criomdun or Duncriom names disclosed related tribes because of their exchanged before- and afternames. Irish monks would duly have recorded unpleasant fates for saints Criomdun and Duncriom. But the puncrafted prehistoric pagan names gaelicized from Crampton, the bizarre biographies and the uniquely linked place names would disclose who these tribes were and where they lived and trekked in antiquity.

AFTERWORD

The Basque-Gascon-Irish Connection

Here's how Butler dealt with combined tribal ancestors and their neighbours to detect the Irish-Basque connection. 'Thus when some Celts and some Iberians in Spain became Celtiberians, an ancestor appeared, Celtiberius ... ' He mapped the territory of the Celtiberians. Its north-east sector neighboured the Vascones and the Vescitani, whom he considered early forerunners of the Basques and Gascons. We now know the Basques were an ancient tribe perhaps descended from Paleolithics and Mesolithics. He first suspected the Vascone-Basque connection when he investigated the Ui Draignech of Connacht, a tribe kin to the continental Dragani, known to the Romans as Draganum Proles. They lived on the Bay of Biscay next the Basques and Veneti. When the Bradley team found the male Atlantic gene peaked at 89 per cent for Spanish Basques and at 98 per cent for Irishmen from Connacht, they authenticated Butler. This Basque-Irish gene association also fit Ireland's human habitat history of over 7500 years.

The 'sc' Sound

Before the male Atlantic gene connected the Basques, Irish, Welsh, Scottish and English, Butler observed:

> There are very few place and tribal names in ancient Spain that contain the 'sc' sound and they almost all occur in or near the Pyrenees – Osca, Menosca, Biscargis (Biscay), Muscara, Cascantium, Virovesca – and among the tribes we find the Vascones, the Vescitani and the Conisci. The Vescitani are obviously a variant of their neighbours the Vascones, and Virovesca must be derived from an amalgamation between the Vescitani and their powerful Celtic neighbours the Verones or Berones. This sound 'sc' seems equally rare in Irish proper names. [TTS pp. 108–9]

Support for Butler's hypotheses comes from two meticulous linguists, Ernst Lewy and Joshua Whatmough. Lewy found portions of Irish vocabulary considered non-Indo-European and identified structural relationships between Irish and Euskera, the language of the Basques. Whatmough identified the 'sc' sound in ancient Gaul including pre-Celtic Ligurian territory abutting the Pyrenees, today's Gascony and Basqueland.

In his detailed 1999 study of the Basques, Mark Kurlansky suggested that Euskera possibly is a New Stone Age language. Like Hungarian, another of Europe's four non-Indo-European languages, Euskera agglutinates by adding more and more suffixes in a style reminiscent of ancient Irish genealogic tales. One Basque legend holds that Iberia was peopled by descendants of Tubal, grandson of Noah, after the Flood receded, and that Basque place names resemble Armenian ones where the ark beached. This legend derives some support from the rise of frequency of the Atlantic male gene from 25 per cent in Armenia to 30 per cent in Hungary and to 89 per cent in Basqueland. Butler continues:

> Indeed among the tribes we only meet the 'sc' sound among the Basc- Musc- Esc- or Uisc- peoples, and evidence of the kinship suggests that all these people belonged to the same tribe, whose name was differently pronounced. Cairbre Bascain, the ancestor of the Dal Bascind was the brother of Cairbre Musc, the ancestor of the Muscraige, and the Dal Bascind are called Dal mBascind and equated with the Dal nOengus Muscae. Among the saints the same picture is apparent. St Mescan (St Patrick's brewer) and St Bresca (St Patrick's chaplain) were both culted on the river Faughan in Co. Derry, and certain scholars have said they were the same. [TTS p. 109]

Butler's proposed descendants of the Basques in Ulster correlate with the male Atlantic-Basque-Irish gene's frequency of 82 per cent in the province.

Interestingly, the habitat of the Muscraige Tire tribe, visited by St Patrick or one of his ninth-century successors on a trip through north Munster, lay in north-west Tipperary opposite the Shannon's Clare shore where dwelt the Corcu Bascainn tribe, their Basque cousins with Munster's 94 per cent association with the male Atlantic gene. Forty-seven 'sc' tribes, ancestors, beforenames, place names and heroes, bridge Ireland and Iberia in Butler's chapter 'Saints of the Vascones'. Finally one surmises that the Basques' northern neighbours, the Gascons, who also include the 'sc' sound in their tribal and place names, may well merit testing of their genes for their contribution to both Irish and other European genomes. The *Atlas Routier France-Belgique-Luxembourg* shows over twenty 'sc' place names in Atlantic Gascony.

Butler strengthened Co. Clare's western Shannon connection with the Basques. The 'sc' sound persists here, too. He noted Mata Muiresc, daughter of the king of Scotland, 'was the ancestress of the Clann Morna of Clare and had seven children, all of them obviously tribal ancestors of Connacht', by Magach, a male not her husband. Butler recorded one child, Bascall, 'would appear to be a Vasconic hybrid'. Butler's Glossary indicated that the Vascones include the Basc folk. As noted earlier, the male Atlantic gene links to the Basques that confirmed Butler's work were 98 per cent in Irishmen in Connacht and 94 per cent in

Irishmen in Munster. The male Atlantic Irish gene also connected Basques and Scotsmen in known Celtic surname territory with frequencies of 73 per cent in Scotsmen, 72 per cent in the Hebrides, and 60 per cent in Orkney and Shetland. Again the distribution of the Basque Atlantic gene supported Butler.

In Butler's Index the rare unique identifying 'sc' or 'sk' sound of Basque appears in 45 of 736 names of ancestors and heroes, 8 of 392 names of saints, 10 of 334 names of Irish tribes and their ancestors, and 16 of 265 names of continental tribes and their ancestors, in each group under 1 per cent. *The Ordnance Survey Road Atlas of Ireland* includes 3223 tabulated names of communities and hundreds of untabulated place names for hills, mountains, lakes, bogs and cross roads. The 'sc' or 'sk' sound appears at 182 sites, 68 in Munster, 56 in Connacht, 36 in Leinster and 22 in Ulster. However, these numbers and percentages should be cautiously interpreted as purely Basque or Gascon since some 'sc' and 'sk' sounds in names possibly descended from Scythian or other tribes when they neighboured the Basques in Iberia or Munster. Nevertheless one ought not to overlook possible Basque-Scythian connections since the male Atlantic gene occurs today in 89 per cent of Basques and 43 per cent of Ossetians (Scythians).

Butler also connected the Vascones and the Basques because the letters 'v' and 'b' interchange. The aspirated 'b' (phonetically 'v') shows the genitive of 'b' and hence, for example, 'Corcu Baiscinn' would quite naturally yield 'Corcu Bhaiscinn', or 'Corkovaskin' when anglicized, to designate the 'people of Baiscinn'. Since the Corcu Baskin tribe who lived in Corcovaskin, south-west Clare's extension north of the Shannon, were said to be Basques, he suggested that it was 'the Vascones who left their name to the Basques and the Gascons, and who covered in classical times the same Pyrenean region where the Basques were located'. In the year 2000 the Hill-Jobling-Bradley team found the male Basque Atlantic gene in 89 per cent of Basque men and in 94 per cent of Irishmen in Munster and thus confirmed Butler.

Basques and Gascons connected by more than Butler's illumination of shared 'sc' and 'sk' sound of place names and Gascony's proximity north of Pays Basque and the Pyrenees. Gascon differs distinctly from nearby Occitan dialects due to linguistic influence of a non-Celtic pre-Roman population, most likely the Gascons' non-Indo-European language neighbours, the Basques.

Gascon and Basque names interrelate through phonetic interchangeability between the Frankish 'v' or 'w'. The modern French 'gu' is a commonplace of French morphology from the antecedent of 'war' to the modern *'guerre'* or from the antecedent of 'to watch for' to the modern *'guetter'*. These linguistic mutations from 'v' to hard 'g' (Vascone to Gascon) as well as from 'v' to aspirated 'b' (Vascone to Basque) show elements of Butler's methods. These linguistic changes imply that gene samples from contemporary Gascons might connect more firmly to Irish, Basque and other European genomes.

The finding that half the Frenchmen sampled north of Gascony have the same male Atlantic gene as the Basques and the Irish supports exploration of Gascon men's genes. In keeping with the male Atlantic Irish gene's frequent presence in Atlantic Europe, coastal place names with 'sc' and 'sk' sound litter the Northern Isles, Hebrides, north and west of Scotland and Skye in *The AA Big Atlas of Britain*. The same sound turns up in Welsh place names but occurs less often in Cornish ones.

Basque Atlantic Travels

Butler noted that the Phocaeans of Asia Minor, Massilia and Iberia founded Massilia (Marseille in modern France) by their leader's marriage to the daughter of the king of Liguria. Coincidentally *Blood of the Isles* informs us that Ireland's major clan mother came from northern Italy. The male Atlantic Irish gene also occurred in 44 per cent of Italian men. 'It seems likely that Phocaeans from Iberia or Massilia reached Ireland [...] of all the Iberians, they as the greatest navigators would have been the most likely to reach Ireland, of which undoubtedly they already knew.' Moreover, 'Pytheas, a Phocaean from Marseilles, cruised round the north of Scotland.'

Not only did Butler track the Basques to Ireland, but also to Scotland. 'The Basclenses, who were the Basques of the Bay of Biscay, rounding the Orkneys, colonized Ireland.' Basques possibly settled then in the Northern Isles and the Hebrides where the male Atlantic Irish gene occurs in 60 and 72 per cent of men, or perhaps the Atlantic Irish gene came with later Irish spreading to Scotland also tracked by Butler. The Vascones and Vescitani of north Spain, reputed ancestors of the Basques, were thought to have held Spain before the Iberians. Their tribal affinities included the Vescini in Latium, the Vestini on the Adriatic, the Bastarnae from the Black Sea, the Bastertini of lower Italy, the Bastetani of east Spain and the Bastuli and Bascali of Gibraltar. These tribal associations reach back to the Near East whence began the male Atlantic gene's progression to the west and north to Ireland shown by Bradley's team.

The Irish genome backs Butler's well-considered speculations of Irish origins in prehistory. The male Atlantic gene and the female genes of the

European clan mothers diffused to Ireland from people who sailed the coasts from the Black Sea to Ireland via the Mediterranean coasts north and south, the Straits of Gibraltar and west Europe, the Iberian peninsula, Brittany, France, Cornwall, Wales, Scotland and the Isle of Man.

In the Atlantic zone from north Iberia to west Scandinavia gene analysis of the female European clan mothers showed shared ancestry and confirmed earlier reports of the male Atlantic gene that linked the Basques and the Irish. Maternal and paternal gene lines also came up the Danube to central Europe before spreading north, south and west. Thus both Butler in 1972 and Quinn in 1986 in their cultural analyses anticipated genetic proof of Irish ancestry.

From Ancient Tribe to Modern Surname

Butler supplied a linguistic way forward for today's archaeogenetic population analysis. Irish surnames indeed have discrete, still localizable, ancient tribal origins.

For example, the Draignean tribal name in the Monaghan parish of Donaghmoyne evolved to the surnames O'Drynan and Drennan and many similar local place names. In Cromwell's time *draighean*, which means blackthorn in Irish, was anglicized to Thornton. As for the name of the Draignean tribe, Butler points out: 'Among the familiar nomadic tribes of early Europe, most resemble that of the tribe known to the Romans as the Draganum Proles which lived on the Bay of Biscay before the Celts and traced their descent from Draganes.' Butler then hypothesized that Draig, Traig or Trega, their Irish ancestor figure, might also be the punned ancestor of the Thracians. If so, then the Draganum Proles were not Celtic, but hybrid Thracians.

His conclusion here and elsewhere in *Ten Thousand Saints* supports Stephen Oppenheimer's 'Celto-scepticism' described in *The Origins of the British*. The Draganum, when pressed by the Celts from the north-east, left for Ireland. Later, acculturized by the Irish and Irish language, they kept their *draighean* name with its blackthorn and Thornton connection. Since the Draganum Proles neighboured Basques in the Iberian peninsula, Algarve, Gascony and Gironde, and in Ireland, the family surnames O'Drynan and Drennan might provide further useful genomic data about Irish origins if these families consented to gene tests, as have other families in Leinster, Munster and Ulster studied by the Bradley team, and now entered into the Leinster Modal.

AFTERWORD

The Stammerers of Ossroy

Over forty saints and their secular kinsmen were dumb or stammered. Those of the kingdom of Ossory at his doorstep piqued Butler's curiosity. Ossory, composed of Co. Kilkenny enlarged to the north by several baronies in Laois and Offaly, had a large unexplained number of dumb and stammering kings, heroes and saints. He thought that Goidelic speakers or Q-Celts met presumably indigenous mixed leftovers of earlier P-Celtic invasions. Because their language was incomprehensible to them, the Goidels labelled the Ossorians 'dumb' or 'stammerers'. The Brythonic-speaking tribes, the Cruthin, kin to the Picts of Scotland, dwelt in north-east Ireland and the Erainn dwelt in south-west Ireland. The Cruithin and Erainn tribes, as earlier immigrants than the Goidels, possibly spoke a vernacular Q-Celtic, and continuous tribal crossings of the Irish Sea gave ample opportunities for linguistic exchange and innovation.

From Sykes' summary in *Blood of the Isles* we know the dominant Atlantic-Basque-Irish paternal clan's gene is found in 79 per cent of Picts in Tayside and 83 per cent of Picts in Grampian. The Atlantic male gene also associates Basques and Irish with Scotland (73 per cent), Orkney and Shetland (60 per cent), and with north-east (82 per cent), south-west (94 per cent), western (98 per cent) and south-eastern (73 per cent) Ireland.

Butler found over thirty Ossorian chieftains and notable men called 'dumb' or 'stammering'. Scanlan was the 'stammering' king of Ossory. Two other eminent stammerers had 'sc' sound names: Cuscraid the Stammerer of the Ulaid (the Ulstermen of the Saga), who once were P-Celts, and Itharnaisc, saint of Clane, Co. Kildare. To Butler, stammering implied spoken language different from indigenous or newly dominant tribes in the region. He noted 'a tradition in county Kilkenny that the descendants of Scanlan did, in fact, stammer'.

Finally Butler wondered 'who was the Scal Balbh and why was his name attached to the Leac an Sceal Bhaildh,' Ireland's tallest portal tomb (four and a half metres high with a huge entrance and five metre capstone) in south Kilkenny? He thought Lug an obvious candidate as the chief god of the ancient Celts of Gaul, with a strong presence in France, Holland, Switzerland, Austria and Silesia in addition to Spain, Wales and Ireland, known to be a foreigner and a stammering spirit. Butler cautioned: 'It would be premature, though tempting, to build a theory of racial origins on facts such as these. The most one can do is to draw attention to their oddity and to hope that its significance will be better understood.' The 2011 Eircom 05 area telephone book lists 41 Scan- and Scal- surnames in Ossory. And there are 104 more in Ossroy's contiguous counties of Carlow, Kildare, Tipperary, Waterford, Westmeath and Wexford. Since localization of the male Atlantic Irish gene and the Irish clan mothers' female gene has shed new light on Irish origins and surnames, the present-day Scanlan families of Kilkenny, Laois and Offaly merit genetic investigation from Butler's clues to their possible link to the Basques. These surnames qualify for the Leinster Modal. Of 132 before-, principal and after-names in the Modal pedigrees, forty-nine (37 per cent) appear in Butler's analyses.

Four Irish Saint Fursas and Suffolk, Gaul and the Low Countries

The wanderings and fates of the Frisian tribe and the four Irish St Fursas in Munster, Connacht, Ulster and Leinster caught Butler's attention. Pepin the Frank, Charles Martel and Charlemagne each in their time brutally suppressed the pagan Frisians and forced Christianity upon them. The tribal movements symbolized by St Fursa's Irish and continental journeys concurred with Ireland's high degree of male Atlantic gene association (Basque 89 per cent to Irish range of 73 – 98 per cent) and also genetic spread from or to Ireland. Today we find the male Atlantic-Basque-Irish gene in the coastal populations of East Anglia (51 per cent), Scotland (73 per cent), the Hebrides (72 per cent), the Orkneys and Shetlands (60 per cent), northern France (50 per cent), the Low Countries (Belgium 63 and Netherlands 43 per cent) and Germany (40 per cent), attesting to the travels of the four St Fursas and the Frisian tribe.

History and Cultural Anthropology

Paralleling Butler's lines of inquiry in *Ten Thousand Saints*, Bob Quinn probed diverse origins in Irish prehistory. He produced three remarkable documentary films (1985) and wrote *The Atlantean Irish* (1986, 2005), which elucidated Irish oriental and maritime roots. Like Butler's research, Quinn's work was and still is greeted with professional silence from the academic archaeological world including bio-archaeologists. He wrote: 'I had to travel to Dublin and deliver copies of the original book to individual newspapers to encourage them to review it.' His research constitutes another triumph for the persevering, informative, entertaining amateur scholar who must surmount the tunnel vision of over-specialized, closed-minded, protective denizens of the groves of academe or the film world. He carefully assembled many cultural connections among Irish, Middle Eastern, Iberian and North African people, some of which date deep into prehistory. He showed how sailing the Mediterranean and Atlantic coasts brought people into contact and occasionally conflict. He collated singing, musical instruments, illuminated art, Aran weaving patterns, boats, sails, rigging, sailors, smugglers, pirates, influences of Arab, Persian, Welsh, European, Viking, Phoenician, Carthaginian and Berber people, stories of St Brendan and Sinbad the Sailor, *sheela-na-gigs* and Coptic Christianity with Irish prehistory and history. Unlike Butler, who died a decade before his portrayal of Irish origins in *Ten Thousand Saints* was confirmed by the Bradley gene team, Quinn lived to see the Trinity College team substantiate his work.

These pre-Celtic Atlantean roots of the Irish enlarged upon the lexicographical archaeological analysis found in *Ten Thousand Saints*. Since Butler deduced movements of prehistoric Irish tribes from genealogies, heroes, place names and Christian myths, his findings support Quinn's observations. Sykes' genetic correlations of maternal and paternal European clans in *Blood of the Isles* matched Butler's and Quinn's portrayals of tribal wanderings.

A Mixed Reception for Ten Thousand Saints

Butler's work may have been difficult for some to fathom. On the other hand, when he reported his research about Irish and European tribes, heroes, ancestors and saints, Butler sensed closed-mindedness and indifference. He felt anathematized by academia in its failure to challenge or question him. As we shall see, his friend Conor Cruise O'Brien's remark on being Irish surely applied: 'Irishness is not primarily a condition of birth or blood or language; it is the condition of being involved in the Irish situation and usually of being mauled by it.'

Arland Ussher recommended Dervla Murphy as a reviewer. The patronizing review that followed in *The Irish Times* disparaged *Ten Thousand Saints* and had little to do with his scholarship. The review ignored his sensitive, thoughtful, deep appreciation of Irish saints and how and what they symbolized in terms of their druidic genealogical predecessors. His unpublished correspondence with Terence de Vere White and Dervla Murphy, their review and his unsent letters speak for themselves.

He wrote from Maidenhall, Bennettsbridge, Co. Kilkenny to Dervla Murphy at Clairvaux, Lismore, on 21 November 1972:

AFTERWORD

Dear Miss Murphy,

My old friend Arland Ussher tells me you might review my book. I've never published a book before, at least only translations as well as countless articles in journals, so I don't know if this is a very improper suggestion for me to make. Perhaps if I am to do any backstage intriguing I ought first to write to the newspaper suggesting your name, but surely I ought to know if you would be ready to review it first?

It won't be out until next Friday and I've only the enclosed copy of an I.T. article to show you what it is about. I've written on the subject more lengthily and relevantly since, but I've no copies, and I haven't changed my approach much. I've always longed to be severely contradicted by some Celtic scholar, so that I would have a chance of hitting back but I think their total silence is evidence that the subject bores them or that they know nothing about it and are ashamed to say so. So I think the field is open to the man or woman of wide interests, who isn't an 'expert'. I share many of your interests, but if I said how I react to your writings it would look like an attempt to suborn you.

I am by the way a classical scholar, quite a good one in my day, and this obsession has perhaps made the middle part of my book on the stodgy side for those who don't share it. But I think you might enjoy the beginning and the end.

If you would review it would I send the book to you or what?

Do you ever review for The Daily Telegraph? *I have an old friend H. D. Ziman, who was literary editor. He is probably retired now but would have influence. He used to ask me and my friends to review for him.*

But perhaps you'd hate even the thought of reviewing for The Daily Telegraph?

Yours sincerely, Hubert Butler

Letter from Terence de Vere White, Literary Editor, *The Irish Times*, to Butler on 6 December 1972:

Dear Hubert:

Thank you very much for your letter and of course the book. I am really delighted for you that it is now published. Liam de Paor is the man who does this particular kind of thing for us and so I am sending it to him. As to his being against you I think one can all too easily imagine feuds. I think Liam de Paor is above that kind of thing.

Yours sincerely, Terence de Vere White.

Letter from Dervla Murphy to Butler from Clairvaux, Lismore, Co Waterford, Eire on 8 December 1972:

I must quickly tell you that I sat up into the small hours two nights running enjoying the Saints. An utterly enchanting book and I shall be VERY annoyed if Terence does not allow me the privilege of reviewing it for I.T. Ireland would not be in the state it now is if there were just a few more Irishmen like you.

Admiringly and respectfully, Dervla.

AFTERWORD

The review, 'Hammering The Holy Men', by Dervla Murphy, appeared on 13 January 1973 in *The Irish Times*:

I remember, as a child watching people going to St. Carthage's well in Lismore on 14 May and filling whiskey bottles, from which the labels had been respectfully removed, with blessed water; its consumption would, it was believed, do good in various unspecified ways during the year ahead. Kindly neighbours used to present pints of this holy but often murky water to my mother, who was an invalid – the only reason, it was assumed, for her not going to the well in person. This was my first intimation that catholicism exists on two levels. I curiously asked: 'Why won't you drink it?' and my mother – an exceptionally devout Catholic, but also exceptionally fastidious – was thus forced to admit that her faith in St. Carthage was not stronger than her distaste for murky water.

I was, however, sternly warned not to betray her to the donors of the water lest their feelings might be hurt or their faith weakened. My mother, I think rightly, never condemned such customs as worthless superstition: she regarded them as part of a spiritual tradition more ancient by far than Christianity. But my father, who was less imaginative and saw no good reason why everybody should not be familiar with the works of Thomas Aquinas by the age of fifteen, used to forecast austerely that the days of Irish catholicsm were numbered because most Irish theologians couldn't tell a saint from a leprechaun. Both my parents would have enjoyed, in their different ways, Hubert Butler's *Ten Thousand Saints*.

The holy men of early Christian Ireland take a terrible hammering from Mr. Butler. On the evidence of place names and family names, he argues that they were 'a Christian by-product of the dying art of ancestor-making ... an art that surpassed any succeeding mode of chronicling what would otherwise have been forgotten. If we were to read the ancient notation correctly, we would one day learn of the wanderings and minglings of all the great tribes of Europe and how every Parish in Ireland and many in Britain and in Europe were settled'. He mentions with approval Marcus Keane's theory that 'a limited quantity of imported deities had acquired different attributes and personalities in different regions so that when the time had come for christianising them, a handful of gods and goddesses dissolved into many thousands of saints'.

By now it will be clear that *Ten Thousand Saints* is the work of a man obsessed. But Mr. Butler's obsession is much to my taste, though, being too unlearned to help him with his gigantic jigsaw puzzle, I was sometimes bored while watching him arranging the pieces. He describes himself as 'a country scholar ... writing primarily for country scholars,' and I must confess a strong bias towards enthusiasts who operate without lavish grants from formidable foundations, or vast laboratories, or armies of assistants, or horrible computers. I can take even his many misprints though this form of amateurism usually irritates me to savagery.

But alas! all this goodwill towards *Ten Thousand Saints* does not qualify me to pronounce on its soundness as a work of scholarship. In his foreword, Mr. Butler complains about not now being able to buy 'the most obvious books like the '*The Martyrology of Òengus* and *Silva Gadelica*,' and this really broke my nerve. I had never even heard of the last two of these 'most obvious books' – nor, indeed, do I fancy they form part of the bedside library of many readers of *The Irish Times* – so what business had I to be sitting down to review *Ten Thousand Saints*?

However, a general dogsbody like myself can always go boldly forth in the armour of the Average Reader, and thus protected from the lances of Mr. Butler's scholarly enemies (if he has any) I admit I am completely convinced by the argument that our ten thousand saints were 'not real people but ingenious and necessary fabrications of the mind'. Clearly they played an enormously important part in the intellectual and emotional development of our ancestors and so deserve something better than dismissal as the crude vapourings of credulous minds. And so far no one, I am pretty sure, has devised a more rational and consistent explanation of their significance than Hubert Butler's.

Scholars can, of course, triumphantly demonstrate almost anything if they try hard enough. For instance, Mr. Butler mentions Father Shearman, a nineteenth century genealogist, who demonstrated that 'both St. Mochop of Kilchop and St. Aedan, the Leper, were distant cousins of Queen Victoria'. (I suppose we are all, if it comes to that, distant cousins of Aristophanes.) But Mr. Butler's own demonstrations are rather more to the point than Father Shearman's and, though not easy going, are frequently enlivened by the eccentricities both of the author and his subjects. If one does not suffer from pious hang-ups many of the Irish saints, idols and ancestor-figures have all the ludicrous charm of Edward Lear characters; there was even one – Fer Caille – who had 'a nose that could be looped across a branch of a tree'.

> There was an old man of Kilkenny,
> Who never had more than a penny;
> He spent all that money, on theories so funny,
> That wayward Old Man of Kilkenny.

On 16 January Butler wrote but did not send this letter to White:

Dear Terence,
Extraordinary about that review! Look at the enclosed from Dervla. [Vide supra 8 December 1972.] *Somebody must have got at her.*
That silly headline was a gift to those readers, who know me as 'the chap who insulted the Nuncio' & had 'the bee in his bonnet about Steppynack and the Crotes'.

AFTERWORD

Fortunately David Marcus of Irish Press *& Kevin Faller of* Irish Independent *took the book seriously. I think you ought to look at my review (*Irish Times *9 December, 1958) of Liam de Paor's* Early Christian Ireland, *a book that I found a boring rehash of the common-place. I recognized him as a fellow archaeologist, & conveyed my total dissent without in any way disparaging him or his work...*
Yours ever, Hubert.

(Not sent. A better one than I did send?)

Butler next wrote but sent no one:

'See Dervla Murphy's review in The Irish Times, *January 13, 1973.'*
   'There was a fair maid of Lismore
   Who exclaimed, 'There's a book I adore!'
   Then a little White bird
   Cheeped 'The book is absurd!'
   So she rewrote what she'd written before'.
   'Alternative to line 3: Then a Paor little bird'
 'I think Dervla, who wrote me the note [vide supra 8 December 1972] after receiving the book, telephoned to either Terence White of The Irish Times *or Liam de Paor, who persuaded her to change her mind.'*

Butler's letter to White on 30 January 1973 reads:

Dear Terence,
 Robert Jacob rang me a few nights ago to say that he was writing to I.T., suggesting that Ten Thousand Saints *be given a proper review as well as Dervla's and I believe that after Dr. Arkell's letter (four others of which one, Arkell's, was printed, were sent to I.T. and there were many letters and telephones to me here). Dervla herself could not object. She visited us here and said she felt the book should have been reviewed by a scholar. Would this be in your power to contrive?*
 [AJ] *Arkell* [Professor of Egyptology, University College, London] *is a high-powered English prehistorian, his book on the excavations at Meroe is more significant than anything done by our prehistorians here, and he is founder and first Director of the Egyptian Museum at London University.*
 When Dervla had read the book, she wrote a note, overleaf [vide supra], of which Peggy made copies for Julia etc. so that they should look out for the I.T. review. Dervla also gave me a great deal of enthusiastic advice about English reviewers etc. They did look out and you know what they saw.
 It is profitless to guess what happened between the reading and the writing, but the circumstance of the review, caused me to speculate ... people don't take such sensational somersaults without a push from behind.
 By the way, you were quite wrong when you supposed that I thought Liam de Paor had anything against me. I merely predicted, accurately as it proved, that he would not wish to review my book. One reason for this was that I had reviewed his

book, Early Christian Ireland, *in I.T. 9 December, 1958. I had pointed out how his view of that period differed from that of various English prehistorians and how some of his conjectures were based on a mis-reading of Latin texts. But if you look at my piece (please do, I think you owe it to me, as Dervla's review was damaging and you were very friendly to the book in those Colin Franklin days), you will see that I took great pains not to say anything to harm the sales of his book. As the founder of a flourishing archaeological society, I know how very precarious Irish archaeology is and that the Minister of Finance or, in my case, the Papal Nuncio, could destroy all fresh life with the stroke of a pen.*

I eagerly hoped, in 1958, that Liam de Paor would reply to my criticism in the I.T., but as he didn't, I knew he would be even less likely to tackle me on my own ground in 1973. Why not urge him now to write about it in one of his weekly articles? And see that I get an opportunity to reply? Or, if he won't do it, then Ian Blake.

Anyway, can you do anything about a re-review, or, at the very least, see that R. Jacob's letter is published?

I would not make this fuss if I were not certain that my view of Irish prehistory (with many modifications, of course) is bound to prevail as did the truth about the Croatian massacres after twenty years of ostracism for those who told it. You know the three gambits of the expert confronted with a new idea? First, he says 'It's false', then 'It's true, but unimportant'. Then, 'It's true and important but we knew it all the time!' This is all as predictable as the stratification of geology and will go on until archaeology is de-professionalized.

Hubert.

White replied on 31 January 1973:

Dear Hubert:

Dervla Murphy was your selection. We had to take the book back in order to fall in with your wishes. I'm afraid to publish a second review is out of the question.
Yours sincerely, Terence de Vere White.

Butler wrote White again on 2 February, but did not send this letter:

Dear Terence,

When I was review editor on The Bell *problems like this constantly arose, but I do not think I was ever so uncandid or arrogant with an old friend whose writings I had liked. I would have returned that review to the writer and I would not have permitted that vulgar heading.*

I gave the book to Dervla, whom I had never met, on Arland Ussher's suggestion. You know her and she told me that you had talked to her about my book. I showed my trust in your goodwill by suggesting that you should be the reviewer.

I think you will agree there is no more to be said.
Sadly, Hubert

It seems quite likely from Butler's sent and unsent letters that he learnt that de Poar had not reviewed *Ten Thousand Saints*. Two weeks after Butler wrote his last unsent letter to White, Murphy wrote to him that she took full responsibility for the review and the closing limerick.

Did other early critics of Hubert Butler's Irish cultural anthropology simply mock him as above? His view was the many wrote favourably, but never engaged in discourse. He, like Dr Samuel Johnson, 'would rather be attacked than not noticed'. He longed for vigorous rational arguments on interpretation of Irish prehistory.

Science Sides with Butler

Butler's intuitive brainwork on prehistory predated molecular bio-archaeology. Three years after he published his magnum opus at his expense, W.M.S. Russell, reader in Social Biology at Reading University and a member of the British Social Biology Council, recorded the potential of Butler's work for confirmation by blood group tests of populations. He wrote:

> In a short article, it is impossible to do justice to the wealth of detail in Butler's book, the multiplicity of examples, the checking and cross-checking, the elaborate catalogues, tables and maps, the glossary of Irish pun-words classified under the relevant tribal groupings. It is the accumulation of interlocking evidence that carries conviction. But quite apart from the evidence Butler has gathered himself, there are many considerations that support his thesis. To begin with, everything we know or can surmise about the prehistory of the British Isles and Europe fits perfectly. Fortunately, Butler's patterns of tribal distribution are so detailed and specific that the cruder sources of error would be automatically controlled, especially if a considerable number of genetic systems were studied at once.

Russell then suggested that Butler's 'hypotheses be tested by independent measures of relationship such as blood group frequency distributions'.

Later human population archaeogeneticists like L.L. Cavalli-Sforza combined linguistics, archaeology, topology, geography, demography and blood-group distribution tests with molecular analysis of genes and their distribution and frequency in populations. As pointed out by Professor Daniel Bradley in the Royal Irish Academy's advisory committee on genetic anthropology: 'The drawing of secure inference about the past from genetic research is no easy task and requires the collaborative efforts of many scholars including archaeologists, geographers, linguists and historians.' Butler's scholarship incorporated these disciplines and emphasized linguistics. He lacked only the support of DNA-driven molecular archaeogenetics, a non-existent science in his time.

In 1981 Lino Rossi, a physician-scientist of Milan, like Butler an amateur archaeologist and a serious scholar of the toponymy and topography of the Ligurian Appenines and Alps and their valleys all around the Po plain, read *Ten Thousand Saints*. He wrote to Butler that he was right and that the Celtae and Ligures territory encompassed 'a wide area of south-west Piedmont, Liguria and eastern Provence. Certainly these Celto-Ligurians were great travellers and no wonder their numerous tribes reached Ireland and left their names to be 'extrapolated' into 'traditional' saint-sages in a way that is completely different from the case of most 'continental Christendom's saints'.

In 1995 John O. McCormick, a friend, long-term supporter and fellow amateur Irish archaeologist, wrote to Butler's widow Peggy:

There has been a tendency even among good friends of Hubert's to dismiss Ten Thousand Saints and his other essays on this topic, 'Influenza in Aran' from Grandmother and Wolfe Tone and [two] articles on puns from In The Land of Nod, as merely the product of playful relaxation from his serious work of journalism, as pardonable frivolity, perhaps even as evidence of a 'bee in the bonnet', about which the less said the better. Of course it is in the record that Hubert, as a follower of the famous T.F. O'Rahilly, showed an early and more conventional interest in 'tribal groupings', when in two articles published in learned Irish journals [Antiquity, 1949 and J. Royal Soc. of Antiquaries of Ireland, 1950] (as he recalls in Chapter 2, p. 28 of TTS), [present edition p. 13] he investigated the question of 'The Dumb and Stammerers in Irish History'. It thus should have been obvious that Ten Thousand Saints, published twenty-two years later, was the outcome of prolonged reflection and study. That it also involved a great deal of detailed research now appears from the 'Charts of Irish Tribes, Saints and Heroes', 1971 [Manuscripts Department, Library, Trinity College Dublin]. Clearly whatever the world might think, Hubert took his work in this field very seriously. There was lack of learned discussion when TTS appeared. We both, and no doubt many of Hubert's friends, are aware that he was much disappointed at the complete silence in the academic world which greeted the book on its publication. Hubert was aware that it might cause fluttering in several dovecotes, and he was ready to receive criticism. [After Butler's death Tim Robinson alleged Butler's theses were inaccurate and lightweight, in Stones of Aran, Labyrinth, The Lilliput Press, 1995, and in 'Butler Among the Saints', Unfinished Ireland, 2003.] He would indeed perhaps have welcomed some such controversy, believing that he could make some show of answering his critics. But this was not to be.

We cannot now tell why this happened, though the most charitable explanation, apart from the rather thin argument about shortage of references, is that members of the academic profession, overwhelmed by the vast and growing amount of published research, do not feel it their duty to welcome or oppose new theses unless these are put forward by fellow professors or by persons sponsored by academic bodies. If this is the reason for the silence of the academic fraternity when the book first appeared in 1972, it may be that the laurels which Hubert has since won for his more recent books (which as I mentioned contained brief examples of his 'tribal' writings) will make it easier for some enterprising pre-historians or other experts to break what has so far seemed an unnatural silence. By what mechanism this end can be achieved I do not know – perhaps by some sort of informed symposium (on the brilliant first eight chapters) or by a new edition of the book. Whatever the means, an informed discussion of the fascinating topics broached by Hubert would surely be of great interest, not only to those professionally engaged in the many disciplines involved, but also to a wider public ever curious about that tantalizing subject, the remote past.

John O. McCormick

Butler's Reflections on his Research of Tribes and Saints

In the Maidenhall Commonplace Book on 4 June 1956, Butler wrote:

In the June number of *The Twentieth Century* I have published an article on the event which ended my association with the Kilkenny Archaeological Society. What else has happened since 1952? I have practically finished my charts on the saints and tribes and have written two or three chapters, defending my view that the saints were for the most part tribal ancestors and that ancient Irish place names mainly derived from the names of tribes, as did the nicknames of saints and heroes. The major tribes concerned seemed to me to be the Briges, Veneti, Thracians, Sardi, Ligurians, Iberians, Carpi, Vellauni, Suebi, Frisians, Sikani, Silures, Mygdones, Thyni, Dumnonians, Kempses, Getae, Geloni, Kynesioi, Morini, Nemedes, Scythians, and others, whom I have classified as Carians, Milesians, etc., without really believing that there could be anything but the most indirect relationship between the famous tribes of Asia Minor and such groups in Ireland, as seemed to me remotely to correspond to them. I have shown a little of my work, a couple of years ago, to Myles Dillon and Dan Binchy. Myles was sympathetic and struck by the correspondence which I have exhibited between the *Da* words and the names of tribes. Binchy was polite and friendly but absolutely dismissive. I have explained to him that I knew no Irish to speak of but that my argument did not depend on such knowledge. However, by his comments he showed that he had not a notion what I was driving at, was rather irritated by the idea that I should attempt such an investigation at all without a knowledge of Irish, and so put excited-looking exclamation-marks and once 'only too typical!' against some insignificant misprints or misspellings which had nothing whatever to do with the arguments. I sent an article on the Draganum Proles to *The Journal of the Royal Society of Antiquaries of Ireland* but got an extremely snubbing refusal, which they would modify, when I asked them to make some comment on what I had written. I also sent article to the *Ulster Journal of Archaeology*, to the *Proceedings of the Society of Antiquaries of Scotland*, and one or two others. The Scottish and Ulster editors replied very politely but were obviously bewildered. A Welshman [Emrys G] Bowen of [University College of Wales] Aberystwyth, a Professor of Archaeology, was most interested until I sent him some fragments. Then he never replied and never sent them back. I detect, in all this, embarrassment and indifference and distrust of me as an outsider. My arguments are based on intricate and often very local facts, which it is impossible for them to verify or to contradict. Nobody has managed to undermine in the very faintest degree my absolute conviction that my method of approach is the right one and that twenty years from now the general scheme of my argument will be universally accepted. I think I started my work on the Irish saints about the same time as I started this diary so I've been working on this intensively for over ten years. Often I have done six or seven hours a day, but I have had no recognition yet at all. Two articles were published in *Antiquity* and *JRSAI* [*The Journal of the Royal Society of Antiquaries of Ireland*], one in *The Bell*, a lighthearted attack on the Pundits, but I got no money for any of these and, in the case of *Antiquity* had actually to pay out money, as I made alterations in the proofs and the printers sent a bill. I say all this not in any spirit of resentment. After all I have been attacking sacred shibboleths and criticizing established views and I must expect to be ignored and disapproved, but I am thinking of my family and this house, which is in increasing disrepair. I have invested income of about 300 pounds *p.a.* and this year I was 540 pounds overdrawn. Had I not been working on the saints I would surely have been earning money so that I could provide Julia with an income and keep our house, garden, orchard and fields in good order. Once my work is recognized I will endeavour to be remunerated as I ought to be remunerated. The whole of early history in these islands will appear differently in the light of my discovery – every textbook will have to be revised; it is right that I who have worked this revolution should be compensated for my long effort and that I should have power, whether through money or authority, to develop the researches which I have started. I observe that I have not mentioned Eric Dorman O'Gowan of Bellamont, Cootehill, who has always supported me and believed in me and to whom I owe more than to anyone else. He has encouraged me and has taken charge for me of the carbon copies of the charts, though he thinks on quite different lines. Tomorrow he and I and Myles Dillon are going to start on a short trip around Monaghan, Cavan, Leitrim, Fermanagh, Sligo. We will base ourselves on Annaghmakerrig and Bellamont.

Butler continues on 6 March 1959:

Since I last wrote, I have been to China, Russia and, last year with Peggy, to Spain. Now I am alone in the house. Peggy has gone to London and I join her in a few days. Then Julia and Dick Crampton, whom I have not yet met, come back with us for Easter. I spent the afternoon collecting things for country-market tomorrow. The potting shed is full of sprouting broccoli, white broccoli, and boxes of pansies, bachelor's buttons, lupins, the dining room has wild cherry lilies bursting out of bud, and an enamel basin full of Lent lilies and blue anemones. In the morning I was revising and changing for the third time the contribution *Saints and Scholars* which will be published in the anthology, which Terence White is compiling for Routledge. Each alteration, it seems to me, makes it feebler, but I see that it has to be done. It is very difficult though for me to realize that proofs and possibilities, arguments, conjectures, which for me are full of excitement, are for the general reader quite flat and dull. I have not written about the saints and tribes to Eric O'Gowan for over a year, but he still has the box of my carbons of the charts. I have had very encouraging support from Bill Allen of Cappagh, and he has mentioned my work with respect in a *Caucasian Magazine*. But apart from that I am working alone and lack the stimulus of a single intelligent and interested critic; I do not blame anyone for this, because Myles Dillon and the others can help me very little, even if they were willing. I have not, for a couple of years at least, talked to any of the Irish scholars whom I know on the subject which absorbs me, because I have not – as the correspondence with Myles Dillon, Daniel Binchy, and Jim Carney which I have preserved will show – succeeded in making clear to them, in the smallest degree, what I mean. Am I overwhelmingly conceited and arrogant? I do not feel that I am. I long to have someone to challenge my beliefs, violently disagree and correct me in some detail, but nothing happens. I wrote in *The Irish Times* lately two long articles on Powell's book on the Celts and on *Early Christian Ireland* by the de Paors. I made many challenging statements in both articles, hoping that I might at least rouse some scholar to disagree, but one cannot provoke them into defending their own beliefs. They are imprisoned in their own self-satisfaction. On my visit to China, David Greene, Professor of Celtic at TCD [Trinity College Dublin], was with us. I felt vibrations of jealousy and resentment coming from him to me the whole time, and it would have been quite impossible to try to discuss with him a subject which to me is an absorbing enthusiasm and to him a profession. Yet I would so gladly have discussed it with anyone: indeed last year I harangued Elizabeth [Bowen] on the subject for a quarter of an hour at Bowen's Court. I had been to get some aspirin for her at Thornhill's, the chemist in Kildorrery. I had asked Mr Thornhill, whether his name had originally been O'Drynan; he proved to be the local antiquary, and he answered excitedly that I was right and took me into his parlour to explain that his name in Irish meant 'blackthorn'. I told him how in Monaghan O'Drynan is Thornton, and when I got back to Bowen's Court I tried to explain to Bitha about the Draganum Proles, St Victor and the Blackthorns at Donahmoyne, the Thorntons and O'Drynans. I do not think I made much of an impression. A fortnight ago, Angus Wilson was here to lecture for the Arts Council to the Kilkenny Arts Society. I talked to him too, so desperate am I for an audience, and I felt that I could persuade him more easily than a more academic type. For my arguments are based on reasoning and common sense, and I deliberately address them to those who are unfamiliar with any specialist jargon. Perhaps I interested him a little.

A further recollection was written four days later:

Then I remember an episode which brings my story half way allegory to matter of fact reality. In the last year of my archaeological secretaryship of the Kilkenny Archaelogical Society I tried to start work-party outings on the antiquities of Kilkenny. I hoped we might, for example, organize a group armed with scythes, choppers, rakes and hoes, to clean up the graveyard of St Mary's, which has now been closed. The fine Shee tombs are covered over with ivy and are cracking. We chose for our first experiment Kilmodimogue ruined church on the way to Ballyfoyle. It interested me because of the supposition that the two neighbouring churches of Kilmodum and Kilmodimogue derived from two saints, St Mo Diomog (10 Dec.) of Clonkeen in Ara, Tipperary and St Mo Dumma, or, as another local legend describes them, the two sons of Dumma. I think they record a Dumnonian colony in Slieve Margy. A different St Dimmoc (Diarmuid) was culted at Killeshin not far away. There was no one with whom I could share these ideas, though for me they gave a secret, special excitement to the beauty and friendliness of that lovely afternoon. I do not think I could ever here simply enjoy the mauve clouds, their southern edges dipped in pink, the bright green fringes to the field, where submerged briars keep the cattle from grazing, the evening light which turns the distant grey stone buildings to white against the dark hills, details which I have, like this, to dredge laboriously out of an undefined rapture. I am not capable of simple aesthetic enjoyment, it comes to me as an unsoughtful auxiliary pleasure to the pleasure of speculating, planning, organizing. Tom Hoyne was there with his flame gun, the rest of us with slashers and we walloped the old elder trees from the nave and chancel and focused a roaring jet of fire on the trunk of the ivy, which overwhelmed the east window. Tom Hoyne said that the flame would have damaged the mortar as well as the ivy and that we must return some day with a bag of cement to repair the rescued wall. I agreed to this and decided that we could put down the cement to the society's expenses and return some other day. But that day never came. In the autumn the Papal Nuncio walked out of the meeting at the Shelbourne Hotel. Because I referred to the forced conversion of the Orthodox in Yugoslavia, I was denounced by special meetings of the Kilkenny Corporation and Kilkenny County Council and the chain of events began which drew me from all this pleasant constructive planning for the revival of archaeology in Kilkenny. I, in *The Twentieth Century* periodical, Paul Blanshard, in his book *The Irish and Catholic Power*, have only told a very little of it and later on I want to describe all that happened afterwards, a sequel of which I am proud enough, because I have stood by what I believed and hit back at those who damaged me only a little but damaged truth a great deal. I'll tell about the first Kilkenny Debate, which was in a sense a deliberate attempt to get elected to Kilkenny County Council, the insults that were thrown at me, when the results were announced, the successful legal action, which I took against Tom Walsh – small episodes, which belong to my neighbourhood and its history, but which, if I do not relate them myself, will be buried like the Dumnonians in Ballyfoyle in reach-me-down mythmaking. A couple of years ago I went back with Maurice Craig to Kilmodimogue and I saw that the east end of the church had completely collapsed as Tom Hoyne had predicted. It was as though Dr. O'Hara, who had ceased to be Nuncio soon after Blanshard had campaigned against him, had leant his bulky body against that precarious wall, and at the same time demolished the carefully devised equilibrium of our society. I had hoped that it would be with this society that I could one day discuss St Mo Dumma, and St Mo Dimogue but this will not happen. Nobody minds this now but one day they will.

On 4 June 1961 Butler noted:

In the last month I have worked very hard on the saints and tribes and have done chapters on Morini, Kynesioi, Carpi, Siguni, Cicones, Sardi, Budini, Ligurians. I still have to do Thracians, Veneti, Suebi, Vellauni, Vascones, Getae, Benntraige, Briges, Carians, Dacians, Dumnonians, Frisii, Kempses, Milesians, Mygdones, Nemedes, Silures; will I ever finish them and complete the introductory chapters before we go to the U.S.A?

On 1 October 1962 he wrote:

As regards my two enthusiasms, I had a smashing attack on my Saints and Tribes theory from Professor [Eric P] Hamp [Departments of Linguistics, Slavic Languages and Literature, Psychology, University] of Chicago. It was so ignorantly confident that, to restore my own confidence, I had to reply. I sent the attack and reply to David Grene [Professor at the University of Chicago and brilliant translator of Herodotus] who has been a tremendous and valuable ally to me. I stayed with him in Chicago and he spent a couple of days with us here.

A decade later, on 1 July 1972, he wrote:

How has Peggy endured my endless preoccupation with the saints? Now after nearly thirty years I am printing a book about them at my own expense at the Wellbrook Press, Freshford. I will have to sell 500 copies if I am to get my money back. I have never met a single scholar who understood what I was working at or gave me encouragement. The nearest to do this was Myles Dillon who died last week when we were in Dublin. Yet I know I am right and will one day be justified.

I have xeroxed my charts and made three books of them, a green one I have been using myself and it will be Julia's, a grey one (I think it is grey) I have left with Eleanor [Burgess] and a red one which Joe [Hone] can have if he wants (John McCormick has it, H.B., 3 September 1982). Obviously unless my work is justified these books will be just useless, inscrutable encumbrances. But I want them kept and not given away and, if their value realized, I wish all copyrights to rest with Julia. I am just sending off to Eleanor six or seven chapters, so that Eleanor will have a complete set at Boreham [Essex]. My present book, to be published in a few weeks, will only deal with about a third of what I have written. Had I had any support it would have been published fifteen years ago.

At Last in Print

Butler dedicated *Ten Thousand Saints* to his intellectual and spiritual predecessor Jacques Boucher de Perthes, 1788–1868, 'the Customs Officer of Abbeville', an amateur scholar who 'grew prize pears, wrote plays that were never produced, joined the Kilkenny Archaeological Society, shunned scientists and founded the science of prehistory'. His recognition of Boucher de Perthes' struggles to gain acceptance of prehistory poignantly highlighted his own efforts to overcome academic indifference to his own work. He insisted that his hypotheses and conclusions would be confirmed eventually by others if they assessed these data, 'which raise fascinating problems, which take us back behind the frontiers of recorded history to the remote wanderings of European peoples, to the clash of tribes and tongues'.

Butler's plight resembled that of other country scholars. Niel Stensen, the first geologist to show what seashells in sedimentary stone on mountain tops meant, was overlooked, ridiculed and forgotten. As Deborah Cadbury noted, Gideon Mantell's seminal discoveries of dinosaurs were considered 'not of sufficient importance to be printed'. A country scholar of geology who wrote a popular text, Robert Bakewell, not admitted to the Geological Society, observed: 'There is a certain prejudice among members of the Scientific Societies in London and Paris which makes them unwilling to believe that persons residing in provincial towns or the country can do anything important for science.' William Smith, pioneer of geological strata in England, indicated that: 'The theory of geology was in possession of one class of men and the practice of another,' as did Boucher de Perthes in France. Gregor Mendel experimented well, aired ingenious results at his local natural history society and in its journal and notified European scientists who ignored him. Twenty years after Mendel's death, his seminal genetic discoveries began a revolution in science that continues today. Butler's only contemporary, the brilliant novelist Vladimir Nabokov, was a scholarly amateur lepidopterist. Yet entomologists scoffed at his theory of evolution of blue butterflies. Thirty-three years after he died, Roger Vila and colleagues sequenced the DNA of blue butterflies and confirmed Nabokov's sixty-five year old report. By chance Butler's voluminous data base and original hypotheses were to prove relevant to studies of prehistoric and historic Irish and European origins ten years after he died.

Butler Owed Much to These Few

Butler was forced to publish privately what he considered his most important work. For eleven years up to seven hours daily he laboured to clarify Irish and European origins. Worried about finances, he struggled to make ends meet, selling produce from his garden and orchard and renting rooms and occasionally his house. He persevered with help from his wife Peggy, and Eleanor Burgess, A.J. Arkell's daughter. Burgess not only helped Butler as both a contrarian and supporting scholar, but also typed the book from Butler's tiny handwriting. His wife drew the maps and illustrations. The first edition's cover was designed by Damien Harrington. Desmond McCheane printed the book. Butler recorded: 'Writing as a country scholar, I am proud that my book is printed and its cover designed by friends and neighbours in my own county.'

Butler's few strong supporters discussed and constructively criticized his research. They included Eric Dorman-O'Gowan, 'a solitary scholar of Cavan' who as General Dorman-Smith made the winning battle plan for El-Alamein, and Eleanor Burgess, 'who both understood what I was trying to say and helped

AFTERWORD

me to say it'. John McCormick, his friend and fellow amateur archaeologist, of Newcastle, Co. Wicklow, found Butler's work engaging and applicable to disciplines involved in prehistorical research. Others attracted to Butler's work were David Grene, professor at the University of Chicago; Gerald Hanley, writer and expert on East African tribes; Lino Rossi, amateur archaeologist and physician-scientist of Milan; and W.M.S. Russell, social biologist.

In 2000 the Bradley team's report in *Nature* provided the first archaeogenetic DNA proof of Butler's Basque-Irish and Basque-Irish-Scythian-Scottish-Welsh-English-Frisian connections, twenty-eight years after *Ten Thousand Saints* was printed.

Conclusion

From recent bio-archaeologic research, Irish legend and science have met. We now know that Butler had thought the way through very complex linguistic entropy. He understood and revealed how one tribe's heroic ancestor dominated another's and how two tribes amalgamated ancestors to keep relations peaceful. He appreciated the sequential changing of tribal meanings and names implicit in the receding drift of pre-Celtic and Celtic languages of prehistoric Ireland, Scotland, Wales, England and France (Gaul and Gascony). His postulated Basque-Irish and Basque-Irish-Scythian-Scottish-Welsh-English-Frisian connections were fortuitously validated by archaeogenetic examination of Irish and European male and female genes. Butler would certainly not be astonished, and he would perhaps be pleased, that confirmation came from the technical, statistically empowered, molecular DNA analytical, 'hot' science of bio-archaeology. Yet how ironic, and like the fate of research by Stensen, Mantell, Bakewell, Smith, Mendel and Nabokov, that meticulous examination of molecular fragments by archaeogeneticists confirmed Butler's research of Irish legends a decade after his death. The data base and the analytic methods found in *Ten Thousand Saints*, 'Charts of Irish Tribes, Saints and Heroes', and 'The Colours of the Winds' offer opportunities for further scholarly exploration of Irish and European tribal genomes. The substantiation of Butler's other hypotheses about Irish and European origins remain an unmet challenge.

AFTERWORD

Acknowledgments

Butler showed me, and I first admired, this work in progress in the 1960s. Before Professor Daniel Bradley's team at Trinity College Dublin [TCD] connected the Basques and the Irish by the male Atlantic gene, parts of my assessment dealing with Butler's verbal archaeological methods comprised my talk to the Kildare Archaeological Society at Maidenhall on 19 July 1998. Eleanor Burgess reminded me of the relevance of the work then, emphasized important details of Butler's meticulous methodology and made helpful suggestions. Then the Bradley team's brilliant report in *Nature* propelled me to explore further. Professor Bradley kindly introduced me to the Irish and European archaeogenetics of DNA. Professors Paddy Cunningham and David McConnell provided constructive skepticism and germane references. Bryan Sykes' *Blood of the Isles* helped me pursue Butler's leads with its classification and distribution of the five paternal and seven maternal clans of Western Europe. Likewise Stephen Oppenheimer's *The Origins of the British* was an invaluable source. The late Billy O'Sullivan, retired librarian of TCD, a great friend of Butler's, gave me Ernst Lewy's work that linked Basque and Irish languages, relevant books and gentle constructive criticism. The late John McCormick gave me his analysis of Butler's research and Joshua Whatmough's *The Dialects of Ancient Gaul*. I thank especially Professor Barbara Wright of TCD, who greatly improved my text, asked provocative questions and made invaluable suggestions about language, phonetics and tribal origins. Robert Tobin eased my task by meticulous organization of relevant papers. I thank Joseph Gilbert, director, and the staff of The Scholars' Lab, Alderman Library, University of Virginia, for the scan with optical character recognition of the first edition of *Ten Thousand Saints*. Anne Makower's proofreading smoothed my text. Julia Crampton cheerfully endured and reread my typescripts. She often calmed my wayward computer's misbehaviour, and the miscreant writer who caused it. I thank Kitty Lyddon of the Lilliput Press for her skilful management of the second edition of this complex study of Irish tribes, saints and heroes. Her intelligent organization, proofing, cross-checking, and invaluable suggestions made work on this book a pleasure. I thank Antony Farrell, Hubert Butler's editor and publisher, who first introduced his essays to the international literary scene. The Lilliput Press's re-issue of *Ten Thousand Saints* ensures that what Butler considered his most important work is again available to play its part in uniting Ireland's pre-history with modern science.

Bibliography

Albarella, Larson G., et al, 'Ancient DNA, pig domestication and the spread of the Neolithic into Europe', *The Proceedings of the National Academy of Sciences USA*, 104 (2007), pp. 15276–81.

Bauchet M. et al, 'Measuring European population stratification with microarray genotype data', *The American Journal of Human Genetics*, 80 (2007), pp. 948–56.

Blackmore, Susan, *The Meme Machine* (Oxford University Press, Oxford, 1999).

Butler, Hubert, 'The dumb and the stammerers in early Irish history', *Antiquity*, 23 (1949), pp. 20–31.

Butler, Hubert, 'Who were 'the stammerers'?', *The Journal of the Royal Society of Antiquaries of Ireland*, 80, Part 2 (1950), pp. 228–36.

Butler, Hubert, 'Charts of Irish Tribes, Saints and Heroes' (privately printed, Maidenhall, 1971), Butler Papers, Trinity College Manuscripts Library, Dublin, Ms. 10304/75/69–105.

Butler, Hubert, *Ten Thousand Saints: a Study in Irish and European Origins* (The Wellbrook Press, Kilkenny, 1972).

Butler, Hubert, 'In the Land of Nod: puns and tribal ancestors in the Old Testament', *In the Land of Nod* (The Lilliput Press, Dublin, 1996), pp. 247–54.

Butler, Hubert, 'Woe unto thee Bethsaida: puns in the New Testament', *In the Land of Nod* (The Lilliput Press, Dublin, 1996), pp. 255–62.

Butler, Hubert, 'The writer as independent spirit', *In the Land of Nod* (The Lilliput Press, Dublin, 1996), pp. 207–8.

Cadbury, Deborah, *The Dinosaur Hunters, A Story of Scientific Rivalry and the Discovery of the Prehistoric World* (Fourth Estate, London, 2000). Cited: Bakewell and Smith, pp. 92–3, 336–7.

Canon J., Garcia D., Garcia-Atance M.A., Obexer-Ruff G., Lenstra J.A., Ajmone-Marsan P., Dunner S., The ECONOGENE Consortium: 'Geographical partitioning of goat diversity in Europe and the Middle East', *Animal Genetics*, 37 (2006), pp. 327–34.

Capelli C. et al, 'A Y chromosome census of the British Isles', *Current Biology*, 13 (2003), pp. 979–84.

Cavalli-Sforza L.L.: Piazza A., Menozzi P., Mountain J., 'Reconstruction of human evolution: bringing together genetic, archeological and linguistic data', *Proceedings of the National Academy of Sciences of the USA*, 85 (1988), pp. 6002–06.

Cavalli-Sforza L.L., *Genes, People, and Languages*. Translated by M. Seielstad (North Point Press, New York, 2000).

Crampton, Richard, 'Working on the saints: clues to the Irish genome' in C. Agee (ed.), *Unfinished Ireland. Essays on Hubert Butler, Irish Pages* (Belfast, 2003), pp. 119–35.

Cymbon T., Freeman A.R., Isabel Malheiro M.: Vigne J.D., Bradley D.G, 'Microsatellite diversity suggests different histories for Mediterranean and Northern European cattle populations', *Proceedings of the Royal Society of Biological Sciences*, 272 (2005), pp. 1837–43.

Dawkins R. and Wong Y., *The Ancestor's Tale, a Pilgrimage to the Dawn of Life* (Weidenfield & Nicolson, Great Britain, 2004).

Dennet, David, *Consciousness Explained* (Little, Brown, Boston, 1991).

Dennet, David, *Darwin's Dangerous Idea: Evolution and the Meaning of Life* (Simon & Schuster, New York, 1995).

Dillon, Myles, Chadwick, Nora K., *The Celtic Realms* (Weidenfeld and Nicolson, Great Britain, 1967).

Falush, Daniel, et al, 'Traces of human migrations in Helicobacter pylori populations', *Science*, 299 (2003), pp. 1582–5.

Forster P., Toth A., 'Toward a phylogenetic chronology of ancient Gaulish, Celtic, and Indo-European', *Proceedings of the National Academy of Sciences of the USA*, 100 (2003), pp. 9079–84.

Greenberg J.H., Turner C.G. II, Zegura S.L., 'The settlement of the Americas: a comparison of linguistc, dental, and genetic evidence', *Current Anthropology*, 27 (1986), pp. 477–97.

Hill E.W., Jobling M.A., Bradley D.G., 'Y-chromosome variation and Irish origins. A pre-neolithic gene gradation starts in the Near East and culminates in western Ireland', *Nature*, 404 (2000), pp. 351–2.

Kurlansky, Mark, *The Basque History of the World* (Alfred A. Knopf, Canada, 1999).

Larson G. et al, 'Ancient DNA, pig domestication, and the spread of the Neolithic into Europe', *Proceedings of the National Academy of Sciences of the USA*, 104 (2007), pp. 15276–81.

Lewy, Ernst, 'Der bau der Europaischen sprachen', *Proceedings of the Royal Irish Academy*, XLVIII, section C (1942), pp. 15–117.

Masceretti, Silvia et al, 'How did pygmy shrews colonize Ireland? Clues from a phylogenetic analysis of mitochondrial cytochrome b sequences', *Proceedings of the Royal Society London*, 270 (2003), pp. 1593–99.

McEvoy, Brian, Bradley, Daniel G., 'Y-chromosomes and the extent of patrilineal ancestry in Irish surnames', *Human Genetics*, 119 (2006), pp. 212–19.

McEvoy, Brian, Richards M., Forster P., Bradley D.G., 'The longue durée of genetic ancestry: multiple genetic marker systems and Celtic origins on the Atlantic facade of Europe', *The American Journal of Human Genetics*, 75 (2004), pp. 693–702.

McEvoy B., Simms K., Bradley, Daniel G., 'Genetic investigation of the patrilineal kinship structure of early medieval Ireland', *The American Journal of Physical Anthropology*, 136 (2008), pp. 415–22.

Moore L.T., McEvoy B., Cape E., Simms K., Bradley D.G., 'A Y-chromosome signature of hegemony in Gaelic Ireland', *The American Journal of Human Genetics*, 78 (2006), pp. 334–8.

Newbigin, Marion, *Plant and Animal Geography* (Methuen, London, 1936) pp. 89–91.

Oppenheimer, Stephen, *The Origins of the British, the New Prehistory of Britain and Ireland from Ice-age Hunter-Gatherers to the Vikings as Revealed by* DNA *Analysis* (Constable & Robinson, London, 2006).

O'Riain, Padraig, 'Saint Patrick in Munster: the journey that never was', Lecture, Cambridge Group for Irish Studies, Queens College, Cambridge University, 6 February 2001.

Pereira F. et al, 'Genetic signatures of a Mediterranean influence in Iberian peninsular sheep husbandry', *Molecular Biology and Evolution*, 23 (2006), pp. 1420–6.

Quinn, Bob, *The Atlantean Irish: Ireland's Oriental and Maritime Heritage* (The Lilliput Press, Dublin, 2005).

Richards, Martin, et al, 'Tracing European Founder lineages in the Near Eastern mtDNA pool', *The American Journal of Human Genetics*, 67 (2000), pp. 1251–76.

Rosser, Zoe H. et al, 'Y-chromosomal diversity in Europe is clinal and influenced primarily by geography, rather than by language', *The American Journal of Human Genetics*, 67 (2000), pp. 1526–43.

Rossi, Lino, Letter to Hubert Butler from Milan, 18 July 1981.

Ruhlen, Merritt, *The Origin of Language: Tracing the Evolution of the Mother Tongue* (John Wiley & Sons, New York, 1994).

Russell, William M.S., 'Saints, tribes and ancestors', *Biology and Human Affairs*, 40 (1975), pp. 118–30.

Somerville-Large, Peter, *Irish Eccentrics* (The Lilliput Press, Dublin, 1990).

Sykes, Brian, *Blood of the Isles, Exploring the Genetic Roots of our Tribal History* (Bantam Press, London, 2006).

Troy C.S., et al, 'Genetic evidence for Near-Eastern origins of European cattle', *Nature*, 410 (2001), pp.1088–91.

Vila, Roger, et al, 'Phylogeny and palaeoecology of *Polyommatus* blue butterflies show Beringia was a climate-regulated gateway to the New World', *The Proceedings of the Royal Society of London* B (2010), doi: 10.1098/rspb 2010.2213.

Viney, Michael, *Ireland* (Blackstaff Press, Belfast, 2003).

Whatmough, Joshua, *The Dialects of Ancient Gaul: Prolegomena and Records of the Dialects* (Harvard University Press, Cambridge, 1970).

Webb, David,'The flora of Ireland in its European context', *Journal of Life Sciences, Royal Dublin Society*, 4 (1983), pp.143–60.

Wilson J.F., Weiss D.A., Richards M., Thomas M.G., Bradman N., Goldstein D.B., 'Genetic evidence for different male and female roles during cultural transitions in the British Isles', *Proceedings of the National Academy of Sciences of the USA*, 98 (2001), pp. 5078–83.

Glossary

BENNTRAIGE	Binit	rennet
	Beann	mountain peak, horn
	Bean	woman
	Binn	sweet
	Beannacht	blessing
	Bantracht	female company
	Inbanda	effeminate
	Ban	white
	Banbh	sucking pig
BRIGES	Brughaidh	farmer
	Brigh	strength
	Breac	speckled, trout
	Breag	deceit
	Breith	judgement
	Briathrach	wordy
	Breach	wolf
	Broc	badger
	Brog	shoe
	Breo	flame
Brit folk	Brit	speckled
Brad-Bard folk	Bradan	salmon
	Bard	poet
Blat-Blad folk	Blad	fame or portion
	Bled	whale
	Blath	flower
	Blathach	buttermilk
	Blath	meal
Bacc-Bocc-Buac	Bac	bend
	Bacach	crooked, crippled
	Bachlagh	a rustic
	Bachall	crozier
	Buachaill	boy
	Boc	he-goat
Beg-Bec folk	Beg, beag	little

GLOSSARY

	Beach	bee
Fraech folk	Fraoch	heather
Bron-Bran folk	Bron	grief
	Bronach	sad
	Bro-bron	mill-stone
	Bru-bronn	breast or belly
	Bran	raven
	Brean	fetid
	Braen	drop
Ber-barr folk	Barr	crest
	Berach	acute
	Bior	spit, skewer
	Biorra (biolar)	water cress
	Bearraim	shave
BOII	Bo	cow
	Beo	lively
BUDINI	Buan	lasting
	Buidhe	yellow
	Buaidh	victory
	Bod	penis
	Both	hut, booth
	Bot	fire
	Bodhar	deaf
	Badhbh	raven
	Baeth	silly
	Beith	birch tree
	Bith	the world, everlasting
CAERINI	Caora	sheep
	Cearr	crooked
	Carrach	scabby
	Cuaran	sandal
	Cior	jet, comb
	Gair	shout
Carthach folk	Carthannach	loving
	Caorthann	rowan tree
Clar folk	Clar	board, flat
	Cleireach	cleric
CORNAVII, CREONES		
Corn, Crann, Crinn folk	Cearn	victory
	Carn	heap, cairn
	Cornu (Latin)	horn
	Cron	dark

	Crion	withered
	Crann	tree
	Grian	sun
CARPI	Carbad	chariot or jaw
CARPETANI	Corbadh	incest, corruption
	Coirpthe	corrupt
Garb folk	Garbh	rough
Gabal folk	Gabhal	fork
Croeb folk	Craobh	branch
	Crobh	paw
	Craibhtheach	pious
	Crub	hoof
Gob-cub folk	Gob	snout
	Gabha	blacksmith
	Gaibhleann	white-loined (cow)
	Goibhneann	'of the smith'
	Gubha	mourning
	Cobhair	help
	Ciab	onion
Crech folk	Crioch	boundary
	Creach	plunder
	Cre-criadh	clay
	Cearc	hen
	Corcair	purple
	Garg	fierce
	Graigh	mare
Crom-crim folk	Crom	bowed, crooked
	Creamh, cneamh	garlic
	Cruimther	priest
	Cruimh	worm
Cnamh folk	Cnamh	bone
Gaman folk	Gamhnach	stripper (cow not in calf that gives milk)
Corr folk	Corr	crane
	Coire	caldron
	Cor	choir
	Coir	genuine
Cerd folk	Ceard	craftsman
	Ceart	just
Cruith folk	Cruth	shape
	Gruth	curds, cheese
	Gruadh	cheek

GLOSSARY

	Croidhe	heart
	Cruadh	hard
	Cruach	rick
	Criotharnach	palsied
	Cruitire	harper
	Cruithneacht	wheat
Cloth folk	Cloch	stone
	Clog	bell
	Cleithe	ridge, pole
	Cliath	hurdle
	Cliabh	basket
	Cleith	concealment
	Cluiche	game
	Cluas	ear
DACI		
Dag-Ded folk	Dagh	good
	Daigh	flame
	Dead	tooth
	De	smoke
	Dath	colour
	Doid	fist
Dess folk	Deas	right hand
Tec-Teth folk	Teachtaim	I possess, take
	Teach	house
	Tead	rope
	Toidiu	water course
	Teith	smooth, sweet
	Tuagh	axe
	Tuath	tribe or left hand
	Togha	election
Da-Duach folk	Da	two
	Taoi, To	silent
	Deoch	drink
	Dia-de	god
DUMNONII	Domnach	church, Sunday
DAMNONII	Domhan	world
	Dumnos, Dubnos	deep
	Damh	ox, a sage
	Domus (Latin)	home
	Deamhan	demon
	Damhan	calf
	Donn	brown

291

GLOSSARY

Dub folk	Dubh	black or ink
Tem-Ten folk	Tamhan	a stump, blockhead
	Tim	weak
	Tamhnach	green field
	Teine	fire
	Tonn	wave
FRISII	Fras	shower
	Feart	virtue, tomb
	Fearsad	shaft, ford
	Ursus (Latin)	bear
GELONI	Ga-gae	spear
	Geal	white
	Gal	feat
	Giall	hostage
	Goll	one-eyed, blind
	Gall	foreign
	Galar	sickness
	Guala	shoulder
	Gual	coal
	Gealt	madman
	Glun	knee
	Glonn	deed
	Glan	clean
Cell-Cal folk	Cell	church
	Cael, Caol	thin
	Coll	hazel
	Codladh	sleep
	Caillc, Cailleach	veil, nun
	Caladh	hard
	Coelum (Latin)	sky
	Cuileann	holly
	Cul	back hair
	Culleum (Latin)	currach
	Culen	whelp
	Coill	wood
GETAE	Cead	hundred
	Cath	battle
	Cat	cat
	Geis, Gedh	swan
	Gad	withe
	Gaoth	wind
	Ceathar	four

GLOSSARY

	Got	stammerer
	Guth	voice
	Gath	spear
Cas folk	Cas	curl
	Ceas	boat
	Gus	vigour
	Casal	chasuble
	Ceis	young sow
	Cos	foot
	Coscar	breaking up
Os-Ass folk	Os, Oisin	deer, little deer
	Osna	sigh
	Os	above
Glas folk	Glas	green, fetter, stream
IBERIANS	Iobhar	yew
	Abhra	eyelash
	Faobhar	edge of blade
ICHT, (P)ICHT PEOPLE		
Ech folk	Each	horse
	Eccond	fools
	Eigeas	poet
	Eidhneach	ivied
	Eidigh	ugly
	Ecintach	innocent
	Ach!, Och!	ach!, och!
Eth folk	Eiteach	flying
	Iothach	thirsty
	Aitheach	rent payer
	Aith	sharp
	Eithiar	spirit
	Aed	fire
	Iocht	healing
Vac-Fec-Fiac folk	Fiach	raven
	Feichin	young raven
(The Vaccaei)	Fiacal	tooth
	Feccadh, Eccadh	turning back
	Facundus (Latin)	eloquent
	Fiach	treasure
Caech folk	Caoch	blind
	Ceacht	plough
Fid-Fad folk	Fiod	wood
	Fada	long

	Fod	sod
	Fuath	phantom
	Fodhord	murmuring
Uath folk	Uath	terror
	Uaithne	green
KYNETES	Cu, gen. Con	dog
CUNESIOl	Ceann	head
	Cain, Caoin	pleasing
	Caine	keaning
KEMPSES or CHAEMI	Caem, Caomh	beautiful
	Caemog	ivory
	Cam	crooked
LIGURIANS	Ligys (Greek)	shrill
	Liguron (Greek)	wailing
	Lingurium (Latin)	amber
	Lingua (Latin)	tongue
	Lingula (Latin)	little tongue
	Liaigh	physician
	Liach	spoon, sorrow
	Liogach	beautiful
	Liaghairne	lazy rascal
	Laogh	calf
	Laighean	spear
	Laightheach	lessener
	Laoch	hero
	Leac	stone
	Leaca	cheek
	Lacht	milk
	Lacha	duck
	St Luke	
	Loch	lake
	Luch	mouse
	Luachair	rush
	Luach	price
	Lua	kick
	Li	beauty
	(S)luagh	host, army
	(S)leacht	prostration
Liath-Lath folk	Liath	grey
	Leath	broad, side, half
	Luath	swift
	Luaith	ashes

GLOSSARY

Ling folk	Lingim	I jump
	Long	ship
	Loingseach	mariner
Lin-Lan-Lon folk	Lionn	ale
	Linn	pool
	Leine	linen garment
	Lan	full
	Lon dubh	blackbird
	Lonan	tale-bearer
	Lon	provisions
	Lonn	impetuous
	Luan, Loin	Monday
	Leana	meadow
Lem-Lam folk	Lamh	hand
	Lom	bare, belch
	Leamh	elm tree
	Loma	boor
	Leim	jump
	Leamhnacht	new milk
Lab-Leb folk	Labhar	talkative
	Lobhar	leper
	Laobh	askew
	Leabhar	book
	Lupaid	sucking pig
Las folk	Lasair	flame
	Lias	shed
	Lus	herb, leek
	Lios	fort
	Loiscthe	burnt
	Lasc	switch
	Luasc	rocking
MILESIANS	Miles (Latin)	soldier
	Mil	honey
	Maol	bald, hornless
	Mall	slow
	Mal	prince
	Molt	wether
MORINI	Muir	sea
	Mor	great
	Muire	Mary
MYGDONES	Muc	pig
	Mogh, Mug	slave

295

GLOSSARY

	Muig	mist, gloom
	Mucaidh	swine-herd
	Mac	son
	Magus (Latin)	wizard
	Magnus (Latin)	great
	Magister (Latin)	master
	Magh	plain
Mid-Med folk	Meath	fat
	Meadh	balance, scales
	Mi-De	bad smoke
	Meadh	mead
	Miach	bag
	Moch	early
	Miodh-	mid
	Medicina (Latin)	medicine
MENAPII	Maon, Menn	dumb, stammering
	Mion, Minn	smooth
	Mionn	diadem
	Maoin	treasure
	Muine	thicket
	Muin	neck, bush
	Mun gen. Muin	urine
	Manach	monk
	Manntach	toothless
	Monach	tricky
	Mong	hair
NEMEDES	Neamhan	raven
	Neamh	heaven
	Neamhann	pearl
	Neimh	poison
	Neimheadh	sacred place
	Niamh	brightness
	Namha	enemy
	Naomh	saint
	Nov	new
Nia-Neid folk	Naoidhe	infant
	Nathair	snake
	Naoi	nine, canoe
	Nua	new
Nar folk	Nar	modest
	Neart	strength
Nel folk	Nuall	shout

GLOSSARY

	Niall	champion
	Neall	cloud
Necht folk	Neacht	pure
	Nocht	naked
	(S)neachta	snow
Nasc folk	Nasc	bond, collar
Ness-Nesa folk	Ni-asa [THU 275]	not sociable
	(C)neas	skin
Nin-Nen folk	Nion	ash tree
	MacNine	son of N, i.e. a writer
	Nin	a wave
SARDI	Sord	pure
SORDONES	Ord	hammer, order
	Odhar	dun-coloured
	Uir	soil
	Uar, (F)uar	cold
	Ara, gen. Aradh	charioteer
	Ard	high
	Art	bear
	Artraigech [LIS II 331]	gouty
	Ara (Latin)	altar
	Airther, Oirthear	eastern
SCYTHIANS	Sciath	shield
	Scath	shadow
	Sceach	thorn tree
	Scoth	flower
SKOLOTI (Scythians, HDT IV 6)	Scal	hero, phantom
SIGINNI	Sego [HOL II 1443]	strength
	Seges (Latin)	corn
	-sech	feminine termination
	Sogh	bitch
	Seagal	rye
Set-Sant-Saith folk	Sento-, Set- [HOL II 1502], [THU 270]	path
	Saith	sufficiency or ration
	Sidh	fairy
	Sioth	peace
	Sanct-(Latin)	saint
	Sead	jewel
Sen folk	Sen	old
	Sionnach	fox

297

GLOSSARY

Scen folk	Sceinne	fugitive
SILURES	Sal	heel
	Salach	dirty
	Saileach	willow
	Suil	eye
	(Cinn) Selach [SG 407]	quarrelsome
	Salvator (Latin)	saviour
	Saile	'the briny'
	Salm	psalm
Selg folk	Sealg	hunt
	Sealgan	sorrell
	Silva (Latin)	wood
El-Ail folk	Eala	swan
	Ealga	noble
	Ealta	flocks
	Ail	stone
	Ailithir	pilgrim
	Hilary, Helen, Eleutherios	Dyonisus, Eros
	Il	very, a buttock
Talfolk	Tal	axe
	Tuile	flood
	Toll	hole
	Tualang	endurance
Dal-Dul folk	Dall	blind
	Dil	dear
	Daol	beetle
Alb-Elv folk	Albus (Latin)	white
	Abhall	apple
SUEBI	Subha	joy
	Subh	berry
	Scuab	broom
	Sabhall	barn
Sleb folk	Sliabh	mountain
SUANI	Suanach	drowsy
SEMNONES	Seim	rivet
	Seimh	subtle
	Snamh	swimming
	Simon and Simeon	
TIGURINI	Tighearna	prince
THRACIANS		
Traig-Treg folk	Traig	foot

GLOSSARY

	Traigh	strand
	Treadhan	three days fast
	Treathan	sea
	Truagh	wretched
	Tri	three
	Triath	nobleman, boar
Torc folk	Torc	boar
	Dorcha	dark
Tres-Dres folk	Treas	conflict
	Treas	third
	Très sainct (French)	very holy
	Dreas	briar
Drag-Draig	Dragan	dragon
	Draighean	blackthorn
	Drucht	drink
Draid-Druith folk	Druth	fool
	Draoi, gen. Druadh	Druid
Derg folk	Dearg	red
	Dearc, Derc	eye, berry, hole, mote
Erc folk	Earc	animal (cow, etc)
	Ore	pig, lap dog
	(S)earc	love
	Eirge	arising
Arg folk	Airgead	silver
	Airgneach	plundering
Tren folk	Trean	strong
	Drean	wren
Torn-Tor folk	Tor	tower, lord
	Torann	thunder
	Taurus (Latin)	bull
Dorn-Dron-Dur folk	Dorn	fist
	Dron	strong
	Dronn	hump
	Dur	hard, stupid
Ern folk	Iarnai	iron
	Urnaidhe	waiting
	Urnaighe	praying
	Airne	sloe
Fern folk	Fearn	alder
Dai folk	Dai gen. Daire	oak
	Der (Deor)	tear
Tart-Dart folk	Dart	heifer

	Tart	thirst
	Tortadh	seizing, striking
Turb-Tarb folk	Tarbh	bull
Treb folk	Treabh	tribe
Sreb-Sren-Srian folk	Sreang	string
	Srian	bridle
	Sriabh	scratch, stripe
	Sraibh	sulphurous fire, lightning
	Serf (English)	
	Searbh	bitter
Tab-Tib-Tob folk	Taberna	booth
	Taobh	side
	Tobar	well
Rig-Reg folk	Riogh, Righ	royal
	Righe	forearm
	Righ (Righim, Rigim)	stretch
	Riagh	gibbet
	Riaghail	rule
Ruad folk	Ruadh	red
Roth folk	Roth	wheel
Rath-Ret-Raed folk	Rath	rath
	Rath	grace, prosperity
	Rathneach	fern
Ros folk	Ros	wood, promontory
	Rosc	eye
	Ros	flaxseed
Ronn-Rann-Ren-Rinn folk	(S)rian	bridle
	(S)ron	nose
	Rinn	spear point
	Rian	track
	Rian	sea
VASCONES		
Basc folk	Bas	death
	Bas	palm of hand
Musc-Mesc- Mess folk	Measc	drunk
	Meas-chu	lap dog
	Measan	lap dog
	Meascan	confusion
	Mo-aisge	my shame
	Meas	fruit or nut
	Meas	edge
	Misneach	vigour

GLOSSARY

Esc-Uisc-Ist folk	Iasc	fish
	Uisce	water
VELLAUNI		
Fael folk	Faoilean	sea gull
	Fail, Failghe	ring
	Faill	cliff
	Faoilidh	hospitable
	Faol chu	wild dog, wolf
	Fial	generous
	Fal	hedge, enclosure
	Fal	phallus
	Fuil, gen. fola	blood
	Fola, gen. foladh	substance
	Fulla	delusion
	Folia (Latin)	leaves
Bel folk	Beal	mouth
	Biail	axe
	Bile	tree
	Ball	spot, birthmark
	Balla	wall
	Biolar	water cress
Bolc-Bolg folk	Bolg	belly, bag or bellows
Olc folk	Olc	evil
	Ol	drinking
	Oll	great
	Ollamh	chief poet
Ulc-Al-Ul folk	Ulcha	beard
	Ulaidh	monument
	Aladh	speckled
	Alla	wild
	Alainn	handsome
Folt-Alt folk	Folt	hair
	Foltchep	kind of leek
	Foltach	rich
	Alt	joint, glen
VENETI		
Finn folk	Fionn	white
	Fine	tribe
	Fuineadh	setting (of sun)
	Fan	slope
	Fion	wine
Ind-Ing folk	Inneoin	anvil

	Inghean	daughter
	Ingneach	having nails
En folk	Ean	bird
	Aon	one
	Eineach	face
	An	brilliant
	Aine	urine
VERONES		
BERONES	Fer (Fear)	man
UNCLASSIFIED		
Cuach folk (Cauci?)	Cuach	cup, cook, cuckoo
	Cock (English),	
	Cucullus (Latin)	cowl
Rem folk (Remi?)	Reamar	fat
	Rime	counting
	Rama	oar
	Ruamach	Roman

Index 1

SAINTS

Abban 119, 169
Aed 79
Aed Mac Breac 79, 83
Aedan 7, 92, 271
Aedlug 37
Aenboin 131
Aerdeyrn 189
Ailbe 67, 115, 119, 156, 160, 202, 205–7
Algisus 223, 226–7, 229
Asaph 183
Attracta 83
Auxilius 99

Baithen 125. 130, 231
Bardanus 103
BarrFinn (Barr Fionn) 213, 124, 135
Benen 94
Beoan 225
Beodan 223, 225, 229
Berach 127–9, 145–6
Berchan Fer da Leithe 199
Bescna 108–9
Bind 23, 104
Bite 169
Blaan (Bledenus) 4, 203
Blath 17
Bolcan, Bolgan 8, 43
Braccan 4, 77, 257
Breac 79, 235
Breaca 79, 235
Brecan 135, 139
Brendan 115, 141, 202–3, 268, 243
Briccin 117,

Brig 56, 78, 83, 100, 139, 151, 202
Briga 78, 156, 202
Brigit 14, 58, 77, 81–2, 130, 203, 206, 235
Bronach 178, 219
Buite 209

Cadoc 163
Caelcu 33, 115
Caelfinn, Caelan 14, 124, 139
Caeltigern 182, 191, 194
CaelFinn (Fionn) 14, 24
Caillin 127, 129
Caindech, Canice 4–7, 56, 116–19, 125, 161, 176–7
Caintigern 184–5, 194
Cairbre 15, 259
Cairbre Crom 162–3
Cairce 158
Canice (Ceanneich) 116–17
Caradoc Garb 167
Carthach 75
Catan 93
Ceannfionnac 117
Cearc, V. 165–6
Cearc, disciple of Columba 165
Cellach 175, 120, 184
Cerbone 145
Cerpan 140
Chebran 149
Chebrien 149
Cianan 118, 227
Ciara 212
Ciaran 3, 4, 8, 15, 102–04, 135, 139–40,

149, 161, 176, 186
Ciaran Mael 15, 176
Ciarascadh 212
Cipia (Cobba, Copia) 169
Cobba (Cipia, Copia) 169
Cobran 135–40, 149
Coemgen (Kevin) 191–2
Colgu 33
Colman (Colmoc) 152, 154, 200, 231
Colman Ela 231
Colman Got 13
Colman Grec 154
Colman mac Luachain 154, 162, 181, 221
Columba 5, 14, 23, 94, 100, 102–03, 124–5, 129, 130–1, 144, 156, 164–5, 177, 196, 220, 229, 240
Columnatan 152
Comgall 35, 162, 186, 202, 237
Comgan mac da Cerda 196
Conchinn, Conchind, V. 27–8, 31, 118–20, 184–5
Copia (Cobba, Cipia) 169
Corba, V. 137, 139
Corban 144, 146, 152
Corbican 140, 146, 166, 223, 227–6
Corbinian 140
Corbiniana, V. 140
Corc, V. (Cearc) 159
Corcan 158
Corcaria 157–8
Cormac 138, 143
Corp 17–18, 74, 138–9, 142, 149, 151–2, 174, 217
Corpnatan 74, 152
Craeban 152
Craebhnat 152
Cramsech 163
Cranat, V. 163, 213
Crebriu 151
Criotan Certronnach 162
Critan 160
Crob Criad 152

Crobhderg, V. 152
Crobnatan 74, 146
Croidan 160
Crom Dithruib 163
Cromm 163
Cronan 8, 29, 75–6, 130
Cronan Clarainech 130
Cruibin Craebdech 152
Cruimine 163
Cruimther Corcrain 159
Cruithnechan 159–60
Crumtheris, V. 159
Cuach, V. 31, 94
Cuana 219
Cubius 167
Cucephas 121
Cudub 115
Cuimin Fada 199
Cuircne 158
Curcagh 158
Curig 155, 159
Cu-Santin 185, 192
Cu Sidhe (Sidwell) 20, 116
Cybi 167, 191
Cyndeyrn 185
Cyngar 167, 192
Cyprian 226
Cyres 155
Cyriacus 155, 157, 159
Cyrus 157

Da Brig 78
Da Celloc 200
Da Cholmoc 200
Da Chua 200
Da Goban 200
Dagan 117, 191
Daig (Daigcerd) 161, 164
Dairchell 29, 76
Damhin 31
Darerca 94, 88, 176, 186
Da Rioc 200

INDEX I: SAINTS

Dartinna 216
David 4, 82, 167, 183, 191, 200, 205, 206
Demana (mac Cuill) 156
Digde 162
Digern, V. 192
Domangen 212
Duach, Archbishop 200
Dub da Leithe 201
Dub da Locha 199
Dub da Thuile 199
Duthracht 82, 192

Edeyrn (Eternus) 189, 191
Elldeyrn 189
Elvan 207
Elvie 206
Emer 177, 219, 220
Emine Ban 23
Enda, Enna 132–5, 139, 140, 146, 167, 192, 202–03, 206, 219
Enna Crom 163
Ennio mac Fiataich 130
Eochaid, King 31, 164, 187, 193
Eogan 81, 151, 188, 235
Erc 31
Erc, V. 88, 93–5, 245
Ercnat, V. 94
Escon 110
Ethcen Dornsalach 14
Etho 166
Etto 223

Faelan 184, 220, 222–3, 226–8,
Faelcu 153
Faeltigern 182, 191, 194
Fanchea 134
Faustus 189
Fechin 8, 163–4
Fer da Crich 155, 193, 199, 104
Fiachra 3–5
Fiachra Cael 14
Fiachra Goll 14

Fiachu Fer da Liach 199
Fid, Bishop (Fith, Ith, Id, Aed) 46–7, 150
Fidairle 46
Fidgus 46
Fidmuine 46
Finan 119–20, 125, 141
Finan Cam 124–5, 203
Finan Lobar 124
Finnbar 124, 205
Findchan 129
Finnchu 124, 243
Findlug, Loga 64, 124–5, 240–5
Fintan 8, 116, 120, 123–6, 128, 167, 169, 192, 249
Fintan Berach 128
Fintan of Clonenagh 124, 126, 170, 201
Fintan of Dunblesc 90
Fintan Maeldub 126, 128
Fintan Munnu 120, 124, 129
Foirtchern (Foirctigern) 187–91
Forseti, Forsee, Fosta 224
Fraech 98, 143, 220
Fro, Fros 224, 229
Frosius 220, 224
Frossach 220
Fursa (Fro, Fros 309) 34, 218–224, 226–9
Fuinche Garb 140–1

Gabhran 149
Gabrian 149
Garban 152, 166
Germanus 33, 98
Gibrian 149
Glascu 115
Gleran, Grellan 151
Glunsalach 14
Gnavan 163
Goban 20, 73–4, 126, 132, 140, 166–70, 200–1, 223, 226–7, 249
Goban Finn 170
Goban Finn Moccu Lama 170
Gobnait 167, 169, 243

Gobran 140, 149
Gobrian 149
Gorba 139, 142
Gortimer 191
Govan 167
Gregory (Grigoir) Pope and Saint 33, 91, 144, 152–5, 157, 159, 228
Grellan, Gleran 151
Guasacht 177, 219
Guillebrod (Willibrord) 33–4, 223–4
Gurthiern 190–1, 193
Gwynan 135
Gwynno 135
Gwynnoro 135
Gwynnteirbron

Hilary, Elair 33, 153

Iariath (Jarlath) 237
Ibar 9, 45, 47, 55, 186, 204
Illdierna
Illtud 192

Jarlath (Iariath) 237
Jestyn 167
Jutwell 20

Kenneth 5, 117
Kentigern 12, 37, 75, 121, 182-6, 189, 192–3, 220
Kentigerna, V. 102–03, 121, 220, 191, 184–5

Lactan 20, 240
Lappan 31, 93
Lasar, Lassar 151, 139, 142, 169, 181, 243–44
Laserian 102
Lawrence 91
Lesru 151
Liadan 139
Liban 23

Liemania 88, 93, 98
Locheni Menn 13, 18
Loga, Findlug 124
Lomman 187
Lon Coisfinn 124
Louthiern, Luchern 186
Lua 33, 200
Luchtigern 186, 194
Lucius 37
Lugid 35, 37, 76
Luke 33, 35
Lupita 88, 91–3

Mac Aible 156
Mac Cairthenn (Carthenn, Carthain) 31, 23, 189, 193, 227
MacCreiche 74, 152, 155–7, 166, 186, 202, 206–7
MacCrithe 160
Mac Croide Ailbe 156
Mac Croide Mochta 156
MacCuill 156, 227
Mac da Cerda 161, 199
Mac Nisse 57, 92
Mac U Greca 154
Maedoc (Mo-Aedoc) 83, 102, 127, 129, 180
Mael, Mel 15, 83, 176
Maelcroin 179
Maelcu 114–15, 175–9, 219
Maeldalua 179
Maeldobarchon 115
Maeldub 126, 128
Maeldun 134
Maelibair 179
Maelodar 14
Maelog 167
Maelruain 180, 253
Maelruba 181, 188
Maelsnechta 220
Maeltiern 191
Maeltigern 194

INDEX I: SAINTS

Magna 167
Maignen 221
Maine, Bishop 31
Mantan 90
Martin 33, 88, 100–3, 153, 184
Martin, Pope 222
Mel (Mael) 92, 176–7, 179, 225
Meldan 181, 223, 225, 229, 252
Mella 177
Mescan 88, 108–9, 262
Mescon 110
Mo-Aedoc (Maedoc) 31, 83, 102, 127, 129, 169, 170, 180
Mobi 130
Mo Brig 78
Mo Chaemog 225
Mo Choche 75
Mo Cholmoc 133
Mochua 8, 75-6, 115
Mochua Ciceach 317
Mo Cua Finn 115
Mochta (Mochta Lug) 156-7
MoChuda 55-6, 75, 158, 212, 259
Mochuta 75
MoConna 102
Mo Cop, Mochop 7, 67, 271
Moelgubi 20, 116, 170
Mo-Frisius 220
Mo Goppoc Artifex 170
Mo Laise (MoLaisse) 8, 23, 184, 244
Mo Laisse Craeb 151
Mo Liba 191
Mo Ling (Moling) 3, 28–31, 35, 76, 99, 241
Mo Lua (Molua) 35–36, 57, 200, 203, 243–5
Mordeyrn (Mortigern) 185, 193
Muiredach 31, 193
Muirgen 225
Munghu 75, 183, 185
Munnu (Mofinnu, Mundus) 11, 124–5, 129, 131, 184

Mura 231

Naindech, son of Maine 161
Nathcaem 102
Nechtan mac ua Baird 99
Nechtan Nair 99
Nehemiah 33
Nem 33
Neman 31
Nessan 8, 90–91
Ninian 101–2, 134, 192–4,
Ninnidh Lamhglan 14
Non 167

Odran 240, 242, 244–5
Oengus 132
Oengus, the Culdee 94, 221
Olcan 43
Onchu 115

Paan 4, 257
Palladius 86
Partholon 39, 41, 58, 78, 106, 256, 259
Patrick 3, 6, 43, 54, 82–6, 88, 90–4, 102–3, 109, 118, 128, 146, 149, 151, 156–9, 163, 165, 169, 177, 187–8, 201, 204, 206, 213, 219, 230, 241–2, 262
Piran 4
Pupaeus 153-4

Riagal (Rule) 220
Ricella 88
Ronan 146, 162, 241
Ruadan 10, 138, 142, 180
Rule (see Riagal) 220

Samson 205
Sannan 88
Sarnait 150
Sciath 208–9, 212–13
Scothin, Scuithin 3–4, 213
Segin Claraineach 130

Seigin Gabal 151, 164
Selyf 167, 192
Senach Garb 141, 159, 166
Senan 8
Servan 183, 189
Setna 139
Sezin 4
Sidwell (Cu Sidhe) 20, 116
Sillan 31
Siltiern (Siltigern) 191–4
Sinell 11, 31
Solomon 192
Srian 203
Suibhsech 31
Swithin 4, 213
Sylvester, Pope 33, 153
Syth 20

Tartinna 215–16
Ternoc 221, 243–4

Teyrnog 193
Tigern 82, 192
Tigernach 23, 102, 104, 185, 189, 192–4, 200, 249
Tigris 88, 91
Torney 193
Trenfer 88, 104–5
Trian 203

Ultan 220–23, 226–8, 231
Ultan Tua 13, 18
Ursula 10
Usaille 99

Victor 88–9, 279
Volcan 43
Vulvella 20

Willibrord (Guillebrod) 33–4, 223–4
Wulfram 33, 223

# Index 2
ANCESTORS AND HEROES

Admaer Trechichech 231
Admilithi 179
Aed Alain 118
Aed Caelcos 219
Aed Dub 127–9, 219
Aed Finn 127–9, 219
Aed Gabalfada 150
Aed Garb 141
Aencos 42
Aengus 42
Aenlam 42, 171
Agni Find 123
Ailbe (dog) 119, 156
Ailbe of Ui Ailbe 206
Ailbe (war-dog of Slieve Crott) 207
Ailbe Gruadbrec 160
Ailill Find 231
Ailill Molt 179
Aillen 207
Aine 41, 150, 132–3, 259
Aine Finn 133
Aithbel 58, 186
Alebion 36, 205
Amalghaid 163, 165
Amalgaid Blaithe 16
Amalgaid Menn 16
Annluan 111
Araide Bibre 54
Art (Artraige) 66, 138
Art Aenfer 105, 131
Artcorb 82, 138, 144
Arthur, King 119, 167, 191
Aulom 118

Baedan Mac Cairill 184
Baeth 26
Bairrche 165
Balor 117
Bardan 100, 103
Barr 186
Bascall 111, 262
Bebrae Fiachach 54
Bec Loinges 30
Belocc 26, 42
Beothach 39, 256–7
Berchan 31
Bergans 77
Bergion 77
Bibrax 53–4
Bibur 54
Binn, son of Ded 23, 28
Bith 39, 60, 96, 256
Blad 31, 115
Bladcu 115
Blat 203
Bloc 42
Bodb Catha 47
Bodmall 120
Bofinda 123
Bolc 42–3
Bolg 42–3
Braca 77
Braccan 4, 76, 257
Braici 83
Bran 203, 245
Breacdolb 81
Breactigern 185, 194

INDEX 2: ANCESTORS AND HEROES

Brec 78
Brecan 76, 78
Bregon 41, 175, 259
Bregu 77
Brendan (Broen-finn) 124, 134, 139, 202–3
Breogan 17, 95
Breotigern 185, 194
Bresal Ainechglas 130
Bresal Breac 79, 217
Bricc 235
Brig 78, 83, 100, 192, 194, 202
Brigans 77
Brigantia 58, 77, 235
Brigit 79, 81–3, 213, 235
Briotan Mael 39, 256
Brocainech 130
Broen-finn (Brendan) 139, 202
Broin-finn (female) 141
Brug 83
Brugaid 83
Bruide 79
Buan 142, 225
Buaidh-beo 88
Buide 196

Caelceis 219–20
Caelfer 42, 105
Caelfinn, Caelan 124
Caer (Ciar, Cuar) 209
Caerenn, Caerfinn 124
Caillech Bere 129, 203
Cairbre 138, 142–7, 151–2
Cairbre Bascain 109, 146, 262
Cairbre Caem 163
Cairbre Crom 163
Cairbre Crom-cinn 163
Cairbre Musc 109, 146, 262
Cairbre Rigfada 49
Cairill 184
Cairpre 143–6
Cairpre Blai 16, 19
Cairpre Cruithnechan 157–60

Cairpre Dercc Oirce 189
Cairpre Dub 16, 19
Cairpre Niafer 105
Cairthenn Dub 16
Cairthenn Finn 16
Cana Garb 149
Capa, grandson of Corb 166
Carbad 138, 140, 142–3
Carban (Corban) 161
Carpent 69, 142
Carthach 75
Carthenn 42, 259
Cas Corach 120
Cas Mac Tail 47
Cass 203
Cassius Tallius 47
Catchern (Catigern) 189–90
Cathal Crobhderg 152
Cathbad 75
Cathluan 162
Ceallach 119–20
Ceann Edig 116
Ceannfaeladh 117
Cearc Bairrche 165
Cellach 120, 179, 184
Celtchair 69, 213
Cennait 48
Cerd Beg 161
Cerberus 149
Cerdan 161–2
Cerdraige 161
Cessair 39, 41, 256, 259
Cet 13, 111, 132, 170, 234
Cett 119–20
Cian 60
Ciar (Caer, Cuar) 209, 212
Cichainech 130
Cichban 231
Cichmaine 231
Cicol 41
Cicol Grigairglun 171, 232
Cindiu 26, 48

Cingit 48, 107
Circe 172–3, 250–1
Cirdubain 237–8
Ciric 172
Ciric, son of Cruidne (Circin, Cirig) 160, 172
Cira 237
Clar, son of Brigit 130
Clarainech 130
Cnama 164
Cnamhfiac 164
Cobfir 105
Cobran 139–40
Codal Corr Chichech 231
Coinne Chichech 231
Colla da Crich 155, 158, 162
Conall Cass 27–28
Conall Cearnach 95, 116, 120, 189
Conall Cu 115
Conall Derg 133, 135
Conall Sciath Bachall 213
Conbel 115
Conchann 120
Conchinn 27-28, 120
Conchinn Cennfada 120
Conchobar 21, 138, 144–5, 166
Condad 118
Congal Ceannfada 120
Congal Claen 119–20
Congal Clarainech 130
Congeilt 179
Conla Cerd 164
Conlaeth 115
Conlead 82
Conleng 30
Conmael 115
Connra 163
Corb 18, 110, 118, 131, 137–8, 142–7, 152, 166–7, 174, 226
Corban (Carban) 139–40, 144, 146–7, 161–2, 167
Corb Gailni 138

Corb Liath (Corp Liath mac Tassaich) 131, 217
Cor(b)mac 138, 144
Corb Olum 152
Corb Ulum 118
Corc, son of Lugaidh 157–8
Corc Duibne 159
Corc Dul 159
Corc Losat 159
Corp (Corb) 17, 74, 138–9, 149, 151–2, 174
Craebh 74, 147, 152, 157
Craebh Finn 152
Crann 76
Craobh 151
Crecan 15–5
Credni 160
Creidne 160, 162
Cridenbel 141, 160, 171, 259
Crimthann Sciathbel 213
Crinna Cerd 162
Crob 74, 147
Crob Criad 152, 162
Crob Finn 152
Croeb 151
Crofinn 152
Croibine 151
Croidh 186
Crom Derg 163
Crom Dub 163
Cronan (Cronn) 29, 76
Cruidne 158, 160
Cruife 152
Cruinbel 171
Cruinn (Cruith) 74, 132, 162
Cruithne 160, 162, 164
Cruithnechan 160
Crutbolc 160
Cu 45, 115–16, 130, 138
Cu Ainech 130
Cuar (Caer, Ciar) 209
Cu Buidhe 115

INDEX 2: ANCESTORS AND HEROES

Cu Catha 116
Cu Cen Mathair 115
Cu Cnamha 117, 163, 165
Cu Congeilt 179
Cu Corb 59, 115, 138
Cucuan 115
Cucullain 115–16, 131–2, 159
Cu Dobuir 115
Cu Duilig 116
Cu Finn 115, 124
Cu Gamna 115, 117
Cu Garb 115
Cu Glass 115
Cuillen 159
Cullen 115
Cunisc 69
Cu Odor 115
Cu Ois 115
Curig 155
Cu Roi mac Daire 48, 212, 232
Cu Santin 184, 192
Cuscraid Menn 13, 90, 234
Cu Sidhe (Sidwell) 20, 116

Da 199
Da Caech 171
Da Creca 155, 199
Da Derga 197, 199
Da Luanus 231
Dael 157–8
Dagda 77
Dai 199
Daig, son of Corc 27, 161–2
Daig Dorn 161–2
Daire 17, 93–4, 142, 213
Daire, son of Dega 161
Dallan 42, 118
Daman 115
Dangal 184
Dara 142, 150
Dargabal 150
Darina 135

Dartad 216
Dartaid 131, 217
Datluath 200
Dau 199–200
Daurthecht 150
Dea 27–8
Deccluaid 200
Ded 23, 27–8, 48, 200
Dedad 200
Degloth 200
Derbind Belfada 23
Dercennus 66
Derg 27–8, 90, 96–7, 163
Dergainech 130
Derinell Cetharchichech 231
Dicuill 188
Digernach 192
Dil Mac da Creca 155, 199
Dimma 20, 93
Dobarchu 115, 203
Dobtha 128
Docha (Toiche) 111
Doigre Dart 216
Doilbh 81
Dolb 235
Dolfinn 123
Donngal 184
Dorn 120
Dorn Corcra 159
Draganes 36, 66, 89, 265
Draichdene 96
Draig 89, 96, 265
Duach Donn 100
Dubad 237
Dub da Boirenn 201
Dub da Crich 129, 201
Dub da Inber 201
Dubhan 129, 237
Dubh da Det 195, 197
Dubh Dead 119
Dubh Dothra 216
Dubhtach 81

INDEX 2: ANCESTORS AND HEROES

Dubhthac 129
Duibfionn 109
Duibne 159
Dula 158
Durthecht (Durthacht) 82, 192

Eber 25–6, 40, 45, 47, 166, 175, 258
Eber Finn 124, 168
Eber Glundub 171
Eber Glunfind 41, 124, 259
Echach 197
Echoaid 187
Echach Fer Aine 105
Echtigern 190, 194
Eirg 83
Eitsen 196
En 111
Encerd 161
Enna, son of Conall Derg 133
Enna Ceinselach 188, 260
Enna Glunliath 27–8
Eochaid, son of Erc 164
Eocho Timin (Leinster) 237
Eochtigern 193
Eogabal 150
Eogan 151, 166
Eogan Breac 81, 235
Eolang 30
Eotigern 190, 192, 194
Erc 94–6, 151, 164
Erc Caelbuidhe 14
Erc Culbuidhe 14
Ercal 96
Ercdroma 96
Ercleng 30
Ercol 58
Erminfinde 228
Estiu 67, 110, 196
Eth Cen 118
Ethedon 150
Etig 116
Ethne 23, 144, 150–1

Ethne Gabalfada 150–1

Faelgus 227
Fainche Trechichech 231
Farsad 224
Fectmagius 91
Fedelmid 187–8
Feindid 124, 203
Fenius 212
Fer 104–7
Feradach Find Fechtnach 158
Fer Aine 104–5, 132
Fer Amhla 106
Fer Baeth 104
Fer Bend 22, 105
Fer Blai 104
Fer Bolg 105–5
Fer Buidi 104
Fer Caille 41–2, 232, 271
Fer Cechech 231
Fer Ceite 105–6
Ferchar 230
Fer Ching (Chinged) 48
Fer Corb 104–5, 107, 142, 145
Fer Crom 104
Fer Cu 104
Fer da Beann 22, 105
Fer da Crich 104, 155, 193, 199
Fer da Gabar 141
Fer da Liach 199–200
Fer Dechet 107
Fer Demmain 105
Fer Det 48, 104
Fer Diad 48
Fer Domnach 48, 104, 106
Fer Dub 104, 106
Fer Fi 105
Fer Fuilli 42
Fer Gaile 106
Fer Gair 105–6
Fergal 229
Fer Garb 104

INDEX 2: ANCESTORS AND HEROES

Fer Glas 104
Fergna 20
Fergna Garb 140–1
Fer Goboc 104
Fergus (Fergus mac Rioch, MacRosa) 117–19, 129, 188, 231
Fergus Dergbotha 96, 238
Fergus Salach 234
Fergus Oiche 203
Fergus Tregbotha 96
Fer Loga 104
Fer Lugdach 105
Fer Mac 48
Fer Mac Ceidi 106
Fer Maise 105
Fer Menn 104, 107
Fer Nuad 105
Fer Rein 106
Fer Ruith 105
Fer Sen 104
Fer Tlachtga 29, 105
Fer Tri 104–5
Fiacha Ceannfinnan 117, 124
Fiachna 184
Fiachra Tort 216
Fianscoth 213–14
Fiatach Finn 123–4
Fidcorb 17, 144
Finbard 100, 102
Finbel 124
Find 124, 129, 151, 203
Findfer 105, 131
Findlug 46, 64, 137–8, 202, 219
Findsciath 213–15
Findtigern 185, 194
Finegas 124
Fingin 123
Finmeda 219
Finn 26, 122–36
Finn, daughter of Lochan 160
Finna 122
Finnbeo 124

Finnbruinne 124
Finncaem 124
Finncas 124
Finnech 124
Finninghean 124
Finnscoth 124
Finntuir 123
Fintan 128–9, 192
Fintat 16
Fionnscothach 124, 213
Foirc (Forc) 95, 189
Forannan 186
Forggo 189
Forsaid 224
Fossan 224
Fothad 29, 120
Fothad Airgthech 165
Fothad Canainne 117, 120
Fuinche (Uinche) 134
Fuirtgern 189

Gabal 150–1, 166
Gabal Glass 150
Gaban 149
Gablan 151
Gabhran 149
Gaedel Glas 60
Galu 171
Garb 74, 140–1, 238
Garban 166
Garbcu 115
Garban (Gablan) 166
Garman 110
Gawain 167
Gelfer 42
Gelgeis 219
Gerg 155, 162, 166
Get 56
Giric 155
Glas, son of Ded 23
Glas Gabhlen 150
Glas Gabhnen 150

Glasgabal 150
Glass, son of Encerd 161
Glassben 23, 27–8
Gleigal Garb (Tiurean) 238
Gleon 171
Gleru 151
Glinne 27–8
Glou 189–90
Glun 28, 171
Glunfind 41, 123, 259
Goban 168
Goibniu 167
Goirmtigern 194
Goirmthigern 191
Goll Glas 150
Gorbonianus 166
Gothnia 60
Graban 152
Grac 154–8
Grec mac Arod 154
Grecus 40, 154, 172, 250, 258
Grian 132
Grim 155, 162
Grogin (bull) 154
Gruibne 158
Gruibo 152
Guaire 179
Guaire Blaith 16, 27
Guaire Garb 16, 27
Gub 166, 174
Gubbi 74, 149, 226
Guithigern 193
Gurguntius 110, 166
Gwydion 167
Gwynn 122, 135

Hercules 27, 36, 58, 62, 77, 93, 96, 173, 186, 205, 209, 215, 245, 250
Horsa 190

Iar 27–8, 119
Iair Conchind 28, 119

Infir (Findfer) 105, 131
Ischomache 112
Ischu 112
Ith 17, 40, 41, 43–6, 76, 95, 171, 258–9
Ixion 112

Jacob 19, 233–4

Laethcu 115
Laidcen Lethcerd 161
Lailoken 183, 185
Lama 92, 170
Lamfin 41, 259
Lamfind 41, 259
Lamgabaid 132, 170
Lamglan 41
Lappan 93
Leamhain 157
Liathan 131, 236
Liban 23
Liger 41, 259
Ligys 36
Ling, son of Mal 29, 30, 76
Linge Dub 16
Linge Finn 16
Lithe 27–8
Lochan 133, 160
Lochru 54
Locrine 37
Loegaire 37, 187
Loingsech 30
Lonan 90
Longbardan 30, 99
Lot or Loth 37, 183, 232
Lot Luath 171
Luan 196
Luch 186
Luchtigern (Mouse–prince) 186, 194
Lud 37
Lug 17, 26–27, 35–8, 40–4, 55, 66, 124, 258–9, 266
Lugaid, son of Ith (Lugith) 17, 76, 40, 258

INDEX 2: ANCESTORS AND HEROES

Lugaid Cal 17, 93
Lugaid Cichech 231
Lugaid, father of Corp 158
Lugaid Corb (Corp) 17, 18, 138, 144
Lugbrand 37
Lugdech 37
Lugid 35, 37, 76
Lug mac Eithnenn 37
Lugmael 37
Lugmind 37
Lug Roth 69
Lugtigern 37, 182, 186, 194
Lulaig 185

Mael 41
Maelainech 132
Maelcu, grandson of Milcu 177
Maelcun 183
Maelfinn 124
Maelgwyn 152
Maelmocheirge 83
Maelruba 188
Maelsnechta 220
Maeltiern 191
Maeve 119, 150
Magach 111, 130, 262
Magdon 56
Maine 14, 157–8, 161
Maine Mal 14, 181
Maine Mall 14
Maine Tai 231
Mal 29, 30, 76, 181
Malling 29
Manannan 184, 238
Marius 182
Martan 103
Mata Muirsce 111
Mathfer 105
Mechdeyrn 191
Meda 219
Mel 176–7, 198, 225
Meldos 225

Mella 26, 177, 225–6
Menn mac Salcolga 13
Mesc 110
Mescorb 110, 238
Mes Deda 110
Mes Delmon 110
Mes Roeda 110
Mes Seda 110
Midgen 58
Mil 26, 41, 111, 175, 179, 181, 212, 259, 258
Milcu 177–8, 219
Miled 37, 130, 175, 178, 225, 258
Miledan 175
Milith 179
Milscothach 214
Milthous 179
Mind 27
Minscothach 214
Moch 83
Mochtigern 194
Moinne 90
Molling, Malling 29, 30, 175
Mong Find 184
Morken 183
Morna 176
Moscegrai, Messgegra 138, 144
Mosscorp, Messcuirb 138
Mugain 176
Mug Corb 105, 111, 144, 150
Mugdorn Dub 161, 237
Mug Ruith 69
Mugtigern 194
Muillethan 199
Muin Menn 90
Muindech Blai 16
Muindech Dub 16
Muirenn 184
Muirenn Mael 175–6
Muiresc 111, 262
Muirinn, Mor-find 111
Muirne Muincaem 176

Musc 109, 110, 262
MacCarthind 189
Mac da Fer 106
Mac da Tho 198
MacErc 95

Nar 110
Nechtan Breac 79
Nechtan Nair (Nar) 99
Nemed 26, 39, 43–44, 173, 250, 256
Nero 69, 143
Nia Corb 138, 144
Nia Mor 105
Niall 187
Niall Frossach 95, 229
Noichride 160
Noichruthach (Noichride) 160
Noinden 21
Noindenach 21
Nuada 135
Nudd 135

Oen Dub 132
Oen Gel 132
Oengoba 170
Oen Goban 132
Oengus mac Nadfraech 135
Oengus Bolg 16, 42
Oengus Dublesc 42
Oenlamgaba 132
Oenlam Gabaid 170
Oensciath 132
OenOlchu 67, 204, 207
Ollmuccaid 98

Porc 95, 189
Proc 95, 189

Radbod 223–4
Rederech 183–4
Redgitus 98
Restitutus 88, 96, 98, 104

Rhydeyrn 191
Ridicus 98
Rig Goban 170
Rigbardan 103
Ruad 18, 97, 178–9
Ruadanus 180, 253
Rusticus 18, 97, 178–9, 259

Salach, Cenel Salach, Fergus Salach 140–1, 198, 234
Saithne na Srian 203
Scath 209, 213
Scathach 209
Scathderc, daughter of Celtchair 213
Scathderg of Leix 213–4
Sciath Amlach 213
Sciath Brec 213
Sciathgabra 214
Sciathglan 214
Sciath Nechtan 214
Scirire 90
Scota, wife of Fenius and Mil 175, 212
Scothniam 214
Scothnoe 187
Segan 188
Segu-Meldos 225
Seim 213
Sem 69, 81
Senach Garb 141, 166
Sentigern 194
Setanta 27
Setna na Srian 203
Sgoith Glegal (Tuirean) 238
Sigebert 227–8
Sigmall 225
Simeon Breac 39, 78, 256
Simon Magus 69
Snedgoba 170
Solmglas 134
Sort 66
Suibne 117, 125, 151, 193
Sylvester 133

INDEX 2: ANCESTORS AND HEROES

Tal 47
Taranis 35
Tassach 131
Tedbendach 23
Teigue 60
Teith or Tet, son of Ded 23, 27, 28
Telbard 100
Teldub 100
Tene 56
Tet or Teith 23, 27, 28
Tigernach 82, 188, 193
Tigernach Dai 199
Tigernach Tedbendach 23
Tigernbard, son of Brig 106
Toiche (Docha) 111
Tomanchenn 54
Tortbuillech 217
Tortchis 217
Tortlugaid 217
Traig 26, 89, 96, 189, 265
Traigia 96
Treg 96–7, 198

Trega 89, 96, 265
Tressi 198
Tri Con 116
Triccdromma 96
Tridene 96
Triscoth 214
Tuathal Maelgarb 141, 199, 234
Tuirbi 168
Tulchan 125?

Ulysses 27, 111–12, 172
Urscothach 214

Valerius Corvus 140
Vercingetorix 48, 107
Verudoctius 107
Vesta 224
Vetir 69
Viricorb 107
Vorsitzer 224
Vortigern 188–91
Vortimer 191

Index 3
Irish Tribes (and their Ancestors)

Aeda Finn, Sliocht (Aed Finn) 127
Aeda, Ui (Aed) 31
Aen Darta, Fir 131, 217
Ailbe, Ui (Ailbe) 67, 206
Ainechglas, Ui (Bresal Ainechglas) 130
Araide, Dal (Araide Bibre) 54
Artcorr, Clann (Artcorb) 82
Artraige (Art) 66–7

Badamna, Ui (Badamna) 184
Baeth, Cenel (Baeth) 196
Baird, Clann 99
Bairrche, Ui (Bairrche) 165
Bardain, Clann (Bardan and Martan) 103
Barr, Sil (Barr) 186
Bascind, Dal (Cairbre Bascain) 109, 262
Bebryces 53, 58, 67
Belchae, Ui (Belocc, Bloc) 26, 42
Benndraige (Fer Bend) 22–3
Benntraige (Fer da Benn) 22–3, 27, 49, 105, 196, 198, 280
Berach Breac 129
Berchain, Ui (Berchan) 31
Bibraige (Araide Bibre, Bebrae Fiachach) 54, 67
Bindigh, Cenel (Bind) 18, 23
Binnig, Cenel (Eochu Binnich) 23
Bladraige (Bladcu, Blad, son of Cu) 31, 115
Blai, Cenel 23
Blait, Ui (Blat) 17, 203
Bodaraighe 196
Bodbain Ui (Bodb) 47

Bolg, Fir (Fer Bolg) 39, 42–3, 105, 142, 225–6, 256–7
Bolgraige 160, 196
Braccain, Ui (Braccan) 67
Bradain, Clann 92
Braici, Ui (Braici) 83
Breacraige (Bresal Breac) 15, 18, 79, 234
Brecdolb 235
Bregdolb 235
Brenaind, Muinter (Brenaind) 235
Bressail, Clann 92–3
Bric, Ui (Bricc) 82, 235
Briges (Brig) 45, 56–8, 78–9, 82, 99, 100, 139, 185, 203, 248, 276, 280
Brigantes 43, 57–8, 66, 77–78, 81, 112, 175, 202, 235
Brigte, Ui (Eogan Brec, Bridget, Breacdoilbh) 81, 130, 213, 235
Briuin Cualann, Ui (Brian) 127, 216
Broc, Ui 82, 196
BroinFind 124
Bronuigh, Ui 196
Brug 83, 98
Brugaid 83
Buain, Dal (Buan) 225
Buidhe, Ui (Buide) 115, 196, 237
Buil, Ui (Oengus Bolg) 42
Buithenaich, Ui (Baethanach) 58

Caba, Clann 196
Caech, Tuath 196
Caelraige 18, 234
Caelrige (Caelfer) 42, 105

INDEX 3: IRISH TRIBES (AND THEIR ANCESTORS)

Caem, Ui 15, 163, 259
Caemain, Ui 67
Caindeann, Ui (Cindiu) 26
Caenraige 121
Cairige 196
Cais or Cass, Dal (Cass) 47, 203
Caillech Bere 203
Calraige (Lugaid Cal) 17, 49, 92, 129
Carbad, Clann 67, 142
Carbraige 138, 143–4
Carthaich, Clann (Carthach) 75
Casraige (Conall Cas) 28
Catcheirn, Cenel (Catchern) 189
Cathair, Clann (Cathair) 21
Cathair Geal (Kerry) 237
Cathrae, Clann (Cathrae) 47
Cein, Dal 115
Ceinselach, Ui (Enna Ceinselach) 188, 260
Ceite, Dal (Fer Ceite) 105
Cell, Fir 33
Cerdraige (Cerdan son of Cerd Beg, son of Cerdraige) 160–2, 196
Chonach, Ui 118
Cianachta (Genus Connath) 118
Ciarraige (Mayo, Roscommon) 237
Cichainech, Ui (Cigaineach) 130, 232
Cinaith, Muinter 118
Cind, Ui (Heads) 117, 164
Cindcamhna, Ui (Cu Gamhna or Bone-heads) 117, 163–5
Cindgamhna, Ui (Cu Camhna or Calf-heads) 117
Ciogal, Muinter (Cicol Grigair Glun) 232
Cirdubain, Clann 237–8
Cirand, Clann 237
Clare, Ui (Clar) 130
Cnaimsighe or Cnamsige Clann 164
Cnamh tribes 117, 164
Cnamhraige 163
Cobain, Ui 105
Coirpraige 138

Conain, Ui 196
Conall Gabra, Ui 217
Concatha, Clann (Cu Catha) 116
Conchind, Ui (Conchinn) 28–9, 43, 118–19, 184
Conchobuir tribes (Conchobar, Noinden tribes, Noindenach) 21
Condath, Dal (Condad) 118
Conduilig, Clann (Cu Duilig) 116
Conmaicne 237
Connacht 116
Connaith, Ui 118
Consithe, Clann (Cu Sidhe, Sidwell) 20, 116
Corbmac, Ui (Cor(b)mac) 138
Corb, Ui (Corb) 131
Corbetraige 139
Corbraige 115, 139
Corcraige 159
Corcrain, Clann (Wexford, Wicklow) 237
Corpain, Ui 138, 142
Corpraige (Lugaid Corp) 17, 144
Coscraige (Lugaid Cosc) 17
Craibi, Fir (Craobh) 151
Cranna, Ui (Cron or Cronan) 29
Creachain, Ui (Crecan) 154
Crecraige (Crecan and Dil Mac da Creca) 154–5, 199, 206
Creide, Sil 166
Crimthann, Ui (Crimthann) 21, 213
Croeb 151
Croibine, Ui (Croibine) 151
Croicni, Cenel 165
Cromain, Clann (Croman) 163
Crommain, Ui 18
Crothrage 160
Cruib Craid, Ui (Crob Criad) 152, 159, 174
Cruimther Corcrain, Ui (Cruibther Corcrain) 159
Cruinbel, Ui (Cruinbel) 171

INDEX 3: IRISH TRIBES (AND THEIR ANCESTORS)

Cruithne (Cairpre Cruithnechan) 73–4, 159–60, 162
Cuaich, Ui (Cuach) 31, 94
Cuain, Ui 115
Cucongeilt, Ui (Cucongeilt) 179
Cucuan, Ui (Cucuan) 115
Cuinn, Ui (Conn) 117
Cuirc, Ui (Corc) 158
Cupraige 74, 149, 226

Daimhin, Clann 31
Dairchella, Ui 76
Dairini or Dairfine (Daire) 161
Dal Mescorb (Messincorb, Mescorb or Lugaid Corp) 110, 138
Dala, Corcu 154
Dallain, Ui, Cenel (Dallan) 42, 118, 196
Damain, Ui (Daman) 197
Dartraige (Doigre Dart) 67, 131, 197, 217
Deda, Dedad, Dedaid, Ui and Clann (Ded) 23, 27, 48, 119, 197
Dega, Degaid, Ui (Daig or Dea) 27–8, 31, 153, 157, 200
Deirg, Clann (Carlow) 237
Demain, Si (Ulster) 237
Derga, Ui 197
Derggain, Ui (Carlow) 237
Dessi 16–17, 192
Dicolla, Ui (Dicuill) 188
Dilmona, Ui (Eochaid Dilmona) 110
Dilraige (Dil) 155, 199
Diugurnach, Ui (Digernach) 192
Dobarchon, Ui (Dobarchu) 115, 203
Dobtha, Cenel (Dobtha) 128
Dolb, Ui (Dolb) 235
Domangen, Cenel (Domangen) 212
Donngal, Clann (Donngal) 184
Dorethain, Dothrain, Dortain, Dorthain, Ui (Dorthon) 216
Dornain, Ui 216
Draignean or Draignech, Ui 67, 88, 261, 265

Duach, Clann (Duach) 199
Dub Daire, Ui (Dub Daire) 92
Dubhda, Ui (Dubhda) 197
Dub(f)lann, Clann 15
Dubhan, Cenel (Dubhan) 129, 237
Dubraige (Mugdorn Dub) 18, 237
Duiblesc, Ui (Duiblesc) 42
Duibne, Corcu (Duibfionn or Corc Duibne) 18, 109, 159
Dula, Corcu (Dula or Corc Dul) 154, 158–9

Ebir, Clann (Eber Finn) 168
Echach, Dal (Eochaid Gunnat) 197
Echtigern, Ui (Echtigern) 193–40, 260
Eistich, Sil (Estiu) 67
Enna, Cenel and Ui (Enna) 131–3, 163, 197
Enna Aine, Ui (Enna Aine) 133
Eochaid, Ui 31
Eothigern, Ui (Eothigern) 194
Erc, Ui 31
Erca, Ui 94
Ercain, Ui (Erccan) 82
Ercal 96

Faelchon Conaille, Ui 110
Fedelmeda, Ui (Fedelmid) 188
Fenna, Ui 55
Fermaic, Ui (Fermac) 48
Fiachra, Ui (Bebrae Fiachrach) 163–4, 197
Fiatach Finn, Dal (Fiatach Finn) 123–4
Fidgenti, Ui (Fiachu Fidgenid) 121, 145, 206
Finain, Ui 121, 144
Finnia, Ui (Find) 170
Findloga, Sil (Findlug) 38, 46, 58
Finechglas, Ui 123, 130
Finn, Ui 18
Findtigern, Ui (Fintigern) 194
Fir da Crich, Ui (Fer da Crich) 104, 193

321

INDEX 3: IRISH TRIBES (AND THEIR ANCESTORS)

Fir Li 22
Fir Tlachtga, Ui (Fer Tlachtga) 69, 105, 145
Fir Tri, Ui (Fer Tri) 105
Fithcellach, Ui (Fithcellach) 21
Flann Dub, Clann 15
Forcc, Ui (Foirc) 189
Fothaid, Ui (Fothad) 29
Fotharta (Eochaid Find Fuath nAirt) 29
Fris, Tuath 229–20
Fuinche, Corcu (Fuinche Enda Uinche) 134

Gabalaig, Ui (Ethne Gabalfada) 149–51, 197
Gabrae, Fir 149
Gabra or Gabla, Ui 149, 151
Gabraige (Gubbi) 74, 132, 149, 170, 197
Gaileoin 39, 43, 257
Gairbheth, Ui 159
Galraige 93
Gamanrige 115, 117
Gamnain, Ui 197
Garban, Clann (Gaban, Garban) 149
Garbraige (Fergna Garb, Gaban) 18, 74, 141, 149, 234
Garrchon, Ui (Garrchu) 31
Gegrige 138
Geirg, Ferann 166
Getae (Celto-Thracians, Get) 56–7, 111, 124, 208–9, 226, 276, 280
Glassin, Ui (Glas) 23
Glasraige 115, 197, 237
Glasraigi Arad 237
Glegeal 238
Gleigal 238
Glunraige (Gluinne) 28
Gobain, Ui 20
Gobbain, Ui (Gobban) 170, 197
Gobraige 74
Gracraige (Grac) 154
Grecraige (Grecus and Grec macArod) 74, 154–5, 157–8, 173, 250
Gruccain, Ui 154
Gruibni, Ui (Gruibne) 152
Gualan, Muinter 197
Gubain, Ui (Guban) 170
Gubraige (Gubbi) 74, 149, 226

Ingeanraige 197
Iste, Aes (Estiu) 110–12

Labrada, Ui (Labraig) 91, 125
Lachtnain, Ui 67
Lamraige (Lama) 67, 92, 132, 170, 197
Lapen, Lappae, Ui (Lappan) 31, 93
Lappae, Ui 93
Li, Fir 22
Li Benndrigi (Liban) 23
Liathain, Ui (Liathan, Lithe) 28, 131, 197, 236–7
Liga, Ui 197
Liliuc or Lulaich, Ui (Lulaich) 185
Linga, Ui (Ling) 29–31, 76, 99
Lipi, Ui (Lappan) 93
Lochain, Ui 197
Loegaire (Fedelmid, St Foirtchern 187
Lonain, Ui (Lonan) 90, 197
Losat, Corcu (Corc Losat) 159
Loscain Cruaich, Ui 165
Lugdach, Ui Oichri Clann 35
Luirg, Fir 197
Lulaig, Clann (Lulaig) 185
Lupae, Cenel (Lappan) 93

MacCnaimhin, Ui 165
Mac Echtigern, Ui 193
Mac Iair Conchinn, Ui (Iar Conchind) 28, 119
Mac Uidir, Ui (Maguires) 237
Mael, Ui (Maine Mal, Maine Mall) 14–15, 18, 92, 170, 178, 180, 234, 259
Maelciarain, Tellach 15, 176
Maelgarb (a), Ui (Maelgarb) 18, 234

INDEX 3: IRISH TRIBES (AND THEIR ANCESTORS)

Maelmiadaig, Ui 176
Mael Mocheirge 176
Maelmocheirgi, Ui 83
Maelodhar, Sil 18, 181
Maelruad 18, 179, 259
Maelruadain, Muinter 180, 253
Maelruain, Muinter 180, 253
Maelruba, Ui (Maelruba) 188
Maeluidhir, Ui 181
Maguires 237
Maic Neamain, Ui 91
Maige, Fir 69
Maille, Ui 178, 259
Maine, Ui (Maine or Maine Mal) 14, 31, 99, 181
Martini 103, 184
Martain, Clann (Martan) 103
Mathra, Dal 105, 115
Meic Caindige, Ui 118
Meic Cainne, Ui 118
Meic Cairthenn, Ui (Mac Cairthind) 31
Meic Cuirp, Dal 138, 174
Meic Maeltine 92
Meidhe, Dal 197
Mella, Sil (Mella) 26
Mennbric, Sil 18, 234
Mennraige (Cuscraid Menn or Maine) 18, 90, 158, 234
Mescorb, Dal (Mescorb or Lugaid Corp) 110, 138, 230
Messincorb, Dal (Mescorb or Lugaid Corp) 138, 144, 238
Mil, Sons of 39, 40–41, 175–81, 212, 225, 257–9
Milchon, Muinter 178, 219
Moccu Crecci, Ui 206
Moccu Greca, Ui 156
Moccu Grecci (Ui) 154, 156, 159
Mochtaine, Tuath 156
Moinrige (Moinne) 90
Moltraige 91, 178
Morna, Clann (Muirne Muincaem, Muirinn, Morna) 111, 176, 262
Muilt, Ui (Molt) 178
Muindech, Ui (Muindech) 16–17, 90
Muinrige (Muin Menn) 90
Muinter Uainidi (Clare) 237
Muiredach, Ui 31
Muirenaig, Ui, Mairenns (Muiresc, Muirinn) 184
Muisge, Dal 110
Muscraige (Cairbre Musc) 49, 109, 147, 262
Mygdones (Magdon) 56, 58–9, 248, 276, 280

Nechtraige 99
Nectan Breac 234
Nemed, Children of 26, 164
Nero 69, 142
Noinden tribes (Conchobuir tribes, Conchobar, son of Noindenach) 21
Noindenach 21

Odoraige (Odran) 115
Odorige 237
Odraige 181, 197, 237
Odorain, Clann 237
Oengusa, Ui (Oengus) 42
Olcain, Ui 67
Olchon, Clann (Olchu) 67
Onchon, Ui (Onchu) 115
Osraige 115

Partraige 217

Rathach, Ui 197
Riaglachain, Ui 220
Rig, Clann (Rig) 197
Rigbardan, Muinter (Rigbardan) 103
Rothraige, (Rothan) 69, 197
Ruadhain, Ui (Ruadhan) 197
Rudraige 18, 234

INDEX 3: IRISH TRIBES (AND THEIR ANCESTORS)

Sai, Cenel 67
Saithne na Srian 203
Salach, Cenel (Fergus Salach) 198, 234
Sciathraige 212
Scotraige 212
Segain, Ui 67, 188
Seimne (Sem) 69
Semon, Tuath 69
Semonraige (Sem) 213
Sillain, Ui 31
Sinell, Ui 31
Siriten, Muinter (Sirt) 21
Sneiden, Clann (Snedan) 170
Sortraige (Sort) 66–7
Sordraige (Sord) 66–7
Suanaigh, Ui 67
Suibne, Clann 31

Tail, Clann (Tal) 47
Tartaisi, Tuath 216
Tassaich, Ui (Tassach) 31
Teith, Aes (Tet or Teith) 23, 28
Temin, Clann (Sligo) 237

Tempall Gael (Kerry) 237
Thenaich, Ui 58
Thyni (Tene) 56, 58, 276
Tigernach, Cenel (Tigernach) 193
Timin, Ui (Eocho Timin) 237
Toi, Tuath 198
Torcraide 198
Tort, Tuath (Fiachra Tort) 216
Tortain, Ui (Tortan) 216
Treisi, Cenel (Tressi) 198
Trena, Ui (Trian) 198
Trenfer, Ui (Trenfer) 104
Tuathal Maelgarb 141, 199, 234
Tuirbe or Turbi, Tuath (Tuirbi) 168
Tuirtre, Ui (Fiachra Tort) 67, 216

Uainidi 237
Uaithne 237
(F)Uinche, Corcu (Fuinche) 134
Uisce Gael (Kerry) 237
Uiste or nUisce, Dal 110
Ulaid (Corcu Aland, Ulster) 237, 266

Index 4
Continental Tribes (and their Ancestors)

Aeneadae (Aeneas) 52, 135
Aeolians (Aeolus) 25
Aesculapius (Asclepios) 27, 111–13
Aestii 112
Alba (Albans) 39, 66, 106, 128, 157-8, 204-5, 207, 257
Albiones (Alebion) 36, 67, 205, 207
Algisus (Clann Faelgus) 223, 226-7, 229
Allo-triges 49
Amazons xviii, 58, 232
Amelek 233
Amelekits 233
Ammonites (Ammon) 25
Arar 27
Arotrebae 62
Artabri 62, 67
Assyrians (Assur) 40, 43, 258
Asturians 108
Atesui (Esus) 26, 35-6, 61
Atrebates 62, 65
Ausetani 64
Ausoceretani 64
Ausoceretes 64

Baiocasses 47, 65, 225
Bardyetani, Barduli 104
Basclenses 110, 264
Basculi 112, 137
Basques 62, 108, 110, 249, 255, 261-7, 284
Basteiani 61
Bastertini 137, 264
Bastetani 61, 264
Bastuli 61, 137, 264

Bastulopoeni 61
Batavi 121
Bebryces (Bibrax and Bebryx) 53-4, 58, 66-7
Belcae 43
Belgae 42-3, 62
Belli 64
Bellocasses 47, 64-5
Bellovaci 64
Berach 127-9, 145-6
Berones 26, 106, 109, 129, 261
Bibroci 53
Bith (son of Noah) 39, 60, 96, 256
Bithyni (Bithynus) 25, 58
Bituriges Cubi 65, 149, 169
Bituriges Vivisci 65, 168
Bodiocasses 47, 65, 225
Bracarii 67
Brigantes (Bergans, Bergion, Brigans, Brigio, Brigantia) xviii, 43, 57-8, 66, 77-8, 81, 112, 175, 202, 235
Briges 45, 56-8, 78-9, 82, 99-100, 139, 185, 203, 248, 276, 280
Brigiani 78
Brigiosi 78
Brigolati 78
Budini 88, 110, 209, 280
Burgundiones (Burgundus) 78

Caerini 95
Caerones 209
Caerosi (Map 2, west) 121
Camponi 59

325

INDEX 4: CONTINENTAL TRIBES (AND THEIR ANCESTORS)

Canaanites (Canaan) 25-6, 233
Caninifates (Map 2, north-west) 121
Cantabri (ans) 108, 119
Carni (Map 2, south) 121
Carnonaceae 95
Carpesii 62, 137
Carpetani, Carpentani xviii, 45, 62, 69, 73-4, 126, 137-8, 140, 142-8, 162, 248 (Carpent 69, 142)
Carpi (c) 18, 45, 62, 74, 137-9, 140-1, 143, 149, 151-2, 159, 162, 166, 168, 172-3, 221, 226, 276, 280
Cassi 47
Cassibodua 47
Castor 53
Catti 95, 111, 194
Catubodua 35, 47, 226
Catuvellauni 20, 65, 226
Cauci 66
Cebren 149
Cebriones 149
Cecropides (Cecrops, Cercops) 172
Celtiberians (Celtiberus) 27, 54, 63-4, 93, 261
Celts xviii, 13, 26-7, 34, 38, 44, 52-6, 59-60, 62, 64, 85, 89, 114, 208-9, 249, 261, 265-6, 278 (Celtos 26, 173, 209, 250)
Celto-Scythians 43, 208
Cempses 59
Cenomani 64 (Map 2, south-west), 66
Cercitae (Circe) 165-66, 172-3, 250-1
Chaemi 64, 67
Chamavi 67
Chatti 47
Cherusci (Cheru) 25
Chuds 56
Cicones xviii, 41, 231-2, 280
Colchi 53, 171-2
Concani 119
Conioi, Cunesioi xviii, 45, 48, 59, 114-21, 124, 179, 184-5, 219
Conisci 69, 108, 261

Consuanitae 57, 64
Cornavii 95
Cotini 64 (Map 2, east-central)
Creones 95
Cretans (Kret) 25
Cu xxv, 20, 45, 48, 59, 75-6, 104, 115-17, 119, 124, 130, 138, 163, 165, 179, 184-6, 212-3, 232
Cu (dog heroes, dog-heads of Ireland) xxv, 20-1, 27, 37, 39, 42, 45, 48, 59, 69, 75-6, 104, 114-21, 124, 130-2, 138, 145, 159, 162, 165, 179, 184-6, 192, 212-13, 232, 256
Cu of Cunotegernos (Kentigern(a)) 12, 37, 75, 102-3, 121, 182-6, 189, 191-3, 220
Cubi 149, 166, 168-9
Cunesioi (see Conioi, Cunesioi)
Cunisc 69
Cuthites 7

Dacians 119, 199, 280
Daii 195–201
Decantae 202
Diicasses 47
Donaghmoyne (blackthorns) 89
Dorians 232
Draganum Proles (Draganes, Dercennus) xviii, 36, 89, 261, 265, 277, 279
Durocasses 47, 66
Duro-triges 49

Eburones 47
Eneti 55, 62, 111, 125, 130, 134, 135, 167
Ennicnioi 130
Epidii 44
Esau 19, 233
Essuvii (Esus) 26, 61
Estiones 67, 112
Exitani 112

INDEX 4: CONTINENTAL TRIBES (AND THEIR ANCESTORS)

Fenni 55
Finns 55, 56
Frisii (Forseti) 95, 280
Frissones 229

Gabali (Map 3, south-central, south-east) 66, 151
Gascons 62, 108, 261–4
Geloni (Gelonus) 26, 33, 42, 124, 129, 156, 171, 173, 179, 250
Getae 56–7, 111, 124, 208–9, 276, 280
Gothones 57
Goths 57
Graeci 159, 173
Greeks (Grecus) 13, 19, 36, 52, 59, 86, 152, 154, 171, 173, 232–3

Hagarites (Hagar) 19
Hebrews (Eber) 19, 25–6, 249
Hecuba 58
Helvecones 62, 207
Helvetii 62, 207
Helvii 62, 66, 207
Hercules 27, 36, 58, 77, 93, 96, 173, 186, 205
Hermiones 64, 228
Hermunduri 64
Histiaeans 112
Hittites (Heth) 25–26, 233

Iberians 26–27, 40, 45, 47, 53–55, 59, 62, 64, 85, 124, 258, 261, 264, 276
Ileates 112
Illyrians (Illyrus) 55
Ingaevones (Ingaevo) 25
Ionians (Ion) 25
Iscaevones (Iscaevo) 112
Istaevones (Istie) 111
Issachar 19, 233, 234

Jacob 19, 233, 234

Lacco-bardi 99
Lacco-briga 99
Lacetani 20, 67
Langobardi 98, 99
Lango-briga 99
Lapiths 112
Latini (Latinus) 172
Lato-brigi 78
Leah 233
Leleges (Lelex) 185
Lemavi 67
Lemovices 66–67
Lemovii 67
Lepontii (Lepontius) 93
Licati 57, 63
Ligures 275
Ligurians xix, 30, 35–8, 44–6, 53–5, 57, 59, 62, 99, 124, 205, 232, 276, 280
Ligyes (Ligys) 36, 54, 57
Lindones 62, 66
Lingones 29–30, 35, 37, 62, 66, 99
Lobetani 66, 93
Lombards 40, 98–9, 258
Longones 62, 99
Longostaletes 62
Lougi 36, 37
Lugii 36, 207
Lugones 36–7, 62
Lungones 36–7, 62, 99
Lusi 26, 62
Lusones 62
Lygii 36
Lycians (Lycius) 25
Lydians (Lydus) 25

Medes (Medea, Medus) 19, 26, 58, 233
Medobithyni 58
Meldi 65, 181, 225
Menapii xviii, 66
Midas 58
Milesians (Miletus) 26, 175, 179, 212, 252, 259, 276, 281

327

INDEX 4: CONTINENTAL TRIBES (AND THEIR ANCESTORS)

Moabites (Moab) 25
Morini 111, 176, 184, 276, 280
Muirenns, Muirenaig 184
Muirinn 111
Mygdones (Mygdon) 56, 58–9, 248, 276, 281
Mysus 25

Nemetavi 25
Nemetes (Nemetona) 26, 44
Nemeturii 44
Neri (Nero) 69
Nervii 99
Nitiobriges 78, 182
Novantes 202

Olcades (Map 1, east-central) 43, 67
Ostidamni 112
Ostiones 112

Persians (Perseus) 19, 26, 233
Phocaeans 215, 264
Phyrges 57, 58, 78
Phrygian family tree 58
Picts 5, 44, 94, 121, 160, 177, 183, 206
Pictones 44, 65
Pollux 53
Priam 58
Pyrene 53

Rachel 233

Saii 67
Salah 26
Salassi (Salassus) 93
Salyes 54
Sardi (Sardus) 62, 66, 276, 280
Saxons (Saxus) 33, 94
Sciopodes 43
Scoti 208, 212
Scotraige 212
Scythians (Scythes) xxvi, 26, 124, 152,
173, 175, 208–9, 212–13, 250–1, 256, 263, 276
Segni 67
Segobriges 78
Segusiavi 67
Semon 69
Setantii (Setanta) 139, 202–3
Sicani 62
Siculi 62
Siginni 20
Sigyni 151
Sigovellauni 20
Silures 54, 59, 116, 191, 192, 276, 280
Sordi 26, 62
Sordones 62, 67
Suanitae 57, 64, 67
Suardones 26, 62
Suarini 62
Suebi (Suebus) 25, 69, 112, 147, 276, 280
Suessiones 62, 66
Suessitani 62
Surdaones 62

Taranis 35
Tarbelli 66, 168
Tartessii 59, 61, 215–17
Taurini 62
Taurisci (Tauriscus) 62, 93
Teuriochaemi 64
Thracians xvii, 53, 56, 73, 78, 89, 96–7, 172, 179, 189, 248, 259, 265, 276, 280
Thyni 56, 58, 276
Tigurini xxvi, 182–3, 185, 191, 194
Tricasses 47, 66
Tricorii (Tricoria) 26, 61
Trinovantes 202
Trojans (Tros) 52
Turboleti 168
Turdetani 59, 61
Turduli 59, 61
Turones (Turonus) 26, 62, 64, 66, 103

INDEX 4: CONTINENTAL TRIBES (AND THEIR ANCESTORS)

Vaccaei 64, 147
Vacomagi 91
Vadicassii 46, 66
Vascones xxvi, 62, 88, 108, 111, 137, 261–4, 280
Vecturiones 158
Vellocasses 65, 227
Vellauni 20, 226, 276, 280
Venedi 33, 55, 145
Veneti xxvi, xxvii, 45–6, 55, 57, 62, 66, 111, 122–5, 127–30, 132–5, 169–70, 185, 202–3, 212–13, 217, 219, 228, 261, 276, 280
Venicones 158
Vennicnoi 122–3, 130–1

Vennones 62
Venonetes 62
Venostes 62
Veragri 106
Veromandui 66, 106–7
Verones 48, 106, 109, 261
Vertacomacori 106
Vescitani 62, 108–9, 137, 261, 264
Vettones (Vetir) 69
Viducasses 46, 66
Vindelici 38, 57–8, 62–3
Viruni 107
Volciani 43

Xerxes 54

Index 5
HISTORIANS AND HISTORIC FIGURES

Alcuin 33, 223–4
Apollodorus 58
Apollonius Rhodius 172
Arbois de Jubainville, d' 55–6
Arribas 55, 62
Avienus 54, 59, 215

Baring-Gould, S. xv, 10, 38, 51, 136, 185–6, 193–4, 223
Bath, Marquess of 89
Beaufort, Dr 7
Bede 189, 218, 222
Betham, Sir William 7
Boniface, St 33
Bosch Gimpera 55, 61–2
Boswell 80
Boucher de Perthes 74, 256, 281–2
Bury, J. B. 83, 85–7, 91, 177
Butler, Hubert xxi–viii, 148, 237–8, 246–76, 278, 280–4
Butler, Richard xvi, 9
Byrne, F 141

Caelcu or Colgu 33, 115
Carney, James xxiii, 30, 85, 278
Carrigan, Canon 140
Chadwick, H. M. and N. K. 100–1, 190–1
Charlemagne 33–4, 224, 267
Chesterfield, Lord 74
Crawford, O. G. S. 14

Davidson, Ellis 224
Dillon, Myles 38, 277–8, 281

Dobbs, M. E. 58

Esposito, Mario 86
Evans, D. E. xxiii, 46–9

Gaedel Glas 60
Garcia and Bellido Maps 61
Geoffrey of Monmouth 110, 189
Germanus of Auxerre 33, 98
Gibbon, E. 100, 160
Giraldus 4, 110
Gougaud, D. L. 227
Graves, James 6
Graves, Robert 113
Gregory the Great (Grigoir) 33, 152–5, 157, 159
Grimm, Jacob 57

Henry II 110
Herodotus 43, 56, 59, 114, 209, 250, 281
Herbert, Algernon 201
Hilary of Arles and Poitiers 33, 153
Hilary, Pope 206
Himilco 204
Hoare, Gregory 154
Hogan, S. J. Edmund 192, 216
Holder, Alfred 29–30, 46, 50, 78, 106, 112, 232
Horace 119
Hubert, Henri 53, 55, 78, 207

Isidore of Seville 43–4

INDEX 5: HISTORIANS AND HISTORIC FIGURES

Jackson, Kenneth xxiii, 12, 75, 183, 185
Jocelyn of Furness 201
Johnson, Samuel 80, 274
Joyce, James 21, 251–2
Joyce, P. W. 111, 165, 195, 212, 217
Julius Caesar 47–8, 55, 182, 207

Keane, Marcus 7–8, 14, 270
Kenney, J. F. 9, 134

Ledwich xxiii, 6–8, 10–11, 16, 36, 86, 169, 176–7
Lehane, B. 202
Livy 140

Macalister, R. A. S. 9–11, 30, 36, 39–44, 53, 123, 171, 213
Mac Cullinan, Cormac 22
MacNeill, E. xxiii, 53, 69, 79–80, 138, 160–1, 212
Martin of Tours 33, 88, 96, 100–4, 127, 153, 184
Martin, Pope 222
Matheson, R. E. 49–50, 74, 117
Murray, Gilbert 52
Murray, John 202

Newman, Cardinal 9

O'Brien, Conor Cruise 268
O'Brien, Henry 7
O'Brien, Michael xxiii, xxv, 15–16, 26, 44, 81, 96, 194, 240
O'Curry, Eugene 6, 93, 116, 161, 235–6
O'Donovan, John 6, 145, 237
O'Hanlon, Canon 9, 40, 51, 86, 88, 95, 104, 122, 130, 141, 166, 169, 176, 216, 218, 225
O'Rahilly, T. F. 13–14, 42, 44, 51, 105, 132, 135, 199, 225, 275
Oengus the Culdee xv, xix, 94, 153, 221, 271

Ormonde, Marquess of 7
Orosius 43–4
O'Siochain 167

Palladius 86
Patrick, St xix, 6, 43, 83–108, 118, 128, 149, 151, 156, 158, 163, 165, 169, 176–7, 187, 201, 204, 206, 213, 219, 235, 240, 242, 262
Paul, St 38, 66, 134
Penda, King of Mercia 228
Pepin the Frank 34, 223, 267
Petrie, George xxiii, 6, 8–9, 168
Phileas 215
Philippon 54, 59
Pierson, Dixon 55
Pliny 61, 69, 205
Plummer, Charles 134, 181
Power, Canon 69, 81–2, 154
Prim, John 6
Prince Consort 7
Procopius 229
Prosper 86
Ptolemy 30, 61, 93, 95, 122, 137, 235

Radbod 223–4
Redwald 227–8
Reeves, Rev. W. 160, 216, 229
Rhys, J. xv, 59, 114, 122, 137, 143,
Ridgeway, W. 56, 78, 137
Rushe, D. C. 89
Ryan, Rev. John 10–11, 135

Scantlebury, Fr. 167
Schulten 61
Shearman, Rev. J. F. 7, 98, 102–3, 153, 200, 271
Sigebert 227–8
Simpson, Douglas 101
Skene, W. F. 78–9, 121, 189
Stokes, Whitley 199
Strabo 43, 52–3, 58–9, 63, 78, 108, 112, 171–2, 199–200, 208

331

INDEX 5: HISTORIANS AND HISTORIC FIGURES

Sulpicius 100–01
Sylvester, Pope and Saint 33, 133, 153

Tacitus 55, 57, 62, 98, 112, 207, 229
Thurneysen, R. 153, 212
Timothy, disciple of St Paul 38
Todd, Dr D.J.H. 85, 188
Trench, W. S. 89

Vallancey, General 6–7, 16

Watson, W.J. 30, 157, 184, 191, 193, 209
Whatmough 38, 261, 284
Wilde, Sir W. 225–6
Willibrord St. 33–4, 223–4
Wulfram St. 33, 223

Zimmer, H. 84

Index 6

MISCELLANY

Afternames (tribal suffix) 13–14, 17–18, 28–9, 37, 41, 129, 234, 248, 250, 252, 259–60
Ahernes, Co. Clare 193, 260
Ancestor–making xxvii, xxviii, 12, 26, 249, 270
Ancestors, amalgamated 19, 24, 27–28, 30, 54, 235, 283
Antiquarian rationalists 3, 6, 8, 169, 176, 249, 250–51
Argonauts 53, 173, 250
Ath Aladh (Louth) 237

Bann River, 22– 23, 151, 170
Bantry Bay 22–23
Basques (Vascones), 'sc' sound x, xviii, 62, 88, 108–11, 137, 249, 255, 261–6, 280, 284
Beforenames (tribal prefix) 15–16, 37, 248, 262
Blackthorn, Donaghmoyne, Draignean tribe, Thornton 67, 88–90, 152, 197, 265, 279

Cabinhogan pun 22, 251
Cael is Goll (other combinations) 14, 21, 33, 42, 105, 115, 124, 129, 139, 143, 182, 191, 194, 219, 220, 234
Caem, Ui, tribe 15, 67, 163, 259
Cairbre Caem, St 15, 163, 259
Cairbre Crom, King of Munster 162–3
Carthac, St 75, 259
Carthach, Bishop 75

Carthaich, Clann 75
Celtic corpus, vast hagiographical 181
Celtic corpus, vast mythological 23, 28, 33, 42, 181, 249
Chapelizod pun 22, 251
Charlemagne and tribal ancestors 33–4, 224, 267
Charles Martel 34, 267
Christianization of stories and saints 10, 12, 32–34, 224, 227, 156
Circe 165–66, 172–3, 250–1
Cluain Alad (midlands) 237
Colours of the Winds, Tribal 159, 233, 235–39, 246, 284
Cu (dog heroes, dog heads of Ireland) xxv, 20–1, 27, 37, 39, 42, 45, 48, 59, 69, 75–6, 104, 114–21, 124, 130–2, 138, 145, 159, 162, 165, 179, 184–6, 192, 212–13, 232, 256
Cu of Cunotegernos (Kentigern(a)) 12, 37, 75, 102–3, 121, 182–6, 189, 191–3, 220

Distortions 74–5
Drennan, Draignean tribe, blackthorn, Thornton (see Blackthorn)
Dumb 13, 234, 266, 275
Dun da Beann, Derry (Fort of two Peaks, Mount Sandel) 22

Echtigern, Ui, tribe 193–94, 260
Enna (Ui) Ceinselach tribe 188, 260 (see Kinsella)

333

INDEX 6: MISCELLANY

Finnegans Wake, puns 21, 251–2

Garvey, O'Garbheth, Ui Gairbheth 141, 159
Goll is Cael (see Cael)

Hagiography, saints to tribes xix, 9, 32–4, 79, 102,
Homonyms 33, 218, 244, 252–53

Incarnation and Pagans 9–10
Ireland, end of habitable world 60
Irish founder saints 4
Irish language origin 60
Irish monastic founders 4

Joyce, James, puns 21, 251–2

Kentigern (Cu of Cunotegernos) (see Cu)
Kilkenny Archaeological Society xvii, xxii, 6–7, 36, 247, 276, 281
Kinsellas, Carlow 188, 260 (see Enna Ceinselach tribe)
Kirkmabrick, Wigtownshire 79

Lake Brigantius 57, 68
Lake Constance 38, 55, 57, 62, 68, 112
Lake Venetus 55, 57, 62

Mac Carthys (Clann Carthaich), Munster 75
Mac Cuillinan, Cormac, Glossary 22
Maelruad, Ui, tribe 18, 179–80, 234, 253, 259
Maille, Ui, tribe (see O'Malleys) 178, 259
Mal is Mall 14–15, 17, 181
Martel, Charles 34, 267
Mayo (see Red Hill)
McCagherons, Co. Antrim 193, 260
Medes (Medea) 19, 26, 58, 233
Mispronounciations 74–5

Mount Sandel (see Dun da Beann, Fort of two Peaks)
Mulroys, Co. Sligo (see Maelruad)

Noinden (dread disease) 21
Numinous beings 8, 250

O'Brien, Michael 15–16
O'Drynan (see Drennan, Draignean tribe, blackthorn, Thornton)
O'Keefes, Co. Cork 15
O'Malleys, Co. Sligo, Mayo (see Ui Maille)
Old Testament 19

Pagans, Incarnation (see Incarnation)
Pepin the Frank 34, 223, 267
Persians (Perseus) 19, 26, 215, 233, 258
Prefix, tribal (see beforenames)
Puncraft xxvii, xxviii, 19, 247, 250, 252–3, 260
Puns, (see Joyce)
Puns, St Kentigern tribal (see Cu)
Puns, tribal 19–22, 29, 49–50, 162, 170–2, 185, 222, 232–3, 251–2

Red Hill (Cusc na Druad, Mullach Ruad, Telach na Maele, Telach Molt) 178–9, 259
Reincarnation and pagans (see Incarnation)

Saints as founders of churches and monasteries 4
Saints, wicked (see wicked saints)
'sc' sound (see Basques)
Seanchas Mor 235, 238
Sheridans 21 (see Muinter Siriten)
Sligo (see Red Hill)
Sociology (social therapy) xvii
Stammerers 13, 266, 275
Suffix, tribal (see Afternames)

INDEX 6: MISCELLANY

Thornton (see Drennan, blackthorn, Donaghmoyne, Draganum, Draignean tribe)
Thrace 39, 44, 52, 56–8, 60, 78–9, 82, 96–7, 99, 232, 235, 248, 254, 256
Tribal distribution 236–8, 274
Tribal prefix (see Beforenames)
Tribal puns (see Puns, tribal)
Tribal suffix (see Afternames, Distortions, Mispronounciations)
Troy (Trojans, Tros) 52
Truth, (ancient, abundant, durable) xix, xxi–ii, xxvii, 5, 10, 21–2, 82, 85, 87, 100–1, 173, 185, 189, 193, 201, 241–2, 250–1, 256, 273, 280
Tuirean, children of 238

Two Peaks, Derry (see Dun da Beann)

Vascones (see Basques), 'sc' sound

Wicked saints: Cianan 118, 227; Da Goban 197, 200; Enda (Enna) 27–8, 131–5, 139–40, 146, 163, 167, 188, 192, 197, 202–3, 206, 219, 260; Four Maels 179; Mac Cuill 156, 227

Wigtownshire (see Kirkmabrick)

Yorkshire 57, 77, 81, 112, 149, 235
Young Ireland and provincial archaeology 6–7

www.ingramcontent.com/pod-product-compliance
Lightning Source LLC
Chambersburg PA
CBHW020828160426
43192CB00007B/566